THE PILGRIMAGE OF GRACE
1536–1537

AND

THE EXETER CONSPIRACY
1538

IN TWO VOLUMES
VOL. I

THE PILGRIMAGE OF GRACE
1536–1537

AND

THE EXETER CONSPIRACY
1538

BY

MADELEINE HOPE DODDS

(Historical Tripos, Cambridge)

AND

RUTH DODDS

VOLUME I

Cambridge:

at the University Press

1915

CAMBRIDGE
UNIVERSITY PRESS

University Printing House, Cambridge CB2 8BS, United Kingdom

Cambridge University Press is part of the University of Cambridge.

It furthers the University's mission by disseminating knowledge in the pursuit of
education, learning and research at the highest international levels of excellence.

www.cambridge.org
Information on this title: www.cambridge.org/9781107502031

© Cambridge University Press 1915

First published 1915
First paperback edition 2015

A catalogue record for this publication is available from the British Library

ISBN 978-1-107-50203-1 Paperback

NOTE

THE authors wish to express their most sincere gratitude to Miss Myra Curtis, Professor A. F. Pollard, Mr I. J. Bell of the British Museum, Mr H. R. Leighton, the Rev. J. Wilson, and Mr T. C. Hodgson for their kind and valuable help in the preparation of this book.

The documents transcribed by the authors from the originals have been given in the original spelling; in those which have been taken from printed copies the spelling has been modernised.

The spelling of proper names of persons and places is that used in the Index to the Letters and Papers of Henry VIII.

M. H. D.
R. D.

July 1915.

CONTENTS

MAPS

ADDITIONS AND CORRECTIONS

PAGE

3 For influence on elections in the King's favour, see "History," October 1914, A. F. Hattersley, "The Real Position of the Duke of Norfolk in 1529-30."

50 *For* Thomas Monkton *read* William Monketon.

79 The church plate of Hull. This method of securing the value of the church plate to the parish became fairly common in the later part of Henry VIII's reign and during the reign of Edward VI. See Cox, "Churchwardens' Accounts" (the Antiquary's Books), pp. 133, 140-1.

91 For the commission to the clergy see Usher, "The Rise and Fall of the High Commission," pp. 15-21.

116 Note E. The Sir Marmaduke Constable mentioned was Sir Robert's brother, not his cousin.

123 Composition of the royal and the rebel forces. See Cox, "Churchwardens' Accounts" (the Antiquary's Books), pp. 325-7, for the parish soldier and the parish armour.

145 "Four docepyers." Not "deceivers," as suggested, but "douzepers," great men. See New English Dictionary, and Lydgate, "Minor Poems" (Percy Society), p. 25:—

> "Where been of Fraunce all the dozepiere,
> Which in Gaule had the governaunce?"

149 The commons of Howdenshire attacked the house of Sir Marmaduke Tunstall, the Bishop of Durham's nephew, but "some more sober than the residue" prevented any serious damage. See "Richmondshire Wills" (Surtees Society), p. 288 n.

184 Spoiling of Blytheman's house. Colins was afterwards accused of being the chief plunderer. See L. and P. xii (1), 1264.

203 Oxneyfield is close to Darlington, where it seems that the townspeople rose and joined the rebels. The dean of the collegiate church commended one of his servants who "was the safeguard of my life, for else I had been betrapped by the commons ere I had known." "Richmondshire Wills" (Surtees Society), p. 40 n. Cf. below, vol. ii, p. 94.

208 The lordship of Middleham, which had belonged to Warwick the Kingmaker, on his death and attainder was granted by Edward IV to Richard Duke of Gloucester, afterwards Richard III. (Gairdner, "Richard III," p. 22.) It is well known that Richard married Warwick's daughter Anne, co-heiress with her sister Isabel, and thus obtained a claim to the lordship not only by grant but also by inheritance. He and his wife were very popular at Middleham, which he called his home (ibid. pp. 28, 259). When Richard in his turn was killed and attainted, Middleham escheated to the crown, but, Anne and her only child being dead, Warwick's line was now represented by the Countess of Salisbury, the daughter of Anne's sister Isabel, who was married to the Duke of Clarence. This expression of affection for the old line may therefore be a reference to the Poles.

209 " Merlione." This is a misreading of " Meliore," i.e. Mallory. The leader of the siege of Skipton was not a peasant with a feigned name, but a member of the family of Mallory.

213 *For* Guisburn *read* Guisborough, as on p. 71. It is not quite clear whether this incident happened at Guisburn or at Guisborough, but the latter seems the more probable.

233 " St Saviour's of Newburgh." The Priory of Newburgh was dedicated to the Virgin Mary, but the canons possessed " the girdle Sancti Salvatoris, which, as it was said, was good for those in child birth." (L. and P. x, p. 137.) This relic was kept in St Saviour's chapel at the Priory, where many pilgrims resorted. (L. and P. xii (2), 1231.) Probably Newburgh was called St Saviour's after the most famous relic which it possessed, though it was really St Mary's, just as Durham was called St Cuthbert's, though it also was dedicated to the Virgin.

233 The message to Darcy from Shrewsbury's camp. After the rebellion was over, when even the executions were almost at an end, Christopher Lassels, who was imprisoned in the Tower with Aske, was heard to say that Aske had told him " very sure tokens" by which the man who sent the warning might be recognised. This remark of Lassels was reported to Cromwell on 22 July 1537, but there is no record to show whether any arrest was made on Lassels' information. (L. and P. xii (2), 321.)

237 *For* " Sir Robert Bowes of Barnard Castle, and his sons " *read* " Robert Bowes and his brothers."

266 The deposition against Hogon is printed in full, with illustrative notes by Furnivall, in " Ballads from MSS," vol. i, pt 2, p. 310 (Ballad Society).

273 Hutton of Snape, probably a misreading of Snaith.

281 Pickering's poem is printed by Furnivall in " Ballads from MSS," vol. i, pt 2, p. 301 (Ballad Society). The editor states that it was published at Ripon in 1843, with a preface by J. R. W. I have not seen this last version, but it appears that neither Furnivall nor J. R. W. knew the author of the poem and its occasion, though they conjectured correctly that it referred to the Pilgrimage of Grace.

317 Henry VIII and the letter. Cf. Chapuys' despatch of 3 November 1533 :—" On 25 October Henry had received Gardiner's letter of the 17th, in which the bishop reported that Clement had refused to dispose of the matrimonial cause in the offhand manner that had been suggested. Henry became pale with anger and crushed Gardiner's letter in his hand, exclaiming that he was betrayed, and that the King of France was not the true friend he had thought. He continued for some time to swear at the pope, and could not regain his equanimity." (L. and P. vi, 1392.)

364 As late as 1596 it was maintained that the long bow was superior to firearms (Sir H. Knyvet, " Defence of the Realme," 1596), but on the other hand as early as 1515 in a paper relating to Ireland it was stated that "the wild Irish and English rebels of all the land doth dread more and feareth the sudden shot of guns much more than the shot of arrows or any other shot of kind of weapon in this world." (L. and P. ii (1), 1366, printed in full Furnivall, " Ballads from MSS," i, pt 1, p. 38 [Ballad Society].)

I

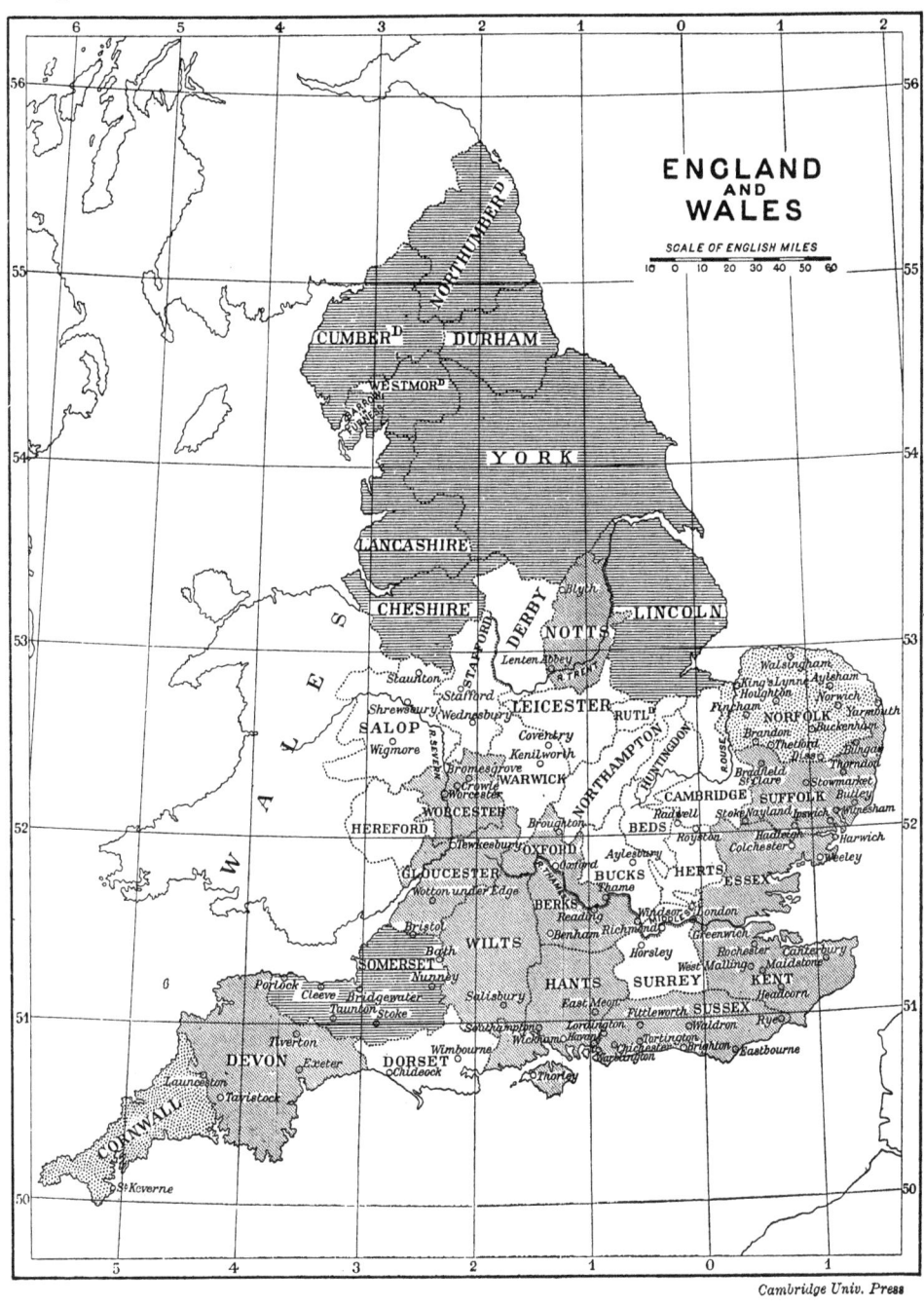

ENGLAND
AND
WALES

SCALE OF ENGLISH MILES

Cambridge Univ. Press

▤ Counties in open rebellion during 1536–7.
▨ Counties where plots were discovered.
▧ Counties where open disaffection was reported.

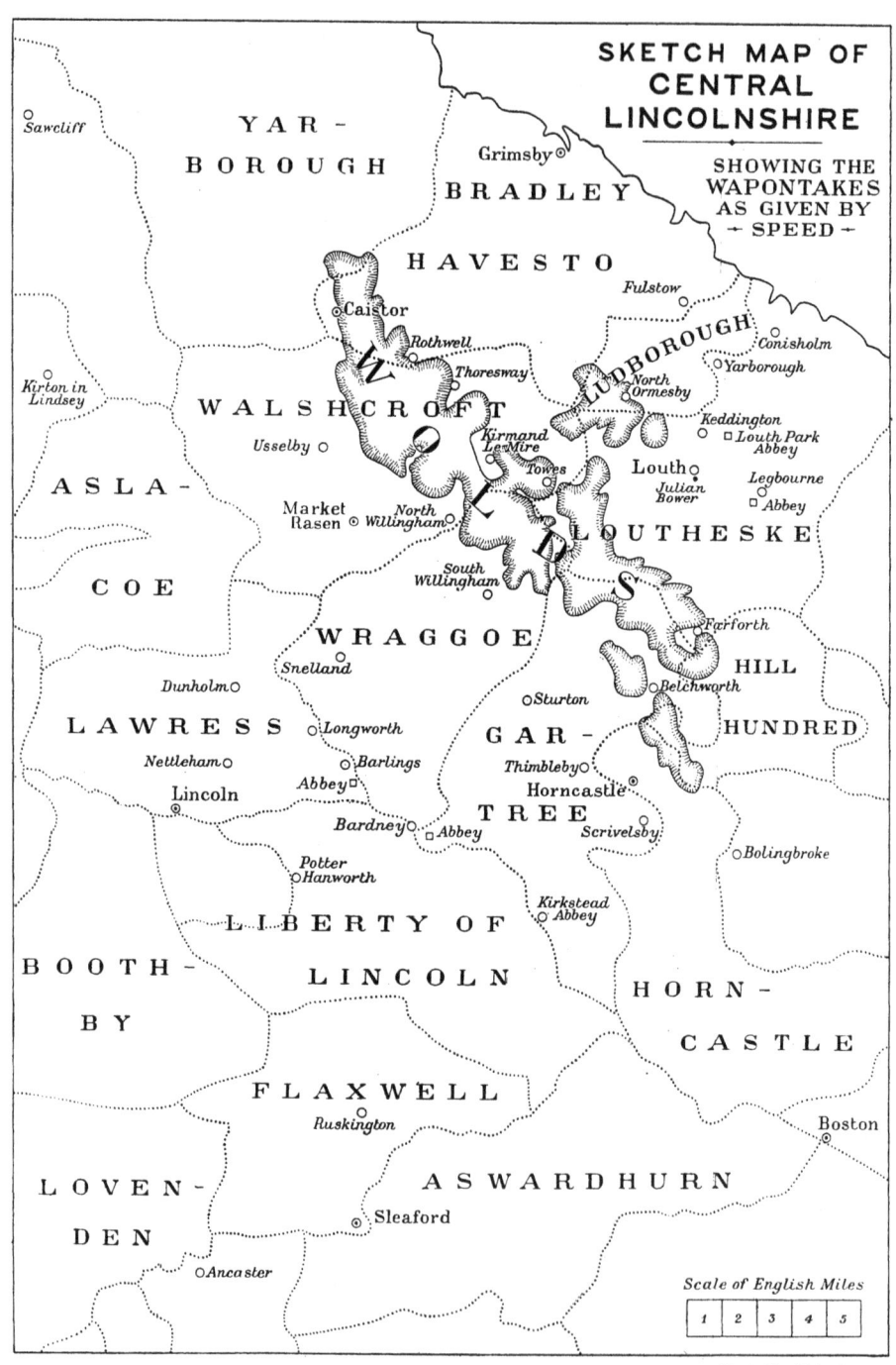

SKETCH MAP OF
CENTRAL
LINCOLNSHIRE

SHOWING THE
WAPONTAKES
AS GIVEN BY
↠ SPEED ↞

Sawcliff

YAR -
BOROUGH

Grimsby○

BRADLEY

HAVESTO

Fulstow

○Caistor

Rothwell

Conisholm

○*Yarborough*

*North
Ormesby*

*Kirton in
Lindsey*

WALSHCROFT

Thoresway

LUDBOROUGH

Keddington
□*Louth Park
Abbey*

Usselby ○

*Kirmand
Le-Mire*

Towes

Louth○

Legbourne

*Julian
Bower*

□*Abbey*

ASLA-

Market
Rasen ◎ *North
Willingham*○

LOUTHESKE

COE

*South
Willingham*
○

WRAGGOE

Fœrforth

Snelland
○

HILL

Dunholm○

Sturton
○

Belchworth

LAWRESS

○*Longworth*

GAR -

HUNDRED

Nettleham○

○*Barlings*

Thimbleby○

Lincoln
○

Abbey□

Horncastle□

TREE

Bardney○

□*Abbey*

Scrivelsby○

Bolingbroke
○

*Potter
Hanworth*
○

*Kirkstead
Abbey*
○

LIBERTY OF

BOOTH-

LINCOLN

HORN -

BY

CASTLE

FLAXWELL

Ruskington
○

Boston
○

LOVEN-

ASWARDHURN

DEN

○*Sleaford*

○*Ancaster*

Scale of English Miles

| 1 | 2 | 3 | 4 | 5 |

Cambridge Univ. Press

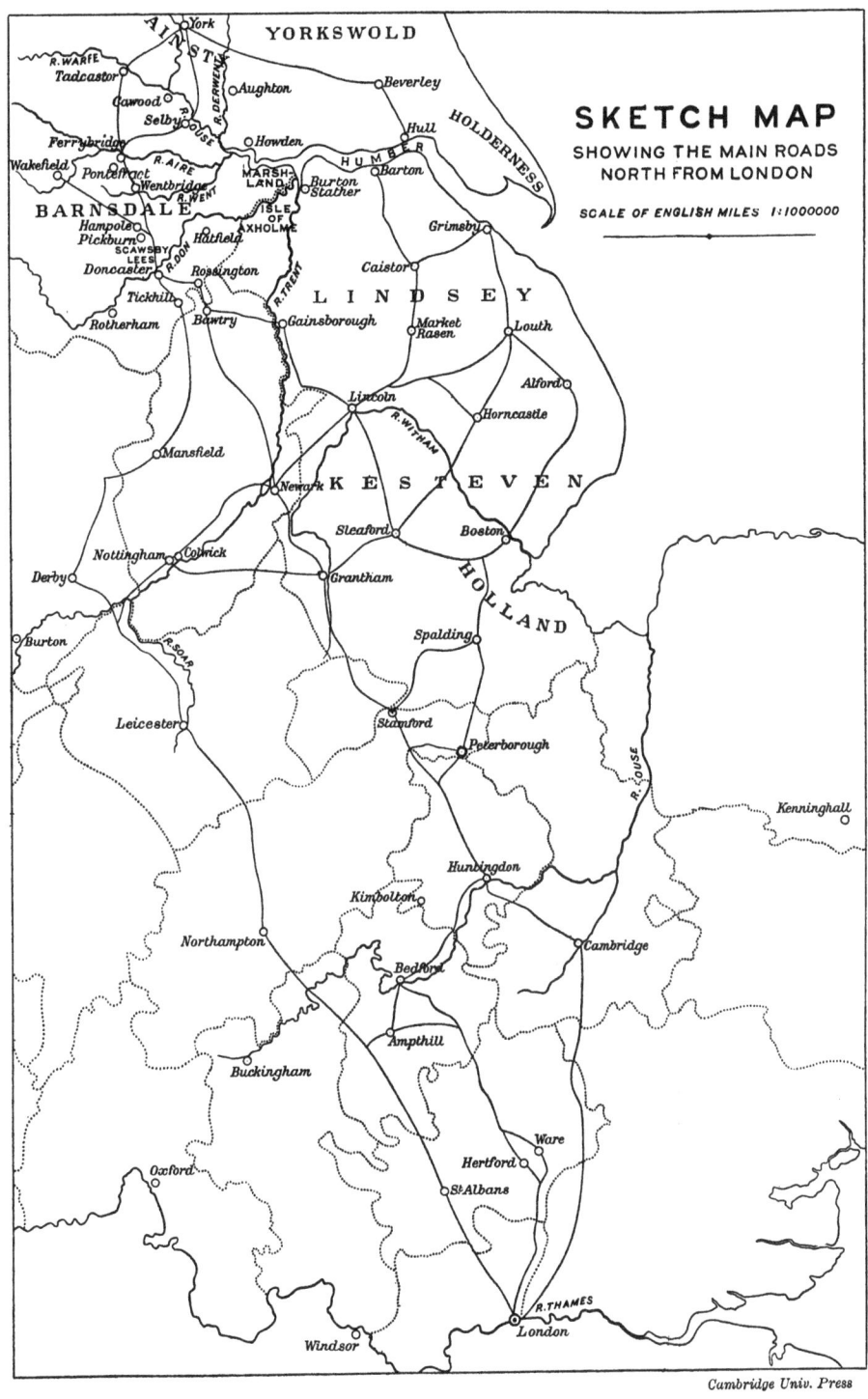

SKETCH MAP

SHOWING THE MAIN ROADS
NORTH FROM LONDON

SCALE OF ENGLISH MILES 1:1000000

Cambridge Univ. Press

Main Roads (Approximate) ━━━━━
County Boundaries ·························

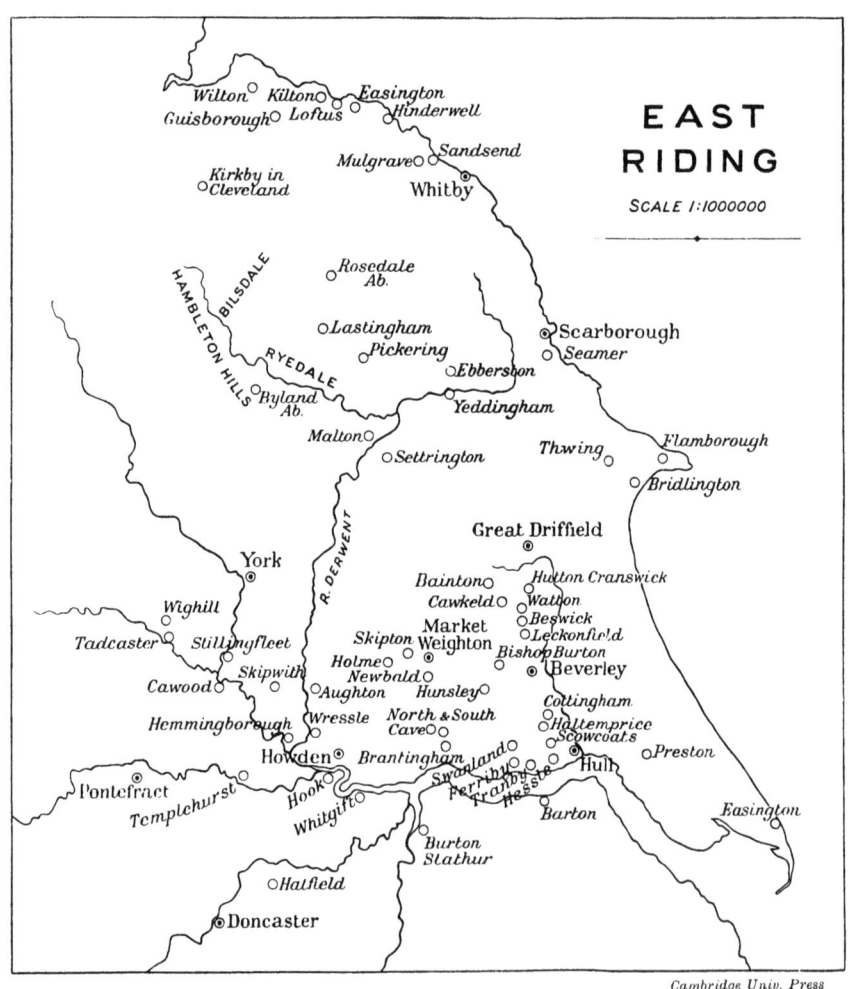

EAST
RIDING

SCALE 1:1000000

Cambridge Univ. Press

V

SKETCH MAP
OF THE
NORTHERN COUNTIES

SCALE 1:1000000

CHAPTER I

THE TURNING-POINT

In order to see the rebellion of 1536-7 in its true perspective it is necessary to make a preliminary survey of the political position in England before the first rising took place. At the end of July 1536 Henry VIII's domestic relations were more settled than they had been for the last ten years. The execution of Anne Boleyn on 19 May had been followed by his marriage with Jane Seymour, who was indisputably his lawful wife. The parliament which met on 8 June declared the two children of the King's former wives, Mary and Elizabeth, illegitimate, and settled the succession to the crown upon the issue of the King's latest marriage: that failing, the King was empowered to determine his heir himself either by will or by letters patent[1]. It was believed that the object of this statute was to bring into the succession Henry's illegitimate son, Henry Duke of Richmond, who, however, died on 23 July[2]. After his death the situation with regard to the succession was practically the same as it had been before the divorce of Katherine of Arragon was proposed. The King was legally married, but it was considered unlikely that Queen Jane would have a child, and unless he acknowledged Mary, his heir by blood was the King of Scotland, whose claim was exceedingly unpopular in England. If the King died it was certain that Mary would be chosen by the nation as their queen, whether she was legitimate or illegitimate. Moreover the power to offer her hand in marriage might be useful to her father in foreign affairs.

A reconciliation between the King and his daughter was effected in July[3], and the greater part of England would have rejoiced if the matter had gone still further[4],—if Henry had acknowledged Mary, beheaded Cromwell, burnt Latimer and the heretic bishops, and reconciled himself with the Pope, who in return would certainly have

---

[1] 28 Hen. VIII, c. 7.
[2] L. and P. Hen. VIII, xi, 148.
[3] Ibid. preface, p. iv, and No. 6.
[4] Ibid. x, 1134, 1150.

been willing to recognise Queen Jane and her possible children. Apart from all other objections to this change of policy, however, there was one fatal obstacle; the King could not afford it.

The characters of the Tudor Kings have made so deep an impression on English history that it is easy to explain the events of their reigns by attributing everything to their personal traits, but Henry's need of money was due to something that lay deeper than his own extravagance and rapacity. The whole of Europe was undergoing great economic changes, in consequence of the discovery of new trade routes and the importation of gold and silver from America, which depreciated the value of the coinage. Prices rose and the spending power of any fixed sum of money diminished. As the royal revenues were almost entirely customary and therefore fixed, it followed that the King was growing poorer while the expenses of government were constantly increasing as the nation emerged from feudal into modern life[1].

One of the most deeply-rooted feudal theories was that "the King should live of his own," that is, that the ordinary revenues derived from the crown lands, the customs and feudal dues, should serve for the ordinary needs of the government, and that taxes should be levied only in time of war, or to meet extraordinary need. This theory had seldom corresponded to facts, and it was now quite untenable, but the tax-payer naturally cherished it. Henry's taxation had already aroused great discontent, but the need for a sufficient revenue did not grow less, and the King could not afford to give up the money which, as supreme head of the Church of England, he diverted from the Pope, or the still more considerable sum that he hoped to derive from the suppression of the monasteries. But while the great mass of the nation desired nothing so much as the remission of all taxes, the educated classes were beginning to realise that this would not be such a very desirable state of affairs. The idea was just beginning to emerge that if the King did not need money he would never call a parliament, and that the liberties of the nation depended on its control of taxation. When the King declared that if only the wealth of the monasteries were in his hands he would never ask his people for money again, there were a few who saw that the King's wealth was a much more serious danger than the King's poverty[2].

The state of affairs on the continent permitted Henry to do as he pleased, for Francis I had again attacked Charles V, and the Pope

---

[1] Cunningham, The Growth of Eng. Ind. and Com. I, chap. v, sections 1 and 6.
[2] L. and P. VIII, 121.

could do nothing while his two champions were cutting each other's throats. Henry therefore continued to carry out the policy expressed in the acts of his two last parliaments, the long parliament which met in December 1529 and was dissolved in March 1536, and its brief successor which met in June and was dissolved in July 1536.

A word must be said about the composition of these parliaments. A Tudor House of Commons was not, of course, representative in the modern sense of the word, for it consisted exclusively of country gentlemen and wealthy merchants, who were in most cases appointed by a small close body rather than popularly elected. The influence of the crown, exercised through the sheriff or through some local magnate, was paramount at the nomination of members, and it does not seem to have been resented, so long as the chosen candidate was a well-known man in the district for which he was appointed. The electors were willing that the King should choose the man most pleasing to himself among perhaps a dozen equally eligible persons, but gentlemen and burgesses alike resented the "carpet-bagger," the stranger sent down from the court, who knew nothing of the place and despised the provincials whom he nominally represented[1]. They also objected to members who held government posts, and, curiously enough, bye-elections were considered an abuse, as it was maintained that when a member died his seat ought to remain vacant until the next general election[2].

The parliament of 1529–36 violated even these elementary conditions of representation; Cromwell, who came into power during these seven years, gradually developed the art of managing the House of Commons to an extent which had never been known before, and the electors were powerless in his hands, because they could not understand what was happening[3]. It must also be noticed that the electors in 1529 had very little means of knowing what measures would be brought before the parliament. They knew of course that the King would want money, and they knew also that the question of the divorce would be dealt with, but even the best-informed can hardly have foreseen the act for the dissolution of the smaller monasteries. It must, therefore, be borne in mind that the acts of this parliament were not passed with the consent, or even with the knowledge, of the nation. Their true originator was believed to be Thomas Cromwell. Whether his rise had been slow or rapid, this remarkable man was now (1536) at the height of his

---

[1] L. and P. xi, 1244.   [2] Ibid. 1182.
[3] Porritt, The Unreformed House of Commons, i, pt iii, chap. xvii.

power[1], and the greater number of this parliament's acts were stages in the progress of his policy. By birth Cromwell came of the English lower middle class, but part of his early manhood was spent in Italy[2], and his character was an illustration of the proverb "An Englishman Italianate is a devil incarnate." He belonged to the new school of political thought which had for its exponents Philip de Commines and Machiavelli, and for its heroes Louis XI and Caesar Borgia. Thomas Cromwell, clothier, solicitor and moneylender, seems genuinely to have believed that it was the duty of any man who by birth, luck or skill became a prince, to make himself absolute, and to guard against any breath of opposition at home as carefully as he did against any hint of attack from abroad. He was really convinced that an absolute autocracy was the best form of government for any country, and that it was the duty of a good subject to do everything in his power to strengthen the hand of the King. Religion meant nothing at all to him. He conformed to the existing usages, whatever they might be, but distinctions between creeds only interested him in so far as they might be used politically. Honour, mercy, conscience, were simply the prevailing weaknesses of mankind, which might be employed for his advantage, just as he might take advantage of drunkenness or stupidity. It was not so much that he disregarded as that he never felt them. With all this moral insensibility he was a singularly efficient administrator. Instead of fearing and slighting the houses of parliament, he manipulated them for his own ends, while his spy system was unrivalled. But this was the darker side of his labours; it was also part of his policy to promote trade, to put the kingdom in a state of defence, to repress crime and violence as well as rebellion. His faults as a statesman were rapacity and a too great desire to interfere in every department of life. It was now six years since his celebrated promise "to make Henry the richest king that ever was in England"[3]; at last the treasures of the monasteries were within his grasp, and his promise seemed on the point of fulfilment.

Cromwell's low birth exposed him to the scorn of his contemporaries, and has been brought up against him even by modern historians; nevertheless if it were necessary to make a choice between his moral character and that of his high-born opponent, Thomas Howard, Duke of Norfolk, it could scarcely be denied that Norfolk was the greater scoundrel of the two. He was simply a courtier and

---

[1] Dictionary of National Biography; Merriman, Life and Letters of Thomas Cromwell, I, chap. VI.

[2] Ibid. I, chap. I.   [3] Ibid. I, chap. IV.

politician, with not a tenth of Cromwell's ability. By inclination
he was conservative and favoured the Old Learning, but if he could
advance himself by denying his politics or his faith he was quite ready
to abandon either. Cromwell at least had a political end in view;
Norfolk merely wished to aggrandise himself and had no other object.

It goes without saying that the two regarded each other with
the bitterest hatred. After the fall of Anne Boleyn Cromwell
managed to procure Norfolk's banishment from the court, but they
were in constant correspondence with each other. Among all the
records of misery, crime and brutality in the Letters and Papers of
the time there is perhaps nothing more horrible than Norfolk's
letters to Cromwell; the sickly expressions of goodwill, the filthy
jokes, the grimaces of thankfulness, make them vile reading. But
not many letters were written in the summer of 1536, for Norfolk
had just been worsted, and Cromwell was completely master of the
situation.

The general course of Cromwell's systematic attack on the Church
is so well known that it is necessary only to recapitulate those
features which chiefly aroused popular indignation.

In 1529, the first year of Henry's long parliament, a very sweeping measure was passed to regulate the clergy. They were prohibited
from holding any land by lease. All leases held by ecclesiastics must
be transferred to laymen before the next Michaelmas. Spiritual persons
were prohibited from trading, except in the case of monasteries
selling the produce of their own lands for their own needs. No
priest was henceforth to hold more than one benefice of value above
£8 yearly, but existing pluralists might retain four; members of
the King's Council, chaplains of the royal family or of peers, and
brothers of peers and knights, were permitted to hold three, and
Doctors of Divinity might hold two. Every priest was required to
reside on one of his benefices, but exceptions were made in favour of
pilgrims, persons on the King's service, scholars at universities, and
royal chaplains. Spiritual persons were prohibited from keeping
breweries and tan-yards[1]. The chief object of this statute was
probably to facilitate the transference of ecclesiastical property to
laymen[2]. It must have caused great indignation among the clergy.
They may have hoped at first that it would not be strictly enforced,
but in 1536 it was re-enacted with still more stringent residentiary
clauses[3].

[1] 21 Hen. VIII, c. 13.
[2] Dixon, Hist. of the Ch. of Eng. I, chap. I.   [3] 28 Hen. VIII, c. 13.

In 1530 the clergy of England were called upon to face the overwhelming charge that they had all offended against the Statute of Praemunire by acknowledging Wolsey's legatine authority. In order to buy their pardon from the King they were compelled to pay a heavy fine. In addition to this the King demanded that they should acknowledge him "the only Protector and Supreme Head of the Church and clergy of England," and that cure of souls was committed to him, "curæ animarum ejus majestati commissæ et populo sibi commisso debite inservire possimus." He made other demands, but these were the most important points. The clergy would only accept the title qualified by the phrase "quantum per Christi leges licet," "as far as the laws of Christ will allow."[1] They applied the same qualifications to the phrase about the cure of souls "ut et curæ animarum populi ejus majestati commissi *dehinc* servire possimus," "and so far (as the laws of Christ will allow) we are able to agree that the cure of the souls of his people has been committed to his Majesty." This acknowledgment was made, as far as can be discovered, only by the southern convocation. The questions were not put to the northern convocation, and it seems that at least three of the northern bishops, Tunstall being one, protested against the new title, even with the modification[2]. However the King was satisfied for the moment by the compromise, and the clergy were solemnly pardoned[3].

It is not necessary to go into the complicated questions of the Petition of the Commons, the Answer of the Ordinaries, and the Submission of the Clergy in 1532, as they were not understood by the people at large[4]. Passing over the anti-papal legislation of the following years, those acts which were protested against by the rebels are the only ones which need be mentioned. The first of these was the Act which conditionally restrained the payment of Annates or First Fruits to Rome in 1532[5], a prohibition which was made absolute in 1534[6]. The fault found with this statute was not that the payments were no longer made to Rome, but that they were still levied by the King.

In 1534 Henry attacked the Church of Rome at a vital point. On 31 March of that year the question was put to the Convocation of Canterbury, "Whether the Roman pontiff has any greater

[1] Dixon, op. cit. I, chap. I.
[2] Ibid.   [3] 22 Hen. VIII, c. 15.
[4] Gee and Hardy, Doc. illus. of Eng. Ch. Hist. nos. XLVI, XLVII, XLVIII.
[5] 23 Hen. VIII, c. 20.   [6] 25 Hen. VIII, c. 20.

jurisdiction bestowed on him by God in the Holy Scripture in this realm of England than any other foreign bishop?" Only four of those present voted for the Pope's authority, and it was consequently resolved by a large majority that he had no such power[1]. On 5 May the same resolution was passed by the Convocation of York without a dissenting vote[2]. Following on this, Henry caused the Supremacy Act to be passed in November 1534. This measure conferred upon the King and his heirs for ever the title of "Only supreme head on earth of the Church of England." The saving clause "quantum per Christi leges licet" was quietly ignored[3].

It must always be remembered that behind this brief summary the great drama of the rival queens, Katherine of Arragon and Anne Boleyn, had been running its course. The anti-papal acts so far had been diplomatic moves. In the more remote country districts they were probably hardly known and not at all understood. But at this point Henry resolved to make the whole nation realise their altered relation to Rome.

In April 1535 Henry issued a mandate which declared that "sundry persons both religious and secular, priests and curates, daily set forth and extol the jurisdiction and authority of the Bishop of Rome, otherwise called Pope, sowing their pestilential and false doctrine, praying for him in the pulpit, making him a god, illuding and seducing our subjects, and bringing them into great errors, sedition and evil opinions, more preserving the power, laws and jurisdiction of the said bishop than the most holy laws and precepts of Almighty God." Any person offending in this way was to be apprehended at once and committed to prison without bail until the King's pleasure in his case was known[4]. Royal letters were sent out on 1 June 1535 to all the bishops to command them to declare the King's new title in their sermons every Sunday, and to cause their clergy to do the same. The name of the Bishop of Rome was to be erased from all services and mass books. This was followed on the 3rd by an "Order for preaching and bidding of the beads in all sermons to be made within the realm." The Pope and the Cardinals of Rome were no longer to be named in the bidding of the beads. The prayers were to be "for the whole Catholic Church and for the Catholic Church of the realm; for the King, only Supreme Head of the Catholic Church of England, for Queen Anne and the Lady Elizabeth, for the whole clergy and temporality, and especially for

---

[1] Gee and Hardy, op. cit. no. LVIII.   [2] Ibid. no. LIX.
[3] 26 Hen. VIII, c. 1.   [4] L. and P. VIII, 623.

such as the preacher might name of devotion; for the souls of the dead, and specially of such as it might please the preacher to name." Every preacher was ordered to preach against the usurped power of the Bishop of Rome, and they were to abstain for one year from any reference to purgatory, honouring of saints, marriage of priests, pilgrimages, miracles[1]. The shock which this measure gave to the nation will be to some extent illustrated in the following chapters. It struck at the very foundations of the existing creed. The papal authority was not always popular in England,—men grumbled at the Pope, sneered at him, criticised him,—but that he was the only supreme head of Christianity was as firmly believed and as confidently accepted as that the sun rose in the east. When simple country priests were called upon to deny weekly a proposition which they had never before dreamed of questioning, they and their congregations might well think that the foundations of society were giving way, and their worst fears seemed to be realised by the Act for the Suppression of the Smaller Monasteries, passed in the following year[2]. It is not necessary to repeat the well-known story of Henry's dealings with the monasteries, and the whole of the following work is a commentary on it.

In the same year the privileges of the palatinate of Durham and other exempted districts were abolished[3].

In the short parliament of June—July 1536 two Acts were passed of considerable importance. By one all bulls, breves, dispensations and faculties from the Pope now within the realm were declared void[4]. In 1534 the clergy had been prohibited from obtaining dispensations, etc. from Rome[5], but those obtained before 12 March 1533 had been expressly declared valid. Now, however, they were required to surrender their papal licences, etc. to the Archbishop of Canterbury before Michaelmas 1537[6]. The Imperial ambassador, Chapuys, reported that this was the statute which the parliament was most reluctant to pass, as it involved serious questions of legitimacy, "but in the end everything must go as the King wishes."[7] The other statute dealt with the question of sanctuary and benefit of clergy. Already several statutes had been passed limiting this much abused privilege[8]. In this statute benefit of clergy was denied to any ecclesiastic who committed the crimes

---

[1] Dixon, op. cit. i, chap. iv.   [2] 27 Hen. VIII, c. 28.
[3] 27 Hen. VIII, c. 14.   [4] 28 Hen. VIII, c. 10.
[5] 25 Hen. VIII, c. 21.   [6] 28 Hen. VIII, c. 16.
[7] L. and P. xi, 148.   [8] 21 Hen. VIII, c. 2; 23 Hen. VIII, c. 1.

specified in former statutes as those for which no layman might claim benefit. The offending priest was to be punished like a layman, without degradation from his holy orders[1].

By the time that this mass of legislation was completed there were very few people in England who knew what they were really intended by the government to believe. In order that the new state of things might be understood, the King as Supreme Head of the Church of England, with the advice and assent of Convocation, published Ten Articles about Religion. They were issued in June 1536, when the year's prohibition of controversy about purgatory, pilgrimages, etc. was at an end[2]. The first five articles stated those points in belief which were necessary to salvation. They were the grounds of faith, as set forth in the Bible, the Creeds as interpreted by the patristic traditions not contrary to Scripture, and by the Acts of the Four Councils; Justification; Baptism; Penance, which included confession and good works; and the Sacrament of the Altar. Thus only three of the seven sacraments were named as essential. The other five Articles dealt with such points "as have been of a long continuance for a decent order and honest policy, prudently instituted and used in the churches of our realm, and be for that same purpose and end to be observed and kept accordingly, although they be not expressly commanded of God, nor necessary to our salvation." These were paying honour to saints, placing their images in churches and praying to them; the rites and ceremonies of the Church; and the belief in purgatory, which involved prayers for the dead[3].

The Ten Articles received the assent of the southern, but not of the northern convocation, although they were signed by the Archbishop of York and the Bishop of Durham[4]. They were supplemented in July by an order of the Supreme Head and Convocation that no holy days should be observed in harvest time, 1 July—29 September, except the feasts of the Apostles, the Virgin Mary, and St George; or in the law terms, except Ascension Day, the Nativity of St John the Baptist, All Hallows and Candlemas; all feasts of the Dedication should be observed on the first Sunday in October, and no "church holidays," which were the feasts of the patron saints of churches, should be observed unless they fell on an authorised holy day[5].

---

[1] 28 Hen. VIII, b. xiii, 1.
[2] Hardwick, Hist. of the Articles, chap. iii.
[3] Ibid. App. i.   [4] Ibid. chap. iii.
[5] Frere and Kennedy, Visitation Articles and Injunctions, ii, 5, n. 3.

In the same month these new regulations were enforced by the first Royal Injunctions of Henry VIII[1]. The publication of these injunctions " was the first act of pure supremacy done by the King, for in all that had gone before he had acted with the concurrence of Convocation."[2] The Ten Articles were a compromise between the Old and the New Learning, but the Injunctions, which were issued in Cromwell's name, went further in the way of innovations. The clergy were ordered to preach every Sunday for the next quarter, and afterwards twice a quarter, on the subject of the King's Supremacy, setting forth the abolition of the Bishop of Rome's pretended authority. They were also to expound and enforce the Ten Articles and to declare the new order for holy days. They were to discourage superstitious ceremonies, and to exhort all men to " apply themselves to the keeping of God's commandments and fulfilling of His works of charity, rather than to make pilgrimages or bestow money on saints and relics." In this the Injunctions went further than the Articles, in which pilgrimages were not mentioned. Another innovation was the order that all servants and young people must be taught the Lord's Prayer, the Creed and the Ten Commandments in English. The remaining injunctions directed the clergy to study, give alms, lead sober lives, etc.

In addition to these measures, any one of which was sufficient to arm all the forces of tradition and religious conservatism against the King, several important political Acts had been passed, which were scarcely more likely to be popular. Among these the three Succession Acts were the most important. The first declared the Princess Mary illegitimate and entailed the succession on the heirs male of the King and Anne Boleyn, or failing heirs male, on the Princess Elizabeth. All were to swear to maintain this act, under penalty of high treason[3]. The second Succession Act confirmed the first and supplied a form of oath to be taken[4], but this was superseded by the third, which has been described above. The Treason Act gave a new definition of high treason. It was declared to be high treason " if any person......do *maliciously* wish, will or desire by words or writing, or by craft imagine, invent, practise, or attempt any bodily harm to be done or committed to the King's most royal person, the queen's or their heir's apparent, or to deprive them of their dignity, title or name of their royal estates, or *slanderously and maliciously*

---

[1] Frère and Kennedy, Visitation Articles and Injunctions, II, 1 et seq.
[2] Wriothesley, Chronicle (Camden Soc.), I, 55, n.
[3] 25 Hen. VIII, c. 22.   [4] 26 Hen. VIII, c. 2.

publish and pronounce, by express writing or words, that the King our sovereign lord should be heretic, schismatic, tyrant, infidel or usurper of the crown."[1]   This act was passed only after prolonged debate in the House of Commons, and the King was forced to permit the word "maliciously" to be inserted; this was done in the hope of saving those who could not conscientiously call the King Supreme Head of the Church, but did and said nothing to prevent others from giving him the title[2].

It was for offences against these statutes, the second Succession Act and the Treason Act, that Sir Thomas More and Cardinal Fisher were put to death in July 1535.   Pope Paul III, roused at last by this deliberate defiance of his authority, prepared a bull of interdict and deposition against Henry in the autumn of the same year[3].   But he had not sufficient faith in his own curses to launch them at Henry without adequate secular support.   If he had had the courage of a medieval pope, he would have published the bull with perfect confidence that it would accomplish its own work, without earthly aid; what is more, it would very likely have been effective, as will be shown hereafter.   Paul III, however, endeavoured to back up his supernatural threats by physical force, and failed.   Francis I protested vigorously against the publication of the bull, as he was Henry's ally, while Charles V was not in a position to lend his aid, and the Pope suspended it for the time[4].

Returning to the unpopular statutes of the long parliament, the financial situation must be briefly considered.   Henry's money troubles have already been mentioned.   The usual levies by direct taxation, the Fifteenth and the Tenth, had originally been the actual fraction of the tax-payer's possessions, but since 1334 they had become fixed payments levied from each county without reassessment, and therefore did not represent the wealth of the nation[5].   In addition to the usual Fifteenth and Tenth, the long parliament granted to the King a general subsidy of 1*d.* in the £ on incomes above £20 a year, levied by commissioners who were sent into every shire to discover through the constables the amount which each person ought to pay[6].   In Henry's reign at any rate a real

[1] 26 Hen. VIII, c. 13.

[2] L. and P. VIII, preface, p. xxxiv, n.

[3] Froude, Reign of Henry VIII, II, chap. IX; Cal. of Venetian St. P. v, no. 125; Pollard, Henry VIII, chap. XII.

[4] Froude, loc. cit.

[5] Cunningham, op. cit. chap. v, section 6.

[6] Dowell, Hist. of Tax in Eng. I, Bk III, chap. I, pt II, sections 1 and 2.

assessment was made, and the measure was consequently exceedingly unpopular.

Another act which was designed to increase the revenue was the Statute of Uses[1]. The object of this statute was to preserve intact to the King the feudal dues from estates which were held directly from him in chief. Such estates might not be given by will, but their holders usually provided for their families by leaving a rent charge on the estate to the use of their younger children or other dependents. The statute abolished such uses entirely, and thus deprived the whole family, except the eldest son, of any income from an estate held in chief from the King,

These statutes were all passed at the direct instance of the King, and chiefly for his profit, but statutes of a more disinterested character were not more popular. Tudor statesmen were firmly convinced that it was their duty to regulate the trade of the nation in every possible way. Their constant interference in minute points must have been most exasperating to tradesmen, and although their object was always the common good, such unwise meddling produced bad results more often than good ones, and therefore was detested not only by the sellers, but also by the buyers, whose interests it was supposed to protect. Moreover the common people had no confidence in the government, and were always ready to believe rumours that these acts would turn out to be new forms of taxation.

A statute which aroused great indignation in the eastern counties was passed in 1535. Clothiers were ordered to weave into their cloth their respective trade marks, and to specify the length of each piece of cloth on a seal attached to it. Until this was done the aulnager was not permitted to seal the goods. At the same time the legal breadth of various kinds of cloth, which had been regulated by previous statutes, was increased, except in the case of Suffolk set cloths. The provisions of the statute did not apply to the county of Worcester[2].

In order to check the evils of enclosures, which were increasing rapidly[3], it was enacted that no grazier might keep a flock of more than 2,000 sheep[4], and by another statute landowners who had abandoned husbandry for sheep-farming since 1515, were ordered to re-erect or repair the houses of husbandry on their lands under

---

[1] 27 Hen. VIII, c. 10.   See F. Pollock, The Land Laws (The English Citizen Series), 89—104; Holdsworth, Hist. of Eng. Law, I, 241.
[2] 27 Hen. VIII, c. 12.   [3] See below, chap. IV.
[4] 25 Hen. VIII, c. 13.

penalty of forfeiting half the land to the crown[1]. These two statutes were intended to check the depopulation caused by sheep-farming enclosures, and were therefore popular in intention, but they were naturally resented by the landowners, and rumours spread that both cattle and sheep were to be taxed or confiscated.

Other measures with an equally good object had equally unfortunate results. Ever since 1529 the government had been endeavouring to keep down the price of meat. As all prices were rising rapidly during this period, owing to causes beyond the control of legislation, these efforts had exasperated the butchers, while they left the purchasers in a rather worse case than before[2]. In 1534 by one of several statutes dealing with the subject the Lords of the Council were empowered to issue proclamations "from time to time as the case shall require to set and tax reasonable prices of all such kinds of victuals" as "cheese, butter, capons, hens, chickens," etc.[3] It seems possible that this statute, together with the ineffective regulations which accompanied it, gave rise to the rumour that all poor men were to be prohibited from eating "white meat" unless they paid a tax to the King on every chicken, capon or such-like[4]. But whether the rumour may be traced to this statute or not, it will be seen in what follows that the butchers sought their revenge on the King by taking an active part in the insurrection.

From this brief review it is obvious that the government had been pursuing a remarkably daring policy in all departments of national life. In the following chapters an attempt will be made to show how the different classes were affected by this varied mass of legislation, and what their feelings were towards its originators, the King and Thomas Cromwell.

[1] 27 Hen. VIII, c. 22.
[2] Leadam, Select Cases in the Court of Star Chamber (Selden Soc.), II, pp. xxxviii—liv.
[3] 25 Hen. VIII, c. 2.   [4] See below, chap. IV.

CHAPTER II

PLOTS AND TOKENS

Before the Act dissolving the Lesser Monasteries was passed, in March 1536, the opposition to Henry's policy was too much broken up by class distinctions to be very formidable; nor did the chief of the conservative nobles ever encourage the popular movement. Henry was able to crush his opponents separately, when a united attack might have shaken even his weight from the throne.

In the first place he was opposed by the party of the Old Nobility. By this we do not mean Norfolk and other time-servers of his opinion, but another and weaker faction, the remaining members of the Yorkist nobility, who had survived the Wars of the Roses. The religious problems of Henry's reign somewhat obscure its connection with the history of the century before it. The days of Cranmer and Pole seem so far removed from those of Warwick the Kingmaker and Richard Crookback that it requires an effort to realise that Henry had to deal with a legacy of trouble from the earlier period, as well as with his own share of the difficulties of the new age. The previous storm had not yet passed away when the new cloud appeared on the horizon and the two broke in full fury upon the unfortunate house of Pole.

Margaret, Countess of Salisbury, the only living child of George, Duke of Clarence, was chief among the old aristocracy, who were now sometimes called the party of the White Rose. Katherine of Arragon had been warmly attached to the Countess and her family. The tender-hearted queen believed that Margaret's brother was sacrificed in order to bring about her marriage with Prince Arthur. The Countess' eldest son, Henry, Lord Montague, married Jane Neville, daughter to Lord Abergavenny, while her daughter Ursula became the wife of Lord Stafford, the Duke of Buckingham's son. It was even whispered that higher honours awaited the Poles. The Countess became governess to the Princess Mary, and Queen Katherine would gladly have seen a marriage between her daughter and her friend's son Reginald, who was a promising lad of sixteen when Mary was born in 1516. The family was closely connected by blood and friendship with Edward Courtenay, Marquis of Exeter, and his wife Gertrude. The Marquis was the son of Katherine, the youngest daughter of Edward IV, and therefore heir to the throne, after the Tudors: a very dangerous position[1].

Henry had learnt his lesson from his father too well to allow this state of things to continue. For the last hundred years the nobles had kept the kingdom in a turmoil. Northumberland, Warwick, the second Duke of Buckingham, had in turn made and unmade kings at their pleasure; now the day of reckoning had come. The two Henrys performed in England the work that Richelieu was to achieve in France a century later; they made the nobles realise at the cost of much bloodshed, that there was to be one king in the country, not half-a-dozen. No one can deny that they triumphed only by means of cruelty and injustice, and that their motives were selfish. But when it is considered how greatly the nation benefited, and when the fate of countries like Poland where the work was never carried out is remembered, it seems ungrateful to abuse the kings who did so much for their country at the cost of their reputation.

Buckingham was executed in 1521 and his son was ruined[2]; Montague and Abergavenny were thrown into prison[3] and made to pay heavy fines. The reason was simply that they were powerful enough to be dangerous, and Henry was powerful enough to crush them.

So far the King had acted from the old motives and guarded against the old dangers; with the divorce of Katherine new factors came into play. The Pole family was devoted to the Queen, and would in any case have opposed the divorce. In addition to this motive the Countess was a very devout woman and had brought up her sons to be pillars of the Church[4]. In 1532 Reginald Pole with some difficulty obtained leave to go abroad, to escape acquiescence in the divorce.

Reginald Pole was a man of quiet, amiable and studious disposition. He had been educated at the King's expense, and was genuinely fond of his patron. There seems to be little doubt that if

---

[1] D. N. B., Pole and Courtenay.
[2] Ibid. Stafford.   [3] L. and P. III (1) 1293.
[4] L. and P. XI, 92.

he had been left alone he would have been content to live peacefully in Italy with his friends and his studies. There he could have deplored the misfortunes of his country without attempting to remedy them by any more dangerous means than the vague, ineffectual plots at which legitimists always excel. But he was shaken out of his tranquillity by Henry himself. Early in 1535 Starkey, the King's chaplain, who was a friend of Pole's, sent him a royal command to state in writing his opinion on the royal title of Supreme Head of the Church of England. Henry wished to force Pole to take up a definite position. If he was friendly he might be useful; if hostile, he was dangerous, and the King was determined to know how to regard him. Pole was at first reluctant to undertake the task, but once he embarked on it he worked hard, and indulged to the full in the dangerous satisfaction of giving the King a piece of his mind. The book "De Unitate Ecclesiastica" was finished by the end of the year, but it was not despatched until Pole received the news of Anne Boleyn's fall. Then, imagining, that the King might now be induced to change his policy, he sent it to England, at the end of May 1536, by the hands of his trusted servant Michael Throgmorton. It was, as its name implies, a vigorous defence of the one and indivisible Catholic Church under one supreme head, the Pope. The language of the book does not exceed the bounds of controversy as then observed; though, considering the King's figure, the comparison between Henry and an unclean barrel was rather tactless. But Pole stated with perfect frankness his very strong disapproval of the King's proceedings. From that time forth there was no hope that Henry would ever be reconciled to his kinsman[1].

The interest of the book to a modern reader lies in its revelation of Pole's point of view. He had an essentially medieval mind; throughout his writings he assumes the political ideal of the middle ages, which pictured the Pope and the Emperor as the spiritual and secular heads of Europe. If any lesser king withdrew his allegiance from the Pope it was the Emperor's duty to make him return to the fold. Hence it was the obvious duty of Charles V to reduce Henry to obedience. It never seems to have occurred to Pole that any life which there might once have been in this theory was now extinguished, and that the condition of affairs in medieval Europe had passed away for ever. After Katherine's death Charles had no more justification for invading England simply because he disapproved of the English government than England had for invading France

---

[1] Haile, *Life of Reginald Pole.*

because she disapproved of Napoleon.   Besides, what with Francis I,
the Turks and the German Reformers, Charles had so many em-
barrassments that it was in the highest degree improbable he would
ever be free to attempt the subjugation of England.   But Pole was
blind to all this, and he and his English friends continued to put
their trust in foreign princes with disastrous consequences to themselves.

Pole had written his book at the King's express request, stating
his opinions quite honestly; he believed his country was going to
perdition, and that a patriot's only hope lay in force.   From the point
of view of the English government the book was certainly treasonable.
It clearly and expressly urged all Englishmen to take up arms against
the King, and exhorted two foreign princes to invade the country
and help the rebels.   Pole, however, was very careful that the
manuscript should not be copied or printed, and its contents were
only known to three or four of his friends[1].   It is unnecessary to
describe the King's anger on receiving the book, or the letters of
remonstrance which he forced the Countess of Salisbury and Lord
Montague to write to the offending author.   He himself dissembled
his anger, and summoned Pole to return home and there confer with
wise men on the subject, about which he was misinformed.   Pole was
too prudent to accept this royal invitation[2].

The policy of the White Rose party is embodied in " De Unitate."
The plan at the root of all their scheming was that Charles V
should invade England, marry Mary to Reginald Pole[3], force Henry
to acknowledge Katherine, and establish a sort of regency, leaving
Henry only the title of King.   There were two serious flaws in this
scheme.   First, the conspirators overlooked the fact that an invasion
was sure to cause a violent reaction in favour of Henry, who was at
least an Englishman: they were, indeed, hopelessly out of touch
with the feeling of the nation at large.   Secondly, nothing was more
unlikely than that Charles would consent to a marriage between
Mary and Pole, for he regarded her as his property and would be
sure, if he had the opportunity, to bestow her hand on some dependant
of his own.   Ruling, as he did, over so many different countries,
he could not realise how strong national feeling was in such an
isolated kingdom as England, and how desirable therefore an English
husband would be for Mary, if she was ever to become Queen.

---

[1] Haile, Life of Reginald Pole, chap. ix.   [2] Ibid. chap. x.
[3] See note A at end of chapter.

Thus the White Rose party was following quite the wrong path, intent on will-o'-the-wisp hopes of the Emperor's help when they should have turned to the mass of the nation for assistance. After Katherine's death the prospect that Charles would interfere in English politics was very distant. King Henry did not "wear yellow for mourning" for nothing[1]. But Exeter and the Poles looked only to the Emperor, and while they did this Henry had little to fear from them. Other members of the party saw their mistake after a while. First among these was Lord Darcy.

Thomas, Lord Darcy, was the son of Sir William Darcy by his wife Euphemia, daughter to Sir John Langton[2]. On his father's death (1488) he came into the lands in Lincolnshire which had belonged to the Darcys since Doomsday Book was compiled, and also those lands in Yorkshire, including the family seat of Templehurst, which had come to the family by marriage in the reign of Edward III. He was already over twenty-one and had probably married Dousabella[3], daughter to Sir Richard Tempest of the Dale, who was the mother of his four sons, George, Richard, William and Arthur. Darcy was raised to the peerage in 1505. In the same year he was made steward of the lands of the young Earl of Westmorland. This young man became Earl in 1523. The Earl's character has left few traces upon history. Norfolk described him as "of such heat and hastiness of nature as to be unmeet" to hold the office of Warden of the Marches[4]. He was connected with the White Rose party by his marriage with Katherine, daughter to the unfortunate Duke of Buckingham. His mother was Edith, sister to William, Lord Sandes.

Darcy's great influence in the north was in part owing to this connection with the Nevilles which was strengthened by his second marriage, to Lady Neville, the young Earl's mother. Darcy held various offices of trust on the Borders during the reign of Henry VII. The King kept a watchful eye on his powerful servant, and in 1496 he was indicted at Quarter Sessions in the West Riding for giving various people his badge, "a token or livery called the Buck's Head." However, Henry by his well-known system of compensation created him Deputy Warden of the East and Middle Marches (16 Dec., 1498) and later Warden of the East Marches

---

[1] Pollard, op. cit. chap. XIII.   [2] D. N. B., Darcy.
[3] See note B at end of chapter.
[4] L. and P. XII (1) 667; printed in full, Papers of the Earl of Hardwicke, I, 41.

(1 Sept., 1505). On the accession of Henry VIII his offices were confirmed to him[1].

Early in the new reign occurred the strangest adventure of Darcy's life—his expedition to Spain. Ferdinand had asked his son-in-law for the aid of 1500 English archers in his war against the Moors. Darcy at his own request was appointed leader of this force. The troops were mustered on 29 March, 1511. The expedition, consisting of five companies of 250 men each, sailed from Plymouth in May and arrived at Cadiz on 1 June. There was in Darcy something of the spirit of his crusading ancestors; but the time for a crusade had passed. The English were unruly and quarrelled with the Spaniards so much that Ferdinand was only too glad to seize the excuse of a truce with the Moors to pack them off home again. They were in Spain little more than a fortnight, and on 17 June re-embarked without having loosed a shaft against the enemy. Darcy was bitterly disappointed and to add to his troubles the voyage home was long and stormy: on 3 August they had only reached St Vincent and he was obliged to spend large sums on victualling the ships and paying his men. His life-long friend, Sir Robert Constable, was one of the five captains under him who shared the humiliation and expense of it all. Such an experience might have made him shun all further dealings with Spain, but on his return to England the Spanish ambassador dealt liberally with him in the matter of money and overcame his resentment. The archers who went out to fight for a Christian prince against the Moors wore as their badge a curious device called the "Five Wounds of Christ."[2]

Darcy took no part in the war with Scotland in 1513. He was not on the glorious field of Flodden, where the future Duke of Norfolk, then Lord Admiral, won such fame that for long years he was beloved through all the north. Darcy had gone with the King to France, where at the siege of Terouanne some accident caused the rupture from which he suffered for the rest of his life. He returned to the strenuous work of governing the Borders, of which more will be said hereafter. During the period of Cardinal Wolsey's power, Darcy was on good terms with him; but in July 1529 he drew up an indictment of the falling favourite. This, in the form of articles, was signed by the Peers in Parliament, on 1 Dec. of the same year. Exactly how much discredit attaches to him for thus acting against a man for whom he had long professed friendship, must be decided by others. The case against Darcy is made rather worse by the fact

[1] D. N. B. loc. cit. [2] Ibid.

that he was at first ready to forward the divorce of Katherine of Arragon. He signed the Memorial of the Lords to Clement VII, and even appeared as a witness at the Queen's trial, although he had no evidence of any importance to give. On the other hand, he must have disapproved of Wolsey's policy for some time, and the tie between the two men never seems to have been very close. Like others he was slow to realise the lengths to which Henry was prepared to go in order to get what he wanted. He did not foresee that Wolsey's policy might lead to a policy of still more daring innovation. But when the situation was plain to him he fully declared himself. In January 1532 Norfolk made an appeal to a private meeting of persons of importance to defend the Royal Prerogative against foreign interference, with the suggestion that matrimonial causes, i.e. the divorce of Katherine, ought to be considered a matter of temporal jurisdiction. Darcy answered. In his speech he maintained that such causes were undoubtedly spiritual, and therefore the Pope was the supreme judge in them. He further insinuated that the King's Council were trying to escape the responsibility of deciding on a course of action by dragging others into the matter[1]. He also addressed the Lords on the fitness of parliament to deal with matters touching the Faith, but the date and purport of this declaration are uncertain[2]. The result of his boldness was that he was informed that his presence was not required at the succeeding sessions[3] of the parliament.

Nevertheless he was not allowed to return to the north, but was kept in London, much against his will, from the winter of 1529[4] till at least as late as July 1535. The King would have been well advised to remember the proverb about idle hands. Darcy, the statesman and warrior, was kept some five years with nothing to do but brood over the changes which were taking place around him, and over the violation of his deepest and most honourable feelings. Cromwell and the King might have foreseen the result. Darcy had a strong sentiment of personal loyalty to the King; he could not bear it to be thought that "Old Tom had one traitor's tooth in his head." But as an honest man and a good Christian he felt he could not stand by and see the Queen and her daughter dishonoured, the Church destroyed, and the land brought under an absolute despotism, without making an effort to save them. The doctrine of the responsibility of the minister salved his conscience; it was easy to

[1] L. and P. v, 805.   [2] L. and P. xii (1) 901, p. 410.
[3] L. and P. vii, 121.   [4] L. and P. xii (2) 186 (63).

believe that if only Cromwell could be removed, Henry would turn
back from the strange and dangerous road along which he was being
led.

Darcy was on intimate terms with Lord Hussey, a member of one
of the new official families which sprang up so plentifully under the
Tudors. Sir William Hussey, father to John, Lord Hussey, was Lord
Chief Justice of the King's Bench in 17 Edward IV[1]; his parents
are unknown. John Hussey assisted in putting down Lovell's
Rebellion in 1486, and obtained a footing at Court. He was partner
to the exactions of Empson and Dudley, and on the accession of
Henry VIII was obliged to obtain a pardon, but he did not lose
favour with the King. He received large grants of land in Lincolnshire, where his seat was at Sleaford[2]; there he was unpopular with
his neighbours, who accused him of arrogance and ostentation[3]. He
served in France in 1513, and was employed on diplomatic missions
until in 1529 he was summoned to the House of Lords as Baron
Hussey of Sleaford. Through the whole of his career he had been
a loyal and unquestioning supporter of the government as it was.
His promotion was probably due to the King's desire to strengthen
his party in the House of Lords. He did what was required of him;
he signed the document requesting the Pope to sanction the divorce
of Katherine, and gave evidence for the King at the Queen's trial.
But Darcy, who was really opposed to the divorce, had done as much
as this. There is no doubt, however, that Henry believed Hussey to
be a man whom he could safely trust, for in 1533 he was appointed
chamberlain to the King's daughter Mary, who had just been declared
illegitimate[4]. It was to his tender care she was confided for the time
of insult and desolation her father had in store for her. Unfortunately
for Hussey a warm friendship sprang up between Mary and his wife
Lady Anne, the daughter of George Grey, Earl of Kent[5]. Hussey
himself, though fairly hard-hearted, seems to have been touched
by the sufferings of his helpless charge. It must have been this
sympathy which drew him into communication with the White Rose
party.

About midsummer 1534 Darcy dined with Hussey at his London
house, and his old friend Sir Robert Constable was there as well.

[1] Tonge's Visitation of Yorks. (Surtees Soc.), p. 22.
[2] D. N. B., Hussey.
[3] L. and P. xi, 969.
[4] D. N. B. loc. cit. J. H. Round, Peerage Studies, Henry VIII and the Peers.
[5] L. and P. vii, 1036 ; op. cit. vol. xi, no. 222.

They talked of a sermon preached by Sir Francis Bigod's priest; Bigod was a young man of great lands in the north, who inclined to the New Learning; his father had been among Darcy's friends. In the sermon under discussion the chaplain had "likened our Lady to a pudding when the meat was out." Not unnaturally shocked by such an expression, they all declared they would be "none heretics" but die Christian men. There by Hussey's account the matter ended; but in September of the same year he was in communication with the Imperial ambassador[1].

Hitherto one of the King's most unfaltering supporters, Hussey at this time unquestionably indulged in treasonable practices. All the disaffected nobles carried on secret correspondence with Chapuys, and Hussey among the rest begged him to urge the Emperor to invade England[2], where everyone was ready to welcome him. Chapuys' correspondence reveals the fact that the nobles, at least, were at that time thoroughly out of sympathy with the King's policy. Sir Geoffrey Pole, the younger brother of Lord Montague and Reginald, was anxious to leave England, and offered to enter the Emperor's service in Spain. He gave up the plan when Chapuys pointed out that he would leave his friends in the greatest danger; they were already regarded with enough suspicion[3].

Meanwhile Darcy was making every effort to obtain permission to quit the Court and go home[4]. But this was steadily refused. In July (1534) he was upon the jury of peers which acquitted Lord Dacre from a charge of high treason[5].

In September he was the most considerable of all the peers who were secretly urging on Charles V an invasion of England[6]. This is the most indefensible part of Darcy's conduct. To attempt to change the policy of the government, even by force if no other way is possible, may be justifiable. But it was very different to invite a foreign prince to invade England, and it was a pity that Darcy was so much swayed by the prevailing policy of the White Rose party as to consent to the scheme. Doubtless the excuse he would have offered was the position of Katherine and Mary. They were helpless in the King's hands. They were inconvenient to him, and people who inconvenienced Henry seldom lived long. A national rising would only add to the danger of their situation; but if Charles joined the rebels the Princesses would at

---

[1] L. and P. XII (1) no. 899; printed in part by Froude, op. cit. II, chap. XIV.
[2] L. and P. vol. VII, no. 1206.   [3] Ibid. VIII, 750.
[4] Ibid. VII, 1206.   [5] Ibid. 962 (x).   [6] Ibid. VIII, Preface, pp. ii—iv.

worst be held as hostages while a sudden raid might snatch them from Henry's grasp[1]. With this object Darcy requested Charles to send a small force to the mouth of the Thames, for Mary was at Greenwich. Katherine at Kimbolton was so much further from the Court that the rebels might hope to rescue her themselves. For the rest, the old lord only asked the Emperor to come to some understanding with the King of Scots, and to send to the North some money, which was very scarce there, and a small number of arquebus men[2]. Both he and Hussey believed the discontent to be so widespread that a national rising would soon effect all that was required without any further assistance from abroad. But Charles was too busy to send even this slight aid. He instructed his ambassador to hold out vague hopes to the White Rose party and to do nothing[3].

For some time this policy succeeded. There was much passing up and down of messages and tokens, and nothing at all was done. Darcy gave Chapuys "a gold pansy, well enamelled" during the autumn. The pansy was the badge of the Poles and was to prove a sign of doom to that unhappy house. At Christmas he presented him with a handsome sword, which Chapuys supposed to indicate indirectly that the times were ripe "pour jouer des couteaulx." His brother-in-law, the brave Lord Sandes, sent expressions of sympathy; and even the Earl of Northumberland, who was believed to be the most loyal of the nobles, sent his physician to Chapuys to assure him that the King was on the brink of ruin[4]. But time wore on; winter drew to spring and spring to summer—the bloody spring and summer of the executions under the Supremacy Act[5]. The Carthusians fell, Sir Thomas More and the gentle Fisher. Still Darcy was detained in London. Nor was he suspected without good reason, for he had long since told Chapuys that once back in the north he would secretly prepare for a general rising. In May he sent an elderly relative of his[6] to the Imperial ambassador, whom the latter described quaintly as "of more virtue and zeal than appears externally." This man proposed to go in person to the Emperor to discover whether he really meant to send help, for if he was only deluding the English they were determined to act for themselves. Chapuys warned him that he would bring Darcy into danger, but he replied that once his master was in the north he would not care a button for any suspicions[7].

---

[1] L. and P. viii, 355.   [2] Ibid. vii, 1206.   [3] Ibid. viii, 272.
[4] Ibid. i.   [5] Ibid. Preface, pp. i–ii.
[6] See note C at end of chapter.   [7] L. and P. viii, 750.

Hussey, who was still trusted by the government, was at his house in Sleaford about midsummer 1535. A Yorkshire gentleman, Thomas Rycard, came to visit him. He found Hussey walking in his garden, and they talked about the spread of heresy in Yorkshire. Rycard said that as yet there was little of it, "except a few particular persons who carried in their bosoms certain books." He prayed that the nobles might "put the King's Grace in rememberance for reformation thereof." Hussey answered that there was no hope of their suppression unless the two counties, Yorkshire and Lincolnshire acted together, and he himself thought it would be necessary to fight for the Faith[1].

In July (1535) Chapuys reported that he had seen Darcy's cousin again, and that "the good old lord" (his by-name among the Imperialist party) was about to go home at last[2]. It appears from a letter to Cromwell, dated at Templehurst, that he was at home by 13 Nov. The year date is not given but it must have been 1535[3].

It is not necessary to describe the character of "Old Tom" at length, for it stands out from the records so vividly that more than any of his contemporaries he seems a living man; we learn to know his out-spokenness, his grim humour, his high sense of honour at a time when the very meaning of honour was almost forgotten. It was a very cruel fate which placed him in an age when it was impossible to live according to his motto, "One God, One King, One Faith." From the day on which Darcy rode north there was something stirring in the land far more serious than any court intrigue, or any wild scheme of the Emperor's interference.

To do the White Rose party justice they were less concerned with hopes of their own advancement than with anxiety for Katherine and Mary. On 6 Nov. 1535, Chapuys wrote to the Emperor: "The Marchioness of Exeter has sent to inform me that the King has lately said to some of his most confidential councillors that he would not longer remain in the trouble, fear and suspense he had so long endured on account of the Queen and the Princess, and that they should see at the coming Parliament, to get him released therefrom, swearing most obstinately that he would wait no longer. The Marchioness declares that this is as true as the Gospel, and begs me to inform your Majesty and pray you to have pity upon the ladies."[4] A few days later he related the sequel: "The personage who informed me of what I wrote to your Majesty on the 6th about the Queen and

---

[1] L. and P. xii (1) 576.   [2] L. and P. viii, 1018.
[3] L. and P. vii, 1426; ibid. viii, Preface, p. iii.   [4] L. and P. ix, 776.

Princess[1]—came yesterday to this city (London) in disguise to confirm what she had sent to me to say, and conjure me to warn your Majesty, and beg you most urgently to see a remedy. She added that the King, seeing some of those to whom he used this language shed tears, said that tears and wry faces were of no avail, because even if he lost his crown he would not forbear to carry his purpose into effect."[2]

It is evident that Henry had purposely alarmed and distressed some of Katherine's friends by threats of an outrage which even he could scarcely have ventured to commit. Was the Marquis of Exeter himself one of the councillors who wept? Someone must have told the Marchioness about the King's threats of getting rid of the Queen and Princess, either her husband or another of the confidential councillors. And she herself, if not her informant, was deliberately communicating the "secrets of the realm of England" to a foreign power. If the King knew this he was quite justified in regarding the Courtenays with suspicion and expelling the Marquis from the Council. The Marchioness acted treasonably, though she did only what any good woman would have done under the circumstances. But Henry could not be expected to see that. Katherine soon gave her friends no more care, for she died in January 1536. In the same month Henry's long parliament met for its last session, that in which the Act for the Suppression of the Lesser Monasteries was to be passed.

Lord Hussey begged to be excused attendance, pleading ill-health, but really, in all probability, because he knew it would be expected to pass acts against the Church. He came joyfully to the new parliament in June, assembled on the fall of Anne Boleyn. Mary was now safe and would probably be restored to the succession; and, on the fall of the late queen, it was universally hoped that a reaction would take place in ecclesiastical matters. Here Hussey's inclination to treason seems to have ended, and his after connection with the rebellion appears to have been sheer bad luck. Or perhaps his wife, an ardent rebel, is to be blamed. She came up with him to London, and at Whitsuntide went to visit her former mistress, the Lady Mary, with whom she had exchanged tokens from time to time since they parted. While she was with the disowned princess on Whit Monday (5 June) she was overheard to call for a drink for "the Princess," and on Tuesday she said "the Princess" had gone walking[3].

---

[1] See note D at end of chapter.   [2] L. and P. ix, 861.
[3] Ibid. vii, 1036.

As Mary's only legal title was "the Lady Mary," Lady Hussey was arrested and sent to the Tower[1]. The charge must have been that "the Princess" meant the Princess of Wales; Mary never was created Princess of Wales, but the title was sometimes informally given to her before 1529. In England the daughters of Kings were not called "princesses" until later times. Chapuys, writing on the first of July, said that the real reason of her imprisonment was the King's suspicion that she had encouraged Mary in her refusal to acknowledge the Acts of Supremacy and the Succession. When he heard that Mary had refused "he made the most strict inquiries, and the Chancellor and Cromwell visited certain ladies at their houses, who, with others, were called before the Council and compelled to swear to the statutes; one of them, the wife of her chamberlain (Lady Hussey), a lady of great house, and one of the most virtuous in England, was taken to the Tower, where she is at present."[2]

The question naturally arises, how much did Lady Hussey know of all that was brewing in the North, and what did she tell Mary? But it can never be answered, though it is certain that whatever her husband's views Lady Hussey was strongly in sympathy with the rebels. Mary's refusal to subscribe to the Acts caused an immense sensation at Court. The King was furious and swore in a passion that she should suffer the extreme penalty. Exeter and Fitzwilliam were excluded from the Council, because they were suspected of sympathy for her. Even Cromwell was not safe, for since Anne's fall he had been bidding for Mary's good-will, in anticipation of her return to Henry's favour. Chapuys assured Mary that she was in immediate danger[3], and that any oath she took under the circumstances would not be binding. Much against her will she yielded to his entreaties, and signed the form her father sent her, without reading it. The result was an almost immediate return to her father's favour and she consented to dissemble in future, whenever it was necessary[4]. Lady Hussey remained in the Tower throughout July, and her health suffered from the confinement[5]. On 3 August she was examined[6], and by the beginning of October she had been released and had gone home to Sleaford[7].

---

[1] L. and P. xi, 222.
[2] Ibid. 7.
[3] Ibid.
[4] Ibid. 219; 220.
[5] Ibid. 10.
[6] Ibid. 222.
[7] Ibid. 969.

NOTES TO CHAPTER II

Note A.   Although Pole was created a Cardinal in 1536, he was not ordained until 1556, after Mary's marriage with Philip of Spain.

Note B.   The Dictionary of National Biography makes Edith his first wife and Dousabella his second, but see Letters and Papers XII (2) Index under Darcy, Dousabella and Edith.

Note C.   He was possibly Dr Marmaduke Walby, a prebendary of Carlisle, who was closely connected with Sir Robert Constable.   After the rebellion had broken out, Darcy proposed to send Walby to the Netherlands for help, because he knew the Imperial ambassador[1].   From this it seems probable that Walby had communicated with the ambassador on the present occasion.

Note D.   The cautious language is characteristic of the Chapuys corre-spondence.   The ambassador never mentioned a name when a substitute was to be had.   "He of whom I told you" is a very common phrase ; Darcy is almost invariably "the good old lord."   This may show that Chapuys feared his letters might fall into the wrong hands, or it may be merely a diplomatic habit.   Letters of such vital importance must have been sent by the most reliable messengers, but there was always a risk of miscarriage.   Yet if they were discovered it does not seem likely that the thin veil of anonymity could have saved those who were compromised.

[1] See chap. x.

CHAPTER III

AFFINITY AND CONFEDERACY

Between the nobles of the Court and the husbandmen in the fields stood that great and influential class "the gentlemen." On it the Tudor government in the main depended. The gentlemen had no more sympathy with the out-of-date dynastic dreams of the White Rose party than with the economic grievances of the commons, but they had their own grudges against the government. They were hard-worked, and gained little thanks, as Henry went on the truly royal principle that it was honour enough to be allowed to serve him. They were worried by clumsy legislation, such as the Statute of Uses; they were angry at the interference with the House of Commons; and their better nature was outraged by the suppression of the monasteries founded by their ancestors, of which they were themselves the pupils and patrons. But the guiding principle of the country gentlemen was their devotion to landed property. They hated rebellion, because, sooner or later, it was followed by confiscation of property. They feared a rising of the lower classes because it endangered their property, even when it was not originally directed against themselves. The German peasants in 1524–5 had risen against the monasteries and the Church; but out of that movement had developed a bloody civil war between the rich and the poor. If fear of loss deterred the English gentlemen from opposing the government, no less did hope of gain. When they realised that the dissolution of the monasteries meant a general scramble for more property, most of them forgot their religious scruples; but this realisation did not come all at once.

So much can safely be said, but there is very little evidence as to the discontent among the gentlemen. It is possible to discover the attitude of the discontented nobles from the letters of Chapuys, which often give us a delightful feeling of eavesdropping across four centuries. Nor is there any doubt as to the feelings of the commons

—scores of informers bear witness to their disaffection. But there is no key to the confidence of the gentlemen. They were more cautious than the labourers, less easily watched than the nobles. Their private opinions were known only to their friends, who would not, of course, inform against them. In the few cases (all after the rising) when gentleman did inform against gentleman, there was generally a feud of some standing between them. We are reduced to arguing backward, as Henry did. The gentlemen, especially in Yorkshire, were the leaders of the Pilgrimage of Grace. We cannot really accept their own subsequent explanation that they acted against their will in fear of their own tenants. There is abundant evidence that risings of the commons alone were very easily put down.

In this chapter we attempt to sketch the histories of half-a-dozen northern families of gentle or noble blood, in order to give some idea of the state of the north at the time and to outline the lives and antecedents of the leaders of the rebellion.

Local government in Henry VIII's reign depended to a great extent on the peers. Each nobleman was responsible for the behaviour of his own district or "country" as it was called; under his supervision the gentlemen kept order, each on his own lands. The lord's private friendships, feuds and marriages had a widespread influence on the lives of all whom he ruled. North of Trent the gentlemen naturally grouped themselves into three clans round the three great houses of Clifford, Percy, and Neville, the heads of which were respectively the earls of Cumberland, Northumberland, and Westmorland. It is necessary to know something of genealogy in order to understand the history of a period when marriages were arranged to suit family politics rather than the inclination of the parties, and consequently a man was born to an hereditary friendship with one family, a feud with another, and perhaps depended on a third for all hope of advancement.

All the noblemen of the northern counties took part in the strenuous task of governing the Borders. The border counties, Northumberland, Cumberland, Westmorland and the Bishopric of Durham, formed a district totally different from the rest of England. Scotland was a troublesome neighbour, and the men of these counties were a hardy race, famed for their soldier-like qualities and especially for their skill as scouts and skirmishers. Then again these counties were exempted from taxation on account of the Scots' ravages and their own special burdens of defence. Finally a state of lawlessness frequently prevailed, which in peaceful times never even threatened the south. The Wardens of the Marches were usually noblemen such as Lord Darcy, Lord Dacre, and the Earl of Northumberland. The power entrusted to them was regarded with much suspicion by the King, while it was quite insufficient to maintain order. As early as 1522 a secret council, under the presidency of a royal lieutenant, was organised on the Borders. In 1525 it was re-organised and placed under the presidency of Henry's natural son the Duke of Richmond[1]. The powers of the Council naturally roused much opposition in the north. Among Lord Darcy's papers there is a draft of a petition complaining of its authority. The petitioners protested their loyalty, and declared their willingness to prove it against any insinuations. Seeing that they were so loyal, and that the country was quiet, with no rufflings as in the days of King Henry and King Edward, "but both the titles and all lovings to God (joined) in your Grace," the petitioners begged they might be left under the ordinary jurisdiction of the Westminster Courts, which extended all over the kingdom except in the county palatine of Durham, instead of being at the mercy of the members of the Council, who might call any man before them on the slightest pretext. They complained that so long as things went well the Council alone was praised, and if affairs went badly, wheresoever the fault might be, the whole blame was laid on the gentlemen. Moreover, the petition continued, the Council was composed of spiritual men, who were not fit to judge murders and felonies, suppress sedition, or see to the defence of the realm, "and as great clerks report, there is no manner of state within this your realm that hath more need of reformation, nor to be put under good government, than the spiritual men." If this were true, it was not meet that they should rule under the commission they now possessed "for surely they and other spiritual men be sore moved against all temporal men." The petition ends with protestations of loyalty, after which Darcy wrote in a note that the like commission had been tried by "my Lady the King's grandam," and proved greatly to the King's disadvantage in stopping the lawful processes at Westminster Hall. From this petition it appears that Darcy, and probably other northern gentlemen, was ready to make use of the King's anti-clerical policy for his own ends, arguing, perhaps, that though he was as loyal a son of the Church as any man, yet priests ought not to meddle in secular matters[2]. This draft was drawn up in the year 1529,

---

[1] Lapsley, County Palatine of Durham (Harvard Hist. Studies), p. 259.
[2] L. and P. xii (2), 186 (38).

before any of the acts aimed at the clergy had been passed, and before Darcy himself had chosen his side in the struggle between King and Pope. It was probably never presented.

Some such body as the Council of the North was absolutely necessary if any approach to law and order was to be maintained on the Borders. In proof of this it is only necessary to describe one case out of a dozen. Humphry Lisle, whose father Sir William Lisle of Felton, had led a brief but crowded career as a freebooter in 1527–8, was run down and condemned to death with his father and most of their band in 1528, when he was only thirteen. He subsequently confessed that he had assisted in an attack on Newcastle gaol, by which nine persons were liberated; that he had taken part in four cattle raids, the burning and spoiling of five farms and villages, and four highway robberies; that he had helped to capture a number of prisoners to be held to ransom, and had been present at the murder of a priest[1]. His life was spared by the Earl of Northumberland, who had captured and hanged his father, but Humphry was sent to the Tower. In 1532 he was back on the Borders and a knight, but almost immediately afterwards he was outlawed and fled to Scotland[2].

Careers of this sort being rather the rule than the exception on the Borders, the office of Warden of the Marches called for a strong man. But one could seldom be found, and the quarrels of the northern nobles among themselves embroiled matters still further. The divisions of the house of Percy, for instance, caused infinite trouble. The fifth Earl of Northumberland, surnamed the Magnificent, died in 1527, leaving numerous large debts. He had three sons by his wife Katherine, daughter and heiress of Sir Robert Spencer[3]. The heir, Henry, born about 1503, was feeble in body and, like all such men in that hurrying age, was constantly the creature of those in power. From his earliest years he was either led or bullied, first by his father and Cardinal Wolsey, in whose household he was educated, later by Cromwell and Cromwell's dependent, Sir Reynold Carnaby. When Henry Percy was a page in the Cardinal's service the incident occurred by which he is best known, his poor little love affair with Anne Boleyn. He seems to have offered to marry her; but the King had already shown the maid of honour favour. The Earl of Northumberland forbade his son to

---

[1] L. and P. iv (2), 4336.
[2] De Fonblanque, Annals of the House of Percy, i, chap. ix.
[3] Ibid.

foster so dangerous a passion and hastened on his marriage with the Lady Mary Talbot, daughter to the Earl of Shrewsbury[1].

In 1527 Henry Percy became Earl of Northumberland, and on the fall of Cardinal Wolsey he was freed from the man who had exercised most influence over him. It is characteristic of Cromwell's methods that he worked the Earl as he wished by means of the young nobleman's own favourite, Sir Reynold Carnaby[2]. While this man retained his position the King could rely on Northumberland, who was reputed to be one of the most loyal of the peers. He was at one time in secret communication with Chapuys, but this was probably a mere freak. Darcy described him as "very light and hasty" and not to be trusted[3]. His loyalty seems to have sprung from abject fear of Henry, and he probably would have been glad enough of the King's overthrow, though he would rather die than venture to assist in it.

The Percy estates were rich, though burdened with debt, and the castles were very strong. With them in his hands the King could keep the north in subjection and even hope to abate the confusion on the Borders. But if they were used against him by some capable commander, such as the Earl's brother, Sir Thomas Percy, the results were sure to be serious; if foreign help were sent to the rebels, perhaps fatal. Cromwell, with Sir Reynold Carnaby to forward his plans, saw the chance of enriching the crown by the whole of the Percy lands. The Earl's life was uncertain; his marriage turned out unhappily and there was no prospect of an heir; he was on bad terms with his brother Sir Thomas, and Carnaby took care that he should not forget the quarrel[4]. It was not surprising that the brothers should disagree, for Sir Thomas had all the conspicuous vices and virtues of his race, which were completely absent in the invalid Earl. An instance of their constant disputes occurred in 1532, when the Earl appointed Lord Ogle Deputy Warden of the Marches. Ogle was allied to Carnaby, and Sir Thomas together with his younger brother, Sir Ingram Percy, refused to recognise his authority and forbade their tenants to do so. Sir Thomas issued proclamations declaring that he was the true Warden, and Lord Ogle postponed his first Warden's court for fear that the brothers would break it up[5].

[1] De Fonblanque, Annals of the House of Percy, I, chap. IX; cf. Wriothesley, Chronicle (Camden Soc.), Introduction, vol. I, p. xxxviii.

[2] L. and P. VIII, 80, 255, 1143; XII (2) 1090.

[3] L. and P. VIII, 1, 121.   [4] L. and P. VIII, 166.

[5] L. and P. V, 727; cf. XII (1) 1090.

Sir Thomas on his side complained that the Earl had not given him the lands left to him in his father's will until he was on the eve of marriage[1]. His wife was Eleanor, daughter and co-heiress to Harbottle of Beamish; by her he had two sons, Thomas and Henry, and a daughter. Their home was generally at Prudhoe Castle on the Tyne[2].

It does not appear that the breach between the brothers was irreparable until about 1535, in which year the King gave the child-less Earl licence to appoint any one of the Percy name and blood heir to all his lands[3]. But when Sir Thomas, his natural successor, was proposed, the King raised objections[4]. The result was that in February 1535 the Earl made the King his sole heir, and an Act of Parliament was passed "concerning the assurance of the possessions of the Earl of Northumberland to the King's Highness and his heirs[5]." Nothing could have made the Earl more unpopular, and it was probably this alienation of the family property rather than his personal extravagance and inherited debts that earned him his surname "the Unthrifty."[6] Sir Thomas was provided for in the Act, but he could hardly be grateful for a pension when he felt himself heir by right to an earldom and the broadest lands in the north[7]. No appeal was possible when the King gained by his loss. A petition which he sent to Cromwell in July 1535 shows his helplessness. In this he related how the lands at Corbridge so tardily allowed him, which he "with great labour" had defended from the Scots, had now been granted by his brother to Sir Reynold Carnaby. Sir Thomas naturally refused to give them up, and went to remonstrate with his brother in person. But he was not allowed even to see the Earl and was rudely turned from his house. He concluded by begging that Carnaby might be removed from the Earl's service, as he was the cause of his master's quarrels with his wife, brothers and nearest relatives[8]. Cromwell was not likely to remove Carnaby from the place where he had been of so much use; and it was Cromwell and Carnaby whom Sir Thomas secretly denounced as the authors of his wrongs when he, with Sir Ingram, swore to be revenged on the Earl's favourite as "the destruction of all our blood."

Perhaps the most curious part of the whole matter is the Earl's hatred of his brother. The reason may lie in some long-forgotten

---

[1] L. and P. VIII, 1143.
[2] De Fonblanque, op. cit. I, chap. IX; L. and P. XII (1), 577.
[3] L. and P. VIII, 166.   [4] L. and P. XI, 714.
[5] 27 Hen. VIII, c. 47.
[6] De Fonblanque, op. cit. I, chap. IX.
[7] L. and P. X, 246 (12), (13).   [8] L. and P. VIII, 1143 (4).

offence, but as far as can be known there were wrongs on both sides in their early quarrels. Sir Thomas was the more deeply injured when his brother set aside his claim and that of his young sons to inherit his lands; yet he seems to have felt a kind of personal loyalty to the Earl as head of his house, while the Earl constantly refused even to speak with his brother. Easily swayed in most matters, he had all a weak man's unreasoning obstinacy when driven to desperation. To modern eyes he seems a pathetically frail figure; but it was an age of strong men, and he inspired more curses than pity then. Sir Thomas Percy was the darling of the people, always sympathetic to the disinherited; he was the favourite of his mother, the dowager countess, to whom he was much attached[1]; it was to him rather than to the Earl that the helpless appealed in times of trouble[2]. Like his father, the Magnificent Earl, he delighted in gorgeous array and warlike adventures[3]; he was fearless and honest as Hotspur himself. But he was as lawless as the Border thieves who were often his followers and allies. Feuds were still pursued with great earnestness in the north, but his methods were rather out of date. On the first opportunity he followed the rude old plan of spoiling his enemy's goods, laying waste his lands, and chasing him into his fastnesses with blood-curdling threats.

Whatever may be thought of the Percys' habits, they were no worse than those of the Cliffords, the staunch supporters of the government. Henry Clifford, first Earl of Cumberland, was the son of Henry Lord Clifford, the "Shepherd Lord," by his wife Anne, daughter of Sir John St John of Bletsoe. The future Earl was born in 1493, and brought up with the sons of Henry VII. He married first Margaret, daughter of the Earl of Shrewsbury, and second another Margaret, daughter of the fifth Earl of Northumberland, the Magnificent Earl; his second wife was the mother of his children. In disposition the Earl of Cumberland resembled his grandfather "the Butcher"—the Black Clifford of "Henry VI"—rather than his father, "the Shepherd." In his youth he was extravagant, and supplied his need of money by robbery and violence[4]. After he succeeded his father, he followed the same course of action. Several cases were brought against his unruly servants in the Court of Star Chamber[5]. The Earl himself was too great a man to be touched, and the local courts were powerless

---

[1] L. and P. xii (1), 491, 393; printed in full, de Fonblanqne, op. cit. i, chap. ix.
[2] L. and P. xi, 785.   [3] L. and P. xii (1), 1090.
[4] Dic. of Nat. Biog., Henry Clifford, 1st Earl of Cumberland.
[5] Star Chamber Proceedings, Henry VIII, Bundle xxx, no. 6; and see below.

to supply any remedy for his aggressions. He was a hard land-lord and well hated in his own county, but he enjoyed the King's favour without interruption, and his son Henry, Lord Clifford, was permitted to marry Eleanor the daughter of the Duke of Suffolk and Mary Tudor, the King's sister, a somewhat dangerous honour[1].

In 1534 the Earl of Cumberland accused Lord Dacre of high treason, having seized his goods long before the trial. This was merely the last move in a feud of some standing. Dacre was tried, but acquitted[2]. He was the only nobleman acquitted on a charge of high treason during Henry VIII's reign; but he was heavily fined, which was presumably all that the government wanted. It was, how-ever, rather shortsighted policy, for something between shame and suspicion prevented the King from employing Dacre again. The Earl of Cumberland succeeded him in his office of Warden of the Western Marches, but he was hampered in the execution of his office both by his personal unpopularity and by the embittered feud with the Dacres and their allies among the Cumberland gentlemen. The Cliffords were the most powerful family on the western borders after the disgrace of the Dacres. The Earl's brother, Sir Thomas Clifford, was deputy captain of Berwick-upon-Tweed[3]; the Earl's illegitimate son Thomas Clifford held the same office in Carlisle[4]. If the younger Percys were in league with the mosstroopers of North Tynedale, so were the Cliffords with the broken men of Esk and Line[5]. The thieves of the Borders were used for or against the King simply as the noblemen who bought their services pleased. It is necessary to bear this in mind in order to understand the position not only of the King but also of his opponents.

Southward from the Borders lay the county of Durham, always spoken of as "the Bishopric." For centuries it had enjoyed the privileges of a county palatine within which the Bishop reigned supreme. But in 1535 all such extraordinary jurisdictions were abolished, and Durham was reduced in many respects to the rank of an ordinary shire[6]. Bishop Tunstall was not a man who could in any circumstances have opposed such a King as Henry VIII. He was timid, gentle and studious, and wins our affection by the quiet persistence with which he refused to burn heretics. To their shame be it said, his moderation irritated alike the Protestants and the

---

[1] L. and P. xi, 1236 ; printed in full, State Papers, i, 521.
[2] L. and P. xii (1) 372, and see Dic. Nat. Biog. loc. cit.
[3] J. Scott, Berwick-upon-Tweed, chap. vii.   [4] L. and P. xii (1), 419.
[5] L. and P. xi, 993 ; xii (1) 439.   [6] See above, chap. i.

Romanists. He seems to have taken the change in his estate with perfect equanimity, but the abolition of the ancient palatinate was resented by the people of Durham, who had been used to pride themselves on their position as "haliwerfolk," the people of the holy man, St Cuthbert[1].

The Hiltons and the Lumleys were the principal families in Durham, and their influence extended to the town of Newcastle-upon-Tyne, which, lying on the north bank of the Tyne, was a county in itself. In the south of Durham the chief gentlemen were Conyers of Hornby and Bowes of Streatlam near Barnard Castle on the Tees.

The Bowes family had acquired their estates by marriage with an heiress of the house of Balliol early in the fourteenth century. After the fall of Warwick the Kingmaker they became the chief family in the neighbourhood. Old Sir Ralph Bowes, living in 1508, was sheriff of Durham for twenty years. He married Margaret daughter of Sir Richard Conyers; we are concerned with two of their large family, Richard the fourth son who married Elizabeth daughter and co-heiress of Roger Aske of Aske; and Robert, the third son, who married Alice daughter of Sir James Metcalfe[2]. In 1511 Robert Bowes was mentioned as a suitable bridegroom for Elizabeth Aske, aged seven, if his brother Richard should die[3]. Failing the income to be derived from marriage with an heiress, Robert became a lawyer[4], and no doubt made the acquaintance of Robert Aske, William Stapleton, Thomas Moigne, and the other young lawyers who played an important part in the rebellion. They were carrying on the tradition of those lawyers of an earlier age, concerning whom it is written:

"We see at Westminster a cluster of men which deserves more attention than it receives from our unsympathetic, because legally uneducated historians. No, the clergy were not the only learned men in England, the only cultivated men, the only men of ideas. Vigorous intellectual effort was to be found outside the monasteries and universities. These lawyers are worldly men, not men of the sterile caste,—they marry and found families, some of which become as noble as any in the land ; but they are in their way learned, cultivated men, linguists, logicians, tenacious disputants, true lovers of the nice case and the moot point. They are gregarious, clubable men, grouping themselves in hospices, which

[1] L. and P. xi, 503.
[2] Foster, Durham Visitation Pedigrees, Bowes.
[3] Plantagenet-Harrison, Hist. of Yorks., Aske of Aske.
[4] L. and P. xi. 1143.

become schools of law, multiplying manuscripts, arguing, learning and teaching, the great mediators between life and logic, a reasoning, reasonable element in the English nation."[1]

The attitude of these men—intelligent, well-educated, unlikely subjects for wild hopes and popular enthusiasms—is one of the most striking features of the rebellion. Robert Bowes, though probably one of the youngest, was not the least brilliant, while, unlike the others, he came through safely and even with credit. Norfolk said of him, "Bowes has no equal in the north both for law and war."[2] His appointment on the Council of the North after the rising was the beginning of a long career in the government service, during which he justified the Duke's estimate.

In the North Riding of Yorkshire the influence of the three northern Earls was about equal.

Wilton, near the mouth of the Tees, was the seat of the Bulmers, who were allied to all the neighbouring great families, the Hiltons, the Evers, the Tempests. Sir William Bulmer of Wilton married Margery daughter of Sir John Conyers, by whom he had three sons, John, Ralph and William[3]. He was present at the battle of Flodden, where he distinguished himself by attacking and routing with a much inferior force the Scots troops under Lord Hume[4]. In November 1519 he was summoned before the Court of Star Chamber on a charge of rioting, together with Sir William Conyers and others[5]. The King presided in person at the trial, and was very much enraged because it appeared from the evidence that Sir William Bulmer " being the King's servant sworn, refused the King's service and became servant to the Duke of Buckingham." Henry exclaimed "that he would none of his servants should hang on another man's sleeve, and that he was as well able to maintain him as the Duke of Buckingham ; and what might be thought by his departing, and what might be supposed by the Duke's retaining him, he would not then declare.... The knight kneeled still on his knees crying the King's mercy, and never a nobleman there durst intreat for him, the King was so highly displeased with him."[6] Buckingham was as angry as the King. He saw that he himself was in danger of imprisonment, and he was afterwards accused of having sworn to stab the King to the

---

[1] F. W. Maitland, The Year Books of Edward II (Selden Soc.).
[2] L. and P. xii (2), 100.
[3] Tonge's Visitation of Yorks. (Surtees Soc.), p. 25.
[4] L. and P. i, 4462.
[5] Star Chamber Proc. Henry VIII, vol. ii, no. 134 ; L. and P. ii, 2733.
[6] Hall, Chronicle, ann. 1519.

heart if the order was given to commit him to the Tower[1]. Sir William, however, was pardoned[2], and in the following year his son, Sir John Bulmer, served under the Earl of Surrey, afterwards Duke of Norfolk, in Ireland[3].

On October 6, 1531, Sir William Bulmer made his will, a long, elaborate document, full of tragic irony considering the later history of the family. The gold chain weighing 100 pounds which was to be an heirloom for the children of his eldest son must have disappeared into the King's coffers when that son was attainted; the chantry of St Ellen where four poor bedesmen and one woman were to pray for ever for the founder's soul can only have stood a few years. The supervisors of the will were "my especial good lord, my lord of Westmorland, my lord Conyers, and my son Sir Thomas Tempest."[4] Westmorland had married the Duke of Buckingham's daughter[5], and the Bulmers may have transferred their allegiance to the Earl on the Duke's execution. Sir William made his three sons, who were all knighted by this time, his executors, but at the end of the will he added another clause: "Also, as I have named my son, Sir John Bulmer, to have been one of my executors, I will that he be none of them, but he to suffer his two brothers lovingly to occupy and minister all and every my goods favourably without any interruption of him and he to have for his so doing and suffering £300 and my chain and household stuff at Wilton, which before I have bequeathed him; and in like manner he to suffer his brothers to have melling at my chantry at Wilton, and to see the priests and bede men there to have that they should have, and all other my servants, according as I have bequeathed them."[6]

Sir John Bulmer, the heir, married Anne daughter of Sir Ralph Bigod, and their eldest son Ralph married before 1530 Anne daughter of Sir Thomas Tempest[7]. On 11 June 1532 it was stated that Sir John was forty years old and upwards[8]. Some examples have already been given of the marriage customs which prevailed at that time. In the case of heirs and heiresses, the contract was often drawn up while the parties concerned were still in their cradles, and he marriage was consummated as early as possible, before the young

[1] Brewer, Reign of Henry VIII, i, chap. xiii.
[2] Ibid. i, chap. xi.
[3] Halliwell-Phillipps, Letters of the Kings of England, i, Hen. VIII to the Earl of Surrey.
[4] Raine, Testa. Ebor. (Surtees Soc.) vi, 306.
[5] See above, chap. ii.   [6] Raine, loc. cit.
[7] Tonge, op. cit. 25.   [8] Raine, op. cit. vi, 306.

people acquired sufficient independence to upset the arrangements of their guardians. Much of the domestic unhappiness of the time may be traced to these child marriages, concluded without any regard for the character and feelings of the parties. It may be inferred that Sir John Bulmer's was such a one, as five of his six children were married before 1530[1], when he was not much above forty years old. His conduct requires the excuse of this bad custom. His father's position in the service of the Duke of Buckingham must have brought Sir John into contact with a girl named Margaret, who is frequently described as the illegitimate daughter of Buckingham himself[2]. But her son in 1584 stated that she was the illegitimate daughter of Henry Stafford[3]; if he could have glozed over the stain on her birth by the rank of her father he would probably have done so, and it is safer to conclude that Henry Stafford was some relative of the Duke. Margaret herself was "a very fair creature and a beautiful," as even her enemies were forced to confess[4]. She was married to William Cheyne of London, but Sir John Bulmer bought her from her husband and made her his mistress[5]. Two daughters were the offspring of this connection, but about 1536 Lady Bulmer and William Cheyne[6] seem both to have been dead and Sir John married Margaret. In January 1536–7 was born their son John[7], afterwards John Bulmer of Pinchinthorpe, who declared in 1584 that he was born in lawful matrimony[8]. The marriage was recognised by Sir John's relatives[9], which may indicate the low state of morality in the north, or the power of Margaret's charms, or the existence of extenuating circumstances.

Sir Ralph Bulmer, one of Sir John's brothers, married Anne, daughter and co-heir of Roger Aske of Aske[10], and was thus brother-in-law to Richard Bowes.

The other brother, Sir William Bulmer, was, like Sir John, unfortunate in his matrimonial experience. His wife Elizabeth, daughter and heiress of William Elmedon of Elmedon, Durham, was married to him in 1505, when she was eleven years old and he

---

[1] Tonge, op. cit. 25.
[2] Ord, Hist. of Cleveland, Pedigree of Bulmer; Brenan and Statham, The House of Howard, I, chap. v.
[3] Foster, Yorkshire Visitation Pedigrees, Bulmer of Pinchinthorpe.
[4] Wriothesley, Chron. (Camden Soc.) I, 64.
[5] Grey Friars' Chron. (Camden Soc.) p. 41; see note A at end of chapter.
[6] L. and P. XII (1) 1199 (2).   [7] Ibid. 236.
[8] Foster, op. cit., Bulmer of Pinchinthorpe.
[9] L. and P. XII (1), 66, 236.   [10] Tonge, op. cit. 25.

probably not much older[1]. The marriage turned out unhappily;
Sir William squandered his own estates and involved his wife's by
his extravagance, and the couple usually lived apart[2]. It will be
shown hereafter how the lady revenged herself on her husband.

The Bigods of Settrington, though their seat near Malton was
between thirty and forty miles south of Wilton, were none the less
neighbours of the Bulmers, for they had both lands and influence on
the north coast of Yorkshire, especially about Whitby. This family
might well seem to be under a curse. Two Bigods, father and son,
fell at Towton Field in 1461[3]; the son, Sir John Bigod, had married
Elizabeth daughter of Henry Lord Scrope of Bolton, and left a son,
Ralph Bigod, who was thrice married. His family seem to have
been the children of his second wife, Margaret, daughter of Sir Robert
Constable of Flamborough[4] and aunt of Lord Darcy's friend Sir Robert
Constable. One of these children, Elizabeth, married Sir John Aske,
of Aughton and was the grandmother of Robert Aske[5]—another,
Anne, married Sir John Bulmer[6].

Sir Ralph Bigod's eldest son, Sir John Bigod, married Joan,
daughter of Sir James Strangeways[7]. He was probably killed at
the battle of Flodden in 1513[8], and his eldest son died with him in
the war against Scotland[9]. He left three children; Elizabeth, who
was afterwards the wife of Sir Stephen Hamerton[10], Francis, and
Ralph.

Two years after Flodden old Sir Ralph Bigod died; his will was
proved 7 April 1515. He made several charitable and religious
bequests, and left a yearly rent of £5 to his younger grandson Ralph[11],
who died unmarried in 1551[12]; but there is no mention of Francis
who, at the age of seven, was heir to his manor of Seton and all his
lands in various parts of Yorkshire[13]. The executors of the will were
Agnes, Sir Ralph's third wife, Sir Ralph Evers, and Thomas and
William Constable of Settrington. The supervisor was Lord Darcy.

In 1529 Francis Bigod came of age and had livery of his lands;
shortly afterwards he was knighted[14]. Before his coming of age he
had been in the service of Cardinal Wolsey, and when, on coming

---

[1] Dur. Cursitor's Rec. portf. 171, no. 2.

[2] L. and P. xiii (1) 366, 707.   [3] Raine, op. cit. iv, 215 n.

[4] Tonge, op. cit. 67.   [5] Ibid. 64.   [6] See above.

[7] Raine, op. cit. v, 306 n.   [8] Archaeologia Aeliana (new ser.) iii, 214.

[9] L. and P. viii, 135.

[10] Raine, op. cit. vi, 68 n.; Yorks. Arch. and Top. Journ. viii, 404.

[11] Raine, op. cit. v, 55.   [12] Ibid. vi, 223.

[13] Dic. Nat. Biog., Francis Bigod; Raine, op. cit. v, 55.

[14] Dic. Nat. Biog. loc. cit.

into his estates, he found himself in financial difficulties, he applied
to his fellow-servant, Thomas Cromwell, for assistance[1].

Sir Francis Bigod married Katherine, daughter of William, first
Lord Conyers, and in 1530 they had one daughter, Dorothy[2]. Their
home was at Mulgrave Castle in Blackmore, on the coast about three
miles north of Whitby. Sir Francis was made the Steward of Whitby
Strand by the Earl of Northumberland[3], and in the execution of this
office he must soon have come into conflict with the Abbot of Whitby,
John Hexham or Topcliffe, who began his career as a Canon of
Hexham and became Abbot of Whitby in 1527[4]. Some account
of the Abbot's doings may not be out of place; they are not only
interesting in themselves but also give a most spirited picture of the
more turbulent phases of life in a little seaport town, and of the
feuds and intrigues which agitated a great monastery.

The first story is gathered from a fragment of a Star Chamber
case; it is undated, and the Abbot of Whitby may have been one of
John Hexham's predecessors. This Abbot lodged a complaint against
certain poor mariners and artificers of the town of Whitby for
making a riot. Only the townsfolk's side of the case remains. It
had been the custom "tyme out of mans remembrance" in Whitby
and all the other haven towns thereabouts, for the fishermen and
mariners to keep the feasts of Midsummer Even, St Peter's Even,
and St Thomas' Even with the following rites. "All maryners and
masters of ships accompanied with other yong peple have used to
have carried before them on a staff half a tarbarell brennyng and the
maryners to follow two and two having such weapons in their hands
as they pleased to bring, and to sing through the streets to resort to
every bonefire and there to drink and make merry with songs and
other honest pastimes."

But one St Peter's Even (31 July) as they went singing through
the streets "entending no harm nor displeasure to the said Abbot"
and "being in good peace of our sovereign lord the King," about
twenty of the Abbot's servants set upon the merrymakers and "did
shamefully and cruelly beat and hurt" divers of them. They thought
this must be by the Abbot's command, though, as they declared,
he had no cause to use them so. When they complained to him, he
assured them he knew nothing of the matter, which was not of his
will, and asked them all to come up to the Abbey on St Thomas'
Even (20 December) "and there he would give to them half a

[1] L. and P. VIII, 135, 735; XI, 23.   [2] Tonge, op. cit. 67.
[3] L. and P. XII (1) 271.   [4] Yorks. Arch. and Top. Journ. II, 246–51.

barrel of beer to drink and make good cheer." But when on the appointed evening they came singing through the town and began to go up the "great hill having a very narrow way towards the said Abbey," the Abbot's servants from the top of the hill "riotously cast down a great number of great stones as much as they could lift" upon the mariners. They "entreated in good and gentle manner the said servants of the Abbot to keep the King's peace and cease their strokes," and seeing they were not welcome, they turned back to a friend's house, to help him with his bonfire and brood upon the lost half-barrel of beer. Here their enemies attacked them again. The cautious mariners admitted that some of the Abbot's servants might have been hurt in the second fray. Some of the mariners themselves certainly were injured. The defence ends with the usual protestation that the defendants had done nothing wrong, and in any case had a pardon for it[1].

In 1528 it was the Abbot of Whitby, John Hexham, who had to defend himself in the Star Chamber. He was accused of being in league with William and John Loder, two French pirates, who on 10 July 1528 seized a Dantzig vessel, the "Jesus," Hans Ganth master, while she lay in the Humber, took her to Whitby, and there sold her to the Abbot, John Conyers, Gregory Conyers, John Ledam and John Pecock, who bought her "perfectly knowing the same ship and goods to be the proper goods of your suppliant," and who refused to give her up when claimed by her rightful owners[2]. The Abbot's defence is lost, and he may have been able to clear himself, but the circumstances look awkward. Gregory Conyers, of whom more will be heard, was the servant and close ally of the Abbot. It is uncertain how he was related to the great family of Conyers to which Sir Francis Bigod's wife belonged, but there is no doubt about the deadly feud which he waged with Sir Francis until he hunted his enemy to death. In 1536 the Abbot of Whitby accused Sir Francis of a great riot committed against the convent of Whitby, and in revenge Bigod and his servants quarrelled with Gregory Conyers and other servants of the Abbot at Whitby Fair on 25 August, St Hilda's Day, and would have killed him had not some of the other gentlemen interfered[3]. The Abbot begged that Conyers and Bigod might be reconciled, but naturally no formal reconciliation had any effect. As in the matter of the piracy we do not know the Abbot's defence, so in this case we do not know Bigod's, but it is

---

[1] Star Chamber Proc. Henry VIII, xxvii, no. 131.
[2] Yorks. Arch. and Top. Journ. ii, 246–51.   [3] L. and P. ix, 216.

certain that Sir Francis was in debt to the Abbot, which would probably aggravate the young knight still further, whatever the original rights and wrongs may have been.

In 1535 Sir Francis Bigod by persuasion or threats induced Abbot Hexham to resign his office to his young kinsman, William Newton, a monk of Whitby. This did not at all suit Gregory Conyers or the other monks, and they insisted that he must withdraw his resignation. Both sides appealed to Cromwell, to whom Bigod wrote on 7 January 1535–6 that " the monks watch him (the Abbot) like crows about a carrion, and will not suffer the monk (Newton) or me to speak with him alone."[1] Cromwell, as usual, was ready to settle the matter in favour of the highest bidder, who in this case seems to have been the Abbot[2]. Sir Francis was examined in Hilary term and warned to trouble the monks no more. Nevertheless on 19 June 1536 the Abbot wrote to Cromwell to ask that Bigod might not occupy the office of under-steward, or, if he must surrender it to him, that the condition might be made "that he make no use of it to revenge himself on us, as we hear he intends.... If Sir Francis occupy that office, and James Conyers the bailiwick, the two being so maliciously bent against us, we shall be brought into continual trouble. The bailly is a very uncharitable and angry man, and so aged that he is almost past reason."[3]

Bigod was better educated than most men of his age. He had spent some time at Oxford, and although he did not take a degree he was something of a scholar. He had leanings towards the reformers; his first book was an attack on the monasteries, and he corresponded with Bale, Latimer, and other advanced thinkers[4]. In June 1535 he was employed in taking down to the northern bishops the King's letters of admonition for the declaration of his title as Supreme Head of the Church of England[5], and he reported the pains that he took to see that the statute was " preached sincerely" and understood by the people. At the same time he informed Cromwell of the suspicion he entertained concerning the loyalty of the monks of Mountgrace Priory, and he procured the arrest of a "traitorous monk" at Jervaux, who saw visions of St Anne[6]. This man was executed at the next York Assizes, for which it is hard to forgive Sir Francis, as the evidence against the monk was very slight[7].

---

[1] L. and P. x, 47—49, 238.   [2] Ibid. 611, 679.   [3] Ibid. 1167.
[4] Dic. Nat. Biog. loc. cit.   [5] L. and P. viii, 849, 854, 869, 1082.
[6] Ibid. 1025, 1033, 1069.   [7] Ibid. ix, 37.

In 1536 Bigod wrote to Cromwell about two priests and a man named Anthony Heron, whom he had caused to be imprisoned at York for their Popish opinions. The letter incidentally reveals the horrible state of York prison; Sir Francis observes that as Anthony Heron was walking in the yard in the open air, he was able to speak longer with him than with the priests who were within. He showed some humanity, however, by giving alms to his prisoners, and he tried to obtain their release as soon as he was convinced that they repented of their errors[1]. Later in the year he wrote a very curious letter to Cromwell, which throws much light on his character. He begged that he might be given a licence to preach, or, if that was impossible, that he might become a priest, in order to utter the truth to the ignorant people of the north[2]. Yet he was now a married man with children !

Sir Francis Bigod appeared to have been in every way a convinced supporter of Cromwell's policy; by birth, by interest, by conviction he was not merely inclined to acquiesce passively, but to promote actively " the innovations." How did such a man come to die a traitor's death ? Froude curtly dismisses him as a fool and a pedant, but such a summary judgment does not dispose of a peculiar character. It may be more just to look upon Sir Francis as a portent of a rising power,—in short, as the first of the Puritans. He hated the Church of Rome, but he hated equally the Erastianism of Henry and Cromwell; what he sought was the Presbytery, and had he been gifted with genius, he might have been the forerunner of Calvin and Knox. Religious liberty was as intolerable to his exact, legal mind, as it was to most of his contemporaries; he must have church, priesthood, dogma, all down in black and white, and all distinct from the state. When it came to choosing between church and state, any church, even a thoroughly bad one, seemed to him better than a purely state religion. Born out of his time, with no power to mould the time to his needs, his baffling figure shows half-seen among the more strenuous leaders of revolt, perplexing others because he was himself perplexed.

Passing southward down the coast from Whitby, we find that the next great family was that of Evers. Young Sir Ralph Evers was the keeper of the King's castle of Scarborough. Later the family was raised to the baronage, but at this time they were not so influential as their neighbours, the Constables of Flamborough.

---

[1] L. and P. x, 49. [2] Ibid. 742.

Sir Marmaduke Constable, surnamed the Little, was the head of this house from 1488 to 1518. He served under two kings in France, and won fame on the Scots Marches. His wife was Joyse, daughter of Sir Humphry Stafford of Grafton; by her he had four sons, Robert, Marmaduke, William, and John, and two daughters, Agnes and Eleanor[1]. Agnes' second husband was Sir William Percy, the Earl of Northumberland's uncle.

Robert, Little Sir Marmaduke's son and heir, was born about 1478. He seems to have spent a wild youth before he succeeded to his estates. The minster of Beverley was held in great veneration, having been founded by the local saint, St John of Beverley. It enjoyed many privileges, and the neighbouring gentlemen were quite in the habit of having feuds about their places in the procession on St John's Day (25 October)[2]. One of these privileges was "granted...unto the church of Beverley by Our Holy Father the Pope of old time and since many times confirmed, that whosoever doth infringe or break or interrupt any liberties of the church of Beverley he is on so doing accurst without any further sentence of any judge." This was no mere nominal power, but had been executed on "divers transgressors." An unknown accuser addressed Sir Robert Constable thus: "You yourself in times past, violating and breaking the said liberties by your hunting there, and knowing yourself to have fallen into the sentence of excommunication for so doing, did resort to the Archbishop of York then being, to be absolved thereof, and so as you have reported were also absolved."[3] But more serious charges can also be brought against him. Froude says, "he was a bad, violent man. In earlier years he had carried off a ward in Chancery, Anne Grysanis, while still a child, and attempted to marry her by force to one of his retainers."[4]

Whatever his early shortcomings, Robert Constable was ready to fight for the King on the first opportunity. In 1497, when the Cornishmen rose and marched on London, he was with the royal army, and so distinguished himself at Blackheath that he was knighted on the field of battle. He married Jane, daughter of Sir William Ingleby[5]. In 1511 he sailed with Lord Darcy's expedition to Spain[6].

---

[1] Tonge, op. cit. 68.

[2] Gentleman's Mag. 1835 (1), pp. 151—2.

[3] L. and P. xii (1), 851 ; see note B at end of chapter.

[4] Froude, op. cit. ii, chap. xiii.

[5] Dic. Nat. Biog., Robert Constable.   [6] See above, chap. ii.

At Flodden Field Sir Marmaduke Constable appeared surrounded by his "seemly sons."[1] Accounts of the battle give no details of their part of the fighting, but two of Sir Robert's brothers, Marmaduke and William, and William Percy, who fought beside them with the tenants of the Earl of Northumberland, were all knighted by the Earl of Surrey after the day was won[2].

Sir Robert Constable was Knight of the Body to Henry VIII[3], and he was in attendence on the King at a gorgeous banquet at Greenwich in 1517[4]. But the following year Sir Marmaduke the Little died, and his son Robert succeeded to his lands and position. Sir Marmaduke's tombstone is still to be seen in Flamborough church, the inscription is an irregular ballad on the vanity of earthly honours, telling of his battles and prowess, with the refrain:

"But now, as ye see, he lieth under this stone."[5]

A more terrible fate awaited his son.

When Lord Darcy resigned his offices as steward of the lordship and constable of the castle of Sheriff-hutton, in 1520, they were bestowed on his friend Sir Robert Constable. Darcy bade his servant in charge deliver the castle and all within it to his "brother," the new constable, and to "do this favourable and lovingly."[6] About the same time the hand of Elizabeth, the only child of Darcy's second marriage, was given to Sir Robert's eldest son Marmaduke. Darcy told his steward to hasten the payment of her dowry to Sir Robert, on account of his "dangerous" disposition[7]. He must have meant that his friend was hasty tempered, and there is abundant evidence that Sir Robert was fierce and quarrelsome.

The Earl of Surrey (afterwards Duke of Norfolk), who was sent to the north in 1523 to inspect the administration of justice, described to Wolsey how, while sitting with the justices of York, he "found the greatest dissensions here among the gentlemen, who would have fought together if they had met." By the advice of the judges he sent for all the parties, and insisted on a promise that they would compose their disputes and keep the peace. Among the rest, Sir Robert Constable and his adherents were almost at war with young Sir Ralph Ellerker and Sir John Constable of Holderness[8].

---

[1] Arch. Ael. (new ser.), vol. III, p. 214.   [2] Ibid. p. 225.
[3] L. and P. II, 2735.
[4] Ibid. 3446.   [5] Gentleman's Mag. 1835 (1), p. 153.
[6] L. and P. III (1), 654—5.   [7] Ibid. 1236, 1260.
[8] L. and P. III (2), 3240; cf. Brown, Yorks. Star Chamber Proc. (Yorks. Arch. Soc. Rec. Ser.), I, nos. IX and LXXXI.

The latter may have been Sir Robert's younger brother, but was more probably a cousin.

In 1533 Sir Robert Constable's differences with his brother-in-law, Sir William Percy, developed into a Star Chamber case. The feud was a long-standing affair, in spite of the intermarriage, which may have been a fruitless effort to put an end to the ill-will. It was well known in the county of York that the families had been in great displeasure with one another, even before the death of the late Earl of Northumberland. Sir William Percy presented before the Court a list of accusations against Sir Robert, beginning with a string of petty wrongs about pasture and impounding cattle, through which he worked up to the chief quarrel. This began in a quaint manner. A traveller picked up a buckler on the King's highway, and sold it to one of Percy's servants, Simon Banister, called Simon Burdythe. Simon wore the buckler at Driffield Assizes, where Christopher Constable, one of Sir Robert's nephews, claimed it as his own. Banister refused to give it up, though Sir Robert, who had given it to his nephew, offered to identify it. After this the servants of the two houses never met without quarrelling. If Italians were as touchy as Englishmen, the feud of the Montagues and the Capulets is certainly no exaggeration, as this story proves. The affair came to a definite issue in March 1534, when the Justices of Assize were sitting at York and the rival families were both in the city in full strength. After preliminary abuse and violence in a tavern, Banister, who had offered considerable provocation, and a party of his fellow-servants were attacked by the Constables in the street. Banister was slain in the fray, and several were wounded on both sides, including Sir Robert Constable's son Thomas. After some scattered street fighting, the Constables escaped through a friend's house into the White Friars and there took sanctuary. They were presently removed to the town gaol, where all their kinsmen and allies flocked to visit them. Public sympathy was on their side, but it had been obtained, said Sir William Percy, by bribes to the mayor and citizens. The coroner was so corrupted that a murder could not be found against them, and the high sheriff was no more incorruptible, for when he appointed a jury to inquire into the case, most of the men on it were kinsmen of the Constables and the rest had seen the colour of their money. Unless the King could find a remedy, the murder and mayhems were like to go unpunished: so Sir William Percy concluded his case. The details of Sir Robert's defence, which has for once been preserved, are too long for repetition here. His accuser himself admitted that Sir Robert took no part in the fray, and it was not proved that he had inspired it[1]. But the principals were equally to blame for encouraging the quarrels of their kinsmen and servants, instead of putting an end to the dispute at the very beginning.

In 1535 Sir Robert Constable was more respectably engaged in befriending the widowed Lady Rokeby against their common opponent Gervase Cawood[2]. This dispute probably brought him into displeasure with Robert Aske, as Cawood was Aske's friend and acted as his secretary during the rebellion[3].

Among the ghosts of the records—the names without men—Sir Robert Constable stands out as a substantial figure; he was a worthy head of a warlike house, fierce and reckless, versed in the ways of war and of courts, full of the wild, independent spirit of the north, but none the less a true son of the Church (in spite of all lapses), a strong and just ruler, above all a good enemy, and a better friend, true to his motto, " Soyes Ferme."

Young Sir Ralph Ellerker of Risby, with whom Sir Robert Constable was at feud, was one of the captains of Hull, his father, old Sir Ralph Ellerker, being the other. It was no wonder that the Constables and the Ellerkers quarrelled, for they were the most influential families in the sea-board districts of the East Riding. Old Sir Ralph Ellerker also contended with the Archbishop of York for supremacy in Beverley. In May and June 1535 there was trouble over the appointment of the Twelve Men of Beverley, who were the aldermen of the town. The burgesses themselves had very little to do with the matter, and on this occasion the Archbishop appointed one body of twelve and old Sir Ralph Ellerker another. It is not easy to discover which side had the popular sympathy in the contest which followed, but as the people of Beverley always opposed the Archbishop on principle, they probably supported Sir Ralph's selection. On 30 November 1535 an order was made in the Court of Star Chamber for the government of Beverley. It was a triumph for the Archbishop. Old Sir Ralph Ellerker and certain of his adherents were prohibited from ever again seeking election to places among the Twelve Men, and an injunction was sent to him never to meddle again in the matter on pain of a fine of five hundred marks[4].

[1] Star Chamber Proc. Henry VIII, bundle 22 no. 162.
[2] The Plumpton Letters (Camden Soc.), vol. IV (1839), pp. 227—8 ; Brown, Yorks. Star Chamber Proc. (Yorks. Arch. Soc. Rec. Ser.) I, no. XXVII.
[3] L. and P. XIII (1) 708.
[4] A. F. Leach, Beverley Town Documents (Selden Soc.), preface, p. xxxvi, pp. 64, 65.

The Askes of Aughton on the Derwent were friends and allies of the Ellerkers. They had long been settled in the county, but were rather esteemed for piety and quiet respectability than noted for any brilliant qualities. The founder of the family was Richard, a cadet of the Askes of Aske[1]. He married the heiress of Aughton, and in 1363 built and endowed the chantry at Howden which bore his name. A love of building and beautifying seems to have run in the family. Nothing remains now of the manor house at Aughton but the site surrounded by traces of a moat[2]; in 1584 the house had stained-glass windows, in which were blazoned twenty-six shields of the arms of the Askes and their relations[3]. From Richard Aske sprang a flourishing branch of the family tree, which begins to concern us in 1497, when Sir Robert Aske, the eldest son of Sir John Aske and Elizabeth, daughter of Sir Ralph Bigod, succeeded to Aughton on the death of his father[4]. Sir Robert's two elder sons, John and Christopher, were born before that date, for their grandfather bequeathed a gold spoon to John and a horse to his brother,—though neither was much more than three years old[5]. Sir Robert's wife was Elizabeth, daughter of John Lord Clifford[6]. Probably they were married after 1485, when her brother, the "shepherd lord," was restored to his lands and titles. Her children were thus the first cousins of the Earl of Cumberland. Nine of these children survived their parents—three sons and six daughters.

Early in 1507 Sir Robert Aske's sister Dame Katherine, widow of Sir John Hastings of Fenwick, died at her brother's house at Aughton and was buried among the Askes in Aughton Church. She was childless and bequeathed most of her worldly possessions to her own kin. To her sisters and nieces she left beads of coral and white jasper, "hooks of silver and gilt," and other bits of finery; her best gowns of velvet, black damask and tawny chamlet were to become altar cloths in certain churches; but for each of her kinsmen she had made a shirt, and among these fortunate legatees Robert Aske is mentioned for the first time[7]. Dame Katherine's brother-in-law, Sir George Hastings, the father of Sir Brian Hastings, who was to be sheriff of Yorkshire in 1536, refused to give up her money to Sir Robert Aske, her executor[8].

[1] Yorks. Arch. and Top. Journ. viii, p. 401.
[2] Archaeological Journ. xxv, 170.
[3] J. Foster, Glover's Visitation of Yorks. p. 441.
[4] Tonge, op. cit. 64.   [5] Raine, Testa. Ebor. (Surtees Soc.) iv, 123.
[6] Tonge, op. cit. 64.   [7] Raine, op. cit. iv, 257.
[8] Ibid. vi. 21.

The children of Sir Robert Aske may be treated in some detail, less because his third son Robert was the captain of the Pilgrimage, than because they are good examples of ordinary men and women of their class. Though their share in the rising was nothing compared to their brother's, their history shows how a great event affected private lives in the days when a change of ministry could only be forced on the government by an effective appeal to arms. Julian, the eldest daughter, married Thomas Portington of Sawcliff, Lincolnshire[1]; when those of her Yorkshire nephews who were studying the law set out for London after their vacations, they spent the first night of their journey under her roof[2]. Anne, the second daughter, seems to have married slightly below her station, for her husband, Thomas Monkton, was the constant companion of her brother Robert, and seems to have acted as a kind of superior servant[3]. At a time when compromising letters might fall into an enemy's hands, men naturally entrusted the most important parts of their communications verbally to a messenger; consequently it was necessary to have reliable servants, bound by the strongest ties to keep faith with their master; poor relations were often put to this use, with varying degrees of success. This reason for the constant use of credence applied more to noblemen such as Darcy and Cumberland than to private gentlemen, but another motive for it was the fact that many of the Yorkshire gentry could write and read very little[4]. Private affairs, which seemed to them very difficult to express in writing, could easily be explained by an intelligent servant, and as a servant had to carry every message, he might as well communicate it by word of mouth. The result of this was the habit, so irritating to the historian, of sending the very kernel of the message by credence, with the consequence that it is now lost for ever.

Agnes Aske formed an important alliance by her marriage with William Ellerker, one of old Sir Ralph's younger sons. The Ellerkers always contrived to maintain an appearance of loyalty, and they rose when the fortunes of the Askes declined. Margaret Aske married Sir Robert Bellingham, a Cumberland knight about whom little is known.

John Aske, Sir Robert Aske's eldest son, succeeded his father

---

[1] For the marriages of the Askes see Flower's Visit. of Yorks. (Harl. Soc.), xvi, 7; B. M. Add. MS 38133, fol. 45 b—46 a.

[2] See below, chap. vi.   [3] L. and P. xi, 622; xii (1), 852.

[4] L. and P. xii (1), 191.

in 1531[1]. His wife was Eleanor, daughter of Sir Ralph Ryther, and in 1530 he had a family of five sons and three daughters[2]. His eldest son Robert was a law student in 1536, but he was destined never to be lord of Aughton, and died before his father in 1542[3]. John Aske suffered from ill-health, which was probably the reason why he was never knighted. Like most country gentlemen he had only two ideas—his lands and his family. He was indifferent to the Reformation, as it did not injure either of these objects, but he strongly disapproved of the rebellion which endangered both. His brother's sympathy for the monasteries did not affect him; on the contrary he took advantage of their fall to consolidate his Yorkshire estates, and in 1541 exchanged certain manors which he owned in Sussex for the priories of Ellerton and Thicket and other church lands in Yorkshire[4].

Christopher Aske, Sir Robert's second son, was only a year or two younger than John[5]. He was in the household of his cousin, the Earl of Cumberland, with whom he was in high favour. His will, dated 1538, gives a pleasant picture of the easy bachelor life of a cultured gentleman. His room in Skipton Castle was well furnished with books on genealogy, the Scriptures, and the noble art of hunting, as well as French romances; while in his room at the "new lodge," the building of which he was superintending for the Earl, was his "cloth of the great mappa mundi" and a tapestry embroidered with the history of St Eustace. The chase, like the right to bear arms, was the special privilege and study of the gentry; his horses, his falcons, his "best beagle called Oliver" were worthy of his most honoured friends, his noble cousins the Earl and Countess. He bequeathed keepsakes to all his family, and mentions his black velvet gown, richly furred, and his gold chain and crucifix. Most of the Askes were short-lived, and Christopher died in 1539, willing a priest to pray for his soul for seven years, and also for the souls of all his "benefactors and predecessors," especially certain of his dead friends[6]; among these was one of the Hamertons. Sir Stephen Hamerton, his friend and fellow in the Earl's service, had died a traitor's death little more than a year before[7]. Christopher Aske's sister Dorothy had married Richard Green of Newbury, and Christopher bequeathed "to my brother Greene my falcon in his keeping, and to my sister his wife a silver spoon of the Apostles."[8]

---

1 Durham Cursitor's Rec. portf. 177, no. 9.   2 Tonge, op. cit. 64.
3 Raine, Testa. Ebor. vi, 165.   4 L. and P. xvi, 653; xvii, 8, 283 (8).
5 Raine, op. cit. iv, 123; L. and P. xii (1), 1186 and 1321.
6 Raine, Mem. of Hexham Priory (Surtees Soc.), i, App. p. clxii n.
7 L. and P. xii (1), 1321.   8 Raine, loc. cit.

Green was also in Cumberland's service, and it must be frankly admitted of his followers that if

> "On Sundays they were good,
> On week-days they were minions."

The Earl of Cumberland was at feud with John Norton of Norton. The quarrel seems to have begun with some dispute about the manor of Rylston, which Norton held in right of his wife. At some time in 1528 a band of the Earl's servants broke into the warren at Rylston and hunted Norton's deer. They beat and shot arrows at two keepers who dared to oppose them, and carried off one of them to Skipton Castle, where he was imprisoned for two months. The other keeper was afraid to stay in that part of the country and fled because his life was threatened in the Earl's name. As to the deer park, no one dared to go near it but Cumberland's servants, who hunted there at will; the chief among them was called by John Norton "Richard Grame," but possibly this is a misspelling of "Richard Green." Norton took his complaint to the Court of Star Chamber because "the said Erle is a noble man and of great possessions gretly alied with the most parte of the noble men of ȝt Cuntry and your seid subiect (John Norton) a pore man and of small power and not abell to meynteyn his sute nor the tryall of the trouth in the premisses by the common law in the same cuntie for the records of his damage."[1] Two years later he was obliged to resort to the Star Chamber again. John Norton had farmed in the most legal manner the lordship of Kirkby Malzeard in Netherdale, where it was agreed that he should hold the manor court. But on the day of the first court (17 April 1531) Christopher Aske and Richard Green, at the head of about sixty armed servants of the Earl's, appeared at the place where the court was held and declared that the Earl would have all rule within the lordship and that any man who attended a court which the Earl had not appointed would do so at his peril. After breaking up the court, they carried away the court rolls[2]. Unfortunately it is impossible to discover how this case ended, but the Earl and his servants certainly did not mend their ways.

In 1535 John Proctor, whose offence against the Earl is not known, was carried off and imprisoned in Skipton Castle, while "his

---

[1] Star Chamber Proc. Henry VIII, Bundle xxvii, no. 143.

[2] Star Chamber Proc. Henry VIII, Bundle xxvii, no. 135; cf. Bundle xviii, no. 164, printed in full, Yorks. Star Chamber Proc. (Yorks. Arch. Soc. Rec. Ser.), ii, no. 15.

goods were spoyled destroyed and lost by brute beasts, and also not so contentyd but they drove away his cattle and beasts."[1] In this case the Earl seems to have sent inferior servants; only a really serious piece of lawlessness, such as stealing the court rolls, called for the presence of gentlemen. Thomas Blackborne, who was the chief defendant against Proctor, must have been some relation to William Blackborne, the vicar of Skipton, to whom Christopher Aske left in his will a horse rejoicing in the name of Grey Hodgeson[2].

Christopher Aske's friendship with Sir Stephen Hamerton involved him in a very curious affair. Sir Stephen's mother, Dame Elizabeth Hamerton, after the death of John Hamerton her first husband, married again; her second husband, Edward Stanley brother to Lord Monteagle, had carried his father's banner at Flodden. He was lame, perhaps from wounds received there, and seems to have expected to provide for a comfortable old age by his marriage, for Dame Elizabeth, as he said, was enfeoffed of Hellifield Peel. Unfortunately his wife did not agree with him. Hellifield had always belonged to the Hamerton family, and it is difficult to see how Dame Elizabeth could have had more than a life interest in it. In September 1536, when Stanley rode home after a visit to his brother, he found the door of the Peel barred against him. His wife, who was watching his approach, ordered stones to be thrown down from the upper windows, and one struck his servant's horse. Having made it plain that he was not welcome, "she dared him to enter her son Sir Stephen's house and bade him go to the Earl of Cumberland." Not knowing what to do he obeyed her, though as he believed her son and Christopher Aske to have counselled his wife to defy him, he had little hope of help there. The Earl refused to interfere. By this time the rebellion had broken out, and Stanley, seeing that resistance was useless, entered into a bond with Hamerton and Aske by which he undertook to leave his wife in undisturbed possession of Hellifield during her life, while she allowed him a share in the rents. After Sir Stephen Hamerton's execution Stanley petitioned Cromwell that he might have the Peel granted to him, but his petition had no effect[3]. In 1538 Christopher Aske bequeathed his goods at Hellifield Peel, after the death of Dame Elizabeth, to Roger Hamerton, one of Sir Stephen's nephews[4]; Sir Stephen's only son had died of grief after his father's execution[5].

[1] Star Chamber Proc. Henry VIII, Bundle xxx, no. 6.
[2] Raine, Mem. of Hexham Priory, I, p. clxii.
[3] L. and P. XII (1), 1321.   [4] Raine, op. cit. p. clxii.   [5] See below, chap. XIX.

In spite of his lawless exploits, Christopher Aske was a gentle-man,—the English gentleman of Henry VIII's reign. It is he, rather than the timid and colourless John, rather than Robert, who was too ardent and too honest for success, who seems to embody the very spirit of his age. He wrote a dashing account of his fortunes during the rebellion[1], and in it he is revealed, brave, clever, well-educated, faithful to his cousin, a lover of gallant and daring adventures, and, as became a man when Cromwell ruled England, worldly, unscrupulous, a believer in blowing his own trumpet. He evidently inherited the family love of bricks and mortar. Not only did he supervise the Earl of Cumberland's new buildings at Skipton, but he added to Aughton Church a tower in Perpendicular style, adorned with shields bearing the Aske quarterings and his own rebus[2]. One inscription on this tower rouses a curiosity that can never be satisfied. It is in black letter and runs as follows: "Christofer le second fitz de Robart Ask ch'r oblier ne doy Ao Di 1536."[3] No one can tell what may be implied by the words. Perhaps they quaintly express the gratitude of the steeple itself to the man who built it, or "oblier ne doy" may be the motto of the Askes, fitly placed above the church where they lie; or are the words a memorial of that Aske who does not lie among his kinsfolk? Whatever they meant so long ago, to those who know the story of the Pilgrimage of Grace they will always speak of Robert Aske and the year in which he triumphed and failed.

Robert Aske, the youngest of the three sons[4], was born about the beginning of the century. From his father's will it appears that an estate at Empshot in Hampshire had been settled on him for the term of his life[5]. This property must have been valuable, as he paid a yearly rent of £8 to his brother John, and was in good circumstances[6]. Part of his early life was spent in the service of the Earl of Northumberland[7], which he probably entered through the influence of the Countess of Cumberland, the Earl's sister. He was with Northumberland in 1527, the year in which he was admitted at Gray's Inn[8]. He must have left the Earl some years before the rebellion, as there is no reference during it to the fact

---

[1] L. and P. xii (1), 1186.   [2] Arch. Journ. xxv, 171.
[3] Ibid.; facsimile in Gentleman's Magazine, Aug. 1754. See note C at end of chapter.
[4] See note D at end of chapter.
[5] Raine, Testa. Ebor. vi, 21; Exch. Inq. ser. 2, 983/4.
[6] L. and P. xii (1), 1223, 1224.
[7] Notes and Queries, 11th ser. vol. iv, p. 441.   [8] Ibid.

that he had been one of the Earl's followers, while it is quite clear that he was a practising barrister. His enemies called him "a common pedlar in the law,"[1] and though he had studied to other purposes besides making money, he speaks of his "great businesses" in London. He had the lawyer's gift of words—the "filed tongue' that wins the heart of lord and commoner alike; even in his answers and manifestos, written in times of stress, on horseback or in prison, and couched in a language now so changed, there are many passages that stir the heart. While the conservative lords were in correspondence with the Emperor's ambassador, the commons binding themselves by secret oaths, and the most steadfast of the religious dying on the gallows, things must have passed among the young lawyers of the Inns of Court that had much to do with the Pilgrimage of Grace; but Aske, Moigne, Stapleton, even Bowes, kept their counsel, and nothing more of their secrets will ever be known.

The home of Robert Aske was always his brother's house at Aughton, where he was born and brought up, but he spent much of his vacation visiting his sisters and other friends in Yorkshire. In 1536 he was about five and thirty years of age and unmarried, although even younger sons generally found wives long before that time of life. Marriage in those days had very little to do with favour, otherwise Aske's confirmed bachelorhood might be attributed to the plainness of his personal appearance. The Court chronicler, Hall, declared in an outburst of loyal indignation that "there lived not a verier wretch as well in person as in conditions and deeds,"[2] and this hostile testimony is to some degree confirmed by the fact that Aske had only one eye. Sir Francis Brian during the insurrection protested his loyalty to the King in these words, "I know him (Aske) not, nor he me, but I am true and he a false wretch, yet we two have but two yene; a mischief put out his t'other!"[3] Whatever his personal disadvantages, he was certainly a man of great physical strength, able to spend day after day in the saddle with little time for food or sleep. It is not necessary to describe his character in detail. In the following pages his own words and actions shall speak for themselves.

The attitude of the northern gentlemen to the Church is one of the greatest interest. It was love of the monasteries which caused them so far to forget their fear of the lower classes that they made

[1] L. and P. xi, 1175.   [2] Hall, Chronicle, ann. 1536.
[3] L. and P. xi, 1103.

common cause with their tenants on behalf of the monks. One
result of the immense influence of the Church was that priests were
continually involved in the quarrels of laymen. In the complicated
case of Sir Richard Tempest and the vicar of Halifax, Tempest,
a supporter of the old religion, accused his enemy the vicar of
treasonable practices, and, when the rebellion broke out, forced him
to fly to the King. This is a chapter of digressions, and at the cost
of another we will relate the story, which at least gives a picture
of the manners of the times.

Sir Richard Tempest was the King's steward of Wakefield. His
feud with a neighbour, Sir Henry Saville, led to an almost endless
string of Star Chamber cases, as one or other of them was constantly
oppressing the unfortunate inhabitants of that town[1]. Robert
Holdesworth, the wealthy and influential vicar of Halifax, was Sir
Henry Saville's staunch ally. He was in trouble with the government in 1535, but he obtained a free pardon, and boasted that he
had "cast such a flower into the Queen's lap," that he would be
heard as soon as Sir Richard Tempest[2]. He had scarcely returned to
Yorkshire, when the judges of assize were informed that he had found
£300 in the wall of an old house which he was rebuilding at Blackley,
co. Worcester, another of his benefices[3]. Meanwhile Sir Richard
Tempest was still busy against him. Sir Richard had assisted in
arresting the vicar when he was sent to London, and on his triumphant
return Holdesworth delivered to Tempest and his supporters injunctions to keep the peace and not to burn his house under penalty of
500 marks. In revenge for these injunctions, which they regarded
as an insult, certain of his parishioners who belonged to Tempest's
party drew up a petition accusing the vicar of being a fomenter
of quarrels in the parish, and also charging him with neglect of his
duties, with false returns about his tenths and firstfruits, and with
an attempt to sell his lands, implying that he did this with a view
to flight. This petition was presented to Sir Richard Tempest, who
caused about a hundred persons to sign it, and sent it to Cromwell
with a letter warning him that Holdesworth and others of the
spiritualty had "full hollow hearts" towards him[4]. Tempest enclosed
a further accusation, from which it appeared that the vicar had said
he had lost 80 marks in mortuaries taken by the King from that one
benefice, and that if the King reigned much longer he would take all
from the Church. Holdesworth had also repeated a sort of proverb,

[1] See note E at end of chapter.   [2] L. and P. viii, 475, 892; ix, 463.
[3] L. and P. ix, 37.   [4] Ibid. 463.

" A pon Herre all Yngland mey werre " (upon Harry all England may war ?)[1].

Sir Richard Tempest's letter was written on 28 September 1535. At the York Assizes in March 1536[2] Holdesworth was accused of shameful and treasonable words, " for which, if true, he deserves imprisonment for life."[3] While the vicar was away defending himself against this charge, John Lacy, Sir Richard Tempest's son-in-law, raided the vicarage and carried off all the cattle and spoil he could find[4]. The vicar must have been acquitted, for in April he returned to his plundered vicarage, bringing with him over £800 of money. Part of this may have been treasure trove, but some at least was his own savings[5]. To keep this treasure, all in gold, safe from his enemies, he determined to bury it. He put the money into " a brass pot with little short feet," in which he also placed a little box containing a strip of parchment with the amount written on it. In the hall of the vicarage, under the stairs, was a patch of naked earth, and here the vicar dug a hole just deep enough to hide the brim of the pot when the earth was put back and stamped down. Then he heaped firewood over the place, and shortly afterwards left for London. He had some cause for anxiety as several people were in the secret, his sister and her son, who had helped him to bury the treasure, his parish priest, Alexander Emett, and his friend Sir Henry Saville[6]. The fortunes of the brass pot during the rebellion will be afterwards related. The point to be noticed here is that to some of the gentlemen private feuds were of more importance than any question of religion. The vicar of Halifax and Sir Richard Tempest were both opposed to Cromwell's policy, but no political sympathy could bring them to take the same side.

When the influence of the religious was exercised against the government it produced great results, as in the following case. The Stapletons of Wighill, near Tadcaster, were a family of position, followers of the Earl of Northumberland. Christopher Stapleton, the head of the family, was a chronic invalid, who passed the summer of 1535 at Beverley, for the sake of his health. He stayed in the house of the Grey Friars, and there he met Thomas Johnson, otherwise called Brother Bonaventure, one of the Observant Friars, who had been sent from York to Beverley when the houses of the Order were made conventual. The friar easily acquired influence over the

---

[1] L. and P. IX, 404.   [2] See note F at end of chapter.
[3] L. and P. VIII, 457.   [4] L. and P. XII (2), 369 (3).
[5] Ibid. 316, 369.   [6] Ibid.

sick man and his childless wife, and when they went home to Wighill he visited them there[1]. Next summer, 1536, Christopher came to Beverley again, bringing with him Sir Brian Stapleton, his eldest son by his first wife[2], and his brother William Stapleton. William, Christopher's brother, was a lawyer of Gray's Inn, and a friend of Robert Aske; he spent his vacation with his brother, and at the beginning of October, when he was about to return to London for the Michaelmas term, Beverley became the headquarters of the rebellion, and William Stapleton, at Brother Bonaventure's suggestion, was chosen captain of the commons[3]. It is beyond doubt that the influence of chaplains and confessors was used to encourage the gentlemen to join the Pilgrimage, though it is not so certain that the whole agitation can be attributed to them.

While the conservative priests were using persuasion the reformers often unwittingly helped them by provoking violence. Religious differences may lie at the bottom of a mysterious affair which took place at Marston. Leonard Constable, the parson of Heyton Wansdale, otherwise called Marston[4], brought a complaint before the Court of Star Chamber in either 1525, 1531, or 1536. Unfortunately it is impossible to discover which of these dates is correct, as the case is undated. Constable stated that on 25 April Sir Oswald Wolsthrope and Sir Robert Waid, clerk, procured that he should be attacked as he was performing the service in the parish church by Sir Thomas Applegarth, clerk, and eight other armed and riotous persons. They "violently came and took the chalice from the Altar, where your said subject (Constable) was standing, and said, 'Thou horson polshorne priest, thou shalt not say mass here, and therefore get thee out of the church, or we shall make thee repent it'." Afterwards the rioters broke into the parsonage and "put in a certain person into the same to the intent to keep your said subject out of the same, and said he should dwell there whether he would or no." On Sunday 30 April, Sir Oswald came to the parish church himself with sixteen armed men. "And then and there the said Wolsthrope, your said subject being at mass, and had almost celebrated the same, said with a high voice these words following, that is to say, 'You horson priest, if I had come betime I would have nailed thy coat to thy back with my dagger.' And

---

[1] L. and P. xii (1), 392; printed in full, J. C. Cox, William Stapleton and the Pilgrimage of Grace; see note G at end of chapter.

[2] Yorks. Arch. and Top. Journ. viii, p. 403.

[3] L. and P. xii (1), 392, see below, chap. vii.

[4] Now Hutton Wandesley in Long Marston parish.

after that your said subject had finished his mass, and kneeled down at the Altar, saying his orations and prayers, the said Sir Oswald Wolsthrope...came riotously to your said subject and plucked him down by the hair backward, and gave him many opprobrious and unfitting words, and put him in fear and jeopardy of his life." The cause of this behaviour on the part of Sir Oswald is not explained. It cannot have been a dispute over the patronage of the rectory, for Constable had been instituted in 1518, seven years before the earliest date to which the dispute can be assigned[1]. If Constable had provoked Sir Oswald by innovations and heretical practices, it is surprising that he did not mention Sir Oswald's disloyalty, unless perhaps his own opinions were not those imposed by the government. But although this riot cannot with certainty be attributed to religious differences, it possibly gives the other side of the picture drawn by an admiring martyrologist of a contemporary Yorkshire gentleman, Sir William Mallory, who "was so zealous and constant a Catholic, than when heresy first came into England, and Catholic service commanded to be put down on such a day, he came to the church, and stood there at the door with his sword drawn, to defend that none should come to abolish religion, saying that he would defend it with his life, and continued for some days keeping out the officers so long as he possibly could."[2]

A powerful bond between gentlemen, priests and commons was their intense hatred of Cromwell. He was above all else detested as a heretic, but the gentlemen also shared the contemptuous feelings of the nobles for an upstart of low birth, and the northern gentlemen had a special grievance against him, for which, doubtless, parallel cases could be found in other parts of the kingdom. One of the most onerous duties of the landowners was the administration of justice. Cromwell was anxious to strengthen the hands of the judges against local anarchy, in pursuit of his policy that England should have only one tyrant, but he was by no means scrupulous as to the quality of the justice administered in the royal courts. In March 1536 a case occurred at York Assizes which roused helpless anger throughout the county. A certain William Wicliff was charged by Mrs Carr of Newcastle-upon-Tyne with the murder of her husband, Ralph Carr. The sheriff assured Christopher Jenney, one of the judges, that the jury had been chosen by Carr's friends, all except one man "who was thought indifferent," yet even this jury acquitted

[1] Yorks. Arch. Journ. xx, 362.
[2] Morris, The Troubles of our Catholic Forefathers, 1st Ser., The Bapthorpes.

Wicliff. The names of the jurors were sent up to Cromwell, and they were bound under a recognizance of £100 each to appear before the Court of Star Chamber on 20 May. Wicliff remained in prison, as Mrs Carr sued an appeal for murder against him[1]. The jury were fined. This excited general indignation in the north; Aske said that " the Lord Cromwell...for the extreme punishment of the great jury of Yorkshire, and for the extreme assessment of their fines, was and yet is, in such horror and hatred with the people of those parts, that in manner they would eat him, and esteems their griefs only to arise by him and his counsel."[2]   Another gentleman declared that "the said traitor (Cromwell) constrains men to be perjured by extreme fines as Sir George Conyers, Sir Oswald Wolsthrope and their fellows were if they would have consented and esteemed their goods above the truth and worship."[3]   Although Wicliff is not mentioned in the latter instance, it is probably a reference to the same case.

The affair of Wicliff is typical of the crimes which were familiar to the King, but almost incomprehensible in the north. A northern gentleman did not hesitate to attack and kill his enemy in the street, but he would not perjure himself and condemn an innocent man to death " for four of the best dukes' lands in France." Abundant evidence has been given of the lawlessness which prevailed in the north, but some virtues flourished there also, which were absolutely necessary in the absence of law. A gentleman spoke the truth and held his word sacred. It was unthinkable that the King, the greatest gentleman of all, did not observe the same code.

In the uncivilised north the Church still performed her old functions, and religion was accepted with a childlike faith which, although tending to superstition, was a decided influence for good. The simple moral and religious principles of the northern gentlemen are not altogether unworthy of respect, but they formed a poor preparation for a conflict with Henry VIII.

[1] L. and P. viii, 457; see note F at end of chapter.
[2] L. and P. xii (1), 6; printed in full Eng. Hist. Rev. v, 330 et seq.
[3] L. and P. xi, 1244.

NOTES TO CHAPTER III

Note A. The authors of "The History of the House of Howard" say of Lady Bulmer "her character (was) foully, and, as has since been shown, lyingly, attacked by the King's lawyers," but we have failed to discover the defence of her character. Her own son did not deny that his sisters were born before his parents' marriage[1].

Note B. The document which accused Sir Robert Constable of breaking the liberties of Beverley is undated. Among the Letters and Papers it is placed with the evidence given at his trial. The reference to "Our Holy Father the Pope" shows that it must have been drawn up at least some years earlier.

We have been unable to discover the case of Anne Grysanis, and it is possible that this Sir Robert Constable may not have been the villain. There were so many Constables.

Note C. Possible translations of the inscription on Aughton church tower :—

(1) "I (the tower) ought not to forget Christofer, second son of Robert Aske, knt, A.D. 1536."

(2) "Christofer, the second son of Robert Aske, knt. I ought not to forget, A.D. 1536."

Note D. Robert Aske is called Sir Robert's third son in Tonge's Visitation of 1530, but in 1507 he had a brother Richard, who seems to have come between Christopher and Robert, but died in childhood[2].

Note E. Star Chamber Proceedings.

Bundle XVIII, 252.	Sir H. Saville v. Sir R. Tempest.	
„ „ 153.	„ v. „ [3].	
„ XVII, 256.	Sir R. Tempest v. Sir H. Saville[4].	
„ XXII, 58 and 147.	„ v. „	
„ XXI, 174.	Robert Holdesworth v. John Lacy, Thomas Saville, Richard Holdesworth, Nic. Brodly.	
„ XXII, 201.	Sir H. Saville v. Sir R. Tempest.	
„ „	Sir Thomas Tempest v. Sir H. Saville.	
„ XXIII, 86.	Isabel Jepson v. Sir R. Tempest and Sir T. Tempest and others for murder of her husband.	
„ XXIV, 238.	Sir R. Tempest v. Sir H. Saville.	
„ „ 380.	Rex v. Sir R. Tempest.	
„ XXV, 37.	Sir H. Saville v. Sir Thomas Tempest.	
„ „ 45, 55.	Inhabitants of various places v. Sir H. Saville.	

---

[1] G. Brenan and E. P. Statham, op. cit. I, chap. v ; Foster, loc. cit.

[2] Raine, Testa. Ebor. (Surtees Soc.), IV, 257; B. M. Add. MS 38133, f. 45 b—46 a.

[3] Printed in full, Yorks. Star Chamber Proc. (Yorks. Arch. Soc. Rec. Ser.), II, nos. xiv, xxiii, xxvii.

[4] Printed in full, Yorks. Star. Proc. (Yorks. Arch. Soc. Rec. Ser.), I, no. lxxxii.

Note F.   Christopher Jenney's letter[1], dated 27 March but without the year, is placed in 1535 by the editor of the Letters and Papers, but from the reference in it to Thwaites the vicar of Londesborough, who was examined in November 1535, it seems that the letter more probably belongs to 1536.

Note G.   J. C. Cox in his transcript of William Stapleton's Confession[2] identifies Thomas Johnson, Brother Bonaventure, with Thomas Johnson one of the monks of the London Charterhouse, but this identification is very improbable for the following reasons :—

(*a*)   It rests only on the name, which is too common to be a proof of identity.

(*b*)   William Stapleton evidently knew Brother Bonaventure well and would not be likely to mistake his Order.

(*c*)   It was contrary to the rules of the Charterhouse for any monk to wander about the country alone, but this was the usual practice of the friars.

(*d*)   Dom Thomas Johnson was not one of the four monks who were sent from London to the Hull Charterhouse in May 1536, but was still in London on 18 May 1537.   In June that year he died in Newgate[3].   As the monks of the London Charterhouse had been under close supervision since May 1536, it is incredible that one of them should have escaped to the north in October, remained there for some time, and then returned again to prison.

---

[1] L. and P. viii, 457.   See below, chap. iv.

[2] William Stapleton and the Pilgrimage of Grace, Trans. of the East Riding Rec. Soc., vol. x.

[3] Gasquet, Hen. VIII and the Eng. Mon. i, chap. vi.

CHAPTER IV

FACTS AND RUMOURS

The great events of the year 1535 were the executions of the Charterhouse monks and of More and Fisher in June and July, followed by the visitation of the monasteries by Cromwell's commissioners in the autumn. There is no need to retell these stories, for the object of this chapter is neither to extol the martyrs nor to defend Cromwell's visitors, but rather to try to discover the feeling of the nation at large, manifested by the words of numberless forgotten men and women, who often paid for their devotion to the religion of their fathers with their lives[1].

All up and down the land the friaries were storm-centres of revolt, and the King's first attack upon them only increased their influence. The Friars Observant were the most recently reformed branch of the Franciscan Order. They had been introduced into England by Henry VII, and had only six houses in the country, Greenwich, Richmond in Surrey, Cambridge, Southampton, Newark, and Newcastle-on-Tyne[2]. Their house at Newcastle had formerly belonged to the conventual brothers of the Order until Henry VII replaced them by the Observants[3]. It was natural that this Order, newly established in England, should contain the most uncompromising enemies of Henry VIII's policy, and they denounced the divorce so resolutely that their houses were suppressed in 1534[4]. The friars were transferred to the conventual houses of the Order, but the result of this was that they infected the whole body with their own discontent. But the other friars, though as yet not directly attacked, were not ready to accept the new state of affairs

---

[1] Merriman, Life of Thomas Cromwell, i, chap. vii.
[2] Gasquet, Henry VIII and the English Mon. i, chap. v.
[3] Brand, Newcastle-on-Tyne, i, 335 n.
[4] Gasquet, loc. cit.

quietly. On the contrary, of all Cromwell's opponents, they most
hated the Act of Supremacy. This was passed in the autumn of
1534, and throughout the following year popular indignation grew
and grew, as the agitation against the new laws was secretly carried
on. A friar who had embraced the New Learning[1], hot against all
"superstitious and popish remembrances," described the methods
of his unconverted brethren to Cromwell. In many church windows
was pictured the story of St Thomas of Canterbury, and he had
heard the pardoners relate how the martyr was slain for resisting
the King, in defence not only of the liberties of the Church, but also
of the rights of the poor; for he would not grant the King that
"whosoever set his child to school should pay a tribute, nor that no
poor man should eat certain meats except he paid a tribute....These
words and divers others remaining in the people's heads, which they
call the articles of St Thomas." Then the preacher would point to
the window where the penitent king knelt naked before the martyr's
shrine, and leave the listeners to draw their own moral. The friars
mendicant "living by the alms of the King's subjects" were received
everywhere by the poor as friends and teachers, although Cromwell's
correspondent declared them to be all "unlearned and without discretion." They would seek out the "aged and simple" and "drive
them into admiration with such words as—Oh, father or sister, what
a world is this! It was not so in your father's days. Ye may see it
is a parlous world. They will have no pilgrimage. They will not
we should pray to saints, or fast, or do any good deeds. Our Lord
have mercy on us! I will live as my forefathers have done, and I am
sure your fathers and friends were good....Therefore I pray you
continue as you have done, and believe as your friends and fathers
did; whatsoever the new fellows do, say and do for yourself while ye
be here." The reformer considered that these friars "do much hurt
and will do, except they be otherwise provided for, that they may no
more so scatter abroad." He concluded by asking for a dispensation
from his habit that he might "preach God's word."[2] It may be
imagined that his sermons would little please his old brethren, and
as a commentary on them or their like may be quoted the words of a
certain White friar, who said "that we should see a new turn of the
Bishop of Rome if we lived; that we were a many wretches of this
realm, without any charity, thus to blaspheme him, seeing that he
does not write against us, but we, malicious wretches, write and rail

[1] See note A at end of chapter.
[2] L. and P. viii, 626; the document is quoted by Froude, op. cit. chap. xiv.

against him without any charity; and though some of his predecessors were evil, he is a good man."[1] The Pope referred to was Paul III. The friars were above all wandering preachers, and reports of seditious sermons by Black, White, or Grey brethren were sent to Cromwell from Norwich, Canterbury, Bristol, Kingswood in Wiltshire[2], and Newcastle-on-Tyne, where the prior of the Black friars preached a series of Lenten sermons in 1536 against the Royal Supremacy and then fled to Scotland[3]. Some of the friars were simple and ignorant enough, but no less powerful among the people for all that; others were more like one of whom Latimer complained,—"wilily witted, Dunsly learned, Morely affected, bold not a little, zealous more than enough,"[4] i.e. learned in the lore of Duns Scotus and holding the opinions of Sir Thomas More.

As an instance of the sort of conversation that went on within the friaries there is the case of the Grey Friars of Grantham, which was remarkable as being the northernmost house in which there was a treacherous brother. Friar John Colsell, in his deposition of 23 August 1535, tried to fasten a charge of treason upon the Warden and other brethren, though his motive was rather private malice than any love of the New Learning. The Warden stated in his defence that he had rebuked two unruly friars, who threatened to complain to the general visitor, whereupon he said, "Well, this fashion will not last always. I trust we shall have the correction of our own religion again, for it hath done a hundred pounds worth of hurt since it was otherwise; for now, if they be checked for their misorder they will threat a man to complain of him, and yet in the end, after he know the truth, I trust the same visitor will take them as they be." Another of the accused friars had remarked, concerning the erasure of the Pope's name from the service books, "If every Act were as well executed as this, we should have a merry world." One of the refractory friars asked, "Be they not so?" "No, for there was an Act made concerning the Statute of Array, that no man should wear satin, velvet nor damask unless he were a man of lands or a burgess, which be now broken." The aldermen of Grantham and other men of influence in the town gave evidence in favour of the Warden, among them Gervase Tyndale, the master of the free school. Tyndale was by no means inclined to favour friars in general[5],

---

[1] L. and P. VIII, 624.   [2] L. and P. VII, 595; VIII, 480; IX, 189, 315.
[3] L. and P. X, 594; Gasquet, op. cit. II, chap. VII.
[4] L. and P. IX, 1118, printed in Latimer's Sermons and Remains (Parker Soc.), II, 373.   [5] L. and P. IX, 179.

for in November 1535 he wrote to Cromwell asking for money, as he was employed in the business of certain friars who were about to practise necromancy. In the same letter he complained of a "doctor" who had preached in the town on All Souls' Day about purgatory, saying that earthly fire was to the fire of purgatory as a picture is compared to a man, and that one penny given to a priest would release souls from purgatory. Tyndale remonstrated with him, but the preacher had the support of the congregation. He called Tyndale a Saxon heretic behind his back, and drove away all the boys from the free school, lest their master should infect them with his opinions[1].

The preaching, however, was not all one way, for there were a few "heretics" wandering up and down the country, friars of a new creed. These poor men were greatly to be pitied, standing as they did between two fires. Henry and Cromwell were willing to use them, but regarded them with the utmost suspicion, and were always ready to pounce upon them if they transgressed the very narrow limits allowed. The ordinary clergy and the mass of the people regarded them with hatred and contempt. Their acts at first seem simply to have stirred up opposition, though here and there are signs that their teaching was beginning to produce an effect[2]. Any earnest soul simply and honestly trying to find a satisfying religion must have been much confused by the laws provided for his guidance. The parson of Staunton in Gloucester was in trouble for saying that "if the King our sovereign did not go forth with his laws as he began, he would call the King Anti-Christ;"[3] while Wotton-under-Edge in the same county was full of discord "by reason of divers opinions"; and one John Plummer was accused of saying "there shall be a new world or Midsummer Day," by which he meant, as he explained, that he hoped "the King in his Parliament would make some order of punishment for those who neither fast nor pray."[4]

The questing soul would have found that it was just as dangerous to speak for as against purgatory[5]; and if he dared to call images idols he was not only likely to be attacked by his indignant neighbours, but was also within reach of the law[6]. The law indeed permitted the reading of the Scriptures in English, but public opinion was so much against it that a layman complained of being

---

[1] L. and P. IX, 740.
[2] L. and P. x, 462.
[3] Ibid. 1027, 1099.
[4] Ibid. 790.
[5] L. and P. VIII, 480; IX, 704.
[6] L. and P. VIII, 20; x, 296.

set in the stocks for having an English psalter[1], and the Prior of Haverfordwest appealed to Cromwell against the Bishop of St David's, who had forced him to give up his English testament "as if to have a testament in English were horrible heresy."[2] So strong was this feeling that even the Bishop of Lincoln, Longland, who was accounted a heretic, complained to Cromwell of "Sir Swinnerton" and other preachers who were bad characters and encouraged people to read English books; the men of Lincolnshire "much grudged" against them[3].

But wandering preachers, whether heretic or papist, were only the skirmishers of the religious fray; the reformers were weak in numbers, but they poured their books and tracts, like an unceasing fire of heavy artillery, from their foreign batteries; also they had an immensely powerful, though suspicious, ally in the King. The romanists, on the other hand, always hoped for but never received reinforcements from the Pope. But they had numbers and tradition on their side, and their army was very efficiently officered by the parish priests. The steady, quiet opposition of these men was much the most effective defence attempted against the King's ecclesiastical policy. They had been ordered to blot out the name of the Pope in all prayer and service books, and to repeat a collect for the welfare of the King and Anne Boleyn[4], but Cromwell's informers continually reported cases of disobedience[5]. The vicar of Stanton Lacy, Salop, was accused of covering the Pope's name by a piece of paper fastened down with balm, instead of erasing the words[6]. All the religious were very loath to reform their mass books. They could not believe that the quarrel with Rome was more than a passing cloud. "When the King is dead all these fashions will be laid down," was the general belief[7]. Richard Crowley, curate of Broughton, Oxford, was accused of calling the Bishop of Rome Pope, and of comparing him to the sun, the King to the moon and the people to the stars, with the application that "the moon takes her light from the sun and as the light of the sun is taken from us, so the world is dark and the people in blindness." He offered his parishioners pardon "during the utas" at the feast of the Name of Jesus (7 August), declared that the power of the Pope was as great as ever, and professed

[1] L. and P. IX, 1130.   [2] Ibid. 1091.
[3] L. and P. X, 804, 891.
[4] Dixon, Hist. of the Church of Eng. I, chap. IV.
[5] L. and P. IX, 100, X, 14.
[6] L. and P. IX, 408.   [7] L. and P. VIII, 406.

himself ready to die for the true faith, like More, Fisher, and the fathers of Zion[1]. Only a few were as bold as he; others, who "would rather be torn with wild horses than assent or consent to the diminishing of any one iote of the bishop of Rome his authority, of old time and always holden and kept in this realm,"[2] were content to speak their minds and then seek safety overseas[3]; but the greatest number were like the curate of Rye, who, though he had taken the oath to the King, had "done the contrary," and spread tracts against the Royal Supremacy[4].

So few people as yet favoured the New Learning that most of our knowledge of the discontent is due to local disputes. If a priest quarrelled with his parishioners, they would bring accusations against him which, however true in themselves, would never have been laid against a popular man. An example of this occurred at Harwich, Essex, at the end of the year 1535, when thirty-two of his flock brought a variety of charges against the priest, Thomas Corthrop, such as that he had not erased the Pope's name from his mass book, that he had called Dr Barnes "false knave and heretic,"[5] that he had preached Anti-Christ and not shown who Anti-Christ was, and so forth. He had also said in a sermon at Bethlehem without Bishopgate, London, that "these new preachers nowadays that doth preach their three sermons a day have made and brought in such divisions and seditions among us as never was seen in this realm, for the devil reigneth over us now." The root of the complaint, how-ever, lies in the last two articles :—"That when the young men of the parish entered the church on December 26 to chose them a Lord of Misrule with minstrels to solace the parish and bring youths from cards and dicing, the said priest had taken the pipe out of the minstrel's hand, and struck him on the head with it, and did next day preach a sermon that the Children of Israel came dancing and piping before idols"; and that he falsely accused his parishioners of hunting and bowling instead of coming to church[6]. If it had not been for his puritanism in these respects, most likely nothing would have been heard of his conservatism in others.

[1] L. and P. ix, 46 ; xii (2), 518.
[2] L. and P. ix, 1066.
[3] L. and P. viii, 480 ; ix, 789.
[4] L. and P. viii, 589, 770, 776; ix, 846; x, 1140; xii (2), 505.
[5] Barnes was afterwards (30 July 1540) put to death at Smithfield on the famous occasion when three heretics, of whom he was one, and three romanists were executed together.
[6] L. and P. ix, 1059.

The preachers were chiefly concerned with the relations between England and the Pope, but the commons looked at the matter from a more personal point of view. Queen Katherine was universally beloved, while Queen Anne was detested. It was the divorce and the slaughter of the monks that roused popular indignation rather than the abstract question of the supremacy. A woman of "Senklers Bradfield,"[1] Suffolk, was accused of rejoicing because Anne's child was still-born (February 1535), and of calling her "a goggle-eyed whore," adding, "God save Queen Katherine for she was righteous queen, and she trusted to see her queen again, and that she should warrant the same."[2]

Henry himself fully shared the ill-will showered upon his new wife. A Buckinghamshire man declared "the King is but a knave and liveth in adultry, and is an heretic and liveth not after the laws of God," and also "I set not by the King's crown, and if I had it here I would play at football with it."[3] A yeoman named Adam Fermour, of Waldron in Sussex, had just returned from London. His friends asked what the news was. "What news, man?" said he. "By God's blood! evil news, for the King will make such laws that if a man die his wife and his children shall go a-begging. He fell but lately and brake one of his ribs, and if he make such laws it were pity but he should break his neck."[4] The act that roused his indignation must have been the Statute of Uses[5]. A few laymen, perhaps, took exception to the Royal Supremacy, but most contented themselves with abusing the King and Queen[6]. Others again reviled the King's favourites, and, of course, Cromwell first of all. The vicar of Eastbourne said to an unreliable friend, while walking in the churchyard, "They that rule about the King make him great banquets and give him sweet wines and make him drunk," and then "they bring him bills and he putteth his sign to them, whereby they do what they will and no man may correct them." He lamented the execution of the Bishop of Rochester (Fisher) and of Sir Thomas More, saying that they would be sorely missed, for they were the most profound men of learning in the realm[7].

[1] Bradfield St Clare.
[2] L. and P. viii, 196, quoted by Merriman, op. cit. i, chap. vii; see note E at end of chapter.
[3] L. and P. viii, 278; quoted by Merriman, loc. cit.
[4] L. and P. xiii (2), 307.
[5] See above, chap. i.
[6] L. and P. viii, 844; ix, 864, 1123; x, 1205.
[7] L. and P. xi, 300 (ii); quoted by Merriman, loc. cit.

As time went on, disloyalty steadily increased.   At Coventry in November 1535 the royal proclamations were torn down from the market cross[1].   At Chichester in April 1536 a seditious bill was posted up[2].

From Crowle in Worcestershire came several reports of treasonable speeches.   In August 1535 Edmund Brocke, an aged husbandman, walking home from Worcester market in the rain, was heard to say, "It is 'long of the King that this weather is so troublous and unstable, and I ween we shall never have better weather whiles the King reigneth, and therefore it maketh no matter if he were knocked or patted on the head."[3]   A year later accusations were brought against James Pratt, the vicar of Crowle.   Witnesses deposed that on the Sunday before St Bartholomew's Day (24 August) he had said in an ale-house "that the church went down and would be worse until there be a shrappe made, and said that he reckoned there were 20,000 nigh of flote, and wished there were 20,000 more, so that he were one, and rather tomorrow than the next day, for there shall never be good world until there be a schrappe.   And they that may escape that shall live merry enough."   Statistics were very roughly calculated in those days, but the 20,000 men whom the vicar believed to be "nigh of flote" appear again and again in the report of the rebels' forces, and perhaps he had some grounds for his prophecy, though he was probably drunk when he made it.   If not strictly temperate he was at any rate brave and loyal to his friends; when examined by torture, he would confess nothing but that he had heard divers persons, whom he would not name, say the Church was never so sore handled[4].   Earlier in the same year (1536) Thomas Sowle, a priest of Penrith in Cumberland, had wandered south to Tewkesbury, where he said in an ale-house, "We be kept bare and smit under, yet we shall rise once again, and 40,000 of us will rise upon a day."[5]   By degrees the mutterings of discontent became more definite.   Thomas Toone, parson of Weeley, Essex, came home from a visit to the north at the beginning of September 1536 in harvest-time.   Two of his parishioners went with him one day into the fields called "Lambeles Redoon" and "Wardes" to gather tithe sheaves.   "There shall be business shortly in the north," said the priest, "and I trust to help strength my countrymen with 10,000

[1] L. and P. IX, 883.   [2] L. and P. X, 722.
[3] L. and P. IX, 74; quoted by Merriman, loc. cit.
[4] L. and P. XI, 407; Merriman, op. cit. II, nos. 161, 164; L. and P. XII (1), 109.
[5] L. and P. X, 693 (ii); see note F at end of chapter.

such as I am myself, and that I shall be one of the worst of them all."
The labourer answered quietly, "Little said is soon amended." The
priest added hastily, "Remember ye not what I said unto you right
now, care ye not for that, for an Easter come, the King shall not
reign long." The priest went on up the furrow gathering the tithe
sheaves, and the two countrymen agreed together to say nothing
of the matter for the present[1]. They waited, like hundreds of others,
ready to applaud the priest if he succeeded, or to accuse him if he
failed.

Such was the state of the south on the eve of the rebellion. The
general opinion was that "the new laws might be suffered for a
season, but already they set men together by the ears and in time
they would cause broken heads."[2] In the north the discontent was
all the more dangerous because less is heard of it[3]. It was by no
means less active than in the south, but there were fewer informers.
In 1535, Layton, one of Cromwell's hated visitors, wrote to his
master on the religious state of the northern counties, where he was
about to begin his visitation of the monasteries: "There can be no
better way to beat the King's authority into the heads of the rude
people of the north than to show them that the King intends reformation and correction of religion." He described them as "more
superstitious than virtuous, long accustomed to frantic fantasies and
ceremonies, which they regard more than either God or their prince,
right far alienate from true religion."[4] And there are a few indications
of the trend of popular sympathy.

Edward Lee, the Archbishop of York, though usually entirely
subservient to the King, once or twice protested against the granting
of licences to heretic preachers, who spoke against purgatory, pilgrimages, and so forth "wherewith the people grudge, which otherwise all
the King's commandment here obey diligently, as well for the setting
forth of his title of supreme head as also of the abolition of the
primate of Rome."[5] In spite of this assertion, when the parish
priest of Guisborough, Yorkshire, was reading the articles of the
King's Supremacy in church on 11 July 1535, John Atkinson, alias
Brotton, "came violently and took the book forth of the priest's
hands, and pulled it in pieces, and privily conveyed himself forth
of the church." A search was made for him, but perhaps not a very
exhaustive one; at least he was not found[6].

[1] L. and P. xii (1), 407.   [2] L. and P. viii, 386.
[3] See note E at end of chapter.   [4] L. and P. viii, 955.
[5] L. and P. ix, 704, 742; x, 172.   [6] L. and P. viii, 1024.

Very touching are the words of the priest of Winestead, who on Midsummer Day 1535 begged his people to pray for him, "for he had made his testament and was boune to such a journey that he trowed never to see them again. And it is said there is no Pope, but I say there is one Pope." He was committed to the Archbishop's prison at York and his fate is unknown[1].

The Royal Supremacy was attacked in books as well as by action and example. On 7 July 1535 Bishop Tunstall wrote to tell Cromwell that a book called "Hortulus Animae," but printed in English, had been brought to him from Newcastle, and that he found in the calendar at the end of it "a manifest declaration against the effect of the act of parliament lately made, for the establishment of the King's succession...which declaration is made... upon the day of the decollation of St John Baptist, to show the cause why he was beheaded."[2] It was easy to draw a sufficiently trenchant parallel between Herod, Herodias, and St John on the one hand, and Henry, Anne, and the Catholic martyrs on the other. Later in the same year other books were "taken up," which treated of purgatory and magnified the power of the Pope[3].

The depositions against William Thwaites, parson of Londesborough, form the fullest case remaining against a Yorkshire parish priest, and they are especially interesting because the circumstances must have come under the notice of Robert Aske. His brother Christopher had lands in Londesborough, and John Aske was the magistrate who heard the second set of depositions on 13 November 1535. John Nesfield, the bailiff of Londesborough, was the principal witness. He charged the vicar with saying "about the Invention of Holy Cross last" (3 May 1535) that he was glad to hear of the subsidy "for now shall ye temporal men be pilled and polled as well as the spiritual men be." He also said that England had now no allies but the Lutherans, and that an interdict on the realm lay at Calais and other foreign ports. If it were brought into the country, there would be no more Christian burial for men than for dogs, "howbeit the King will not obey it." He had refused to attend when summoned to appear before Archdeacon Magnus on 29 June 1535 at Warter Priory, when the other curates of the deanery were given briefs to declare every Sunday; these must have been the briefs for the Royal Supremacy[4]. Thwaites never published

[1] L. and P. VIII, 1020.
[2] Ibid. 1005; printed by Strype, Eccles. Mem. I (ii), 274.
[3] L. and P. IX, 135.   [4] See above, chap. I.

his copy until the Sunday before Holyrood Day (14 September), when his parishioners began to murmur. There were three other witnesses who had heard him say that the King would be destroyed by the most vile people in the world "and that he should be glad to take a boat for safeguard of his life and flee into the sea, and forsake his own realm; and, masters, there hangs a cloud over us, what as it means I know not." He also spoke much of prophecies about future battles[1].

Thwaites was tried at the York Assizes in March 1536, and was acquitted on the grounds that the charge was malicious. Nevertheless he was sent up to London to appear before Cromwell next term[2].

Although all classes were to a certain extent hostile to the religious changes, a sharp line was drawn between the disaffection of the gentlemen on account of the new laws, and the unrest of the lower orders under social conditions. The troubles of the commons may be summed up in the one word—change. Everything was changing,—the relations of the landlord to the tenant, of the labourer to the land, of the buyer to the seller, of the layman to the church,—and in most cases the change bore heavily on the poor man. It was all this changing that he resented so profoundly; he disliked to see the abbeys pulled down and the monks turned out, just as he disliked raised rents and sheep-farming enclosures, and an English service in the parish church. About an abstract question like that of the Supremacy he cared little, and if the King had been content with his new title and spared the monasteries, there would probably have been no rebellion, but only a series of isolated disturbances raised by the commons and easily put down by the gentlemen, such as the Craven riots of June 1535. The rioters tore down the enclosures made by the Earl of Cumberland, the most ill-beloved of the northern nobles. Their grievances were the usual ones: fields which when tilled had supported families were turned into pasturage for the lord's profit, and the common lands were shamelessly stolen. The authorities had no difficulty in finding and punishing a suitable number of offenders[3]. In December there was rioting in Galtres Forest by York, but here the sympathy of the gentlemen was with the rioters, for in spite of the evidence the inquest which the Earl of Northumberland appointed to deal with the affair refused to "find a riot,"

---

[1] L. and P. ix, 791.
[2] L. and P. viii, 457. For the date see above, chap. iii, note F.
[3] L. and P. viii, 863, 970, 984, 991; ix, 150, 196, 427.

at the instigation of Thomas Delaryver, one of the jurors[1]; and in April 1536 Sir Arthur Darcy appealed to Cromwell on behalf of the people of Galtres Forest, who were being troubled by Mr Curwen and Sir Thomas Wharton about an alleged riot although it was barley-seed time and they were in great poverty[2].

The people about Snape assembled in April 1536 to attack the commissioners for the subsidy, but when they reached the place they only found the spiritual officers holding a court, and so they dispersed[3]. This assembly must have been promoted by the yeomen farmers, who, being the poorest class included in the subsidy, naturally resented it most.

At the end of 1535, commons, yeomen, and gentlemen were as yet far from forgetting their contending economic grievances in their common religious ones. Darcy himself was involved in a quarrel with his tenants at Rothwell about enclosures[4], and parties with interests so different might never have united, if the dissolution of the lesser monasteries had not welded them into one.

The Act was passed in March 1536[5], and the suppression began in May. News travelled so slowly, and the proceedings of the government were so little understood, that the first intimation of the coming change must often have been the arrival of the commissioners who were to suppress the monastery. The effect on the people may be imagined when they saw the monks turned out, their alms stopped, their lands given to an absentee landlord, their buildings pulled down, or unroofed and left to fall to ruin.

When the idea of dissolving the monasteries was throwing the whole kingdom into a turmoil, it may well be asked how it was received in the monasteries themselves. There is strangely little information on this point. As early as February 1536, that is, a month before the act was passed, Thomas Duke[6], the vicar of Hornchurch, Essex, had been heard to say that "the King and his council hath made a way by wiles and crafts to pull down all manner of religious, and thus they go about to abbots and priors and possessioners and agree with them to deliver up their rights and promise them a sufficient living, a hundred marks or more, and when they have given all over, all other must needs give over, but an they would hold hard for their part, which be their rights, the King could not pull down none, nor all his council."[7] From this and other

---

[1] L. and P. x, 77.   [2] Ibid. 733.   [3] Ibid. 745.
[4] L. and P. vi, 355, 537.   [5] See above, chap. i.
[6] See note B at end of chapter.   [7] L. and P. x, 1264.

evidence it is clear that Cromwell had taken steps to ensure the peaceful surrender of houses[1]. In the majority of cases the monks must have felt very bitterly against those who forced them from their chosen life, and numbers of abbots and abbesses spared neither trouble nor gold in vainly trying to save their houses from the general spoil. Others again simply could not believe that such an order would really be carried out; such a one was the Abbot of Woburn, whose ruthful story Froude has told[2]. In June 1536 the Abbot of Tavistock was heard to say at table, "Lo, the King sends about to suppress many houses of religion, which is a piteous case; and so did the Cardinal (Wolsey) in his time, but what became of him and what end he made for his so doing, I report me unto you; all men knows."[3]

It has often been said that if all the religious had borne themselves as did the Carthusian martyrs, the Reformation would have been impossible. This is perfectly true, and perhaps, religiously speaking, the monks ought to have been prepared to die to a man rather than give way, especially as their training was supposed to be the best possible preparation for martyrdom. But they were handicapped. The King struck so suddenly that they had no time, even if they had the necessary determination, to agree on any common action. There were no positive orders from the Pope, and the immediate superiors whom the monks were bound to obey were often either bribed by Cromwell or turned out to make way for government servants. Then there were discontented monks, and monks who inclined to the New Learning, in many of the houses. Nevertheless there was nothing that could have stayed real enthusiasm if it had swept through the monasteries. The monks of the Charterhouse could die, and the canons of Hexham could take up arms. Others might have done as they did, instead of going forth sadly and lamenting their hard lot. It was not that the religious did not care, but that they did not care quite enough. And yet it is scarcely fair to blame them for lack of zeal. It is impossible, humanly speaking, that a large and scattered class of men and women, united only by the common aim of their lives and schooled in implicit obedience, should be able to defy in solid and unbroken ranks the law under which they live. The case of the romanist priests who suffered during the Elizabethan

---

[1] A. F. Pollard, Henry VIII, chap. xii.
[2] Froude, The Dissolution of the Monasteries, Frazer's Mag. 1857.
[3] L. and P. x, 1221.

persecution is not to the point.   They were enthusiasts who were eager for martyrdom, like the leaders of a forlorn hope.   The religious of Henry VIII's reign were peaceful votaries, and however well the monastic life may have fitted them to praise God, feed the poor, and teach the children, it could not produce men capable of resisting constitutional authority.   People grumbled as much then as now at acts of parliament, and thought of resisting them as little.   The monks were not as a class capable of refusing to acknowledge Henry's supremacy, but they were eminently suited to carry on a long passive resistance, and this was one of the reasons which moved the King to rid himself of them.   Having once recognised Henry as Head of the Church of England, they were helpless against the further attack.   Morally they had admitted themselves absolutely at his mercy; actually they might perhaps have made a better fight than they did, for the people were almost everywhere on their side; but as the whole aim of their way of living had been to cut them off completely from the world, the better they were from the ecclesiastical point of view, the more helpless they were to take any action in practical life.   They were not even convinced that any action on their part was necessary.

The fall and execution of Anne Boleyn in May 1536 was received with universal rejoicing, and conservative people expected the longed-for reaction in ecclesiastical affairs.   But in the very month that rid them of the cause of their troubles the suppression began. Before the end of July they realised that their hopes were not to be fulfilled, and within the next month the country was alive with "rumours," as the royal spies said, though it was really a secret political agitation.   The King was at great pains to trace out these rumours after the rebellion, because he wished to represent that such of them as he had no present intention of carrying out were the only cause of the rising.   Consequently, when the poor, deluded commons discovered how false the tales were, they would at once return to their allegiance, without making any inconvenient demands.   Nevertheless the rumours were usually based on fact, or anticipated measures which were afterwards taken, and the outstanding facts of the Treason Act, the Succession Acts, the subsidy, the Royal Supremacy and the Dissolution of the Monasteries were undeniable and gave colour to the rest.   When the King was actively engaged in robbing a church, what hope was there that he would spare his subjects ?   The commonest rumours were as follows :

(*a*) All the jewels and vessels of the parish churches were to be taken away, and such as were necessary were to be replaced by tin or brass[1]. This report was the natural sequel of the pillaging of the monasteries and the destruction of the shrines. Though Henry himself did not make such a confiscation, it occurred in his son's reign.

(*b*) All gold, coined and uncoined, was to be taken to the mint to be tested, and every man would be obliged to pay for the testing[2].

(*c*) One of the rumours which had least foundation in fact was that parish churches were to be at least five miles apart. Where they stood nearer together, the separate parishes were to be united into one, and the unneeded churches were to be pulled down[3]. Even now there is great local rivalry between parish and parish. At that time it often rose to a positive feud. The idea that the ancient landmarks would be removed and that men would be compelled to worship with their neighbouring enemies was enough to make some parishes take up arms.

(*d*) A tax was to be levied on all horned cattle. Those on which it had been paid would be marked, and any found unmarked would be confiscated[4]. This rumour probably originated in the legislation concerning graziers[5].

(*e*) In anticipation of Cromwell's parish registers, it was said that all christenings, marriages, and burials were to be taxed[6].

(*f*) No poor man was to be permitted to eat white bread, goose or capon without paying a tribute to the King[7]. The probable source of this rumour has already been mentioned[8]. It is a reminder that though the Tudor sumptuary laws seem very quaint now, they must have been a real hardship at the time.

(*g*) Finally, it was said that every man would be sworn to give an account of his property and income. If he falsified the return all his goods would be forfeited[9]. This was simply a complaint against the subsidy in rather an exaggerated form.

Such were the more fantastic of the stories which were passing from mouth to mouth. It is evident that they were no wider of the truth than many political agitations in our own time, and with them were united the real grievances which have already been mentioned

[1] L. and P. xii (1), 70 (xi), 481; xi, 854 (ii), 768 (2).

[2] L. and P. xi, 768 (2); printed in State Papers, i, 482.

[3] Ibid.   [4] L. and P. xi, 828 (vi).   [5] See above, chap. i.

[6] L. and P. xi, 768 (2); printed in St. P. i, 482.

[7] Ibid.   [8] See above, chap. i.

[9] L. and P. xi, 768 (2); printed in St. P. i, 482.

They passed through the country from market to market[1], and can be traced as far south as Devon, where on 5 September a "somner" was accused of spreading them[2]. They circulated chiefly in the midland and eastern counties. Aske declared that they were never heard in Yorkshire until after Guy Kyme brought them with the Lincolnshire articles[3]. Stapleton however heard at Beverley that several parishes were to be made into one and the church jewels taken away[4]; and Breyar was told of the tax on horned cattle and on every "child and chymley" at Sturley and Retford[5]. It is natural that rumours should spread from the south to the north bank of the Humber, and Aske first heard them from the ferryman as he was crossing at Barton[6]. It would be difficult to find a better way of spreading news than by enlisting ferrymen to repeat it to their fares. But though the rumours were certainly known in Yorkshire after the rising began, they do not seem to have spread very far, or to have had much influence there. The newsbearers who carried them need not be accused of ill-faith; in all probability they really believed what they said, and this gave their words all the more weight. Their work may be compared to that of the Evangel-ical Brotherhood in Germany, formed in 1524, whose members each contributed a small weekly sum "to defray the expenses of the bearers of the secret despatches which were to be distributed far and wide throughout Germany, inciting to amalgamation and a general rising."[7] The effect of their propaganda was soon seen.

Early in August 1536 riots broke out in Cumberland, and the Bishop of Carlisle was accused of promoting them[8]. In Norfolk there were stirrings at the beginning of September. An organ-maker "in-tended to make an insurrection" at Norwich, but he was arrested by the Duke of Norfolk, who also took up another "right ill person" who spoke lewd words[9]. Men from Lincolnshire were reporting in other counties that "anyone who would go thither at Michaelmas should have honest living, for diking and fowling," and there were several who took the hint and set out for Lincolnshire as soon as the harvest

---

[1] L. and P. XII (1), 70 (x), (xi).   [2] L. and P. XI, 405.

[3] L. and P. XII (1), 901; see below, chap. VII.

[4] L. and P. XII (1), 392; see below, chap. VII.

[5] L. and P. XI, 841; see below, chap. VII.

[6] L. and P. XII (1), 6; printed in Eng. Hist. Rev. v, 331.

[7] E. B. Bax, The Peasants' War in Germany, 1524–25, p. 37.

[8] L. and P. XI, 319; printed by Raine, Mem. of Hexham Priory (Surtees Soc.), I, p. clvi, n.

[9] L. and P. XI, 434, 470.

was over[1]. The commissioners and their servants were by no means careful to allay the unrest. On St Matthew's Day (21 September) a tall serving-man in Louth church declared that the silver almsbowl was "meeter for the King than for them." Whereupon one of the congregation "fashioned to draw his dagger, saying that Louth and Louthesk should make the King and his master[2] such a breakfast as they never had."[3] It was said at Grimsby that the people of Hull had sold their church plate and jewels and paved the town with the proceeds, in order that the King might not get them[4]. In the Yorkshire dales the people had taken an oath and were on the verge of rebellion, openly speaking treason[5].

It was impossible that rumours should circulate and oaths be taken without some human agency, but the men who were conducting the agitation are difficult to discover. The King's pardon to the rebels only covered the period of the actual rebellion; any treasonable word or action before that time was to be punished. In consequence very little can be learned about the time of preparation. The prisoners naturally declared that they had been taken unawares and knew nothing of the business until they were compelled to join the insurgents. In such a situation a little prevarication is pardonable, and it is scarcely wronging Aske, Stapleton, and others to say that they probably knew more than they would admit about the origin of the rebellion. Sometimes there is a glimpse of a friar or a vicar, such as the priest of Penrith and the vicar of Crowle, and sometimes it is some person indirectly ecclesiastical, a summoner or an organ-maker, who may be suspected of knowing the secret; but of the laymen engaged in the agitation only two can be identified, and very little can be discovered about even these two.

One of them was Guy Kyme of Louth, who was executed at Lincoln after the rebellion[6]. On Saturday 30 September and Sunday 1 October 1536 he was at Grimsby. He said that his business was "about the conveyance of certain suspected pirates of a ship of Feversham to Lincoln,"[7] but several people believed he was already in communication with the disaffected in Yorkshire[8], and during the rising he was sent as a messenger from the insurgents to Beverley[9]. Anthony Curtis, the other agent, is a still more problematic

---

[1] L. and P. xi, 543.
[2] The serving-man's master, i.e. Cromwell.
[3] L. and P. xi, 828 (vii).
[4] L. and P. xii (1), 481.
[5] L. and P. xi, 841.
[6] L. and P. xii (1), 590.
[7] L. and P. xi, 828 (xii).
[8] Ibid. 972.
[9] See below, chaps. v and vii.

character.   He lived in Grimsby[1], and was connected with the Askes[2], though the relationship cannot now be traced.   He was a fellow-lawyer of Robert Aske's at Gray's Inn[3].   Like Kyme he was concerned in carrying news from Lincolnshire to Yorkshire[4]. Both these men, it is to be noted, were from the north of Lincolnshire, and several details seem to point to the fact that this country was the headquarters of the agitation.

In addition to the definite rumours about new taxes and changes, there was the vaguer but perhaps no less influential mass of wandering prophecies.   As early as 1535 a certain hermit of Bristol, returning home after a visit to Lincolnshire, called Katherine of Arragon " the Queen of Fortune," and declared that when the time came she would make ten men against the King's one[5].   During May and June of the same year it rained continually, and it was murmured that this was God's vengeance for the death of monks[6].   In London a prophecy went about that there would be a month " rainy and full wet, next month death, and the third month war,"[7] and another that " the floods flowing in Britain shall cause a great insurrection."[8] The connection between floods and rebellion was obvious; when the rain spoiled the harvest the people starved, and were ready for any mischief.   Before the Peasants' Revolt in Germany it was prophesied that there would be a second Flood in the summer of 1524[9].   Prophecies almost as vague and quite as likely to come true can be found to-day in any newspaper; now, as then, the weather and politics are the two subjects on which mankind always listens to the seer, however often misled.

The story of one of the strangest prophecies was told by a Dorsetshire justice on 20 May 1535.   A servant of his was overheard lamenting first the stormy weather, and then the state of the kingdom, " saying it was a heavy world and like to be worse shortly, for he heard say that the priests would rise against the King." Inquiries were made, and the servant admitted that one of the tenants had told him some such words, which he had from an old man living but three miles from Chideock.   The justice set out to see the prophet, who was too aged to come before him.   When questioned he said it was true he had told several neighbours that

---

[1] L. and P. xii (1), 70 (viii).

[2] L. and P. xi, 1120.   [3] L. and P. xii (1), 392.

[4] Ibid.   [5] L. and P. viii, 809.

[6] Ibid. 949.   [7] Ibid. 771.

[8] Furnivall, Ballads from MS (Ballad Soc.), i (2), 317.   [9] Bax, op. cit. 59.

"the priests should make a field"; he knew this from his master, a very wise man, who had been dead fifty years. The rest of the prophecy ran, "that the parish priests should rule England three days and nights, and then the White Falcon should come out of the North-West and kill almost all the priests, and they that should escape should be fain to hide their crowns with the filth of beasts, because they would not be known."[1] The White Falcon was the badge of Anne Boleyn, and these very adaptable phrases suggest the brief reign of Mary and the Catholic persecutions under "the White Falcon's" daughter.

Anne Boleyn's reign and fall were said to have been foretold by Merlin[2]. "A.B. and C." are of frequent occurrence in the prophecies, even after her death, probably standing for Anne Boleyn and Cromwell. The monks of Furness had a saying "that A B and C should sit all in one seat, and should work great marvels," and that afterwards "the decorate rose shall be slain in his mother's belly." It does not appear how long this saying had been known in the house, but during the winter of 1536 they interpreted it to mean that Henry should be slain by the hands of the priests, for the Church he oppressed was his mother[3]. The prophecies circulated chiefly in the monasteries and among the priests and friars. The Prior of Malton in Rydale described a picture drawn on parchment which he had seen fifteen years before (1512) at Rostendale (Ravenstonedale) in Westmorland; it showed a moon waxing and waning, each moon with the date of the year beneath. Over the full moon was drawn a Cardinal, and under the old moon two headless monks; in the midst was a child "with axes and butchers' knives and instruments about him."[4] This recalls another prophecy of 1512, which made a deep impression on the mind of Cromwell, "that one with a Red Cap brought up from low degree to high estate should rule all the land under the King...and afterwards procure the King to take another wife, divorce his lawful wife Queen Katherine, and involve the land in misery...that divorce should lead to the utter fall of the said Red Cap...and after much misery the land should by another Red Cap be reconciled or else brought to utter destruction."[5]

---

[1] L. and P. VIII, 736.
[2] L. and P. X, 911.
[3] L. and P. XII (1), 841, 3 (ii) and 4. For similar sayings see Furnivall, loc. cit. and Early Eng. Text Soc., Thomas of Ercildoune, vol. 61, p. 61.
[4] L. and P. XII (1), 534.
[5] L. and P. XIV (1), 186; Merriman, op. cit. I, chap. XI.

D.

6

Dr Maydland, a Black friar of London, had discovered by necromancy in November 1535 that the New Learning should be suppressed, and the Old restored by the King's enemies beyond the seas.   He was in hopes that the King would die a violent death, and that he would see the Queen (Anne) burnt, and the head of every maintainer of the New Learning on a stake[1].

It was treason to possess copies of such prophecies.   On 2 April 1536 the parson of Wednesborough was accused of possessing one; other accusations against him were that he was a Scot, and "if well handled" could "declare a multitude of papists[2]."   In June the canons of Tortington in Sussex were accused of reading prophecies[3], and, as mentioned above, the vicar of Londesborough repeated them. In spite of the danger, scrolls of prophecies were often circulated by the owner among his friends, who took copies or committed the striking parts to memory; some made regular collections, borrowing or learning all they could find to add to the rolls, and so, as sayings or writings, the verses spread through a whole district.   One of these collections is preserved among the Lansdowne MS[4]; it seems to have been compiled about 1531 as a whole, but contains later entries[5].   In it is a version of the prophecies of Thomas the Rymer, and it concludes with an account of the great deeds to be done by " a child with a chaplet,"[6] who shall reign for fifty-five years, and after restoring peace in England shall recover the Holy Cross from Jerusalem and bring it back in triumph to Rome, where his bones will finally be buried in great honour.   As long as the King remained a faithful son of the Church there was no harm in this ordinary ballad conclusion, but once Henry had quarrelled with the Pope it wore a very different aspect, and men began to think that the King who was such a welcome guest at Rome could not be Henry himself, or one of Henry's heirs, but his conqueror[7].

The vicar of Mustone was accused before the Council of the North in 1537 of spreading seditious prophecies.   This man, John Dobsone by name, was like nearly all the northern clergy secretly in favour of the Pope.   Doubtless most of his parishioners agreed with him, but three of them, disliking either his opinions or himself, accused him of relating in the ale-house and the church porch that the King would be driven out of his realm, and then return and

[1] L. and P. ix, 846.   [2] L. and P. x, 614.
[3] Ibid. 1207.   [4] Lansd. MS, 762.
[5] E. E. T. Soc. 61, p. lix.   [6] Ibid. 52–61.
[7] See note C at end of chapter.

be content with a third part of it; that the Eagle "which is the
Emperor...shall rule all the land at his pleasure"; that the Dun
Cow "which is the bishop of Rome...shall come into England
jingling with her keys and set the church again in the right faith";
also that "When the Crumme (Cromwell) is brought low Then shall
begin the Christ's Cross row." The vicar denied the charge that he
had any such writings in a book, though he admitted he had seen
such a collection. He also denied that he had ever repeated them in
public, and all the witnesses whom his accusers cited bore him out
in this, and declared he was an honest man denounced from private
malice. The Council, though they committed him to gaol and wrote
to the King for instructions, were inclined to take a lenient view of
his case. But they energetically set to work to hunt out the
originators of such dangerous sayings. The result is like an Arabian
story, tale following tale in endless sequence. Dobsone had first
heard of the prophecies at the White Friars at Scarborough in
October 1536. The Warden of the Grey Friars, who was visiting
there, spoke of a prophecy that was going about, whereupon the
Prior of the White Friars produced a roll of paper on which a number
were written. It was in fact a collection that he had been making
for some years. He lent it to Dobsone, who justified his confidence
by returning it in a fortnight. Another friend of the prior's was not
so particular. He borrowed the roll and it was stolen from his
house during the insurrection, but several accounts of the contents
remain. The prophecies were said to be declared by "Merlion,"
St Bede, and Thomas of Ercildoune, but they were copied from
many sources[1]. The earliest told how "when the Black fleet of
Norway was comed and gone, after in England war shall be never,"
and other things equally harmless[2]. Others were given the prior in
May 1536 by a priest of Beverley, whom he never saw before or
after. They began "France and Flanders shall arise" and perhaps
included the Eagle and the Cow, as well as some obscure forebodings
of battles where "the clergy should stand in fear and fight as they
seculars were," with which a "long man in red" would have something to do. The most interesting relate to the great northern
families, which were indicated by their badges, as is usual in sayings
and ballads. The cock was the crest of the Lumleys, and one prophecy runs "the cock of the north shall be plucked and pulled,
and curse the time that ever he was lord," but after his misfortunes

---

[1] Cf. The Prophecies of Rymour, Beid and Marleyng, E. E. T. Soc. vol. 61, App. 2.
[2] See note D at end of chapter.

"he shall busk him and brush his feathers, and call his chickens togethers and after that he shall do great adventures." "The moon shall lose her light, and after shall take light of the sun again" refers to the crescent badge of the Percies, and the Tudor crest of a rose surrounded by the rays of the sun. The scallop shells of the Dacres "shall be broken and go to wreck." At the end of the roll "Thomas demandeth of Merlion and Bede saying when shall these things be? About the year of Our Lord God 1537." The Council of the North thought the rhyme about Cromwell the most serious, and made every effort to find the author. There were numberless versions, the best lines being:

> "Much ill cometh of a small note
> As (a) Crumwell set in a man's throat
> That shall put many other to pain, God wote;
> But when Crumwell is brought a-low,"[1] etc.

The gentleman who gave it to the prior had learnt it from a priest, who heard it from a brother priest about Michaelmas 1536 "in the buttery at Ayton." The second priest had it from the clerk of a remote parish as they walked together in a country loaning. The investigators might have traced its journey from mouth to mouth all round the country without finding anyone definitely responsible for it; but they gave up the hopeless quest at this point[2].

There lived at this time at Huntington in Yorkshire one Wilfrid Holme, a man with poetical leanings and a favourer of the New Learning. After the rebellion he set to work to write an account of it, or rather he included an account of it in a poem entitled, "The Fall and Evil Success of Rebellion from Time to Time." It is interesting as being the only contemporary history of the Pilgrimage, but Holme gives few details, and though many facts are correct he throws little new light on the subject. His last canto is headed "Of the Mouldwarp," and concerns a prophecy of Merlin's which the rebels applied to the King. Holme never repeats this prophecy, but it seems to have been that the Mouldwarp, "the sixth king," should be coward and caitiff, and have a skin like a goat. Holme states (without giving a reason) that the reckoning must be made from Henry III, and accordingly Henry IV was the sixth king and Henry VIII the twelfth, as he does not reckon Richard III. Therefore the Mouldwarp could not be Henry VIII,—

> "...Except ye skip at pleasure
> To take here one and there one your purpose to defend."

[1] L. and P. xii (1), 318.   [2] L. and P. xii (2), 1212, 1231.

Moreover Henry VIII is neither caitiff, coward, nor hairy. Holme never says what was to happen to the Mouldwarp. That Henry IV was believed to be that monster by Owen Glendower and his fellow conspirators is a tradition preserved in "The Mirror for Magistrates":

> "And for to set us hereon more agog,
> A prophet came (a vengeance take them all!)
> Affirming Henry to be Gogmagog,
> Whom Merline doth a mouldwarp ever call,
> Accurst of God, that must be brought in thrall
> By a wolf, a dragon and a lion strong,
> Who should divide his kingdom them among."[1]

After such a string of doubtful fables the excellent good sense of Hotspur is a pleasing change,

> "...Sometimes he angers me
> With telling me of the moldwarp and the ant,
> Of the dreamer Merlin and his prophecies,
> And of a dragon and a finless fish,
> A clip-wing'd griffin and a moulten raven,
> A couching lion and a ramping cat,
> And such a deal of skimble-skamble stuff
> As puts me from my faith."[2]

Yet one more must be mentioned—the Pilgrims' own prophecy, which was commonly repeated in their host throughout the rising,

> "Forth shall come a worm, an aske with one eye,
> He shall be chief of the meiny;
> He shall gather of chivalry a full fair flock,
> Half capon and half cock,
> The chicken shall the capon slay,
> And after that there shall be no May."[3]

The interpretations of this must have varied at the time, and now they can only be guessed. The lines about the capon and the cock seem to predict disunion among the insurgents themselves such as brought about the failure of the Lincolnshire rising. It has been suggested[4] that in the last line, foretelling the end of the rebellion, the "May" means the badge of Henry VII, the crown of England hanging on a hawthorn tree, and so anticipates the fall of his dynasty. Reading it after the event, it has rather the sense of spring without summer and fair promises unfulfilled.

---

[1] The Mirror for Magistrates, II, 71. The Legend of Glendour.
[2] Henry IV, pt. 1, Act III, sc. 1.
[3] Wilfrid Holme, The Fall and Evil Success of Rebellion.
[4] Longstaffe, Hist. of Darlington, 98, n.

From amid the prophecies, rumours and travellers' tales which were agitating the country during the summer of 1536 one point looms up,—that great events might be expected at Michaelmas. The government was only half aware of what was going on. But the army of the discontented, the starving labourers, the homeless monks, the sincere believers in the old religion, knew that when Michaelmas Day had come and gone they might expect news from the north. The King was at Windsor in September, and on the 27th he bade Ralph Sadler send word to the Lord Privy Seal to summon the Privy Council and attend the King at once. Sadler suggested there might be some delay as the command would not reach Cromwell until late on the following afternoon, and the day after was Michaelmas. "What then?" quoth his Grace, "Michaelmas Day is not so high a day."[1] When so many saints' days had given way to his pleasure, why should the King heed Michaelmas Day? Yet that Michaelmas Day came near to mastering the King.

NOTES TO CHAPTER IV

Note A. Throughout this book the "New Learning" is used in the sense of protestant or anti-papal opinions, not as another name for the classical revival.

Note B. One of his parishioners, John Bird, tried to lay information against him, but Duke had sufficient influence to stop him, and the accusation was not made until after the rebellion, for Bird mentions witnesses to whom he spoke "a month before the rising." There is another deposition by Bird against a priest in L. and P. xii (1), 301, too much mutilated to be intelligible. Cf. xi, 1495.

Note C. Other prophecies of about the same period are printed by Furnivall, op. cit. pp. 316–20, but they are unintelligible.

Note D. The Prophecies of Rymour, Beid and Marleyng[2]:

"When the black fleet of Norway is comen and gone
  And drenched in the flood truly
Mickle war hath been beforne
  But after shall none be.

Holy Church shall harnes hent
  And III years stand on stere,
Meet and fight upon a bent,
  Even as they seculars were."

[1] L. and P. xi, 501; printed in St. P. i, 459.
[2] E. E. T. Soc. vol. 61, App. 2.

Note E. A curious illustration of the feelings with which the north regarded the King's family arrangements is given by the fragmentary story of Mary Baynton, a girl of eighteen, the daughter of Thomas Baynton of Birlington, i.e. Bridlington in Yorkshire. The only document relating to her adventures is undated, but probably belongs to the year 1533. She made her appearance at Boston in Lincolnshire, and represented herself as the Princess Mary fleeing from her father's cruelty. Although she must eventually have been arrested, she seems to have been received with respect and sympathy. Her fate is unknown, and it is impossible to say whether she was a deliberate impostor or a self-deluded lunatic. There is nothing to show that she had any accomplices, but it is interesting to observe that she was connected with Bridlington and Boston, which were two centres of the rebellion. Her story was "that the French queen was her aunt and her godmother, and upon a time the said French queen, being of her pleasure in a bath, and she with her there, looked upon a book and said to her, 'Niece Mary, I am right sorry for you, for I see here that your fortune is very hard; you must go a-begging once in your life, either in your youth or in your age.' And therefore I take it upon me now in my youth, and I intend to go beyond the sea to mine uncle the emperor, as soon as I may get shipping."[1]

Note F. In April 1536 there was a disturbance in Somersetshire about which little is known. On 21 April 1536 John Py informed Cromwell that he had arrested Thomas Towghtwodde of Bridgewater. The prisoner had attempted to fly the country because his apprentice "was one of those who made the business in Somerset." The apprentice was three days with "those who made the business...till my lord Fewaryn sent him home."[2]

In May Cromwell noted among his remembrances "the poor men of Somerset for their pardon,"[3] and on 26 May 140 persons were pardoned for making unlawful assemblies in Somerset[4]. Others were executed for the same offence, and £50 were allowed for expenses to "Serjeant Hinde the King's Solicitor and others that went for the executing of the rebels in the west."[5]

It is probable that this rising was due to social discontent, and not to religious grievances, as the Act for the Suppression of the Monasteries was passed only in March and was not enforced until June, while the rising was early in April.

It is curious that, according to Wriothesley's Chronicle, there was also a rising in Somersetshire in April 1537[6]. The only allusion to this second rising in the Letters and Papers occurs on 13 May 1537, when Sir John St Lo requested Cromwell to contradict the report that the King was displeased with John Horner for "his taking the men imprisoned at Nunney" and causing them to be executed at Taunton[7].

---

[1] L. and P. vi, 1193; M. A. Everett Green, Letters of Royal and Illustrious Ladies, ii, no. xcvii.

[2] L. and P. x, 702. [3] Ibid. 929 (ii).

[4] Ibid. 1015 (26). [5] L. and P. xi, 381 (A).

[6] Wriothesley, Chron. (Camden Soc.), i, 61.

[7] L. and P. xii (1), 1194–95; see below, chap. xix.

It is probable that there were two risings in Somerset, one in April 1536, the other in April 1537. But it is possible that there was only one rising, that in April 1536. After that rising some prisoners were executed and others pardoned, but some may have remained in prison at Nunney, either because they were condemned to perpetual imprisonment or because they were never tried. In April 1537, when there were rumours of a rebellion in Devonshire and Cornwall, the magistrates may have become alarmed and executed the unfortunate prisoners out of hand. It is evident that the execution in April 1537 was hasty and irregular. If this second hypothesis were correct, Wriothesley must have misdated the entry in his Chronicle, or, hearing of the executions in Somerset in April 1537, he may have concluded that there had been a rising. It is simpler and involves less guessing to assume that there were two risings.

CHAPTER V

THE RISING IN LINCOLNSHIRE

"How presumptuous then are ye, the rude commons of one shire, and that one of the most brute and beastly of the whole realm...to find fault with your Prince?"[1]

So wrote Henry VIII to the men of Lincolnshire, and it must be confessed that they were deservedly held in ill repute. The number of cases relating to this county preserved among the Star Chamber Papers clearly shows how little order was kept or justice regarded. There was less excuse for lawlessness there than on the Borders, but the people seem to have lived, among the great tracts of undrained fen, almost as wild a life as the marchmen on their fells and mosses. On the other hand the men of Lincolnshire were not trained to arms so strictly as the moss-troopers. They were rather given to riots than to raiding, which demands a certain amount of discipline. They were very poor and ignorant, and regarded the gentlemen, their landlords and magistrates, with suspicious dislike. In 1517 royal commissioners were appointed in Lincolnshire to enforce the Inclosure Act of 1515[2]. It is rather surprising that the county should have been included in the commission, as the report showed that the enclosures were insignificant in extent and had caused but little eviction[3]. The commission was probably appointed in consequence of the shire's turbulence, and it is to be observed that such enclosure as there was had taken place in the district which was the centre of the rising, the parts of Lindsey, including Scrivelsby, Bolingbroke and Horncastle[4].

The gentlemen were quite as lawless as, and only a little better educated than, the commons. The feuds of such noble families as the Willoughbys not only caused endless discord among their friends

[1] L. and P. xi, 780 (2); printed St. P. i, 463.
[2] Leadam, The Domesday of Inclosures, i, pp. 8, 243.
[3] Ibid. 244.   [4] Ibid. 245, 251, 255.

and enemies, but fomented dozens of petty hatreds among their
dependents. A good thriving feud, fairly rooted in disputed lands,
would in the course of years scatter as many seeds as would afforest
half Lincolnshire. An example of such a minor feud occurs in a
complaint brought before the Star Chamber by Thomas Moigne[1], of
the Inner Temple[2], a gentleman and lawyer of Lincolnshire. He was
seised of the manor of Wyfflingham, but his right to it was disputed
by another gentleman, George Bowgham of Haynton. On 20 Sept.
1534 Bowgham assembled about forty people at his house. They
seem to have been collected haphazard, anyone who wanted a fight
being welcome, and included a pardoner, a weaver, and several
husbandmen. They were armed and set out for Wyfflingham,
summoning others to join them by the way. Moigne was away
from home at the time, and when they reached his house they
found no one but his wife and one of his servants. They cried out
that they would seize all in the place, but as it does not appear
that they carried out their purpose it may be concluded that the
lady of the house successfully defended it against their attack[3].
The characteristic feature of this outwardly pointless affair is that
the rioters assaulted Wyfflingham when the master was away. If
a man could never leave home without the fear that he might
return to find his house in flames and his wife abused, he would
be likely to come to terms about the land. The frequency of this
sort of intimidation does not speak well for the men of Lincolnshire. The story of the rising is even less pleasing. Lincolnshire
might have been expected to take the lead all through the rebellion.
The movement began there, and such signs of preparation as can be
discovered almost all concern Lincolnshire. The rumours circulated
there most freely, and may even have originated there. But if it rose
first, it was the first shire to lay down arms, and this at discretion,
without making any terms. So divided were the insurgents among
themselves by class-hatred, private feuds and mutual suspicion that
their host was never once in a state to offer battle to the most feebly
organised troops. In Lincolnshire alone were serious outrages committed[4], but the rebels showed none of the determined enthusiasm in

---

[1] Froude always alludes to Moigne as Mayne. The name is spelt in many
different ways.

[2] Wriothesley, Chronicle (Camden Soc.), i, 61; cf. Inderwick, Cal. of Inner
Temple Records, i, pp. 94, 104, 107–8, 110–14.

[3] Star Chamber Cases, Bundle xxviii, no. 120. As usual the result of the case
is unknown.

[4] See note A at end of chapter.

the field which might have explained their ferocity. The gentlemen were neither true to the King nor to the cause with which they really sympathised. The commons showed all the worst qualities of an armed mob,—they were savage, always swayed by the last speaker, and incurably suspicious of their leaders, whom they seldom obeyed even when they had chosen them themselves. The whole affair of Lincolnshire leaves the impression that the men of the fens were loud speakers but poor fighters, and almost confirms the King's description. No doubt this feeling is partly unjust. As will soon appear, they had many disadvantages to face, and in particular had no such excellent boundary to defend as the line of the Humber and Don, which was held by the Yorkshiremen.

By Michaelmas 1536 three sets of royal commissioners had swooped down upon Lincolnshire. The first, which had been at work since June, was the commission for dissolving the smaller monasteries[1], the second was to assess and collect the subsidy[2], and the third was a commission of inquiry into the condition of the clergy and their fitness in morals, education and politics for their office[3]. These provided grievances for all classes of the community; the commons were outraged by the suppression of the monasteries, the gentlemen were exasperated by the fresh taxation, and the clergy were infuriated by the examination which the commissioners forced them to undergo. They had been warned of the coming inquiry at the commissary's court held at Louth about three weeks before Michaelmas, when the commissary's scribe, one Peter, told the priests "that his master bade them look to their books, for they should have strait examination taken of them shortly after."[4] The visitation began at Bolingbroke on 20 Sept., and the priests seem to have been roughly handled, for they came away fuming with indignation. The parson of Conisholme said, "They will deprive us of our benefices because they would have the first fruits, but rather than I will pay the first fruits again I had liever lose benefice and all."[5] Simon Maltby, parson of Farforth, reported on his return home that the silver chalices of the church were to be given to the King in exchange for tin ones, and that therefore he and other priests had determined to strike down the chancellor[6], and trusted in the support of their neighbours[7]. The next visitation was to be held

---

[1] L. and P. xi, preface, pp. xi–xii.   [2] Ibid. p. xv.
[3] Gasquet, op. cit. ii, chap. ii.   [4] L. and P. xii (1), 481, 380.
[5] Ibid. 481.   [6] i.e. Dr Raynes, Chancellor of the Bishop of Lincoln.
[7] L. and P. xi, 975 (4).

on Monday, 2 Oct., at Louth[1], and several of the priests from
that district went to Bolingbroke to see what the dreaded examination was like; they came away declaring that they would not be
so ordered or examined in their learning[2].

It does not appear that Thomas Kendale, the vicar of Louth,
was one of those who went to Bolingbroke, but he was as bitterly
opposed to the commissioners as the rest. On Sunday, 1 Oct., he
preached a sermon in the parish church of Louth, in which he told
his parishioners "that next day they should have a visitation, and
advised them to go together and look well upon such things as
should be required of them in the said visitation." The congregation understood very well what he meant, and as they prepared
to walk in procession after three silver crosses which belonged to
the village, Thomas Foster, a singing-man, cried out, "Masters,
step forth and let us follow the crosses this day: God knoweth
whether ever we shall follow them again." The rumour of the
vicar's sermon and Foster's words spread quickly through the place.
Robert Norman, a roper, gave a penny to Jockey Unsained, otherwise John Wilson, a carpenter, to carry the report, and after
evensong an armed company appeared at the choir door, and took
the keys of the treasure house from the churchwardens, saying that
they knew the chief constable meant to deliver the jewels to the
Bishop's chancellor next day. The keys were given into the charge
of Nicholas Melton, shoemaker, or Captain Cobbler, as they called
him, and a watch was kept in the church that night for the first
time, which was taken up again night after night until the end
of the rebellion[3].

The news of what had happened in Louth was heard the same
night in the little village of Kedington by Louth Park, the new
home of William Morland alias Burobe, late a monk in the dissolved
monastery of Louth Park. He had been employed since his eviction
in carrying "capacities"[4] to other expelled monks in various parts
of the country, and in the course of his travels he had heard many
discontented mutterings. On Monday, 2 Oct., after matins, he
hastened to Louth to find out the meaning of the "rufflings." He
went first to the church but was not allowed to enter, for the
commons who had been guarding the jewels were discussing what
course they should follow, and whether they should ring the
church bells and raise the alarm. Morland went to the house of

---

[1] L. and P. xii (1), 481.   [2] L. and P. xi, 975 (4).

[3] Ibid. 854, 828 (1).   [4] See note B at the end of the chapter.

William Hert, butcher, whose brother Robert had been a fellow-monk of his at Louth Park. The three sat down to breakfast "with puddings," in which they were joined by one Nicholas, a servant of Lord Borough's.

Meanwhile "the heads of the town" had gathered in the town-hall to choose an officer for the coming year, as the custom was, and the commons in the church were left to their own devices. The deliberations in the town-hall and the breakfast at the butcher's were both interrupted by the sound of the church bells ringing out alarm. The Bishop of Lincoln's official, John Henneage, had arrived to conduct the choosing of the new town officers. Hearing the tumult, Nicholas remarked that some of those who ordered themselves after this fashion would be hanged; to which the butcher replied, "Hold thy peace, Nicholas, for I think as much as thou dost, but if they heard us say so, then would they hang us." Meanwhile the noise and "skrye" became so great that Morland went out to see what was happening. He found that Henneage had alighted at Robert Proctor's door and had been seized there by an armed mob, who were taking him to the church. Morland and other honest men helped him to take refuge in the choir and locked the choir door. The commons were shouting that he and all who had opposed them the night before must take an oath that they would be true to the commons and do as they did, upon pain of death. This oath was administered to Henneage, Morland, and the honest men by Captain Cobbler, to whom Henneage had tried to speak privately before being taken to the church. After the oath was taken the people began to disperse, when again the common bell rang out and they reassembled to seize John Frankishe, the Bishop of Lincoln's registrar, who had come to hold the dreaded visitation[1]. He was taken at the Saracen's Head, William Goldsmith's house; his books were seized and carried to the market-place, and John Taylor, a webster, brought a great brand and lighted a fire in the Corn Hill. Other books were brought out—copies of the New Testament in English and "Frythe, his book,"[2] a fact which shows that the new creed was penetrating even to this stronghold of conservatism—and the insurgents prepared to burn these heretical works, together with the registrar's papers[3]. Morland was alarmed at their violence,

---

[1] L. and P. xii (1), 380; extracts are printed by Gasquet, Henry VIII and the English Mon. ii, chap. ii.

[2] L. and P. xi, 828 (iii).   [3] Ibid. (1).

and exhorted them from Guy Kyme's doorway, saying: "Masters, for the Passion of Christ, take heed what ye do, for by this mischievous act which ye be about to do we shall be all casten away... will ye burn those books that ye know not what is in them?" He prevailed so far that they took him and six other persons who could read and set them up upon the High Cross, ordering them to read the registrar's papers. Morland got hold of the King's commission, but before he could make it out, the other people on the Cross, terrified by the hideous clamour of the crowd below, threw down the papers that they held, "and every man below got a piece of them, and hurled them into the fire."

Meanwhile Frankishe and Henneage had been brought to the market-place, and the people forced the former to climb up to the highest part of the Cross by a ladder. The poor man no doubt believed they would hang him, and when he was on a level with Morland, he whispered, "For the Passion of Christ, priest, save my life; and as for the books that be already brent I pass not of them, so as a little book of reckonings...might be saved, and also the King's Commission" Morland promised to do his best, took the book of reckonings, and, escaping from the Cross, succeeded in handing the commission to Henneage. The commons cried out that Frankishe must burn the papers himself, which he did. Then they demanded what book it was that Morland carried; with great difficulty he persuaded them to let him keep it. Then, worn out by the fatigues of the morning, he went and had a drink. But when he attempted to restore the book to the registrar, he was set upon by three or four hundred commons, who called him "false, perjured harlot to the commons for saving that book, for therein was contained that thing which should do them most tene (harm)." The book was torn from him, and eventually came to the hands of Captain Cobbler. Morland went to the registrar, explained what had happened, had dinner with him, the registrar paying, and helped to smuggle him out of the town. After this his friends warned him that his life was not safe for the present, so for the rest of the day he kept away from the commons[1].

Sixty parish priests who had assembled at Louth for the visitation were now compelled to take the oath to the commons, and also to swear to ring the common bells of their parishes and raise the people[2]. The heads of the town, who were still in the town hall, were summoned "by the name of churls" to come and

---

[1] L. and P. xii (1), 380.　　　　　[2] Ibid. 70 (1).

take the oath to God, the King, and the commons for the wealth of Holy Church. Some forty of the rebels set out for Legbourne, a small nunnery about two miles away, where the royal commissioners were then at work. By the way they met one of Cromwell's servants, John Bellowe, who was especially detested by all the country. Some of the commons, returning with him to Louth, met Sir William Skipwith of Ormsby, whom they took back with them and compelled to take their oath[1]. Captain Cobbler asserted that Sir William came in of his own free will[2], but this is very improbable, as he had obtained a grant of Markby Priory[3], and whatever the attitude of other gentlemen may have been, he was probably entirely opposed to the rising. After taking the oath he was allowed to go home[4].

The rest of the band went on to Legbourne, and there took the commissioners and their servants, William Eleyn, John Browne, Thomas Manby, and John Milsent[5]. They returned to Louth, taking on their way one George Parker at the town's end. The prisoners were very roughly handled, "all the country crying to kill Bellowe."[6] He and Milsent were put in the stocks, and afterwards cast into prison in the custody of Robert Browne, from which they were released a fortnight later by Suffolk's orders[7]. So intense was the hatred which they inspired that a report flew about the country that one or other of them had been blinded, wrapped in a raw cowhide, and baited to death with dogs. This story was reported to the King on 6 October[8], and was frequently repeated, but it is evidently untrue, for none of the rebels were examined about the alleged murder, and the two men were afterwards released.

While the prisoners were being brought in, Henneage had found an opportunity of slipping away; in his flight he met Guy Kyme at the town's end, returning from Grimsby[9], but would scarcely stop to speak to him for fear of the commons[10]. If Kyme was already in communication with the disaffected in Yorkshire, he probably brought news that they were not yet ready to rise, and that the outbreak must be put off a week or so; but if this was his message he came too late. He went into the town and tried to stay the commons, and his representations were supported by others, but

---

[1] L. and P. xi, 854. [2] Ibid. 828 (1).
[3] Ibid. 324. [4] Ibid. 854. [5] Ibid. 135.
[6] Ibid. 828 (1). [7] See below, chap. vii.
[8] L. and P. xi, 567. [9] See above, chap. iv.
[10] L. and P. xi, 828 (xii).

it was impossible to draw back. Captain Cobbler, when urged to make no more business, replied that " he had otherwise appointed,"[1] while Thomas Noble bade Kyme speak of no stay or they would kill him[2]. The last event of this tumultuous day was a proclamation from the High Cross that all the men of the neighbourhood between the ages of sixteen and sixty must assemble there on the morrow[3].

The news of the rising at Louth was received the same day by Sir Edward Madeson and Lord Clinton, who sent it on to Lord Hussey[4]. The commissioners for the subsidy, of whom Madeson was one, had intended to sit at Caistor next day, but they arranged by messenger to meet outside the town to see how events were shaping before they began to sit[5]. The priests who had been sworn at Louth carried the news all over the country-side.

On Tuesday 3 October Caistor was filled with the constables and head men of the wapentakes, who had come to meet the commissioners of the subsidy, and with priests who had come to attend the commissary's court, to be held there that day. The commissioners held their preliminary meeting on Caistor Hill, while in the town itself Anthony Williamson, Harry Pennell and others " proclaimed aloud that the justices had a commission from the King to take all men's harness from them and bring it to the castle of Bolingbroke." The commons declared that they would not give up their weapons. They went to the church and demanded of the priests, who were assembled there " to the number of eight score," whether they would take the commons' part. The priests received them enthusiastically, went with them to the market-place, and with their own hands burnt their books. The commons had already chosen George Hudswell to be their leader, and the whole body of commons and priests marched out to Caistor Hill to speak with the justices[6].

When they first assembled the commissioners believed Caistor to be quite peaceful[7], but presently news was brought of a new factor in the situation. The town of Louth had been astir since dawn; the common bell rang and the people assembled, prepared to set out for Caistor, as had been agreed the night before[8]. Four spiritual men, of whom William Morland was one, and four laymen were chosen as their leaders, and they marched off[9]. The justices on Caistor Hill heard

[1] L. and P. xi, 828 (iii).   [2] Ibid. (xii).
[3] L. and P. xii (1), 380.   [4] L. and P. xi, 568, 852.
[5] Ibid. 971.   [6] Ibid. 853.
[7] Ibid. 971.   [8] Ibid. 828 (xii).
[9] L. and P. xii (1), 380.

that 10,000 men were advancing upon them[1], a grossly exaggerated rumour, as there were really not more than 3000[2]. Their first idea was flight, but, at the suggestion of Mr Dalison, before setting out, they sent to summon the commons of Caistor to meet them, so that they might explain why the commission would not sit and urge them to go home before the arrival of the men from Louth. The insurgents in Caistor would not come, but a number of people had collected round the commissioners, a hundred or more. To these they explained that the subsidy was to be assessed by the people themselves, and that the rumours about robbing aud pulling down churches were false. Their eloquence did not make much impression, for by this time the church bells of Caistor were ringing against them; and when the people of Louth came in sight the commissioners turned their horses and fled[3].

The Louth company would have come up sooner if they had not paused to decide whether or no they should send on a hundred of their number to confer with the justices. When it came to the point none of the commonalty would consent to stay behind, but about a dozen of the best mounted, with Morland among them, rode forward. On Caistor Hill they met about 1000 men from Caistor "without weapons, but as they were wont to do riding to markets and fairs." While the two parties were discussing the situation, they saw a company of about twenty horsemen, making for the house of Sir William Askew, one of the commissioners. The well-horsed men of Louth rode after them, and asked them to return and speak to the commons for certain matters which they had in hand. Sir William Askew was doubtful: "Trowest thou that if I should come amongst them I should do any good, and be in surety of my life?" he asked. Morland replied, "Let two of your servants lead me between them, and if they do any hurt to your person then let me be the first that shall die." This, however, was not a very good security, as Sir William's servants were clearly on the side of the commons, and one of them indignantly pointed out to Morland that as they talked Sir Thomas Missenden had slipped away and escaped among the furze. Sir William Askew, Sir Edward Madeson and Mr Booth went back with them to the main body and were all sworn at once. Others of the commons had captured Sir Robert Tyrwhit[4] and Thomas Portington[5], but Lord Borough, whom they were particularly anxious

---

[1] L. and P. xi, 971. [2] Ibid. 853. [3] Ibid. 971.
[4] See note E at end of chapter.
[5] Robert Aske's brother-in-law, see above, chap. iii.

D. 7

to take, escaped, having a swift horse, and so did Thomas Moigne. In their disappointment the commons turned on Borough's unfortunate servant Nicholas, crying that he had warned his master. Morland says: "there were so many striking at him as he never saw man escape such danger. At last when he had fled evermore backward from them almost a quarter of a mile, saving himself always among the horsemen, he was stricken down by the footmen of Louth and Loutheske." Morland went to him, confessed him, and had him conveyed to a safe place and attended by surgeons, but he seems to have died of his injuries[1].

The captured gentlemen asked why the commons were making this insurrection. John Porman, a gentleman, replied "with a loud voice," that the commons were willing to take the King as Supreme Head of the Church and that he should have the first fruits and tenths of every benefice and also the subsidy granted to him; but he must take no more money of the commons during his life and suppress no more abbeys; also Cromwell, and the heretic Bishops of Canterbury, Lincoln, Rochester, Ely, Worcester and Dublin (Cranmer, Longland, Hilsey, Goodrich, Latimer and Browne) must be given up to the commons[2]. This answer seems to embody the demands of the commons themselves, untouched by the influence of the clergy or the gentlemen. They cared little for theological questions, but opposed Cromwell's reckless spoliations.

The insurgents carried their prisoners back to Caistor in triumph[3]. By this time their ranks had been swelled by companies from the neighbouring villages. The men of Rasen, Fulstow, Kermounde, Rothwell, and Thoresway were there. In the evening the main body, taking the gentlemen with them, returned to Louth[4].

Tyrwhit, Askew, Portington and Madeson supped at Guy Kyme's house, and after supper were desired to write a letter to the King, begging for a general pardon. It ran as follows:

"Pleasith your highnes these be to advertise youre grace that this thirde day of october we by the vertue of your graciouse commission directe unto us and other for the levacion of your secund payment of the subsidie to your grace graunted by acte of parliament assembled us togeders at the towne of Caster within your countie of Lincoln for the exccucion of the same. Wthere were assembled at oure cummyng within a myle of the seid towne xxiim of your trewe and faithefull (*lege peple crossed out*) subgietts and moo by oure estimmacion and the causion of ther said assemble was as they affirmed unto us that the comon voce and fame was that all the Jewells and goods of the

---

[1] L. and P. xii (1), 380.   [2] L. and P. xi, 853.
[3] Ibid. 534, 568.   [4] Ibid. 568.

Churches of the countrey shuld be taken from them and brought to your gracez councell and also that your seid lovyng and faithful subgets shulde be put of newe to enhaunsements and other importunate charges. Whiche they were not able to bere by reason of extreme pouertie and upon the same they did swere us first to be true to your grace and to take ther parts in maynteyning off the comon welthe and so conveid us with them from the seid Caster unto the towne of Louth XII myles distante from the same (*mark of omission but no insertion*) where as we yet remayne unto they knowe forther of your graciouse plesure humbly besechyng youre grace to be good and graciouse boith to them and us to send us your graciouse letters of generall pardon orells we be in suche daunger that we be never like to se your grace nor owre owen houses as this berer can shewe to whom we besche your highnes to gyff ferther credence And ferther your seid subgietts haith desired us to writte to your grace that they be yours bodies lands and goods at all tymes where your grace shall commande (*torn*) for the defense of your person or your realme[1].

Robt tyrwhyte   Willim Ayscugh
Edward Madeson
Thomas Portyngton."

When this letter had been read to the commons, Sir Edward Madeson and John Henneage were despatched after midnight to take it up to London[2]. Many other messengers were hurrying through Lincolnshire that night. Lord Borough, who had taken refuge at a friend's house, sent off news of the rising to the King[3], to the Earl of Shrewsbury at Sheffield Park[4], who was the nearest representative of the royal authority, and to Lord Darcy in Yorkshire[5]. Thomas Moigne sent a message to Lord Hussey from his bailiff's house at Usselby, where he had taken refuge[6]. Lord Hussey wrote back asking for further news[7], and despatched a messenger to warn the mayor of Lincoln[8].

After sending to Hussey, Moigne ventured to go home to Wyfflingham, where his wife was lying dangerously ill. He found that all the commons of the neighbourhood had joined those of Louth. He therefore ordered his bows and arrows to be brought out. Word of this reached the commons, and for his wife's sake he was obliged to write to Sir William Askew for protection. The house was watched and it was impossible for him to escape[9].

On Wednesday, 4 October, the gentlemen who were held in captivity at Louth persuaded the commons that they could do nothing more till an answer was received to the letter they had

---

[1] L. and P. xi, 534 (St. P. Hen. VIII, vol. 106, p. 250. R. O.)
[2] L. and P. xi, 568.   [3] Ibid. 533.   [4] Ibid. 536.
[5] Ibid. 563.   [6] Ibid. 971.   [7] Ibid. 532.
[8] Ibid. 531.   [9] Ibid. 971.

sent to the King; and they were so successful that Sir William Askew sent a message to Thomas Moigne, which he received at 7 a.m., that he might keep the great court next day at the Isle of Axholme. The lull, however, did not last long. The bailiff of Wyfflingham presently came to tell Moigne that warning bells were being rung at Rasen, and that the towns around were ringing in answer. Moigne directed him to do nothing, and the reason of the alarm was soon explained. A body of men arrived from Rasen bringing with them Sir William Askew's two sons and George Eton, a servant of Lord Hussey[1]. Eton had been captured at Rasen, and two letters were found in his possession, one from Lord Hussey to Tyrwhit and Askew, offering to help to stay the country[2], the other from the mayor of Lincoln in answer to Hussey's offer of help[3]. These letters infuriated the commons so much that they very nearly killed their three captives,—in fact a report went about the country that Eton had been killed[4]. They were now being taken to Louth, and the men of Rasen insisted that Moigne must take the oath and go with them.

They arrived at Louth after mass; Moigne had tried to persuade them on the way to keep the letters secret, but they refused to do so, though he prevailed upon them to conceal the name of the messenger. As soon as their contents were known, the people rushed to the church and rang the common bell, in spite of the efforts made to stop them by Morland and the gentlemen. A rumour spread that Lord Borough was coming over Rasen Moor with 15,000 men to destroy them. This increased the tumult, but at length the gentlemen prevailed on the mob to muster at Julian Bower, where they were to be divided into wapentakes and to choose captains[5]. Morland was despatched to find out if there was any truth in the report about Lord Borough[6]. After Morland had gone, Sir Andrew Bilsby and Mr Edward Forsett were brought in by the men of Alford[7]. The newcomers believed the report about Lord Borough, and assured the gentlemen of it, but the commons' alarm was now appeased and they were induced to go to their dinners. The gentlemen hoped that Lord Borough might arrive without bloodshed. In the afternoon the host assembled again, and was divided into wapentakes, each having for captain the commissioner who dwelt in it[8]. It was agreed that they should muster next day

---

[1] L. and P. xi, 971.   [2] Ibid. 852, 973.   [3] Ibid. 531, 971, cf. 879 (2).
[4] Ibid. 585.   [5] Ibid. 971.   [6] L. and P. xii (1), 380.
[7] L. and P. xi, 967 (xi).   [8] Ibid. 971.

and march on Lincoln, though the gentlemen opposed the advance
as far as they dared[1]. Letters were written to Lord Hussey and to
the mayor of Lincoln, calling upon them to take part with the
commons[2]. At supper-time Morland returned from Horncastle with
grave news. It was true that the report about Lord Borough was
unfounded, but Horncastle had risen, with evil results[3].

As early as Saturday 30 September unrest had manifested itself
at Horncastle[4]. The outbreak came on Tuesday 3 October in
response to the summons of Nicholas Leache, parson of Belchford,
and his brother William. The men of Horncastle marched to
Scrivelsby Hall, and took Sir Robert Dymmoke, his sons, one of
whom was the sheriff, Mr Dighton of Sturton, and Mr Sanderson.
Sir William Sandon was also at the Hall, but refused at first to obey
the commons' summons, until by threats he was forced to come "with
his cap in his hand." In revenge for his delay the commons carried
him to Horncastle and imprisoned him in the Moot Hall. This
so far intimidated him that he went with the company to bring in
Thomas Littlebury and Sir John Copledike. Another party from
Horncastle went to Bolingbroke, where they found Dr Raynes, the
obnoxious chancellor of the Bishop, ill at a chantry priest's house[5].
They made him take the oath "lying sick in bed," and spent the
night there. Apparently their first intention was to carry him to
Horncastle, but he was saved for the moment, partly by his servant,
partly by bribing his assailants[6].

The commons assembled at Horncastle early in the morning on
Wednesday 4 October under the command of Edward Dymmoke, the
sheriff, and despatched two messengers, one to Bolingbroke to order
the commons there to bring in Dr Raynes and another priest called
the surveyor, and the other to Louth to ask for news of Lord
Borough[7]. They mustered in a field near the town, whither the
chancellor was brought by one Gibson and John Lincoln of Hagnaby,
"a very rich man."[8] His appearance was greeted with a yell of
hatred,—he was torn from his horse, set upon, and slain with staves.
His clothes and the money in his purse were divided among the
crowd by the sheriff[9]. The murder was the work of a frenzied mob,
and probably many took part in it. The names of three are preserved,—William Hutchinson, William Balderstone and Brian Stonys.
The last named, in his deposition, laid the blame of the murder on

[1] L. and P. xi, 971.   [2] Ibid. 539.   [3] L. and P. xii (1), 380.
[4] L. and P. xi, 536.   [5] Ibid. 828 (2).   [6] Ibid. 975 (2).
[7] Ibid. 828 (2).   [8] L. and P. xii (1), 70 (ix).   [9] Ibid.

the priests and parsons in the crowd, declaring that they cried continually " Kill him !" and that after he was slain "every parson and vicar in the field counselled their parishioners to proceed in their journey, saying they should lack neither gold nor silver."[1]   As Stonys, by his own confession, was one of the murderers, his statement about the parsons and vicars cannot be considered very reliable, as he may have been trying to win a pardon by accusing those who were obnoxious to the government.   But it must be acknowledged that the character of the Lincolnshire clergy does not appear to have been very high.   William Morland said that when he heard they were to be examined in their learning he was glad, "thinking he might happen to succeed to the room of some of the unlettered parsons."   He also said that "certain lewd priests of those parts, fearing they should lose their benefices, spread such rumours to persuade the common people that they also should be as ill handled."[2] This contemptuous way of speaking may have been partly due to the slight esteem in which the regulars often held the secular clergy; but besides this there is evidence that at least one of the vicars had used threatening language against the chancellor before the rising began[3].   In short it seems fairly clear that the clergy who were present at his death did nothing to help him, and were on the whole pleased by it.

The sheriff and Sir John Copledike were present when Raynes was killed, and Morland, the messenger from Louth, arrived just in time to see William Leache go to them and the other gentlemen and ask them to deliver up to the commons Thomas Wolsey, who had been a servant of Cardinal Wolsey, in exchange for Stephen Haggar.   Wolsey was accused of being a spy and was promptly hanged, in spite of Morland's intercession on his behalf[4].

The gentlemen were not present while this was taking place ; they had withdrawn about a mile, but after a time they returned and read out a list of articles which they had drawn up, expressing the grievances of the insurgents.   The first two needed no explanation,—they required that the King should remit the subsidy and let the abbeys stand.   The next was not so intelligible, as it expressed a grievance which affected only the upper classes.   The sheriff therefore addressed the crowd as follows:

" Masters, there is a statute made whereby all persons be restrained to make their wills upon their lands, for now the eldest son must have all his father's

[1] L. and P. xii (1), 70 (ix).   [2] L. and P. xii (1), 380, 481.
[3] See above.   [4] L. and P. xii (1), 380.

lands, and no person to the payment of his debt, neither to the advancement of his daughters' marriages, can do nothing with their lands, nor cannot give his youngest son any lands."

The commons had not before heard of the Statute of Uses, but when it was explained to them in this way they were quite willing to include an article requesting its repeal. The gentlemen next demanded of the people whether they would ask for the heads of the lord Cromwell, four or five bishops, the Master of the Rolls[1], and the Chancellor of the Augmentations[2], "saying to them the lord Cromwell was a false traitor and that he and the same bishops, the Master of the Rolls, and the Chancellor of the Augmentations, whom they called two false pen clerks, were the devisers of all the false laws. And the commons asked the gentlemen, 'Masters, if ye have them, would that mend the matter?' And the gentlemen said, 'Yea, for these be the doers of all mischief.'" When these articles had been read, George Staines addressed the commons, saying, "Masters, ye see that in all the time we have been absent from you we have not been idle. How like ye these articles? If they please you, say yea. If not, ye shall have them amended." "The commons held up their hands and said with a loud voice, 'We like them very well';" whereupon Staines wrote them out "upon his saddle-bow." He was believed to be the deviser of the articles, which superseded other lists drawn up before. A copy was given to Morland to carry back to Louth[3].

A message was brought by two of Lord Hussey's servants, offering redress if any of the commissioners had exceeded their commission, and requesting the insurgents to send a deputation to speak with him[4]. The servants were asked whether Hussey was not raising the country against them; they replied it was a false tale[5]. No doubt they dared not tell the truth, which was that Hussey had sent messages to stay Holland, and was in communication with Lord Borough, whom he had promised to meet at Lincoln with 300 men[6]. The men of Horncastle, however, were satisfied. They made the messengers take the oath and kept them all night; but they sent three or four men to speak with Hussey[7]. By the time they arrived he had discovered that he could not trust his tenants, for when he sent bidding them to come and advise with

---

[1] Christopher Hales.   [2] Richard Riche.
[3] L. and P. xii (1), 70 (iii, vii, x, xi); ibid. 380.
[4] L. and P. xi, 852.   [5] Ibid. 620.   [6] Ibid. 852.
[7] Ibid.

him, they replied they had more need of his advice and stayed at home[1]. The only answer he could return to the Horncastle men was that he would not be false to his prince, but he could do nothing against them, as none of his people would take his part[2]. The messengers spent the night at Sleaford, and returned next day to Horncastle. On their arrival Hussey's servants were sent home[3].

On Wednesday evening the man who had been sent to Louth came back to Horncastle in time to see the bodies of Raynes and Wolsey "burying in the churchyard."[4]

William Morland had therefore plenty of news when he returned to Louth at supper-time. The gentlemen appointed twelve men to be sent to Lord Hussey and then went to bed meditating upon the murder of Raynes and Wolsey, the Articles of the commons, and the answer of Lord Hussey. Nor was the excitement even then at an end, for about midnight there was a fresh alarm. The commons cried that the gentlemen had betrayed them, and that they would kill them in their beds. However in the end they resolved to prove them further, and the disturbance passed over[5].

The rising was now no mere local affair. The news of the chancellor's murder flew far and wide, and was the signal for a general arming. Beacons were burnt along the south side of the Humber, which were seen and understood in Yorkshire[6], and at 3 a.m. on Thursday morning it was reported at Beverley that all Lincolnshire was up from Barton to Lincoln[7]. Any gentleman who stayed at home was liable to be seized by his tenants to be their captain. The people were particularly anxious that the monks, for whom they were taking up arms, should share their risks and expenses, and messages were sent to the greater monasteries, which had not yet been touched by the King. The turn affairs were taking was known by Wednesday at Barlings[8]; at Bardney[9], where the abbot and his company were required to go with the commons; at Kirkstead[10], where the abbot was told that if he and his monks came not forth the house should be burnt over their heads, " upon which word, about 4 of the clock in the evening the abbot, cellarer, bursar, and all the monks of the abbey able to go, 17 in all, went to the outer gate where they met a servant of the abbey, who said the

[1] L. and P. xi, 969.   [2] L. and P. xii (1), 70 (iii).
[3] L. and P. xi, 620.   [4] Ibid. 828 (2).
[5] Ibid. 971.   [6] L. and P. xi, 563.
[7] L. and P. xii (1), 392; printed in full by Cox, op. cit.
[8] L. and P. xi, 828 (v).   [9] Ibid. (vii).   [10] Ibid. (x).

host had pardoned them for that night, but they must be at Horn-castle next day at 11 o'clock ";[1] and at Grimsby, where "at night, when the commons came home, Leonard Curtis came past the (Austin) Friars' gate in a coat of fence covered with leather, and with a long spear in his hand, and said to two friars there, 'It were alms to set your house of fire; therefore command your prior that you come tomorrow.' They desired him to go in himself, and so he did, and commanded the prior to have his friars ready when called, and afterwards the 'sargyn' brought the same command."[2]

The need for captains was much felt by the commons in some parts, and led to the first appearance of Robert Aske among the rebels. Before Michaelmas the three Aske brothers had been staying at Ellerker in Yorkswold with their sister Agnes and her husband William Ellerker. Young Sir Ralph Ellerker was expected at the beginning of October for some fox-hunting, but he was prevented from coming by his duties as commissioner of the subsidy, so Robert Aske set out for London, in order to be there about the beginning of the law term, accompanied by Robert Aske, his brother John's eldest son, and another nephew. They crossed the Humber at Barton, five miles from Ellerker, and heard from the ferryman of the commons' rising and the capture of the commissioners. On landing they set out for Sawcliff, eight miles away, to spend the night at the house of Thomas Portington. They had only gone two miles when they were stopped at Ferriby by George Hudswell and a band of horsemen, who made them take the usual oath—to be true to God, the King and the Commonwealth. They were allowed to go to Sawcliff, where they found that Thomas Portington had been taken by the commons and was still with them. On this Aske became anxious to go back to Yorkshire, but on his way to the nearest ferry some of the commons met with him "and so intreat him that he was glad to repair again to Sawcliff." There he passed the night—that is the night of Wednesday 4 October[3].

On Thursday 5 October the rebels were early astir. Before daybreak a party of them appeared at Sawcliff, came to Robert Aske's bedside and insisted that he and his three nephews[4] should instantly go with them   Aske induced them to let the three young men go into Yorkshire   because two of them was heir apparents." But it seems possible there were more pressing reasons than mere

---

[1] L. and P. xi, 828 (viii).   [2] Ibid. 593.

[3] L. and P. xii (1), 6; printed in Eng. Hist. Rev. v, 331.

[4] The third was probably Thomas Portington's eldest son.

humanity; did Aske send no messages by them? The commons carried him off to join a company of some two hundred men who were mustering within three miles of Sawcliff and had no gentlemen or captains. They spent the morning in raising Kirton Soke, which had been warned against them ineffectively by Lord Borough. Aske went along Humber side with the horsemen while the footmen went inland, and they met again at Kirton at three in the afternoon[1]. The meeting-place appointed for all the different bands that day was Hambleton Hill, where in the afternoon assembled the host of Yarborough Hundred under command of Sir Robert Tyrwhit[2]; Thomas Moigne with 200 men[3]; the men of Louth, who had mustered at Towse Athyenges (Towse of the Lynge) Heath[4], and those of Horncastle, who had met between Horncastle and Scrivelsby[5]. The last named brought with them a silk banner with Lyon Dymmoke's arms, which they had taken out of Horncastle church the day before[6]. All the monks of Kirkstead, except the abbot, joined the host, the cellarer and the bursar mounted and with battle-axes, the rest on foot. Their serving-men were also carried off by the rebels. The bursar brought money and provisions, and they were all welcomed by the sheriff. The entire muster was estimated to be 10,000 strong. On their way one company had come upon Francis Stonar, priest and surveyor to Lady Willoughby, perhaps the surveyor whom the people of Horncastle wanted to take the day before. He was roughly used, but the gentlemen saved his life, and he ransomed himself by paying £100 to their funds[7]. When all had met at Hambleton Hill the general voice was to march on Lincoln, but Moigne made a speech reminding the people that now was the time to sow wheat and till the fields for the next year, and he therefore advised them to send only a small number forward to represent them. Just then he was told that Nicholas Girlington, Robert Askew, and one Aske wished to speak with him. He knew the two former, and also knew that Aske was a lawyer. Believing they would be on the side of peace, he wished to speak to them alone, but the commons would not allow it[8]. He told Aske that they would lie that night at Rasen Wood, and next day at Dunholm

---

[1] L. and P. xii (1) 6; Eng. Hist. Rev. loc. cit.
[2] L. and P. xi, 853.   [3] Ibid.   [4] Ibid. 828 (i).
[5] Ibid. 828 (2).
[6] See description of Lionel Dymmoke's tomb, G. Weir, Hist. Sketches of Horncastle, 30, and S. Lodge, Scrivelsby, Append. 3.
[7] L. and P. xi, 828, iii (2), 585.   [8] L. and P. xi, 971.

Heath, and directed the commons of Kirton to meet them at Dunholm. Aske took this message to his company at Kirton. He spent the night at Sawcliff and did not rejoin the Kirton men again[1].

The host marched from Hambleton Hill to Market Rasen, and there it became necessary to make arrangements for the night. Some slept in the fields about the town, others made themselves more comfortable. A party led by Edmund, "old Lady Tailbois' chaplain," was advancing to the meeting-place when they met Matthew Mackerell, Abbot of Barlings[2], between Barlings monastery and Barlings Grange. They made him lodge them for the night and he gave them beef and bread and "the meat that was on the spit for his brethren's supper." Numbers of men entered forcibly and slept in the chambers of the monastery and "on the hay mowes" in the barns. The two leaders, whose names Mackerell did not know, commanded him to join them with all his brethren. The abbot offered to go with them and sing a litany; he pointed out that it was contrary to his vow to wear harness, yet the leaders still swore he should go. They terrified him so much that when he turned to the altar to hear mass, he trembled till "he could unnethe say his service." In answer to their threats he gave them each a crown to buy horses. Thomas Kirton of Scotherne then came in, and said that he had met a band of horsemen coming to burn the monastery, but that he had saved it by showing them the men sleeping in the hay. He brought a message from Mr Thomas Littlebury, who advised the abbot to please "this ungracious company"; and he alarmed the poor abbot still more by telling him how "Mr Sampoull, a man of four score," had been taken from his bed to be sworn and forced to send his son with them[3].

If things were moving fast in Lincolnshire, they were not standing still in London. Madeson and Henneage, who had left Louth at midnight on Tuesday 3 October, arrived at court about 9 a.m. on Wednesday 4 October[4]. They brought the first definite news of the outbreak. The King at once perceived that the matter was grave. So great was his anxiety that it even overcame his pride, and he sent, very reluctantly, for the Duke of Norfolk, who was living at Kenninghall in Norfolk, in a state of semi-disgrace for his opposition to Cromwell. The gentlemen in attendance at court were ordered to make ready to march against the insurgents under the command

[1] L. and P. xii (1) 6, Eng. Hist. Rev. v, 333.
[2] See note C at end of chapter.			[3] L. and P. xi, 805.
[4] L. and P. xi, 576, 714.

of Richard Cromwell, the Lord Privy Seal's nephew. Horses were pressed for them by the Lord Mayor of London, who went from stable to stable, taking the horses of both foreign merchants and citizens. This vigorous measure aroused indignation, and as the King did not permit much to be said about the rising in Lincolnshire, the sufferers were told that the Count of Nassau was coming on a visit to England with a great company of men but no horses[1]. The King's uneasiness could only be increased by the letters which must have arrived on Wednesday evening from Hussey to Cromwell[2], enclosing the commons' summons to him, and from the Earl of Shrewsbury[3], who sent word of Lord Borough's flight and the commons' threats to destroy his house at Gainsborough if he would not return and lead them[4]. The Earl had sent out notices to the neighbouring gentlemen, summoning them to assemble on Thursday at Mansfield with as many men as they could collect to march against the rebels[5].

The King pressed on the preparations in London as fast as possible. He was said to distrust the city, and took from it men and horses to strengthen not only his army but also the Tower "which is his last refuge." This action shows the uncertainty under which he laboured: he did not know how much he might have to fear. His daughters, Mary and Elizabeth, were summoned to court, as if he felt it was not safe to let them be out of his sight, and Mary was treated with more kindness and respect than she had known for a long time. "Madame Marie is now the first after the Queen, and sits at table opposite her, a little lower down, after first having given the napkin for washing to the King and Queen." It was said that when the first news of the rebellion came Queen Jane threw herself on her knees before the King and implored him to restore the abbeys, saying that this was a judgment for their putting down. "But he told her, prudently enough, to get up, and he had often told her not to meddle with his affairs, referring to the late queen, which was enough to frighten a woman who is not very secure."[6]

Letters missive were sent out to summon musters[7], and a proclamation was issued to delay for a year the enforcement of the statute regulating the size of woollen cloths, in order to appease the discontent among the cloth-makers[8]. The only person really pleased

---

[1] L. and P. xi, 576; printed also in Cal. S. P. Spanish, v (2), 104; L. and P. xi, 714.
[2] L. and P. xi, 538.   [3] See note D at end of chapter.
[4] L. and P. xi, 536.   [5] Ibid. 537.   [6] Ibid. 860.
[7] Ibid. 557.   [8] Ibid. 545; see above chap. i.

by the news was the Duke of Norfolk. He did not believe the disturbance was anything of importance and doubted that the rebels could raise 5000 men, but he hoped that he could use the opportunity to overthrow Cromwell and bring himself back into favour. Consequently he hurried up to court on the 5th in very good spirits[1].

Cromwell, on the first coming of the news, despatched two emissaries of his own to Lincolnshire to gather information[2]. They were Sir Marmaduke Constable and Robert Tyrwhit[3]. With them went John Henneage, who had carried the commons' first petition to the King[4]. At 9 o'clock on Thursday morning they reached Stilton and sent in their first report. The commons were said to have been 10,000 strong on Tuesday. Their oath was repeated to the writers by "an honest priest" who had been forced to take it. It ran: "Ye shall swear to be true to Almighty God, to Christ's Catholic Church, to our Sovereign Lord the King, and unto the Commons of this realm; so help you God and Holydam and by this book." Constable and Tyrwhit had delivered the letters of summons to several of the gentlemen. They intended to push on to Lincoln, sending a letter to the Lord Steward (Shrewsbury) from Stamford[5]. At eight o'clock that night they wrote again from Ancaster. They had learnt that the rebels were now over 20,000 and expected to be in Lincoln on Saturday. Their petition was that they might receive pardon for rising, that holydays might be kept as before, that the religious houses might stand, and that they might be taxed no more; "they would also fain have you," i.e. Cromwell. The messengers were on their way to Lord Hussey[6]. They arrived at Sleaford late at night, and delivered their letter[7], but they found Lord Hussey quite unable to carry out the orders it contained. He had sent forward some armed servants to Colwick, close to Nottingham, intending to follow them, but when the people heard that he was about to leave them they rang the common bell and about a hundred assembled outside his gate and refused to disperse until they had seen him, crying, "Alas, we shall be brent and spoiled, and all for lack of aid." Lord Hussey came out and asked what they wanted. They answered, "Aid," saying he was their only aid and that they heard he would leave them. He replied he would come and go as he pleased, and "'bade them walk home, knaves,' trusting to see them hanged shortly." He noticed one Bug "with a bill in his hand" and asked

[1] L. and P. xi, 576.
[2] Ibid. 552.
[3] See note E at end of chapter.
L. and P. xi, 561.
[5] Ibid. 552. [6] Ibid. 553. [7] Ibid. 852.

what he wanted. Bug answered, "In faith, my lord, to take your part, to live and die with you." Hussey called him "a naughty busy knave," and sent them all away "amazed," but they declared they would not let him go, and watched his house[1]. Cromwell's messengers dared not stay in this dangerous neighbourhood, and left Sleaford at midnight[2]. Then they separated, Henneage and Tyrwhit going back to the King, while Constable went on towards Yorkshire. They left with Hussey several letters for the knights and gentlemen, who had been "taken" by the commons[3].

Next morning, Friday 6 October, Hussey wrote to Shrewsbury, saying that he was so beset that he could not leave his house, though he was anxious to join the King's forces, asking for orders, and promising to escape whenever he could[4]. He sent this off by a trusty servant and at the same time despatched another servant, George Cutler, to the Louth rebels, with a reply to the deputation which had waited on him the day before. Cutler was also to deliver the letters to the gentlemen with the host, and Hussey bid him "say anything to get himself away."[5] The host was marching from Market Rasen to Lincoln, but they had not gone two miles when disputes broke out. The gentlemen complained that the commons were unruly and said "they should be ordered whether they would or no"; in the end the commons submitted and the host went on. A rumour spread that Lord Borough would join them that day, and though there was no truth in it the commons were much encouraged[6]. The next halt was at Dunholm Lings, where the men of Kirton Soke were waiting, as Aske and Moigne had appointed[7]. Here Cutler came to them[8]. Perhaps the gentlemen were not too well pleased to receive the King's letters at such a time. At any rate Sir William Askew questioned Cutler as to whether Lord Hussey were at home and would take their part; he replied that "he and all his house were at the commons' command."[9] In spite of this prudent answer he was carried to Lincoln with the host[10]. The rebels had sent on a party before them to prepare lodgings in the town, and when they arrived they were well received. The officers of the city gave orders that provisions should be sold to them at reasonable rates[11]. They had so far been without artillery, but in Lincoln they found some guns which, it was believed, had come from Grimsby[12];

---

[1] L. and P. xi, 852, 969.   [2] Ibid. 561.   [3] Ibid. 578, 561.
[4] Ibid. 561.   [5] Ibid. 852.   [6] Ibid. 853.
[7] Ibid. 828 (xii).   [8] Ibid. 853.   [9] Ibid.
[10] Ibid. 587 (2).   [11] Ibid. 853.   [12] Ibid. 828 (2)

had these anything to do with Guy Kyme's business at Grimsby the week before ?

The gentlemen lodged in the Close and the commons in the town[1]. The first to arrive was the company from Louth, and they were joined by the commons of the city with whom they spent a pleasant time in spoiling the palace of the hated Bishop[2]. The host of Horncastle came to Lincoln either this day or early on the morrow. On the march the Abbot of Barlings had met them at Langwith Lane End. In reply to repeated orders he brought them "beer, bread, cheese and six bullocks," and was accompanied by his brethren. When he had given the provisions to the sheriff, he begged that he and his monks might be allowed to go home, but the leaders resolved that six of them must go with the host next day, "seeing they were tall men." The abbot was given a passport permitting him to gather victuals for the commons; his secret intention, as he said, was to use this to slip out of the country[3].

The sheriff summoned the people of Boston to meet "the great host" at Ancaster on Sunday 8 October[4]. On receiving this letter the whole of Holland rose, and the gentlemen were compelled to take the oath, under pain of having their goods seized. Two thousand men rose in Boston, and it was believed that the whole number of the rebels was 40,000 "harnessed men and naked men clad in bends of leather." Those who were latest to rise said "they would do as their neighbours did, for they could not die in a better quarrel than God's and the King's." The list of grievances which they presented to the gentlemen was not quite the same as the one drawn up at Horncastle. The reforms which they desired were (1) that the Church of England should have its old accustomed privileges without any exaction; (2) that suppressed houses of religion should be restored, "except such houses as the King hath suppressed for his pleasure only"; (3) that the bishops of Canterbury, Rochester, Lincoln, Ely, Bishop Latimer and others and the Lord Privy Seal, the Master of the Rolls, and the Chancellor of the Augmentations, should be delivered up to the commons, or else banished the realm; (4) that the King should demand no more money of his subjects except for the defence of the realm[5].

Cromwell had sent Christopher Askew[6], one of the King's gentlemen ushers, to gather news. On Friday he reported that he had advanced into the country as far as he dared, apparently to Spalding.

---

[1] L. and P. xi, 853.   [2] Ibid. 939.   [3] Ibid. 805.
[4] Ibid. 571.   [5] Ibid. 585.   [6] See note E at end of chapter.

His report is a mixture of hearsay and fact; like the gentlemen of Holland he estimated the number of the rebels at 40,000 or more,— 10,000 or 12,000 well harnessed, and 30,000 more, "some harnessed and some not." The journeymen were deserting their masters, and the towns were left defenceless. "About Stamford, Spalding and Peterborough they are very faint in rising against the rebels." In fact they were readier to take the other side, but Mr Harrington showed them the King's commission and they were pacified and glad that the King was coming. Askew advised that more commissions of this kind should be sent. The people murmured among themselves that if they held not together they would be undone, "for it is reported that they shall pay a third part of their goods to the King and be sworn what they are worth, and if they swear untruly other men will have their goods." He had heard the rumours that some had gone to burn Lord Borough's house, and that Bellowe had been baited to death. He also said "they have made a nun in your abbey Legbourn and an abbot at Louth Park." But this seems to be a mistake, for, unlike the Yorkshire rebels, the commons of Lincolnshire made no attempt to restore the suppressed houses. Mr Harrington had commanded the Prior of Spalding to raise as many men as he could for the King, "and he answered he was a spiritual man and would make none." Askew had heard that Hussey's tenants would not rise for him, and it was said he would be taken that night[1].

The last report was well founded. Hussey's servant Cutler met a spy of Shrewsbury's when the rebels took him to Lincoln. Perhaps he did not know this man as a friend; at any rate he told him that Hussey was about to join the rebels[2]. He managed to leave the town that night and warned his master that the gentlemen were going to send to bring him in[3]. Thanks to this news Hussey escaped in the night disguised as a priest[4]. He was just in time, for on Saturday 7 October the host at Lincoln sent out several bands to find and bring in gentlemen[5]. Five hundred men under Sir Christopher Askew were despatched for Lord Hussey[6]. Before they arrived, Anthony Irebye, one of the commissioners of Holland, brought to Sleaford a troop of about eight score men which he had raised to serve the King. He found that Hussey had fled, but in obedience to a letter from him the little troop afterwards joined the

<hr>

[1] L. and P. xi, 567. [2] Ibid. 587. [3] Ibid. 620.
[4] Ibid. 852. [5] Ibid. 971.
[6] Ibid. 854; see note E at end of chapter.

King's forces[1]. When Sir Christopher Askew reached Sleaford he was met by the principal people of the town, including Robert Carre, who begged him not to spoil their houses. Sir Christopher promised to protect them, and made them join his company. Hearing that Lord Hussey had fled, the rebels began to cry, "Fire the house!" but their captain spoke with Lady Hussey and satisfied his followers by making her promise to follow her husband and bring him back[2]. George Hudswell of Caistor was appointed to accompany her, but they did not start that day[3]. After the company had set out for Lincoln, a tempest of rain drove them back, and they took refuge from the weather in the Bishop of Lincoln's castle at Sleaford, where they spent the night, doing much damage. Lady Hussey gave them provisions,—beer, salt fish, and bread[4]. Next morning (Sunday 8 October) she sent more food to them, and offered Sir Christopher twenty angel nobles, which he refused to take[5]. While the rebels made their way back to Lincoln, she and Hudswell set out in search of Lord Hussey, whom they found at Colwick[6]. He refused to go with them to join the rebels at Lincoln, and ordered them to follow him to Shrewsbury, who was to hold a muster at Nottingham next day[7]. Hussey had received an answer to his letter of the 6th which might well make him anxious. Misled by the report of the spy who had been told by Cutler that Hussey was wavering if not actually pledged to the rebels[8], Shrewsbury had become suspicious of his loyalty. He wrote: "My lord, for the old acquaintance and familiarity between us I will be plain with you. You have always shown yourself an honourable and true gentleman, and no man may do the King higher service in those parts by staying these misruled persons and finding means to withdraw the gentlemen and men of substance from among them, when the commons could do small hurt. For I assure you, on my troth, all the King's subjects of the counties of Derby, Salop, Stafford, Worcester, Leicester and Northampton will be with me tomorrow to the number of 40,000 and I trust you will keep us company."[9] In the face of these suspicions it is no wonder that Hussey was angry with his wife when she implored him to return to the rebels. He rode to the Lord Steward with what speed he might.

The rebels stayed at Lincoln all Saturday. Early in the morning they mustered at New Port, and it was agreed to send

---

[1] L. and P. xi, 852.   [2] Ibid. 969.   [3] Ibid. 852.
[4] L. and P. xii (1), 380.   [5] L. and P. xi, 853, 854.   [6] Ibid. 852.
[7] Ibid.   [8] Ibid. 587.   [9] Ibid. 589.

another letter to the King, as no answer had been received to the first[1]. The men of worship held a council at Mile Cross towards Nettleham apart from the host, and drew up a new set of articles, because they considered those made at Horncastle "wondrous unreasonable and foolish."[2] As a matter of fact the new articles seem to have differed very little from the old, unless others had been inserted among the Horncastle articles besides the four given above. The wandering bands brought in gentlemen from the surrounding country,—Sir John Sutton, Robert Sutton and the Disneys[3]. The Abbot of Barlings came with six of his canons, all in harness; but he only delivered his men and went straight home again[4]. Several monks came from Bardney[5], and those pressed at Kirkstead were still with the host.

On Sunday 8 October the host mustered at Lincoln; they had changed Lyon Dymmoke's banner for a white cloth to which was pinned a picture of the Trinity painted on parchment[6]. The commons were growing impatient at the delay, but the gentlemen were undecided as to what course of action they should follow, and wished to hear more of the King's preparations before committing themselves to an advance. The great muster on Ancaster Heath had been appointed for this day, but the gentlemen postponed it, saying they must await the King's answer[7].

The articles which had been prepared the day before were read aloud to the whole host by George Staines, who offered himself as a messenger to take them to the King[8]. No complete copy of these articles has been preserved, but they seem to have been seven in number, as follows:

(1) that the King should demand no more taxes of the nation, except in time of war.

(2) that the Statute of Uses should be repealed.

(3) that the Church should enjoy its ancient liberties and that tenths and first fruits should not be taken from the clergy by the government.

(4) that no more abbeys should be suppressed.

(5) that the realm should be purged of heresy, and the heretic bishops, such as Cranmer, Latimer, and Longland should be deprived and punished.

(6) that the King should take noblemen for his councillors, and give up Cromwell, Riche, Legh and Layton to the vengeance of the commons, or else banish them.

(7) that all who had taken part in the insurrection should be pardoned[9].

---

[1] L. and P. xi, 828 (1).   [2] Ibid. 971.   [3] Ibid.
[4] Ibid. 828 (v).   [5] Ibid. (vii).   [6] Ibid. 828 (2); xii (1), 70 (ii).
[7] L. and P. xi, 971.   [8] Ibid. 828 (v).   [9] Ibid. 780 (2); 828 (5).

The host accepted the articles, but they were not yet despatched to the King.

The gentlemen had established themselves apart from the commons; their lodgings were in the Close and their meeting-place was the Chapter House of the Cathedral, where on Sunday evening they received two letters of the greatest moment. The first was brought by William Woodmansey; it was under the common seal of the town of Beverley and addressed to the people of Lincolnshire. It informed them that, hearing of their rising, the townsmen of Beverley had also taken up arms; they wished to know the Lincolnshire articles and were ready to send help. The gentlemen were obliged to reply, and wrote a letter enclosing the new articles. The papers were entrusted to Guy Kyme and Thomas Donne, who probably set out for Yorkshire with Woodmansey next morning. Meanwhile the news from Beverley had spread, and the whole city of Lincoln was humming with excitement. The commons' one thought was to set forward without delay. Their rear was safe,—why should they loiter? The leaders still insisted that they must wait for the King's reply. In the midst of these discussions two more messengers arrived and came before the meeting in the Chapter House. They were from Halifax, and brought word that their country was up and ready to do as the men of Lincolnshire did. It was a wonder that the gentlemen themselves were not carried away by the surging enthusiasm of the commons. When they had already risked so much they might in that moment of triumph have brought themselves to stake all. But they still counselled prudence. They assured their followers that it would be high treason to march against the King's troops before the King's answer came. It speaks poorly for the intelligence of the host that this ridiculous reason was enough to turn them from their purpose. George Staines was at length despatched to London with the new set of articles. The commons were heartily tired of Lincoln and inaction, but they consented to stay there another day on the understanding that they should be allowed to spoil the goods of any man who did not join the host when summoned[1].

NOTES TO CHAPTER V

Note A. The conduct of the Percys in Northumberland was outrageous enough, but, as good luck would have it, no one was murdered. Moreover the Percys and the thieves of Tynedale were responsible for this, not the gentlemen and commons of the county as a body.

[1] L. and P. xi, 971.

Note B. When one of the lesser monasteries was suppressed, the monks were given a choice of two courses ; they might either be transferred to one of the large houses of the same Order, which was not yet suppressed, or they might receive a paper from the King by which they were released from their vows and received licence to begin life over again as ordinary laymen. These were called " capacities."

Note C. Holinshed identified the Abbot of Barlings with Captain Cobbler. There is no hint of this in any contemporary chronicle, and the most cursory reference to the State Papers shows that it was a mistake. Nevertheless the error has been very generally copied[1].

Note D. There is a curious story that Shrewsbury was very uneasy lest he should be accused of treason for levying men to resist the rebels. It is first told by Holinshed (1577), but no foundation for it can be discovered in contemporary chronicles and documents. Holinshed asserted that he had been told it by " men of good credit that were then present." According to this story, the Earl consulted his friends and legal advisers as to whether he might lawfully muster men. They replied that he might do so. He retorted, " Ye are fools. I know it in substance to be treason, and I would think myself in a hard case, if I thought I had not my pardon coming." Thereupon he sent out orders for the muster, and wrote to the King begging for a pardon. The King sent him both a pardon and thanks. The men assembled expecting the Earl to lead them to join the rebels, but he took a solemn oath before them all that he was true to the King alone[2]. The baselessness of this story appears when it is compared with Shrewsbury's letters. On 4 Oct. he sent news of the rising and asked for orders[3]; at the same time he sent out a summons to the neighbouring gentlemen to muster at Mansfield next day[4]. On the 6th he acknowledged the receipt of the King's letters missive, containing orders to assemble his men, and described the musters which he had appointed[5]. Cromwell wrote a flowery letter of compliments and thanks to him on the 9th, but without a suggestion that any pardon was needed[6]. The King sent him further orders and a new commission on the 15th, but without hinting that he had been over zealous[7]. Noblemen were expected to suppress riots without waiting for orders, and it was made a charge against Hussey that he did not muster his men at the first alarm. The only foundation which there can be for Holinshed's story is some vague memory that the Earl's attitude at the beginning of the rising awakened doubt. He was a devout man, and very much opposed to innovations in any form[8]. Personal loyalty kept him true to the King, but there is every reason to believe that he had much stronger sympathy for the rebels than for Cromwell.

Note E. The reduplication of names is very confusing. Sir Marmaduke Constable was the cousin of Sir Robert Constable of Flamborough, not his brother or his son, although they both bore the same name. Robert Tyrwhit was a different person from Sir Robert Tyrwhit, the commissioner who was taken at Caistor. Christopher Askew, again, was a different person from Sir Christopher Askew, one of the Lincolnshire gentlemen who was most enthusiastic in the rebels' cause.

[1] Holinshed, Chronicle, III, 800.   [2] Ibid.   [3] L. and P. XI, 536.
[4] Ibid. 537.   [5] Ibid. 562.   [6] Ibid. 612 ; printed by Merriman, op. cit. II, 33.
[7] L. and P. XI, 715–16.   [8] L. and P. XII (2), 436.

CHAPTER VI

THE FAILURE OF LINCOLNSHIRE

By Saturday 7 October the preparations in London were fully under weigh. Letters under the Privy Seal were sent out. They announced that the King purposed to advance against the rebels in person, and summoned the noblemen to whom they were directed to meet him at Ampthill each with a specified force. Orders were sent out to the ports to keep watch; arrangements were made for posts; lists were drawn up of those who were to march against the rebels, those who were to attend the King and those who were to guard the Queen[1]. Sir William Fitzwilliam, the Lord Admiral, was despatched to Ampthill. He reported that the country was loyal as far as Godalming and Guildford, and that he had no difficulty in raising men, but that he would only take horsemen as recruits, there being such need of haste[2].

The news of the insurrection was first sent abroad by Chapuys, who wrote to the Emperor on 7 October. The ambassador believed that the insurgents were numerous and the disaffection widespread, but he did not think that they could hold out long, as they lacked both money and a leader. Nevertheless the King seemed dejected, great preparations were going forward, and Cromwell was said to be afraid. His nephew Richard Cromwell had taken quantities of arms from the Tower, and was pressing men, even the masons at work on Cromwell's house; the sanctuary men were being imprisoned for fear they should join the rebels. The Duke of Norfolk dined that day with the Bishop of Carlisle—a special occasion for which wine was procured from Chapuys—and requested his host to help to make some large purchases of cloth which the government was organising to allay the discontent among the clothmakers. The Bishop promised to contribute, and many wealthy merchants and bishops were

---

[1] L. and P. xi, 579, 580.
[2] Ibid. 584; printed in part by Froude, op. cit. chap. xiii.

compelled to do the same. Immediately after dinner Norfolk set
out for his own country to raise men for the muster at Ampthill and
to prevent disturbances[1].

Reports of the rebels' strength and the unsettled state of the
country south of Lincolnshire poured in upon Cromwell[2]. Lord
Clinton had been despatched to the Midlands with letters missive
summoning the gentlemen to keep order in their own neighbour-
hoods and to raise men for the King, who were to meet the Earl of
Shrewsbury at Nottingham on Monday. The Earls of Rutland and
Huntingdon were ordered to join him. Clinton was unable to
deliver the letters to the Lincolnshire gentlemen, and wrote on the
7th that Hussey would probably be taken that day[3]. There was
a rumour that Clinton had raised 500 men who immediately went
over to the enemy[4]. Two friars of Grimsby sent Cromwell information against the prior of the Austin Friars, who had supplied the
rebels with money[5]. The gentlemen of Holland reported the rising
of their country on Saturday[6]. Sir William Hussey, who seems to
have escaped from Sleaford at the same time as his father, rode
straight to London with only one servant. By the wayside they
heard the people "both old and young, praying God speed the
rebellious people of Lincolnshire, and saying that if they came
that way they should lack nothing that they could help them to."[7]
In Windsor itself a priest and a butcher were hanged for expressing
sympathy with the rebels[8]. On Friday Sir Edward Madeson, who
brought the commons' letter to the King, was examined before the
Council, and told them what he knew of the rebels[9], which, as he
had left Lincolnshire on Tuesday night, was not very much.

George Talbot, Earl of Shrewsbury, the Lord Steward, was at
Hardwick in Sherwood on Saturday 7 October[10]. On this day Sir
Arthur Darcy arrived at his camp. He had been sent by his father
from Templehurst with letters which reported the unsettled state of
the country, the risings in Lincolnshire and Northumberland, and
asked for orders, money and ordnance[11]. He found the Lord Steward
"sore crassyd" with sickness, but labouring to muster all his powers
at Nottingham on Monday next. Sir Arthur saw a chance of dis-
tinguishing himself in the coming conflict, and his father's messages,

---

[1] L. and P. xi, 576.   [2] Ibid. 558, 560, 562, 581, 590.
[3] Ibid. 590.   [4] Ibid. 576, 714.   [5] Ibid. 593.
[6] Ibid. 585.   [7] Ibid. 584.
[8] Ibid. 714; printed in "The Pilgrim," ed. Froude, p. 113.
[9] L. and P. xi, 568.   [10] Ibid. 587.   [11] Ibid. 563.

essential as they were to the safety of the north, were at once thrown to the winds.   He wrote to Lord Darcy, telling him that when the Lord Steward gave him a message for the King, "I said I would be no messenger when the King should need; and further that I knew well that he being at so near a point to try his friends that I would be with him, thoff I had but my page and my man."   He therefore asked that his men might be sent up to him "and I shall there be found near the Talbot."   In a postscript he drops from his heroics to domestic details, "Remember a truss bed and my harness for me and my men."[1]   The spy who had been at Lincoln told Shrewsbury that the rebels were about 40,000 strong, but only 16,000 in harness.   He reported the muster to be held at Ancaster, where it was said that Hussey would join the rebels.   He had promised to return to Lincoln and was about to do so.   His watchword was "Remember your promise."[2]   Shrewsbury at Hardwick and Rutland, who had already arrived at Nottingham with his men, were both writing to the King for money and ordnance, "for money is the thing that every poor man will call for."[3]

Fitzwilliam reached Ampthill on Sunday 8 October and "planted his standard and guydon."   Richard Cromwell was again at the Tower and took out "34 little falconets of those made by the King last year"; he set out with them, but the roads were so heavy with the recent rain that when they had gone no more than a mile into the country the horses broke down[4].   Thirteen of the guns were sent back at once, and in the end only sixteen could go forward, together with the necessary stores and supply of weapons[5].   Richard Cromwell pushed on without waiting for the guns.   He reached Ware that night, meeting by the way some recruits and two fugitives from Lincolnshire, who told him the rebels were 40,000 strong, that their numbers were ever growing, and that they were encamped in strong positions[6].

As the reports of the insurrection became more and more alarming, the King altered his plans.   His first idea was that Shrewsbury could easily dispose of the rebels, and that he himself would then make a military promenade through the district.   The Duke of Norfolk had been sent to Ampthill "to exercise the office of High Marshal, and to set the army which shall be then arrived in order, that the King on his repair thither on Monday[7] may view

---

[1] L. and P. xi, 592.   [2] Ibid. 587 (2).   [3] Ibid. 581, 587.
[4] Ibid. 714.   [5] Ibid. 600.   [6] Ibid. 607.
[7] Probably Monday, 16 Oct.

them and dismiss them from time to time with thanks and good enter-tainment."[1] But it was now evident that the campaign would be no mere picnic, and the King was unwilling to expose his royal person to its possible dangers, while the need for haste was so great that it would be unwise to hamper the army by the delays which were inevitable if the King accompanied it. At the same time he did not consider it safe to trust the command to the Duke of Norfolk if he himself were not there, as Norfolk was suspected of leanings towards the old religion[2]. It was impossible to send Cromwell, for while on the one hand he was no general, on the other he was so unpopular that it would have been difficult to find a dozen men who would follow him. The King therefore had recourse to his old comrade Charles Brandon, Duke of Suffolk, who was one of the few persons Henry regarded with something like friendship and confidence. Suffolk had gone to his own country to prevent disturbances, when a message overtook him that he was to set out at once for Hunting-don, where he would find Richard Cromwell with the stores from the Tower. On receiving these orders he lost no time. Leaving the force he had mustered to follow him, he turned northwards, riding all night[3].

Meanwhile letters reached Norfolk countermanding his orders, directing him to send his son, the Earl of Surrey, and his horses to the Duke of Suffolk, and to remain himself in Norfolk to stay the country[4]. He must have suspected that such a slight was due to Cromwell's jealousy, and he wrote at once a vigorous remonstrance pointing out that if he were to send away his son and his horses he could do little towards staying the people. He declared that rather than " sit still like a man of law " he would set out on Tuesday unless he received positive orders to the contrary. This letter was despatched at 1 a.m. on Sunday 8 October from Easterford[5]. By 6 p.m. on the same day Norfolk had reached Stoke and found so many seditious rumours by the way that he had become reconciled to the idea of remaining in that part of the country, but he found it more than ever necessary to keep his son and horses with him. The clothmakers were " very light," and had only been prevented from rising by the proclamation suspending the new statute. Nevertheless the Earl of Oxford would be able to do as much as he towards keeping all quiet, and he con-cluded with a final protest: " I think I had much wrong offered me to send my son and servants from me, considering that he cannot

[1] L. and P. xi, 579 (2).   [2] Ibid. 576.   [3] Ibid. 615.
[4] Ibid. 601.   [5] Ibid.

overtake my lord of Suffolk who will be tomorrow night at Huntingdon, and they shall be fought withal or tomorrow noon by my Lord
Steward."[1]

On Monday 9 October Norfolk was at Woolpit. He reported
that he could raise 2500 men, and that he had "set such order that
it shall be hard for anyone to speak an unfitting word without being
incontinently taken and sent to me." He had heard of the rising in
Boston and Holland and was prepared to meet the rebels if they
attempted to join hands with the discontented clothiers of Suffolk.
If only Oxford were sent down the country would be safe enough,
and he himself was ready to serve under the Duke of Suffolk, whom
he could join in two or three days[2]. Three hours later, when he
was within three miles of his home at Kenninghall, he received
a summons to the general muster, dated the 7th[3]. Probably the
messenger had been despatched on the 7th, had missed Norfolk,
who had been travelling about so much, and had only come up to
him now. But the Duke at once accepted the summons as countermanding the orders that had reached him on the 8th, and wrote to
the Council that he would set out for London that night as soon
as the moon rose[4]. Here we must take leave of my Lord of Norfolk
for a considerable time.

On Sunday 8 October Lord Darcy wrote to his son from Pontefract Castle, urging him to make haste to the King; the Lord
Steward, he said, would understand that Sir Arthur was necessary
to his father, on account of his (Lord Darcy's) debility, and he could
do most service by going to the King at once. In spite of every
effort, Yorkshire was on the point of rising[5]. The King's letters
summoning the northern counties to send help to Shrewsbury were
received at Pontefract that day. The danger of mustering men in
a shire humming with sedition was obvious. However Sir Brian
Hastings, the sheriff, who was with Darcy, set out to gather what
men he could and march to Nottingham[6]. The King wrote to
Darcy on the same day, in ignorance of Yorkshire affairs, simply to
tell him to deny the rumours about parish churches, etc., and thereby
expose the "wretched and devilish intents" of the rebels[7]. Next
day, Monday 9 October, the King did at last receive Darcy's letters.
He thanked him for his warning and politic proceedings, but was
confident that the danger was at an end, and that all Darcy had

[1] L. and P. xi, 603.   [2] Ibid. 625.   [3] Ibid. 626.
[4] Ibid.   [5] Ibid. 605.   [6] Ibid. 662.
[7] Ibid. 598.

to do now was to arrest fugitives and any who spread rumours[1]. This tone of exaggerated confidence perhaps shows that the King distrusted Darcy, for the position of affairs seemed very unpromising from the royal point of view. It was reported in London that Sir Thomas Percy had joined the rebels with 30,000 men to avenge himself on the King for the loss of his inheritance[2]. No doubt this was the first distorted hint of the rising in the northern counties.

The disposition of the royal forces was as follows: at Nottingham were the Earls of Shrewsbury, Rutland, and Huntingdon, with such forces and weapons as they could muster. At Stamford were Sir John Russell and Sir William Parr with a small force in an absolutely defenceless town[3]. At Huntingdon was the Duke of Suffolk, who arrived there at 6 a.m. on Monday morning, almost alone, to find "neither ordnance nor artillery nor men enough to do anything; such men as are gathered there have neither harness nor weapons."[4] He had received from the King letters for the rebels, which reproached them for their disloyalty, denied the rumours, and threatened them with terrible vengeance if they did not instantly submit[5]. These he sent to Lincoln with a covering letter of his own[6]. Even if the rebels refused to surrender he hoped he might be able to prevent their advance until the royal army was in a little better order. But he also wrote to ask for instructions in case they should submit, and to urge that money, of which he was greatly in need, and ordnance, should be sent at once. Many of the troops which he had levied in Suffolk were detained there by the King's orders, and he begged that they might be sent after him under command of Sir Anthony Wingfield, Sir Arthur Hopton, and Sir Francis Lovell. He was expecting to be joined by Sir Francis Brian, who was at Kimbolton with 300 horse. He had written to Parr and Russell to ask whether it would be possible to defend Stamford; if not they were to fall back upon him at Huntingdon[7]. At the same time he wrote to Cromwell for "a herald, two pursuivants, two trumpets and the King's banner."[8]

On Tuesday 10 October Suffolk determined to advance to Stamford instead of halting at Huntingdon. He was joined early in the morning, before he set out, by Richard Cromwell, without the ordnance[9], which was finally despatched from London that very day under charge of William Gonson[10]. Richard had heard a rumour

---

[1] L. and P. xi, 611.   [2] Ibid. 714.   [3] Ibid. 621.   [4] Ibid. 615.
[5] Ibid. 569.   [6] Ibid. 616.   [7] Ibid. 615.
[8] Ibid. 617.   [9] Ibid. 658.   [10] Ibid. 638.

that Suffolk had lost a battle and 20,000 men, and wrote to his uncle to assure him that everything was going well[1]. George Staines was taken by the royal troops on his way up to London with the rebels' second petition to the King, and was sent on under guard by Suffolk[2]. By 8 o'clock on Tuesday night there were assembled at Stamford the forces of Suffolk and Richard Cromwell, Sir John Russell and Sir William Parr, Sir Francis Brian, and the troops from Ampthill under the Admiral, Sir William Fitzwilliam[3].

The letters from the King and the Duke of Suffolk were delivered this day to the gentlemen in the Chapter House of Lincoln Cathedral. They brought the affairs of the rebels to a crisis. It became necessary for the gentlemen to make a definite choice. The royal troops were disorganised and without money or ordnance. In discipline, equipment, and fighting quality they were exactly the same as the insurgents, neither better nor worse; both alike were drawn from the ordinary farm hands of the country and tradesmen of the town. The rebels, being on volunteer service, might be something above the royal troops in spirit; on the other hand the King's men had no voice in the council of war and were more amenable to authority. The commons of Lincolnshire were clamouring to be led to battle, and one small success, which seemed well within their reach, might raise the whole kingdom and leave the King at their mercy. But the gentlemen were afraid. In order to gain that victory they must definitely throw in their lot with the commons, give up the plea that they were with them only on compulsion, and abandon all hope of making peace with the King. If they fought and were defeated those who did not fall in the field would end on the gallows, or at best in exile; their lands would pass to strangers, their children would be left destitute, and the old names would die out. Lincolnshire would be given over to fire and pillage. If they fought and won, it would mean the renewal of civil war in England, after fifty years of peace. The new war would be a religious war, with some prospect of a foreign invasion; England at the hour of her first prosperity, just taking her place among the nations, might be crippled beyond recovery. It was a terrible decision to lie in the hands of a few country gentlemen, who were not, perhaps, very well fitted to deal with such momentous affairs. Cromwell's servant, John Williams, declared a few weeks later that he had never seen anywhere "such a sight of asses, so unlike gentlemen as the most part of them be. Knights

[1] L. and P. xi, 650.   [2] Ibid. 658; see above, chap. v.
[3] Ibid. 658.

and esquires are meeter to be baileys; men void of good fashion, and, in truth, of wit, except in matters concerning their trade which is to get goods only."[1]   This is very prejudiced evidence, but the attitude of the Lincolnshire gentlemen towards the rebellion is a difficult problem.   It is impossible to speak of them all collectively as doing or believing this or that.   The chief distinction that must be noticed is the division of the host into two principal bands, the men of Louth and the men of Horncastle.

The gentlemen who belonged to the Louth district seem on the whole to have been acting from the first against their will; they were for the most part the commissioners taken at Caistor, and they had generally every reason to support the government and fear the commons.   There were exceptions, such as Sir Christopher Askew, but on the whole the commons were right in the suspicions which they entertained of their enforced leaders.   William Morland stated in his evidence that "as far as he could see both all the gentlemen and honest yeomen of the country were weary of this matter, and sorry for it, but durst not disclose their opinion to the commons for fear of their lives."[2]

In the Horncastle host the leaders were not nearly so reluctant. When the people first rose there and went to Scrivelsby Hall they were met, about a quarter of a mile from the house, by the sheriff, Thomas Dymmoke of Carlton, Mr Dighton of Sturton, Mr Sanderson, and Arthur Dymmoke.   They greeted the commons with the words, "Masters, ye be welcome," and when they were told they must take the commons' oath they replied, "With a good will."   When the sheriff was asked whether the bells should be rung, he said, "Yea, and ye will, for it is necessary that the people have knowledge."[3] That night the Sandersons went through the village of Snelland in harness and told the people that they must be at the Horncastle muster next day[4]; they were the bringers of the white banner with the parchment picture[5].   It was the gentlemen of Horncastle who drew up the articles and explained the Statute of Uses to the commons[6].   Nicholas Leache, the parson of Belchford, who was with the Horncastle company, thought "all the exterior acts of the gentlemen amongst the commons were done willingly, for he saw them as diligent to set forward every matter as the commons were.   And further during the whole time of the insurrection not one of them

---

[1] L. and P. xi, 888.   [2] L. and P. xii (1), 380.   [3] Ibid. 70 (x).
[4] L. and P. xi, 828 (xi).   [5] L. and P. xii (1), 70 (ii).
[6] See above, chap. v.

persuaded the people to desist or showed them it was high treason. Otherwise he believes in his conscience they would not have gone forward, for all the people with whom he had intelligence thought they had not offended the King, as the gentlemen caused proclamations to be made in his name.   He thinks the gentlemen might have stayed the people of Horncastle, for at the beginning his parishioners went forward among the rebels only by command of the gentlemen.   The gentlemen were first harnessed of all others, and commanded the commons to prepare themselves harness, and he believes the commons expected to have redress of grievances by way of supplication to the King."[1]

At first the policy of the gentlemen, whether favourable or unfavourable to the rising, was probably much the same.   There would have been no difficulty in making a sudden dash up to London, for there was no force to oppose them on the way; but even if they reached London, as Wat Tyler and Jack Cade did from nearer points, it was difficult to do anything effective there.   The well-wishers of the insurgents might reasonably think that their best chance lay in drilling the commons into some sort of discipline before they advanced, and this was the opinion of all the gentlemen. According to George Hudswell, " Sir William Skipwith said they (the commons) should be ordered whether they would or no, and every gentleman said it shall be well done that they be ruled ";[2] Philip Trotter deposed that " from the beginning to the end of the insurrection the gentlemen might have stayed it if they would, for the commons did nothing but by the gentlemen's commandment, and they durst never stir in the field from the place they were appointed to till the gentlemen directed them what to do; and were cautioned not to stir from their appointed places upon pain of death."[3] Moreover, if the leaders knew that Yorkshire would rise in a few days, they may have wished to put off their advance on London until they were joined by reinforcements from the north.

The fact that the gentlemen counselled delay does not therefore prove that they were really opposed to the rising.   But by Tuesday 10 October the spirits of the most daring seem to have failed.   No doubt rumours of the King's musters had reached them as much exaggerated as the accounts of their own numbers which were repeated in London.   The first effect of the news from Yorkshire had worn off.   The commissioners were men of influence, and when

---

[1] L. and P. xii (1), 70 (xi).

[2] L. and P. xi, 853.   [3] L. and P. xii (1), 70 (x).

the more impetuous of the gentlemen found them opposed to the movement, they probably felt its chance of success was very much diminished. They may have been half irritated and half frightened by the attitude of the commons, who were in a grumbling, dispirited, and yet vicious mood. They feared their allies quite as much as the troops which opposed them; and recollections of the German Peasant Revolt in 1525 would increase their alarm[1]. When it came to the parting of the ways, even those who had at first seemed heart and soul with the rebels wavered; they dared not proclaim themselves traitors and give up the path of retreat which they believed was still open to them. Accordingly they prepared to desert the commons. If they had had a chief captain, a man who thought of neither gentlemen nor commons but only of the cause, this dangerous time might have been tided over. A popular leader might have coaxed the host out of its ill-humour, and inspired the gentlemen to forget the promptings of cowardice and treachery in the greatness of the adventure which they had taken upon them. But there was no leader, and mistrust and disorder took his place in Lincoln.

There was a muster upon Lincoln Heath on Tuesday morning, but it seems to have been ill-attended. The monks of Kirkstead and the men of Sleaford both were given leave to go home[2]. William Morland returned to his home at Kedington, and in passing through Louth saved the lives of Cromwell's servants, Bellowe, Milsent, and Parker, who had been imprisoned in the Tollbooth since Monday 2 October. Their captors, having taken their money and given it into the charge of Robert Brown the jailor, had resolved to put them to death, but Morland and some honest men of the town persuaded the crowd to spare the prisoners and disperse. In recognition of this service Parker and his fellows requested the jailor to give Morland, out of the £6 of their money which he was keeping, "two crowns, the one of 5s. and the other of 14 groats, and to make up just 10s. they gave him 4d. in silver."[3] It is a pity that Morland, who was so good an observer and narrator, was away from Lincoln on this critical day, as only one account of the events now remains, that of Thomas Moigne[4].

On Tuesday afternoon some three hundred of the commons brought in the letters from the King and the Duke of Suffolk addressed to Sir Robert Tyrwhit, Sir William Askew, Sir William Skipwith and

---

[1] See note A at end of chapter.   [2] L. and P. xi, 828 (viii), 969.
[3] L. and P. xii (1), 380.   [4] See note B at end of chapter.

Sir Edward Dymmoke. They carried them to the gentlemen who were assembled in the Chapter House, and insisted on hearing their contents. Moigne began to read the letters aloud, but coming to a part which he knew would anger the commons, he omitted it. The parson of Snelland, standing at his elbow, detected this, and cried out to the commons that the letter was falsely read[1]. The meeting was plunged into confusion; someone cried that it was time to kill some of the justices: if they were hanged for it they would not leave a gentleman alive in the shire[2]; many would have slain Moigne. In the end the wilder spirits were driven out into the cloisters, where, after much debate, they determined to kill the gentlemen. Their plans miscarried, for the gentlemen's servants overheard, and warned their masters that a party was lying in wait to kill them as they came out of the west door of the minster. With the aid of the faithful servants they were smuggled out of the south door to the house of the murdered chancellor, and there they resolved to make a stand, to refuse to go forward, and to defend themselves, if necessary, until the royal army relieved them[3]. According to Moigne this resolution was taken by his advice, but some preparations had been made the day before to render the Close defensible against the commons[4]. The servants carried messages to "the most honest men of their companies" by which they were induced to give up the idea of going forward. Meanwhile the commons outside the minster discovered that they had been tricked, and decided not to attack the gentlemen until morning[5].

On Wednesday 11 October the gentlemen and honest men, in harness, marched down from Lincoln minster and met the commons in the fields, where they stated clearly that they would not go forward, but would wait for the King's answer to their suit for pardon. They had written to Suffolk to ask him to intercede for them, and they would do no more[6]. The commons seem to have been completely bewildered by this turn of affairs. They did not attack the gentlemen, but neither did they choose leaders of their own and go on, nor as an alternative return to their homes in a body. A good many slipped away quietly; Robert Carre of Slea-ford, for instance, went to see his wife, who had taken refuge with her father, put his "evidences" into two chests, gave orders that they were to be hidden in a hole under the thatch if the host came

---

[1] L. and P. xi, 971.   [2] Ibid 975 (3).
[3] Ibid. 971.   [4] Ibid. 939.   [5] Ibid. 971.   [6] Ibid.

by, and rode off to join Lord Clinton at Nottingham[1]. The canons of Barlings went home the same day[2]. William Morland on the other hand returned to Lincoln by way of Louth, where he "made him a cloak of black cloth." It was said in the host that he had gone to Louth to fire the beacons, which shook his credit both with the gentlemen and the commons, until two indifferent men were sent to Louth, who reported that he had done no such thing[3].

Rumours of the rebels' flight soon reached Suffolk's camp, and Richard Cromwell reported them to his uncle. His letter gives an amusing glimpse of Suffolk's headquarters. Richard says that "my Lord Admiral" (Fitzwilliam) and also "my Lord's Grace" (Suffolk) show him great attention, and "my Lord Admiral is so earnest in the matter that I dare well say he would eat them (the rebels) with salt. I never saw one triumph like unto him."[4] It is easy to imagine the nobles, with hearts full of contempt and hatred, showing every courtesy to the young upstart, and taking care that their abuse of traitors grew warmer when he appeared. It was first said that 10,000 or 12,000 of the rebels had fled home, but later in the day one of Sir John Thimbleby's sons arrived at Stamford who halved these figures, but declared that not 10,000 remained in Lincoln. Young Thimbleby's reception was not encouraging; Suffolk at once put him in ward and threatened, if his father did not come in by eight next morning, to spoil all he had and cut his son in pieces. The feeling against Sir John was particularly strong, because Russell and Parr accused him of assembling all his tenants as if to join them, threatening to burn the houses of those who refused to go with him, and then taking his whole company over to the rebels. Suffolk intended to march on Lincoln on Saturday, and afterwards to destroy Louth and Horncastle. Richard Cromwell professed to be very sorry that the rebels were flying, as he had hoped they would be used as they deserved and the whole shire sacked[5]. The ordnance had arrived at Huntingdon[6], so that Suffolk was able to think of advancing. His only wish was to meet the rebels in a pitched battle, but Shrewsbury, at Nottingham, was more politic. He had with him Thomas Miller, Lancaster Herald, whom he despatched to Lincoln with a proclamation which bade the rebels depart to their homes[7]. Lancaster Herald reached Lincoln on Wednesday evening and found everything in confusion, — the

[1] L. and P. xi, 969.   [2] Ibid. 828 (v).
[3] L. and P. xii (1), 380.   [4] L. and P. xi, 658.   [5] Ibid.
[6] Ibid. 661.   [7] Ibid. 694.

gentlemen anxious to make their peace with the King,—the commons without leaders, without plans, without hopes[1]. It was too late to discharge his errand that night.

On Thursday 12 October the host was summoned to the Castle Garth to hear his proclamation[2]. It was in the names of George Earl of Shrewsbury, Thomas Earl of Rutland, and George Earl of Huntingdon, and briefly ordered the rebels to depart to their houses[3]. The herald told the rebels that Shrewsbury was prepared to fight them on Ancaster Heath if they disobeyed[4]. It is not known what further arguments he used, but after much persuasion the commons agreed to go home, while the gentlemen made a formal submission[5] and repaired to Suffolk to sue for pardon[6]. There was still a party which was eager to fight. Its leader, Robert Leache, seized the gentlemen's written submission, and opened and read it before it was delivered to the herald, "saying he would see what their answer was ere it should depart."[7] With the usual irony of slow-fingered indifference the painters had ready that day the banner which the insurgents had designed for themselves. It was a linen cloth on which were painted "the Five Wounds of Christ, a chalice with the Host, a plough and a horn with a scripture." The Five Wounds were to show the people they fought in Christ's cause; the chalice and the Host were in remembrance that chalices, crosses, and church jewels should be taken away; the plough was to encourage the husbandmen; the horn, according to the Horncastle men, was in token of Horncastle, but others regarded it as a symbol of the tax on horned cattle[8].

The news of the herald's success was sent to Suffolk, and he wrote to the King asking for instructions. He was expecting to effect a junction with Shrewsbury on the following Monday[9]. Most of the money had arrived[10], and the ordnance was looked for next day (Friday). He wished to know whether he and the Lord Steward should pardon the Lincolnshire men and advance at once into Yorkshire, or stay and reduce Lincolnshire to complete submission by severity. He pointed out that the Yorkshire rebellion was spreading fast and had better be confronted immediately, and that by an advance the royal troops could prevent a meeting between

---

[1] L. and P. xi, 971; xii (1), 380.   [2] Ibid.
[3] L. and P. xi, 694 (2); printed in St. P. i, 462.   [4] L. and P. xi, 854.
[5] Ibid. 690, 718; printed St. P. i, 468.   [6] L. and P. xi, 971.
[7] Ibid. 843.   [8] Ibid. 828, i, (2); xii (1), 70 (xiii).
[9] L. and P. xi, 672.   [10] Ibid. 680.

the Yorkshiremen and any new rebels in Lincolnshire.   He wrote at midnight, and in the midst of his letter the Dymmokes arrived at the camp accompanied by a messenger from the other gentlemen, who was commissioned to ask Suffolk whether they should come to him in harness and to beg for his intercession with the King.   He replied that they must use their own discretion; he could only keep them in surety until the King's pleasure was known[1].

On Friday 13 October the last of the insurgents dispersed[2]. They despatched the bailly of Barton to Beverley—the last messenger from the Lincolnshire host—to countermand Kyme's message[3]. The men of Horncastle marched sadly home and placed their new unneeded banner in the parish church[4].   All Suffolk's ordnance had now arrived, and though he had only 5000 men he discharged 2000, as he had not enough arms to supply both his own men and Shrewsbury's; he thought such a sign of confidence would make an impression on the rebels.   He sent word to Shrewsbury to advance next day to meet him, but the Earl replied that he could not leave Nottingham without money, and that he wished to know what the King had to say to Lancaster Herald's report before anything more was attempted[5].   Shrewsbury wrote at the same time to Darcy, and sent him a copy of the proclamation which had had such effect in Lincoln.   He said that the rebels now "mind themselves to be the King's true and faithful subjects at all times and from time to time accordingly."   As they would give no further help to the Yorkshiremen, but on the contrary had promised to stop the boats on the Humber, Ouse, and Trent, "so that none shall come over but be glad to return homewards like fools," he trusted that the disturbances in Yorkshire would cease[6].

At this point we must return to Lord Hussey, who had gone straight to Shrewsbury's camp after his escape from Sleaford.   He reached Nottingham on the morning of Monday 9 October, bringing with him his wife and George Hudswell.   Instead of finding himself in safety among friends he had only left one atmosphere of danger and suspicion to enter another.   Shrewsbury's doubts of his loyalty sprang from the constant reports that he had joined the rebels. Depositions against him had been taken as early as the 7th[7]; when Norfolk heard the false report that he was with the rebels he wrote to the King, "if it be true there is folly upon folly.   I pray God

---

[1] L. and P. XI, 672.   [2] Ibid. 854, 691.   [3] Ibid. 854 (ii).
[4] Ibid. 828, i, (2).   [5] Ibid. 808.   [6] Ibid. 694.
[7] Ibid. 587.

there be truth though there be much folly."[1] Hussey's own family unintentionally strengthened the feeling against him. Fitzwilliam advised Cromwell to examine Sir William Hussey as to why he had not reported to the Council the seditious words which, according to his servant's report, he had heard between Lincolnshire and London[2]. On their arrival at Nottingham Lady Hussey created a very unfavourable impression when she implored the Earls of Shrewsbury and Huntingdon to allow her husband to return to Lincolnshire for the sake of the children she had left at Sleaford; "like a fool saying that if she brought me not again the rebels would burn my house and them," said her naturally aggrieved husband[3]. No doubt the poor lady was in great anxiety, and he had brought her with him much against her will. George Cutler, who had carried Hussey's messages to the rebels, was examined that day[4].

The principal evidence as to Lord Hussey's conduct lies in two undated papers, which were probably drawn up about the end of the week. One is his own statement to the Council, whom he begged to intercede for him with the King. After giving an account of the week's events at Sleaford, he concluded with the assertion that he had 300 men now in the King's service, 200 under the command of his son, and eight score under Anthony Ireby; that he remained at Sleaford to stay the country, and that while he was there neither Holland nor Kesteven rose[5]. The other document is the deposition of Robert Carre of Sleaford, the head of the principal local family[6]. The two accounts agree very closely as to the facts, but differ completely in the interpretation put upon them. Lord Hussey represented himself as pacifying those who urged him to join the rebels; Carre accused him of sending away men who offered to fight for the King; for example, " Before the rebels came to Sleaford, the bailiff of Ruskington offered to be, with as many as he could get, under Hussey's command; and my Lord pinched him by the little finger, bidding him come when he sent unto him by that token and not else." At the end of his deposition, which is mutilated, there seem to have been other instances of persons who offered their services to Lord Hussey and "had slender answers."[7] This account is to some extent confirmed by the saying of Richard Burwell, constable of Potter Hanworth, that he asked counsel of Mr Robert

---

[1] L. and P. xi, 625. [2] Ibid. 584. [3] Ibid. 852.
[4] Ibid. 620. [5] Ibid. 852.
[6] Lincolnshire Pedigrees (Harl. Soc.), Ped. of Carr of Sleaford.
[7] L. and P. xi, 969.

Sutton, who answered that he had been with Lord Hussey and could see no remedy but to do as the commons did[1].

Against this must be set Hussey's account of the position; Lord Clinton had fled, the gentlemen returned slack answers to his summons, and he did not believe that he could raise enough men to resist the rebels, but by his influence he was able to keep his own people from rising, while if like Lord Borough and Lord Clinton he had fled at the first alarm, they would have joined the rebels at once[2]. There seems to be little doubt that this was really Hussey's belief, and in itself it was quite reasonable. There are two points which tell against Carre's evidence. In the first place he had been for some days with the rebels,—against his will as he said,—but still the fact was enough to hang him. In the circumstances he would probably be ready to say anything that his examiners wished him to say, and particularly ready to incriminate somebody else. In the second place the whole deposition is conceived in a spirit of the bitterest hatred of Hussey, perhaps on account of some forgotten local quarrel, perhaps from a feeling that Hussey had deserted Sleaford and brought its inhabitants into danger. In one place Carre says "If my lord had gathered men for the King as he had done for his own pomp to ride to sessions or assize, he might have driven the rebels back," an obviously foolish and spiteful remark[3]. The offer of help which he mentions came too late, when the rebels were approaching the town and Hussey had prepared for flight. Carre's deposition seems to have been the chief evidence against Hussey, and at the end of it are written the ominous words, "My lord Hussey, this is perused deliberately." All things considered, the only charge which could be substantiated against Hussey was that he had made himself singular by remaining at his post longer than the neighbouring noblemen.

On Wednesday 11 October the King did not yet know of the Yorkshire insurrection, and though the issue in Lincolnshire was still doubtful, he put a bold face on the matter and wrote to the ambassadors in France, Gardiner and Wallop, such an account of the rebellion as he wished to circulate in foreign courts. The rebels were chiefly boys and beggars, who had been deceived by the false rumours of traitors. He had sent an army under the Duke of Suffolk, which would by this time have disposed of them, and "according to ancient custom" had levied another of "pure tried men" which could not number less than 40,000 and had been

---

[1] L. and P. xi, 975 (4).   [2] Ibid. 852.   [3] Ibid. 969.

conveyed to Ampthill in six days, "and yet the greater part of our realm is not touched."[1] This was a rather loose statement on the King's part, though no doubt good enough for foreign consumption; the first levies at Ampthill had been summoned on the 5th and 6th and had marched to Huntingdon with Fitzwilliam on the 9th, while the second levies, which were just being assembled by Norfolk and others, were summoned on the 10th to be at Ampthill on the 16th[2]. Suffolk's letters of the 12th were not despatched until after midnight; consequently the news of the "sparpling" of the rebels cannot have been generally known in London on the 13th. It was probably on this day that Chapuys' nephew sent an account of the rising to the Regent of the Netherlands. He refers to the events of the 12th, but not to the rebels' capitulation. He gives an amusing account of the progress of affairs,—as they were unofficially reported in London. The King's commissioners, he said, were demolishing 400 (really 40) abbeys in Lincolnshire, when the peasants rose against them on Monday 2 October "under the leading of a shoemaker named William Keing Hardy, a man of persuasive manner." This must be our old friend Nicholas Melton, Captain Cobbler, but it is impossible to say where Chapuys' nephew picked up the extraordinary name. The rebels tried to seize Dr Legh, "a man much hated by the whole country for his arrogance ever since he dared to cite before the Archbishop of Canterbury your late aunt the Queen of England." But Legh escaped, and in their disappointed rage the commons seized and hanged his cook. There is nothing in the depositions about the rebellion to confirm this story. Chapuys also repeats the tale about a man being baited to death, and mentions the rumour of a rising further north, and the execution of two men at Windsor for seditious words. He describes the murder of the Bishop of Lincoln's chancellor, and attributes the commons' hatred of the bishop, to the fact that they regarded him "as one of the principal councillors who raised scruples in the King to repudiate your said aunt." The numbers of the host increased rapidly, and they began to take and swear the gentlemen; "and from that time the said shoemaker began to wear a cloak of crimson satin, embroidered with the words "Je ayme Dieu le roy et le prouffit du commung."[3] The arrival of the news in London and the King's preparations are next described. "On Saturday (7 October) they (the rebels) were more than 50,000, and among them over 10,000

---

[1] L. and P. xi, 656; printed by Tierney, Dodd's Church Hist. of Eng. i, Append.
[2] See note C at end of chapter.   [3] See note D at end of chapter.

priests, monks and religious persons of whom the most learned continually admonish their men to continue the work begun, pointing out the advantages which will come to them of it." The writer himself saw the ordnance taken out of the Tower and the break-down which occurred. The King is levying musters in Kent and the southern counties, but there is great danger that his own men will turn against him, as they sympathise with the demands of the rebels, saying "that they wish to live like their ancestors, defend the abbeys and churches, be quit of taxes and subsidies, and recover those they have paid already more by fear than love, especially that which they lent in the time of the Cardinal, which amounts to a very horrible sum. Finally they demand a shearer of cloths to be given up to them, meaning Cromwell, and a tavern-keeper, meaning the Archbishop of Canterbury, the Chancellor of the country, the Chancellor of the Augmentations, and certain other bishops and lords of the King's Council." The King is taking men from Dover and Sandwich, which will weaken the coast defences and make an invasion easy. The French tailors and Flemish shoemakers in London are being compelled to serve in the army for two groats a day, and one groat as drink money for every five miles they march, while the English receive only 6*d.* and the same drink money. He concludes by pointing out that such a chance may not come again for avenging all the wrongs that Henry has inflicted on the faith and family of the Emperor; he therefore implores the Regent to send from the army now in Zealand 2000 arquebusiers and a supply of ammunition, which should be landed "in the river which goes up to York."[1] Needless to say, this advice was not acted upon.

By the next day, Saturday 14 October, Lancaster Herald was with the King, and the news from Lincolnshire must have been generally known. For the first time since the beginning of the rebellion all parties halted, and nothing was done until the 15th, Sunday, when the King, believing all danger at an end, sent out orders countermanding the musters at Ampthill[2]. Suffolk would delay his advance no longer, but set out for Lincoln, and sent a message to Shrewsbury to do the same. He was obliged to advance slowly, as he took the ordnance with him[3]. He received from the King instructions to occupy Lincoln and to collect there the arms of the rebels[4]; with these orders came a proclamation by which the

---

[1] L. and P. xi, 714; the translation of another copy is printed by Froude, The Pilgrim, p. 113. [2] L. and P. xi, 720–1.
[3] Ibid. 808. [4] Ibid. 717.

King accepted the surrender and promised to show mercy[1]. The gentlemen were to be examined, and their examinations returned in writing to the King; they might then be dismissed with good words, except the most culpable, who were to be sent up to London. Suffolk was to establish order in the shire, and to survey the Cathedral and the Close secretly, as the King thought of placing a garrison there, " to keep them in mind that their forefathers were traitors and for the keeping under of their posterity." If the country submitted there was to be no pillaging, but four captains of Louth, three of Horncastle, and two of Caistor must be kept for execution. Suffolk might expect reinforcements, and was to remain at Lincoln until he received further orders. If all was quiet when he received this letter, he need not publish the proclamation, but the King "took the sending of the herald in good part," for the people respected his coat and he could see more than an ordinary spy. Shrewsbury was to join Suffolk in examining the traitors, and then to disperse his troops and go quietly home, if all went well, but if there were further disturbances in Yorkshire, he was to advance at once to suppress them, taking with him the ordnance, as Suffolk could be supplied with more from Ampthill[2]. The order to Shrewsbury shows that the King was still over-confident. It was Shrewsbury's rash advance, in obedience to it, which afterwards seriously embarrassed the position of the royal troops.

Suffolk sent forward the Admiral with an advance guard, and on Tuesday 17 October was himself at Lincoln. His sudden appearance put an end to the last plans of resistance which the rebels still cherished. Richard Cromwell said that the people of Lincoln were "as obstinate persons as ever I saw, who would scarce move their bonnets to my said lord, and probably would have withstood us if we had not stolen upon them."[3] In his next despatches Suffolk explained to the King that the situation was not so secure as Henry had assumed in his first relief,—the country was still very much unsettled, and beacons were lighted and men assembled in harness on the least provocation. He had ordered the release of Milsent and Bellowe from Louth Tollbooth, but their jailor was obliged to promise that they should be restored on demand before the commons would let them go[4]. On Wednesday 18 October he sent Sir Francis Brian to make a full report to the King. Sir Francis reached Windsor next day, just as a reply was being drawn

[1] L. and P. xi, 718; printed in St. P. i, 468.   [2] L. and P. xi, 717.
[3] Ibid. 756.   [4] Ibid. 854.

up to Suffolk's previous letters, in which he was thanked for his diligence and promised money, ordnance and men, under the command of Sir Anthony Browne. If any further rising was attempted he must immediately attack Louth and "with all extremity destroy, burn and kill man, woman and child, the terrible example of all others." Sir Francis, however, must have explained that if it came to fighting it was by no means certain that the terrible example would not be, so to speak, on the other foot, as Suffolk had only 3000 men of certain loyalty in the heart of a hostile country; the King's postscript, therefore, took a milder tone. Sir John Thimbleby and the other gentlemen were to be told that he "minded nothing less (i.e. nothing was further from his thoughts) than their destruction." All the gentlemen who would come in and serve the King might be promised safety from bodily hurt and the Duke's intercession with the King; proclamation must be made that the multitude could obtain the same terms, if they would denounce their captains and give them up. The King also, at last, sent an answer to the commons' petition which had been sent to him on the 9th. It was to be read openly, and he complacently added that he thought it was "so conceived as of itself to make them repent their follies and ask mercy without further tarrying."[1] The answer was as follows:

"Answer to the Petitions of the Traitors and Rebels in Lincolnshire.

"First, We begin and make answer to the 4th and 6th articles, because upon them dependeth much of the rest. Concerning choosing of Councillors, I never have read, heard, nor known that princes' councillors and prelates should be appointed by rude and ignorant common people; nor that they were persons meet, or of ability, to discern and choose meet and sufficient councillors for a prince. How presumptuous then are ye, the rude commons of one shire, and that one of the most brute and beastly of the whole realm, and of least experience, to find fault with your prince, for the electing of his councillors and prelates; and to take upon you, contrary to God's law, and man's law, to rule your prince, whom ye are bound by all laws to obey, and serve, with both your lives, lands, and goods, and for no worldly cause to withstand: the contrary whereof you, like traitors and rebels, have attempted, and not like true subjects, as ye name yourselves.

"As to the suppression of religious houses and monasteries, We will that ye, and all our subjects should well know, that this is granted us by all the nobles, spiritual and temporal, of this our realm, and by all the commons of the same by Act of Parliament; and not set forth by any councillor or councillors, upon their mere will and fantasy, as ye full falsely would persuade our realm to believe. And where ye allege, that the service of God is much thereby diminished, the truth thereof is contrary; for there be none houses

---

[1] L. and P. xi, 780 (1).

suppressed, where God was well served, but where most vice, mischief, and abomination of living was used: and that doth well appear by their own confession, subscribed with their own hands, in the time of our visitations. And yet were suffered a great many of them, more than we by the act needed, to stand; wherein, if they amend not their living, we fear we have more to answer for, than for the suppression of all the rest. And as for their hospitality, for the relief of poor people, we wonder ye be not ashamed to affirm, that they have been a great relief to our people, when a great many, or the most part, hath not past four or five religious persons in them, and divers but one, which spent the substance of the goods of their house, in nourishing of vice, and abominable living. Now, what unkindness and unnaturality may we impute to you, and all our subjects, that be of that mind, that had lever such an unthrifty sort of vicious persons should enjoy such possessions, profits, and emoluments, as grow of the said houses, to the maintenance of their unthrifty life; than we, your natural prince, sovereign lord, and king, which doth and hath spent more in your defence, of his own, the six times they be worth!

"As touching the Act of Uses, we marvel what madness is in your brain, or upon what ground ye would take authority upon you, to cause us to break those laws and statutes, which, by all the nobles, knights, and gentlemen of this realm, whom the same chiefly toucheth, hath been granted and assented to; seeing in no manner of thing it toucheth you, the base commons of our realm! Also the grounds of those uses were false, and never admitted by any law, but usurped upon the prince, contrary to all equity and justice, as it hath been openly both disputed and declared, by all the well learned men of England in Westminster Hall; whereby ye may well perceive, how mad and unreasonable your demands be, both in that, and the rest, and how unmeet it is for us, and dishonourable, to grant or assent unto, and less meet and decent for you, in such rebellious sort, to demand the same of your prince.

"As touching the Fifteenth, which ye demand of us to be released, think ye that we be so faint hearted, that, perforce, ye of one shire (were ye a great many more) could compel us with your insurrections, and such rebellious demeanour, to remit the same? or think ye that any man will or may take you to be true subjects, that first make a show of a loving grant, and then, perforce, would compel your sovereign lord and king to release the same; the time of payment whereof is not yet come? yea, and seeing the same will not countervail the tenth penny of the charges, which we do, and daily must, sustain, for your tuition and safeguard? Make ye sure, by your occasions of this your ingratitudes, unnaturalness, and unkindness to us, now administered, ye give us cause, which hath always been as much dedicate to your wealths, as ever was king, not so much to set our study for the setting forward of the same, seeing how unkindly and untruly ye deal now with us, without any cause or occasion. And doubt ye not, though ye have no grace nor naturalment in you, to consider your duties of allegiance to your king and sovereign; the rest of our realm, we doubt not, hath: and we, and they, shall so look on this cause, that we trust shall be to your confusion, if, according to our former letters, ye submit not yourselves.

"As touching the First Fruits, we let you weet, it is a thing granted us by Act of Parliament also, for the supportation of part of the great and excessive charges, which we support and bear, for the maintenance of your wealths, and others our subjects. And we have known, also, that ye, our commons, have much complained, in times passed, that the most of the goods, lands, and possessions of the realm were in the spiritual men's hands; and yet now, bearing us in hand that ye be as loving subjects to us as may be, ye can not find in your hearts that your prince and sovereign lord should have any part thereof, (and yet it is nothing prejudicial unto you, our commons;) but do rebel and unlawfully rise against your prince, contrary to your duty of allegiance, and God's commandment. Wherefore, sirs, remember your follies and traitorous demeanours, and shame not your native country of England, nor offend no more, so grievously, your undoubted king and natural prince, which always hath showed himself most loving unto you; and remember your duty of allegiance, and that ye are bound to obey us, your king, both by God's commandment and law of nature. Wherefore we charge you eftsoons, upon the forsaid bonds and pains, that ye withdraw yourselves to your own houses every man, and no more assemble contrary to our laws and your allegiances; and to cause the provokers of you to this mischief to be delivered to our lieutenants' hands, or ours, and you yourselves to submit you to such condign punishment as we, and our nobles, shall think you worthy. For doubt ye not else that we and our nobles can nor will suffer this injury at your hand unrevenged, if ye give not place to us your sovereign, and show yourselves as bounden and obedient subjects, and no more to intermeddle yourselves from henceforth with the weighty affairs of the realm; the direction whereof only appertaineth to us your king, and such noblemen and councillors as he list to elect and choose to have the ordering of the same. And thus we pray unto Almighty God to give you grace to do your duties, and to use yourselves towards us like true and faithful subjects, so as we may have cause to order you thereafter; and rather obediently to consent amongst you to deliver into the hands of our lieutenant 100 persons, to be ordered according to their demerits at our will and pleasure, than by your obstinacy and wilfulness to put yourselves, lives, wives, children, lands, goods, and chattels, besides the indignation of God, in the utter adventure of total destruction and utter ruin by force and violence of the sword."[1]

So ended the insurrection in Lincolnshire, for there is nothing more to tell of it but the King's revenge. It was a most curious movement, both in its sudden outbreak and its still more sudden collapse. It is not surprising that it should have been attempted, but it is that it should have failed so completely. The secret of this failure seems to be twofold. The most obvious weakness was that it had no leader. Perhaps it would have been better if the commons had trusted solely to their own leaders, Captain Cobbler, William Morland, and the others. Knowing that they were committed to the cause, they gave themselves up to it heart and soul, while the gentlemen upon whom the commons attempted to force the responsibility were at best only half-hearted. But the lack of a leader

---

[1] L. and P. xi, 780 (2); printed in St. P. i, 463.

was only a symptom of their real weakness, namely, that they had no definite object in view. The rising was not simply religious, or agrarian, or political, but a little of each. It was as much against an unpopular tax and an unpopular bishop as against the King's religious policy and his chief minister. The rebels protested against the dissolution of the monasteries, but the vital question of the Royal Supremacy was only mentioned once, and then the rebels expressed their willingness to acknowledge the title[1]. The gentlemen hated Cromwell and the Statute of Uses, but they wavered on the question of the abbeys, and were very much afraid of the commons and of civil war. These jarring forces could only be united into an effective opposition by the inspiration of a great leader or a great cause; this was the lesson which the Lincolnshire failure taught, and one man at least learnt from it. In many respects the earlier rising was a hindrance to the Pilgrimage of Grace,—it gave confidence to the government, and confirmed the waverers in the conviction that the King would win in the end,—but his connection with it showed Robert Aske what to avoid. He saw that half-hearted leaders were worse than useless, and he saw also that the only common ground on which all parties could meet was that of religion. Himself sincerely attached to the old faith, he insisted on it as the cause and the sole cause of the insurrection which he led; hence the curious form of his oath—" we rise not for the common weal, but in defence of the Church." His banner did not bear the motley crowd of symbols which the men of Horncastle devised, but simply the Five Wounds of Christ. If he could inspire in others the enthusiasm which he himself felt for that badge, they would lose sight of their conflicting interests, and gentlemen and commons would fight side by side, without thought of high or low. This was what Robert Aske learnt from the Lincolnshire rebellion. It remained to be seen whether he could put it into practice.

NOTES TO CHAPTER VI

Note A. The attitude of the Lincolnshire gentlemen bears a strong resemblance to that of the German nobles who were compelled to join the peasants in 1525. "Princes, lords and ecclesiastical dignitaries were being compelled far and wide to save their lives, after their property was probably already confiscated, by swearing allegiance to the Christian League or Brotherhood of the peasants and by countersigning the Twelve Articles and other demands of their refractory villeins and serfs."[2]

[1] See above, chap. v.   [2] Bax, op. cit. 108.

The peasants captured Gotz von Berlichingen of the Iron Hand and compelled him to become their leader[1]. "Had Gotz been sincere in taking up the cause of the rebellion, there is no doubt that, experienced warrior as he was, he would have been a valuable acquisition. Even as it was some of his suggestions respecting the maintenance of discipline were in the right direction, but the fact remained that he was acting under compulsion in a cause with which he had no sympathy and his one concern was to get rid of his responsibility at the first possible moment, if not actually to betray his trust."[2]

Note B. Moigne's statement refutes Williams' scoffing remarks about the Lincolnshire gentlemen, for it shows that Moigne at least was a very able man. Spirited as it is, there is an air of special pleading about it,—the facts are given, but a particular construction is put upon them. It would be very interesting to compare this with some other narrative of the same events, but no other remains. Examinations of the other Lincolnshire gentlemen seem to have been taken, but are not preserved, and perhaps very little inquiry was made into the affair of the Chapter House, as it reflected too much credit on the loyalty of the gentlemen to be acceptable to the King. The only other reference to it is in an accusation brought against James Atkinson, a tailor, the man who cried out that they ought to kill some of the justices.

Note C. Although Henry exaggerated the number of his forces and the speed with which they had been collected, it is too much to say, with Tierney and Gasquet, that "no such army ever existed." The main facts that the King had levied and sent north one body of troops and was busy levying another were perfectly correct.

Note D. Another allusion to Captain Cobbler's robe occurs in a letter of Wriothesley's to Cromwell, written on Monday (23 Oct.), in which, speaking of the Lincolnshire prisoners, he says, "I perceive, also, his highness would have that traitor in the motley coat well examined, for he (the King) took that part also very well; yet we have no further news."[3] The leaders of the German peasants wore gorgeous clothes—"a red hat and mantle," "purple mantles and scarlet birettas with ostrich plumes,"[4]—but the English commons, except in this case, did not affect such finery.

---

[1] Bax, op. cit. 137–41. [2] Ibid. 141–2.
[3] L. and P. xi, 842; printed in St. P. i, 490.
[4] Bax, op. cit. 44, 108.

CHAPTER VII

THE INSURRECTION IN THE EAST RIDING

If the agitators of the Yorkshire and Lincolnshire risings had been working together for a general rising at Michaelmas, their plans were upset; for in the first place Yorkshire did not take up arms till a week after the appointed day; and secondly the Lincolnshire movement collapsed with such incredible swiftness. It began on Sunday 1 October, and by Wednesday the 18th it was over. But when Yorkshire did rise, events moved so fast that before the insurgents south of Trent had laid down their arms, the commons of the East Riding had entered York in triumph, and so widespread was the sympathy felt for their cause that they might almost be described as masters of the six northern counties. We will now return to the beginning of the month and trace the course of the rising of Yorkshire.

When the hunting-party at William Ellerker's house in Yorkswold broke up on 3 October, 1536[1], John and Christopher Aske rode to join Sir Ralph Ellerker the younger, who was with the King's commissioners of the subsidy at Hemingborough[2]. Robert Aske and several of his nephews, law students, turned south and crossed the Humber into Lincolnshire, ostensibly with no other purpose than returning straight to London for the term[3]. How they were "taken" and sworn by the commons has already been related. On Friday, 6 October, the day after his meeting with Moigne at Hambleton Hill, Robert Aske left his Lincolnshire company and crossed the Trent into Marshland. Here, and in Howdenshire, north of the Ouse, where Aughton lay, Aske was in his own country, among men ready and anxious to rise at his word. He was eagerly welcomed as a bearer of news from Lincolnshire, and at the mere

[1] L. and P. xii (1), 6; printed in full, Eng. Hist. Rev. v, 330 et seq.; see chap. iv.
[2] L. and P. xii (1), 1186.
[3] Ibid. 6, printed in full, Eng. Hist. Rev. v, 331.

sight of him the bells would have been rung, had he not prevented it. All through the insurrection the ringing of bells was the special sign of the rebels—the call to arms against the Government. To sound the alarm, generally by ringing the peal backwards, was to proclaim to all the surrounding country that the parish had risen. Aske advised the men of Marshland not to be the first to stir, but to wait till they heard the bells of Howdenshire. He then crossed the Ouse into Howden and bade the people there listen for the bells of Marshland before ringing their own; and so assured himself, in the simplest way, that the alarm would not be given without his own orders. His motive for this expedition was highly characteristic. He was determined to delay the Yorkshire rising till the answer to the Lincolnshire petitions was known[1]. The King might be inclined to make concessions after all, and Aske regarded rebellion as the last expedient, to be resorted to when everything else failed. But this delay, though doubtless it seemed best at the time, when the commons once let loose might have plunged into any excess, was certainly a mistake. As the two counties had failed to rise together, the sooner Yorkshire gave its full support to Lincolnshire the better. On the other hand, as confusion reigned in the Lincolnshire host, perhaps that brief pause on the brink of rebellion made little difference in the long run.

Aske rode on to Aughton, but finding his brothers were away with the King's commissioners, he turned back to Howden for the night. While he slept certain honest men of the town came to his bedside to tell him that Sir George Darcy "would take him if he tarried." Next day, 7 October, he set out for Lincoln, as rumour said that the King's answer had arrived there. Reaching the town on Saturday evening he found everything in confusion, owing to the mutual distrust of gentlemen and commons. Both parties, he was told, regarded his journey into Yorkshire as a desertion, and "if he tarried he should be slain either by the gentlemen or by the commons." On this warning he left the sign of the Angel, where he had put up, and spent the night in hiding with the host's brother, a priest. Early in the morning he finally turned his face northwards and rode to Burton-upon-Stather ferry. Trent was flooded by the heavy rain on Saturday[2], and he was unable to cross for two days. At length he crossed the Trent about midnight on Monday, 9 October. He had left Yorkshire on the verge of open

[1] L. and P. xii (1), 6; printed in full, Eng. Hist. Rev. v, 333.
[2] See above, chap. v.

revolt; before he returned the plunge was taken. Exactly how far he was responsible for it is one of the mysteries of the Pilgrimage.

At the first word of rising in Lincolnshire the anxiety of everyone responsible for the peace of Yorkshire became painful. Those who were honestly loyal to the King feared for their property and lives; a far larger number secretly sympathised with the rebels, but were too cautious to break with the Government until they were certain of being on the winning side; even those who entirely approved and who had (we suspect) been working for an outbreak, generally made an effort to preserve some appearance of loyalty at the last. The Archbishop of York, who in spite of all his protestations seems to have belonged to the waverers, heard the news at Cawood, his favourite residence[1]. Fearing that some of the "light heads in Yorkshire might be encouraged to do likewise," he wrote to Darcy at Templehurst, to Dr Magnus (a member of the King's Council), Sir George Lawson and the lord mayor of York; to Robert Crake and Sir Ralph Ellerker the younger, to "keep an eye on Beverley where there were some light heads"; he sent besides to Ripon, that in all these places the news might be published that the Earl of Shrewsbury had set forth against the insurgents[2]. Needless to point out, he was also spreading the news of revolt. Sir Ralph Ellerker already knew of the rising[3]; all the north bank of the Humber had been stirred by beacons lighted on the Lincolnshire side on Wednesday 4 October, the very night that Aske had been raising the river side[4], and Sir Ralph had reported the fact to Darcy next day.

Darcy despatched his son, Sir Arthur, to the King with news of the risings in Northumberland, Dent, Sedbergh and Wensleydale and the warning that "greater rebellions were to be feared."[5] He then left Templehurst, his family seat, for Pontefract Castle, as it was customary for the King's steward to repair to his post in time of unrest. The rumour, afterwards reported to the King, that he had fled there from the commons with only twelve horsemen was quite unfounded; as a matter of fact he was obliged to travel very slowly on account of his infirmity, for he was nearly eighty years old; he had as many men as he wished with him and every day more of the loyal gentlemen came in with their followers[6]. Nevertheless his position was anything but secure. Out of a garrison

[1] L. and P. xii (1), 1022.
[2] Ibid.
[3] L. and P. xi, 563.
[4] See chap. v.
[5] See chap. v.
[6] L. and P. xi, 760.

of 300 men hardly a hundred could be trusted if it came to a general rising[1]. The town of Pontefract, indeed all the county, favoured the rebels and hindered his efforts to buy provisions. York itself would certainly welcome any rebel force, if the King could not send troops to overawe the citizens[2]. Darcy had written to the King as early as 6 October for guns and powder[3], as even if victualled the castle was not in a state of defence. But the King had neither money nor arms to spare, and, preoccupied with the affairs of Lincolnshire, did not see fit to despatch either to Yorkshire. Moreover, Darcy's loyalty had long been under suspicion, and Henry probably thought that if things came to the worst it would be better to lose a doubtful supporter than to send arms to a possible rebel. The most single-hearted commander might have been daunted by the prospect, and Darcy had secretly avowed to the Imperial ambassador that his object in coming north was to organize a rebellion. But whatever his motives were he now strove to keep the country quiet. He believed (or at least professed to believe) that the gentlemen were ready to serve the King[4]. He postponed all "commissions, leets and other assemblies...till the King's pleasure is further known"; he issued soothing messages and proclamations, but in spite of the momentary success of these endeavours, on Sunday 8 October the whole of the East Riding flamed up like a pile of dried bracken, at the first spark of open sedition.

That spark was struck in Beverley. As John and Christopher Aske were returning home from Hemingborough on Saturday 7 October, they found "the people drawn out in the fields, awaiting the ringing of Howden great bell to advance." The brothers set out the same night and travelled along the Derwent staying the people[5]; they probably spent the night at Aughton and next day rode to Beverley and dined with Mr Babthorpe[6]; long before they left, the town was in commotion and the alarm bells ringing[7].

The special jurisdiction of Beverley had been abolished by the same act that swept away the privileges of Durham[8]. This the people bitterly resented; and they saw clearly that the days of their beloved St John were numbered. When news first came to Beverley

---

[1] L. and P. xii (1), 1022.
[2] L. and X. xi, 605.　　　　　　　　[3] Ibid. 563.　　　[4] Ibid. 605.
[5] L. and P. xii (1), 1186.　　　　　　[6] L. and P. xi, 841.
[7] L. and P. xii (1), 392; printed in full, J. C. Coxe, William Stapleton and the Pilgrimage of Grace (Trans. of the East Riding Antiq. Soc. x).
[8] See chap. i.

of the Lincolnshire rising, the people in the market began to talk of going to London "to have four docepyers (deceivers?) in the realm," and of bringing home the goods of Cheapside and the south. A gentleman was heard to say that the rebels might be sure of Holderness, where he dwelt; and on Saturday two canons arrived from Lincolnshire and put up at the Tabard Inn, where they spoke treasonable words[1]. No one could cross the Humber without a pass from the Lincolnshire rebels[2]. Either on Saturday or Sunday a letter had come to Robert Raffells "one of the twelve men (i.e. aldermen) of Beverley," purporting to come from Robert Aske, bidding every man of the town to swear to be true to God, the King and the Commonwealth, and to maintain Holy Church[3]. Raffells had kept this secret as long as he could[4], but on Sunday 8 October one Roger Kitchen heard of it and said "he would that day ring the common bell or die for it." An attempt was made to stop him, but too late; the bell was already calling the townsfolk to the market-place. Richard Wilson and Richard Newdyke commanded the burgesses to assemble at the Town Hall, where surrounded by an armed company they read the letter in the name of Robert Aske, and further proclaimed that every man was to take the oath on pain of death[5]. No one demurred, and the whole town was sworn. It was appointed that they should meet, fully armed, in the West Wood field at four o'clock[6].

Among the throng was one William Breyar, a sanctuary man, who was wandering about England in the Queen's livery, to which he seems to have had no special right; after being sworn with the rest he heard a man in the crowd say that Robert Aske and another gentleman had been to dinner at Mr Babthorpe's house; the bailly Stuard replied, "I marvel what Robert Aske doth with Mr Babthorpe, for he is a worshipful gentleman"; rather an ambiguous remark[7]. It was really the two elder Askes who were in Beverley; Robert was waiting with what patience he might at Burton-upon-Stather till the evening fell and the beacons on the north bank of Humber showed him that Yorkshire had not stayed for his coming. Whether or no he wrote the proclamation that raised the country it is hard to say, for he himself "utterly denied making or consenting to" it[8]. On

---

[1] L. and P. xi, 841.
[2] Ibid. 647; append. 10.   [3] L. and P. xii (1), 370; xi, 841.
[4] L. and P. xii (1), 370.   [5] Ibid. 392; printed in full, Coxe, op. cit.
[6] L. and P. xi, 841.   [7] Ibid.
[8] L. and P. xii (1), 6; printed in full, Eng. Hist. Rev. v, 333.

the whole, we incline to accept his word, but fortunately the question, though interesting, is of little importance. Whoever wrote this particular letter to Beverley, there is not the slightest doubt that Aske was from the first the chief leader in the East Riding. If we suppose this letter to have been " forged in his name " it proves him to have been admittedly the man with most influence.

The commons of Beverley duly assembled at four o'clock on West Wood Green, every man that was able with horse and harness; and a council was held for sending letters to allies and making plans for future movements[1]. William Woodmancy was despatched to Lincolnshire with the letter to the commons there under the town seal[2]. A summons was sent to York, probably at the same time, though the document is undated: "my lord mayor and all the commons" were asked to send word "against tomorrow night" to the White Lion at Newborough, whether they would allow the commons of Beverley "to pass through this the King's city with your favour or not, in case we so require."[3] The lord mayor, anxious not to quarrel with anyone, seems to have prudently refrained from sending any reply.

West Wood Green, where the commons met, was near the house of the Grey friars[4], where some visitors were staying,—Christopher Stapleton of Wighill, with his wife, his brother William, and his son Brian[5]. It is William Stapleton's long statement that gives many details of the rising of Beverley and the only full account of the siege of Hull. William had been about to go to London for the law term when the news of the Lincolnshire rising prevented him. When disturbances broke out in Beverley he felt that he could not leave Christopher "ever thinking that it should be slanderous to him to leave his said brother in that extremity, who for extreme fear, being so feeble and weak, neither able to flee nor make resistance, was like without great help to fall in sound (swoon), wherein the said William moved with natural pity, did comfort him, promising not to flee from him, and therein he took great comfort." Orders were given that all the household were to stay indoors, but as the crowds trooped past to West Wood Green, Mistress Stapleton "went forth and stood in a close where great numbers came of the other side of the hedge," and cried to them, "God's blessing have ye, and speed you well

---

[1] L. and P. xii (1), 392; printed in full, J. C. Coxe, op. cit.   [2] See chap. v.
[3] L. and P. xi, 628; printed by Russell, Kett's Rebellion, 33, n.
[4] L. and P. xii (1), 392.
[5] See above, chap. iii.

in your good purpose." They asked her why her husband and his servants did not come out to them, to which she replied, "They be in the Friars. Go pull them out by the heads." Her behaviour increased the "perplexity" of the unfortunate Christopher, who mildly remonstrated, "What do ye mean except ye would have me, my son and heir, and my brother cast away and mine heirs for ever disinherited?" The lady merely retorted that it was God's quarrel.

The commons now devoted themselves to revenging old grudges. An earnest supporter of the Archbishop of York in his recent dispute with the town was nearly killed; and "great quarrels were picked to Robert Raffells of the same part." After dark William Stapleton sent a servant to Christopher Sanderson, advising him to stay the commons if possible, and begging him in any case to show them that his brother was too impotent to help them, and to persuade them to spare him and his household on that account.

Next day, Monday the 9th, the commons assembled again at West Wood Green, and sent to young Sir Ralph Ellerker to ask him to join them. He offered to come and give them his advice if they would not require him to take the oath, for he was, he said, sworn to the King already; but they refused to exempt him. It then occurred to them that everyone in the town had taken the oath except the Stapletons at the Friary. Brother Bonaventure, the Observant friar[1], was among the people, and acted as a messenger between the house and the Green. He told William that the commons were threatening to burn the Friary and those in it if they would not join them, and "was very busy going between the wife of the said Christopher and the said wild people, oft laying scripture to maintain their purpose, noting the same to be goodly and specially to the said William." In the end they sent one or two honest men to take Christopher's oath in the house, and to bring out William and Brian. As soon as the commons saw them they rushed towards them crying, "with terrible shouts"—"Captains! Captains!" And when they had taken the oath the people cried, "Master William Stapleton shall be our captain," "which [he] thinketh came by reason of the said Observant in setting him forth with some praises to the said people or else they would never have been so earnest of him whom they did not know." Seeing how wild and dangerous the mob was, Stapleton thought the wisest thing he could do was to accept the leadership, and they made a bargain that if he would

---

[1] See above, chap. III.

be their captain they would obey his orders in everything not contrary to their oath.   He then stayed old grudges and moved them to proceed in this quarrel as brothers and not make spoil of any man's goods; and sent them home for the night.   Mistress Stapleton and Brother Bonaventure were very much pleased with the way things were going, and the friar went himself in harness with the commons.   As the host was breaking up, Roger Kitchen "came riding forth of town like a man distraught," crying, "As many as be true unto the commons follow me," and led out a party to raise the neighbouring country[1].   They went to fire Hunsley Beacon, but it was lying on the ground; however, they made fires of hedges and haystacks to spread the alarm[2].

The beacons set all the country in a "floughter" as far as they could be seen.   Aske saw them as he crossed the Trent at midnight, after all his weary hours of waiting.   He was in Marshland on the morning of Tuesday, 10 October, and there he found that the gentlemen had received orders from Sir Brian Hastings, the sheriff, to raise men for the King and join him at Nottingham.   Thereupon they called a meeting of the commons in the parish church, but suddenly the bells were rung backward there and in every church in Marshland.   Following Aske's former advice, the bells of Howdenshire answered from their steeples across the Ouse; by nightfall the whole countryside had taken up arms[3].   Aske now wrote and published his first proclamation—the first, that is, which he acknowledged as his own, and the earliest extant.   It is undated, but there is little doubt that it was published during the rising of Marshland on 10 October[4] :—

"Masters, all men to be redie to morow and this nighte and in the mornyng to ryng yor bellis in every towne and to assemble your selfs upon Skypwithe moure and thare apoynte your captayns Master Hussye, Master Babthorp and Master Gascoygne and other gentilmen, and to yeff (*give*) warnyng to all be yonde the watter to be redy upon payn of dethe for the comen Walthe; and make your proclymacion every man to be trewe to the kyngs issue, and the noble blode, and preserve the churche of god frome spolyng; and to be trewe to the comens and ther welthis; and ye shall have to morowe the statutes and causis of your assemble and peticion to the kyng, and place of oure meting and all other of pour (? *word illegible*) and comen welthe in haste; By me Robt. ask cheiff captayn of Marches lande, th' ile and howden shyre Thomas Methm Robt aske yonger. Thomas Saltmerche Wyllm Monketon Master ffranke Master cawood captayns of the same."

---

[1] See map no. 3.   [2] L. and P. xii (1), 392; printed in full, J. C. Coxe, op. cit.
[3] L. and P. xii (1), 6; printed in full, Eng. Hist. Rev. v, 334.
[4] L. and P. xi, 622. Copied from original at R. O.

This was Robert Aske's first assumption of authority; it is interesting to note his title. The Isle is the Isle of Axholme, between the Trent and the Don (as it then was). Marshland, Yorks., was the triangle of country between the Don and the Ouse which formed part of the West Riding. The county boundary still more or less follows the course of the river now removed. So Aske was first made captain of three wapentakes, one in Lincolnshire, one in the West Riding, one in the East, each separated from its neighbour by a great river. As to the other captains, Robert Aske the younger was doubtless Robert's nephew, John's son and heir, a wild young law student. William Monketon, his brother-in-law, was his constant companion all through the stirring months that followed. Saltmarsh and Franke will both reappear hereafter.

At nightfall Aske went to a poor man's house to hide from his followers and get a little sleep, but his place of retreat was discovered and a bodyguard of enthusiastic volunteers burst in and escorted him over the water into Howdenshire, where the commons were clamouring for his presence. No one was thinking of sleep here; a large company of commons were at the house of Sir Thomas Metham, knight, whom they had taken out of his bed the night before to be their captain. Not being in sympathy with the rebels he had fled at the first opportunity, and they were now threatening to burn down his house. Aske exerted his influence to save it, and soon persuaded them to return quietly to their beds for what remained of the night. There was to be a general muster of the Howdenshire men at Ringstanhirst next morning, corresponding to that of the commons of Marshland on Skipwith Moor. Sir Thomas Metham's son and heir became one of Aske's petty captains, perhaps out of gratitude for the saving of his inheritance[1].

Others of high rank were also threatened. The commons of Wressell had risen with the rest of the countryside and cried at the gates of the Earl of Northumberland's Castle, "Thousands for a Percy!"[2] The Earl's health had been failing ever since the execution of Anne Boleyn, and his last illness was already upon him. He had good reason to believe in the King's power, and he was little inclined to take the part of his tenants, who hated him heartily enough, but cared little what he did, once they were convinced he was powerless to act against them. Judging from their cry, they hoped one of his brothers was with him; but Sir Thomas was at

---

[1] L. and P. xii (1), 6; printed in full, Eng. Hist. Rev. v, 334.

[2] L. and P. xii (1), 393; printed in full, De Fonblanque, op. cit. i, chap. ix.

Seamer in the North Riding, the home of the Dowager Countess, and Sir Ingram was in Northumberland. After the first general excitement the invalid Earl was left in comparative peace for a while, though a watch was kept on his movements and correspondence.

John and Christopher Aske had stolen away from Beverley on Sunday 8 Oct. without taking the oath, for Christopher afterwards declared that they were prepared to be "hewn into gobbets" rather than "distain" their allegiance. On Monday they were at Aughton in "great heaviness," for Christopher was in charge of over £100 of the Earl of Cumberland's revenues. The danger of having so large a sum while the country was in such commotion was obvious. After being twice roused from their beds by false alarms on Monday night, the brothers resolved to risk their trust on the road rather than in the heart of the disturbance. They set out at once for Skipton Castle in Craven, forty miles away, where their cousin the Earl was then lying. They rode separately, and Christopher, going first, arrived safely at Skipton in due course[1]. He fell in with Breyar, the sanctuary man, at Tadcaster. This shady individual had also "stolen away" from Beverley, and was now on his way to Cawood. Once there, he hastened to the Archbishop's palace, and, passing himself off as a servant of the King as was his wont, he informed Lee of the events at Beverley[2]. The Archbishop had already been disturbed by rumours of stirrings in the East Riding[3]; Breyar told him that the men of Beverley, particularly the leaders, Wilson and Kitchen, were threatening to march on Cawood and kill him; Lee answered resignedly that he knew it and intended to flee to Lord Darcy at Pontefract, for he was afraid of his own neighbours and tenants. He gave the "pretended King's servant" a horse and twenty shillings to carry a letter to the King[4]. But no sooner was one messenger despatched than another hastened in with the news that the commons of Marshland said they were coming to take the Archbishop for their captain. This seems to have alarmed him even more than the first report. Robert Crake, Mr Babthorpe and other loyalists also arrived from Beverley; and, fearing to be surprised at any moment, the Archbishop determined to set out at once for some place of safety. Pontefract Castle was hardly ten miles off; Lord Darcy was there, and Dr Magnus from York had taken refuge with him. Scarborough, the only alternative, was three times as far off and the country between was rising if not already up.

---

[1] L. and P. xii (1), 1186.   [2] L. and P. xi, 841.
[3] L. and P. xii (1), 1022.   [4] L. and P. xi, 841.

It was natural that Lee and his companions should choose the former place. Darcy allowed the Archbishop thirty servants and with these he took up his abode at Pontefract on Tuesday the 10th, charging those he left behind to "keep out of the commons hands."[1] His tenants rose the same day and captured John Aske, together with Sir Thomas Metham and Portington of Lincolnshire, at Cawood ferry; but John Aske "escaped strangely and took him unto the woods,"[2] being delivered with the other two by Lee's steward and helped by him to pass "over the water out of danger." Next day this man was himself taken by the commons of Selby, Wistow, and Cawood, but he had little difficulty in redeeming himself with money[3].

In Beverley the chief business on Tuesday the 10th was bringing in the neighbouring districts. During the usual muster on West Wood Green messengers came from Newbald and Cottingham, which had been roused by the beacons, saying these villages were willing to follow Beverley's lead and advance with it. The commons were anxious to go forward at once, but Stapleton and the other captains thought it better to wait for the answer to their message to Lincolnshire, which was eagerly expected. William Stapleton chose for his petty captains his nephew Brian, Richard Wharton and the bailiff; the commons agreed to "proceed to no act" without consent of one of these; he made every effort to prevent "spoilings," "for he would never have the name of a captain of thieves." Christopher Sanderson was sent to ask old Sir Ralph Ellerker to come next day and use his influence in the town to prevent outrage[4]. On this day a certain friar and limitor of St Robert's of Knaresborough first makes his appearance. His name was Robert Esch or Ashton, and he had lived at Beverley for some time[5]. Zealous in the cause of the monasteries and popular among the people from whom he begged, he appointed himself, as did other brethren of the same house, a kind of general secretary to the insurgents, attaching himself to no particular chief, but spreading the rumours and the rebels' proclamations up and down the country[6]. At his request Stapleton gave him a "passport" to travel North, where he promised to "raise all Rydale and Pickering Lythe."[7]

On Wednesday, the 11th, after the usual muster, the gentlemen breakfasted at Sanderson's house and held a private council with

---

[1] L. and P. xii (1), 1022.   [2] Ibid. 1186.   [3] Ibid. 1022.
[4] Ibid. 392; printed in full, Coxe, op. cit.
[5] L. and P. xii (1), 1021.   [6] Ibid. 370, 1018.   [7] Ibid. 392.

old Sir Ralph Ellerker, Sir John Milner, and others, who had not taken the oath. While they were at table a letter came from North Cave wishing to know when they should go forward. The gentlemen would not consent to move until news came from Lincolnshire. If we are to believe Stapleton this was a mere excuse to keep the host quiet. After "long persuasions" they carried their point, and orders were sent to the surrounding villages that no advance was to be made until special orders were issued under the Beverley town seal. But at length William Woodmancy was seen riding hard for the town, with the welcome news that messengers from the Lincolnshire host were close at hand, "by whom they had sent their whole mind." Guy Kyme, Antony Curtis and Thomas Donne were these long-expected messengers and were brought before the company assembled on the Green. Sir Ralph advised the gentlemen to hear the letters and credence apart, but the commons insisted that all should be done openly. They hardly wronged their leaders by their suspicion, for "some honest men" had been secretly sent to Hessle to intercept the message "so as to amend it if necessary in opening it to the commons," though they started too late to carry out their intention. Kyme delivered a letter to Sir Ralph[1]; its brief contents and his lengthy credence have already been described[2]. Such cheerful tidings naturally raised the enthusiasm of the people to the highest point. They "counted themselves half ashamed to be so far behind them" of Lincolnshire. The gentlemen were obliged to resign all hopes of further stay. Stapleton allowed old Sir Ralph to depart unsworn to his home, though the commons wanted to keep him by force.

This day John Hallam rode in from Yorkswold seeking news[3]. He was only a yeoman, the owner of the Calkhill farm not far from Watton Priory, but his influence among his neighbours was as great as that of any gentleman. The respect in which he was held seems rather to have been owing to his own fearless and determined character than to any superiority in riches. The general disaffection had already shown itself in his countryside. On Sunday the parish priest of Watton did not announce St Wilfrid's Day, 12 October, and Hallam demanded, before all the congregation, why it was left out, "for it was wont always to be a holyday here." The priest replied that the king had forbidden the keeping of that and other feasts. When mass was over the whole parish was talking of

---

[1] L. and P. xii (1), 392; printed in full, Coxe, op. cit.
[2] See chap. v.   [3] L. and P. xii (1), 201, pp. 89–90.

nothing else; they declared they would never give up their holy-days, and the passing over of St Wilfrid, a north-country saint and an archbishop, was probably regarded as a special slight on Yorkshire. Later in the day the country was further disturbed by the news of the rising in Beverley. Hallam came to the town on Wednesday, and went to the house of John Crow. Here he found a great number of people drinking and discussing the rebellion, with Guy Kyme, Thomas Donne and Woodmancy in the midst of them. The Lincolnshire men described the two hosts of Horncastle and Louth "with six knights in each," and repeated all the rumours concerning the taking away of church jewels and the throwing of five parishes into one. Nobody disbelieved them, for these things seemed hardly more monstrous than the suppression of the abbeys. The Lincoln-shire articles were passing from hand to hand, everyone being anxious to see them and secure a copy[1]. Kyme was asked what they did with suppressed monasteries; he answered "nothing"; and how their men were provided for, to which he answered that those who could afford it went at their own cost and poor men were helped[2]. Kyme suggested that the men of Beverley should go and aid the Lincolnshire hosts against the King's troops. Hallam was sworn by one of the leaders; and he was given a bill summoning the men of Watton to appear at Hunsley on St Wilfrid's Day and take the same part as the men of Lincolnshire. Hallam carried it home, but found his neighbours already warned and willing to attend the muster. Copies of this bill were sent to Cottingham, Hessle and all the townships round; every man was to be at Hunsley Beacon at nine next morning with horse and harness; and that night the beacons were fired at Hunsley and Tranby on Humber side, so that all the country might understand. The summonses were written out by a friar of St Robert's of Knaresborough; as Robert Ashton had left for Rydale this must have been another of this zealous community. They had all the effect that was in-tended. "From that time forward no man could keep his servant at plough, but every man that could bear a staff went forward towards Hunsley."[3] Antony Curtis dined with Stapleton, and after the meal said he must go on into Holderness (the region, roughly speaking, between Hull and the sea) which was not yet up[4].

The whole country met at Hunsley Beacon on the morning of Thursday, 12 October, St Wilfrid's Day. The Lincolnshire articles

---

[1] L. and P. xii (1), 201, p. 90.   [2] L. and P. xi, 828 (xii).
[3] L. and P. xii (1), 201, p. 90.   [4] Ibid. 392; printed in full, Coxe, op. cit.

were read again for the sake of the outlying villages which had now come in for the first time. Guy Kyme estimated the men gathered there at about three thousand. Certain persons were sent to take Smythely, "a man of law dwelling at Brantingham," and among them was his great enemy, Hugh Clitheroe by name. They found Smythely sick in bed, and contented themselves with taking his oath; he sent back with them his clerk, "horsed and harnessed, with many fair words." Some thought that his illness and goodwill were equally feigned, and when Guy Kyme related how Master Skipwith, serjeant-at-arms, was carried in a cart with the Lincolnshire host, they proposed to bring the unfortunate Smythely in the same way. Stapleton dissuaded them from this barbarity. A curious incident now occurred. Stapleton was informed that a great treasure of the King's, the spoils of the monasteries of Ferriby and Haltemprice lay in Beckwith's house at South Cave. "To please the people and save the goods" Stapleton selected certain honest persons, keeping light persons away as much as possible, and rode to the house. He found it in charge of a woman, apparently alone. But after some parleying she admitted that the priest who had the chests in his keeping was hidden in the house. Some swashbucklers had just been there, threatening to spoil the goods and slay the priest, and he wanted no more visitors of the same kidney. But finding Stapleton's party did no active damage he came forth "quivering and shaking for fear." The captain asked him "what treasure was in the two great iron chests"; he replied, "Nothing but evidences." Stapleton remarked to his companions "that it was like to be so, yet it was like to have been plate," and turning again to the priest "bade him be merry, for he should have no harm, and set forth meat if he had any." The priest made them what cheer he could, and begged that they would protect him. Stapleton gave orders that proclamation should be made "at the church style, that no man should meddle with any goods there on pain of death"; anyone who did so was to be brought before him. The grateful priest thereupon produced a letter showing that the chests contained only papers. We cannot help wishing that Stapleton's curiosity had led him to investigate a little further[1].

While he was away on this mission important news had arrived from Aske. He was now at the head of the full forces of Howden-shire, and marching that night to Wighton on the direct road to York. He suggested that the men of Beverley and the surrounding

---

[1] L. and P. XII (1), 392; printed in full, Coxe, op. cit.

country should muster "in the morning at Wighton Hill that he might see us and he would muster on another hill of the other hand of Wighton that we might see him and his company." Guy Kyme and Thomas Donne "much rejoicing thereat, saying they would not unto Lincolnshire with their finger in their mouths, but they would tarry and see our musters and the raising of the countries so that they might be able to declare the same to their host by their own sight and not by hearsay; for they supposed that Antony Curtis had gone over to show their host how far they had gone." They were probably mistaken in this last opinion, and the news which arrived immediately afterwards that "all Holderness was up to the sea side" was a better guide to his real whereabouts[1]. The bells were rung and the countryfolk assembled at Nuttles on this day; the vicar of Preston helped to administer the oath. Holderness was a very large wapentake, and each of the three divisions chose its own head captain—the Middle bailiwick chose Ric. Tenant, the North bailiwick Wm. Barker, and the South bailiwick Wm. Ombler[2]. But though they had their own captains they were not slack in bringing in the gentlemen. They took Sir Christopher Hilliard, one Grinston, one Clifton, a lawyer of Gray's Inn "whom they hurt in the taking," Ralph Constable, John Wright and others. Many gentlemen of Holderness and the surrounding country had fled to Hull, the principal being Sir John Constable and his son, Sir William Constable, young Sir Ralph Ellerker, Edward Roos, Walter Clifton, son of the wounded man, Philip Miffin and John Hedge, the King's servant. They were preparing to defend the town for the King, but, as many thought, against the will of the mayor and citizens.

Evening was falling when these tidings reached Beverley, but four messengers, including Richard Wharton and Wilson, were despatched at once "to know of the mayor and aldermen of Hull if they would do as we did or be against us"; their answer was to be sent next day to Wighton Hill. After holding a council the mayor sent word that he would appoint as the men of Beverley did, but would send a fuller answer next day[3].

Before relating the circumstances of the great muster on Friday, it will be as well to go back and examine the incidents of the rising in Marshland. After the busy night of Tuesday, Robert Aske found an equally busy day before him on Wednesday, 11 Oct. He first attended the muster of Howdenshire at Ringstanhirst as he was on

---

[1] L. and P. xii (1), 392; printed in full, Coxe, op. cit.
[2] L. and P. xii (1), 201, p. 94.   [3] Ibid. 392.

the north bank of the Ouse, and while he was there messengers arrived from Marshland requesting his presence at their muster on Hooke Moor, near Whitgift[1]. He crossed to that town, and there encountered two serving-men who had just brought the Lincolnshire articles to the house of one Walkington, and were reading them to the people. One of these men was in a popinjay green coat, and as this was Lord Darcy's colour Aske assumed that he "belonged" to that nobleman; there is no further evidence that he did. The other was dressed in orange-tawny colour; and they were both describing the musters in Lincolnshire and the numbers of the host[2]. The articles were taken up to the Moor and read to the assembly. Four of them were:

(1) For redress of Abbeys suppressed.

(2) Repeal of the Statute of Uses.

(3) Punishment of divers bishops, especially the bishop of Lincoln.

(4) Release of quindene or tax.

There was another, probably for the putting down of base blood in the King's Council. Aske had not before seen the articles actually written; they were sent "under the hands of divers worshipful men of Lincolnshire into Yorkshire."[3] The messengers could not have been those who appeared at Beverley the same day, for even if Aske did not know Kyme or Donne, and his "cousin" Antony Curtis had not yet joined them, they would have been sure to tell him their mission and he could not have mistaken one of them for a servant of Darcy.

On Thursday 12 Oct. the whole countryside mustered at Howden, and, with the church cross borne before them like a banner, began their march to York. Before starting they sent the messengers to Beverley to arrange the meeting of the two hosts. Wighton was their halting place for the night[4].

Accordingly, on Friday 13 Oct., Beverley marched to meet their neighbours at Wighton Hill. The mayor of Hull had sent the promised messengers, Brown and Harrison who had been sheriffs, Kensey and one Sawl. According to their promise they "made offer of their town by commandment of the mayor and aldermen of the same, with as gentle words as they could speak." But there were some doubts as to the good faith of this friendliness,

[1] L. and P. XII (1), 6; printed in full, Eng. Hist. Rev. v, 334.   [2] Ibid. 852 (ii).
[3] Ibid. 6.   [4] Ibid.

and Guy Kyme significantly described "the extremities they of
Lincolnshire showed towards those who fled from them in spoiling
their goods." All the East Riding was moving towards Wighton;
among others came Robt. Hotham (who brought in a company from
his master the Earl of Westmorland's lands in Yorkswold), James
Constable of the Cliffe, Philip Waldeby, "Lygerd of Hullshire,"[1]
and John Hallam, who had not been idle but had "stirred up all
Watton, Hutton Cranswick and the country between that and
Driffield and was ringleader of them all."[2] George Bawne, who
seems to have been a leader from the North Riding, brought word
that Sir George Conyers, Ralph Evers, Tristram Teshe, Copindale
and others had fled to Scarborough; Sir Ralph Evers, the younger,
was the keeper of the castle and was expected to hold out for the
King; Bawne declared his determination to win it "or hasard his
life."[3] When the muster was complete and the whole host stood in
array on the hill above Wighton, Aske gives their numbers as nine
thousand horse and foot, but then he calls them "Holderness and
Yorkswold"; the main body of Holderness had not yet come up,
so this was probably a good deal above the mark[4].

Stapleton with a party of gentlemen, his petty captains and
the messengers from Lincolnshire and Hull, set forward down the
hill towards Wighton to carry their tidings to the host of Howdenshire. Before they reached the town they met Aske with the two
Rudstons and young Metham coming to speak with them[5]. The
two captains had last seen each other in London the term before[6].
Aske told Stapleton how he had been taken by the commons in
Lincolnshire, and listened eagerly to the news from Beverley and
Hull[7]. He asked Kyme and Donne if they had brought any letter
for him, but their only message was to Beverley, and he was
disappointed to find that they knew no more of the progress of
events in Lincolnshire than he did himself. They then asked
leave to depart, intending to cross the Humber that night at the
tide. Aske "bade them God be with them, saying they were
pilgrims and had a pilgrimage gate to go." This is the first reference to the beautiful name, "the Pilgrimage of Grace," given by the
insurgents to their protest in favour of the old religion[8].

---

[1] L. and P. xii (1), 392; printed in full, Coxe, op. cit.
[2] L. and P. xii (1), 201, p. 85.   [3] Ibid. 392.
[4] Ibid. 6; printed in full, Eng. Hist. Rev. v, 334.
[5] L. and P. xii (1), 392.
[6] Ibid. 901 (28); printed in full, Eng. Hist. Rev. v, 560.
[7] L. and P. xii (1), 392.   [8] L. and P. xi, 828 (xii).

At Aske's request the two Stapletons, Philip Waldeby and Robt. Hotham were elected by the Beverley leaders to represent their company and form with Aske's little party a head council. The friendly messages from Hull were regarded with the greatest suspicion, and in case they proved a mere blind it was determined that Aske's host should advance alone on York, while Stapleton himself, with Robert Hotham to represent the men of Yorkswold, and young Metham and Nicholas Rudston for Howden, should ride down to Hull at once, and make arrangements with the mayor for its formal occupation. The Beverley host was to muster again next morning at Wighton Hill, and be ready either to advance on York or turn back and lay siege to Hull; in either case word was to be sent on immediately to Aske. Once the plan of campaign was settled there was no delay. The men of Howden turned their faces towards York, and lay that night at Shipton. Three of the messengers from Hull were kept as pledges for the safe return of Stapleton's party, who took the fourth, Sawl, with them. This precaution shows they had little hope of a favourable reception.

On arriving in Hull they sent Sawl to the mayor to demand an interview. He returned with the answer that the mayor could not speak with them that night, though he had consulted with the aldermen before sending this reply; "which we liked not," adds Stapleton. Early next morning they were asked to go to speak with "the gentlemen that were fled" in the church. Here the situation was discussed with no little heat[1]. Rudston, Aske's petty captain, who is distinguished from his numerous relations by the epithet "with a perle in his eye,"[2] was chief spokesman for the Pilgrims. He tried to persuade the loyalists to come over to the popular cause. But his efforts were vain, and after a long argument old Sir John Constable declared he would rather die than join them, saying "he had rather die with honesty than live with shame." Apparently no one could cap this beautiful sentiment, and "after long communication," all withdrew to breakfast[3]. After this the messengers were requested to return to the church, where they were formally received by the mayor and aldermen, though the loyal gentlemen were also there. They demanded that the men of the town should be sworn and join the host "with harness, money or ordnance," as the messengers sent from Hull to Wighton had

[1] L. and P. xii (1), 392; printed in full, Coxe, op. cit.
[2] L. and P. xi, 818.
[3] L. and P. xii (1), 392.

promised in the mayor's name[1]. The mayor and aldermen denied any responsibility for the message; "they would keep their town as the King's town," they said. They would allow all who wished to join the rebels full liberty to depart, but such a person should have neither horse, harness, meat nor money provided for him. Young Sir Ralph Ellerker further offered to carry any articles they wished to send to the King, "and either he would do our message truly or else (we might) strike off the heads of Ralph, his son and heir, and Thomas his brother whom we had amongst us, but in no wise he would agree to come in to us." The rest of his party were of the same mind[2].

Stapleton and his companions were in haste to go back to Wighton, but considerable delay was caused by the mayor's anxiety for his "untrue messengers." He refused to let the Beverley captains go without ample security for the safe return of these men, who were indeed in some danger. At length Stapleton and his companions were obliged to swear that they would return to the town and give themselves up if the messengers did not reach home safely before nightfall. When at last they arrived at Wighton "all the country was looking for" them. So great was the excitement that they hastily despatched the false messengers back to Hull "and made them good countenance" before daring to announce that their protestations of friendship had been merely lies to gain time, and that Hull was prepared to hold out. Young Metham was sent forward to carry the news to Aske. We can imagine with what a mixture of indignation and fierce pleasure the men of Beverley heard that their neighbouring enemies were determined to resist them.

The next news that reached Wighton was that the men of Holderness had come to Beverley, and their captains, chief of whom was Sir Christopher Hilliard, had advanced as far as Bishop Burton, where they waited to take council with the Beverley captains. Stapleton with his friends left the company drawn up in array to wait his return, while he arranged with the Holderness leaders how to dispose their men about Hull. They decided to hold a general muster at Wynd Oak near Cottingham at nine o'clock next morning. Rudston returned to the Beverley men at Wighton Hill to give out these orders; he was greeted with general indignation. The commons, weary and irritated with standing to arms all day on the same spot, wanted to know why Stapleton sent and did not come

[1] L. and P. xi, 818.   [2] L. and P. xii (1), 392; printed in full, Coxe, op. cit.

himself? Rudston was a Howden man; where were their own captains? The old suspicions broke out. "The gentlemen," they muttered, "counselled too much and would betray them." So they dispersed grumbling.

Stapleton and his companions had meanwhile ridden straight to Beverley, where they found three hundred Holderness men mustering on West Wood Green under their three captains, Barker, Tenant and Ombler. They were probably obliged to camp there for the night.

As the Beverley men were on the way to Wynd Oak next morning, Stapleton called them together and reproached them with their "unkindness" and suspicions of the night before. They had been pleased to choose him to command them, he said, though he was only a stranger; he thanked them for that, and he had worked harder than any man among them; but now, as they were dissatisfied let them make another captain, and whoever it was he would obey him willingly. The commons had slept off their illhumour, and this appeal had the natural effect. "We will have none other captain," they cried, "and whosoever after speak against the captain, the rest to strike him down." Nor would they hear of anyone else for all Stapleton could say. Seeing his authority much strengthened for the moment, he gave orders "for every man to pay honestly" for what he took. They then advanced to the trystingplace near Cottingham, a village about two miles north-west of Hull. It was agreed that part of the host should follow Aske to York, while the rest besieged Hull. The Stapletons wanted to go with the former, because, as they explained, neither they nor their servants had any defensive armour with them; all their harness was at Wighill beyond York. But the Beverley men would by no means consent to this; if their captains went they would go too. So it was finally agreed that Rudston should follow Aske with the men of Yorkswold, reported to be two thousand strong, and Stapleton should stay and direct the siege, unharnessed as he was. When Rudston had marched, two wapentakes, one being Holderness and the other Hullshire with Beverley and Cottingham, which were all in the same wapentake, though mustered separately under different commanders, remained to surround Hull.

Barker and Tenant with their two hundred horse and all the Holderness footmen were stationed on the east, from the Humber along Hull water; Stapleton with the men of Beverley was on the other side of the water, at Sculcotes on the north of the town;

next him on the west was Thomas Ellerker with the company from Cottingham, and "at Hull Armitage by Humber side" lay Sir Christopher Hilliard and all Hullshire, and with him Ombler and one hundred Holderness horse. The city was thus completely beleaguered on three sides, the fourth being defended by the wide expanse of the Humber, over which the usual traffic had ceased to ply for some days past. Feeling ran high in the Pilgrims' camp; for Hull, comparatively an upstart town, had monopolised Beverley's ancient trade and claimed the sole right to navigate Hull river. Now it seemed a day of vengeance had come. The shipping, the pride and wealth of the town, offered a particularly tempting mark. It was said that a single barrel of burning tar floated down the river on the ebb tide would destroy every ship lying there. Even surer ways might be found. "Certain men of the...water towns" came to Stapleton and offered "to burn all the ships in Hull haven and thereby to burn all that part of the town." He "warned them in any wise seeing it was a high policy not to disclose the same, for if they did, the same should be prevented by policy, but the truth was if it had been opened it had not lain with him to have saved the town." Some windmills stood without the walls near the Beverley gate and Stapleton was at no little pains to save them. He protested that "notwithstanding this great business he trusted both we should have our reasonable requests and the King's highness retake us to his mercy"; and if all went well there was bound to come a day of reckoning for property destroyed.

Stapleton's list of the spoils that did occur is quaint reading. His headquarters at Sculcotes were a house belonging to the mayor of Hull, and here his men made free with some hay and grass for their horses. They also discovered and devoted to their own use a crane, a peacock, a "cade lame" (whatever that may be) and several young swine. The mayor evidently kept a good larder, unless the crane and the peacock were family pets. The commons captured, besides, seventy-five head of oxen, belonging to the Archbishop's brother, which seem to have been considered fair game for some forgotten reason; and Stapleton took ten or eleven wethers which were being driven in to the besieged, but returned them to the owner on the capitulation. It was for everyone's good that stealing should be put down. Some "honest men" told Stapleton that his orders were being disobeyed and begged that the offenders might be punished, "else they should be robbed themselves." Watch was set and two men were taken red-handed, one of whom "had been put in trust to keep their victuals," while the other was "a naughty fellow, a sanctuary man of Beverley and a common picker. Whereupon the whole company made exclamation" and Stapleton caused the two to be taken, and made them believe they should die. A friar was sent to confess them, and they were brought out before all men to the waterside. "The sanctuary man was tied by the middle with a rope to the end of the boat and so hauled over the water, and several times put down with an oar over the head." The other man was a householder of more respectable character, and at the intercession of his friends was reprieved from his ducking; but both were banished from the host. This example put an end to "privy pickings."

Several people offered Stapleton money, but he always refused it; and lacking further evidence we must suppose that here, as in other places, the Pilgrims were provided with ready money by a voluntary tax levied in each township. Wealthy people sometimes gave money and food, and unpopular people ransomed themselves. The Prior of Ferriby distributed twenty nobles among the commons, who wanted him to go with them, as the price of being left in peace. The Priory of Ferriby seems to have been the only suppressed house with which Stapleton interfered, and it was an especially hard case. It was farmed from the King by Sir William Fairfax, though he had not yet removed the goods from it. He was "a man of fair possessions," but of miserly nature, and incurred the anger and disgust of all his neighbours, rich and poor; for he neither took up his residence in the priory nor made any attempt to carry on its ancient hospitality. The men of Swanland, in Ferriby parish, asked Stapleton to protect the valuables of the deserted house from their present owner, and he "bade them put two brothers of the same house to lie within it and to see nothing wasted...till...some way was taken with all the houses."[1]

On Tuesday, 17 October, Horncliff of Grimsby came from Lincolnshire with a letter and the news that the insurgents were dispersing. The commons cried that the letter was a forgery and the man a liar. He was seized and imprisoned. There is reason to believe that Antony Curtis, who had been so active in the first days of the rising, was with Horncliff. At any rate he suffered with him from the unjust if natural anger against bearers of ill-tidings[2].

---

[1] L. and P. xii (1), 392; printed in full, Coxe, op. cit.
[2] L. and P. xi, 1103.

The host despatched a letter to Lincolnshire by William Woodmancy, their first messenger, "wherein…was contained the unkindness of Lincolnshire to them who rose by their motions" in sending them no news. On their side they had plenty to tell, for posts had come in from other parts of Yorkshire. Aske sent word that he had taken York without fighting, and from the north came the news that Sir Thomas Percy had been taken. Shortly afterwards a servant of Percy's came with a message from his master to Sir Ralph Ellerker, "who would be much advised by him" and perhaps induced to join the Pilgrimage. Stapleton reluctantly let him through to Hull, for he came "without letter or passport"; and eventually sent him back to Sir Thomas with a remonstrance against his carelessness "in such extreme business." It does not appear if this man, who gave his name as James Aslaby, was a royal spy or not. Robert Ashton, the friar, returned from the north-west, saying that he had been at the rising of all Malton; that Richmondshire was in arms and Lord Latimer taken; and that he intended to go to the Forest of Knaresborough, but his money was all gone, and the horse he rode was borrowed from the Prior of Malton, for his own had been tired out[1]. He was provided with twenty shillings, and indefatigably set out again.

John Wright, a petty captain of Holderness under Ombler, had been to Hull to negotiate with Sir Ralph Ellerker, and brought word from him to Stapleton that he and Sir William Constable were willing to make terms for themselves. A meeting was arranged at nine o'clock on Wednesday morning at the Charterhouse without the town walls. Only a few of the Pilgrimage captains knew of the appointment and these chose Stapleton, one of the Holderness captains, and at Stapleton's desire, Marmaduke, one of Sir William Constable's own sons, to receive the two knights from Hull. On the morning of Wednesday, 18 October, the meeting in the Charterhouse took place. Sir Ralph Ellerker and Sir William Constable professed themselves willing to come in to the Pilgrims and "do as they did" provided they were neither obliged to take the oath nor to become captains. They intimated that many would come in from Hull on these terms. Stapleton and his fellows readily agreed to this proposal; but they were very doubtful as to how the commons would take it; the men of Holderness were particularly unruly and might refuse consent to anything but an unconditional surrender.

---

[1] L. and P. XII (1), 392; printed in full, Coxe, op. cit.

The captains were summoned and sent to announce to their companies that anyone coming from the town was to be received peaceably and allowed to join their ranks unsworn. To Stapleton's relief the commons were " well pleased " with the arrangement.

Next day, Thursday, 19 October, Sir Ralph again met Stapleton and told him that if Sir John Constable left the town, the mayor and aldermen would certainly yield; let the captain allow Constable to pass secretly through the rebel lines and make his escape, and the town would soon be his. Stapleton was too much a man of honour to listen to this insidious proposal. He replied that he was stationed there to force the gentlemen in the town to join the Pilgrimage and no one should escape with his aid; though if Sir John could get through by himself " God be with him." At this point of their deliberations something chanced which hastened the fall of the town.

On receiving news of Aske's unopposed entry into York, Stapleton had written to him for reinforcements, and in answer to this Rudston now made his appearance on the west of Beverley, near the Hermitage, with four or five hundred men in battle array about to make an attack. His appearance surprised everyone. Sir Ralph Ellerker asked Stapleton " if he knew and could stay them ? " Stapleton thought he could and rode off to speak to the leaders. But the threatened assault had ended the burghers' indecision. Eland and Knolles, two of the aldermen, were sent to yield the town to the Pilgrims. Rudston, meeting no resistance, and no doubt seeing the royal colours flutter down, " lodged his men about and came himself to the Charterhouse to hear the offer of the men of Hull." When he and Stapleton reached the hall they found Sir John Constable and the other loyal gentlemen there before them. The single condition of the surrender was that no one in the town was to be forced to take the Pilgrims' oath. It was mutually agreed that no troops should enter the town till next day because at such a late hour it would be difficult to prevent spoiling. " And that night Sir Ralph Ellerker and Rudston lay together at the Charterhouse."[1]

It chanced on that very day Richard Cromwell in Lincoln was writing to his uncle about the defence of Hull. The letter is so full of details about the state of Lincolnshire, and the sympathy shown there for the insurgents beyond the Humber, that we give it in full :—

---

[1] L. and P. xii (1), 392.

"Master Richard Cromwell to My Lord (Privy Seal)

"Please it your Lordship to be advertised that this daye we have newes that ther is up aboute hull in nomber aboute VI thousand persons intending to wynne the same which if they cannot do woll set fire of it. In which town Sir Rauf Ellerker doth lye to defend the same. And he and his company be nere hand famyshed how be it my lorde's grace hath sent oon of Mr Tyrwitte's sonnes with vitayle gunne powder and such other necessarys (?) as they nede to defende them selfe unto such tyme as they shall have better socore. And these traytors have sent hither into dyvers places within this shyre for ayde desyring them to come and they woll so provyde (?) that they shall have thar own desyres of any gentlemen or other what so ever he be within this shyre. But as yet we here of none in these partes that do assemble but all still. And the moost part of the gentlemen here be come in and do come in hourely and many of them sworne promysing [to] take those that have begon this busyness and treason. And where as the kinge's highness perchaunse thinketh some slakness in my lorde's grace and other how for that they procede not with no greater force against thyse Rebells here, In my poore opynyon if his grace with other of his moost honourable counsail were present here [he] wold do non other then is done considering how busy they are in other parts and also fynding the people here so holow which had rather in manner dye then one to utter another. And how glad they wold be if they might to go to thother Rebells in yorkshire. So that as yet no cruelty may be showed but all wrought with wysdom and delibrate policye. And though it hath pleased his hyhness to say that they were afrayde of their shadows. In faith to advertise your lordship of the treuth I never sawe gentlemen forwarder then they have been and is in this mater nor take greter paynes day and night than they do to devise and Imagyn which way they may best wynne and come by these malefactors and the originalls thereof for surely if they shuld take but ii of them cruelly all the rest (ad id affisand) be so hollowe that they wold to them in yorkshire straight. Ther is but a water betwen and they may in on night go a thousand or more. So that they may niether take their harness away from them nor yet hinder them any thing roughly. But furst wynne them and after knowe the originalles and fynally use them according to their deserts. And doubt ye not but your lordship shall hereafter right well perceyve and knowe that the surmyse that hath been put in his grace's hed is not true. And for that I perceyve my lord's grace and thother of his highness counsoul here be somwhat amased for bicause his highness shuld upon any synyster and untrue report judge that they have not done their duety in this case as I take god to record they have to my poore Judgement, as much as possible is for men. I most humbly besech your good lordship to obtayne the king's moost honorable letters unto them with some comfortable and loving words to encourage them agayn and to avoyde their dolour. Not doubting but herafter his highness shall right well perceyve and prove that they have done thair duetyes and have not been negligent in no case or else let me dye for it. Please it you to be advertised that this day your servants mylysent and bellowe be comen hither unto me who saith that your servant mamby's father was one of the procurors of this treason, wherefor it shall be

well don that ye detayne your said servant ther with you not suffering hym
to depart as yet in to these parts and thus I besech almighty god long to
preserve your lordship in honour. At Lincolne this thursday at VI of the
clock in the after noon.

> "Yo^r humble nephew most bounden
> "(signed)　　Rch. Crumwell."[1]

The King's displeasure with Suffolk and his council was merely
his usual method of getting the greatest possible service out of his
servants by mingling suspicion and threats with favour and fair
promises. The guns and provisions which Suffolk sent to Hull
must have fallen into the Pilgrims' hands. As to the hollowness
of the people and their sympathy with the Yorkshire rebels, that
was only to be expected. Among the Pilgrims, on the contrary,
prevailed a feeling of anger and contempt against Lincolnshire.
After so much talk it seemed ridiculous that the earlier rising
should be ignominiously ended and that without other agency
than the threats of a blazon-coated herald and the blare of his
trumpet; surely there had never been such a fall since the days
of Jericho. And it made a very material difference in the chances
of the rising. Lincolnshire in arms might easily have encouraged
the other midland counties to rise. The royal forces might have
been cut off from their base, surrounded and crushed. But with the
example of Lincolnshire before them and a royal army in their midst
the midlands would hardly venture to show their feelings unless
a decisive victory was won. In fact the northern counties were
obliged to depend on themselves alone; there was no longer the
slightest hope of the movement spreading from shire to shire through
all the land. Tremendous as this idea seems to be, it was certainly
what the Pilgrims expected at first, and, what is more to the point,
it was what the King feared. Strong and cunning as Henry was,
even he might have failed if the men of Lincolnshire had stood by
the men of the north.

On Friday, 20 October, Eland, Knolles and John Thorneton
opened the gates of Hull to the captains of the Pilgrimage, the
terms of the treaty being duly observed on both sides. A council
was held at Hunsley Beacon, the two aldermen representing Hull.
There was no longer any doubt about the dispersal of the Lincolnshire rebels and the advance of Suffolk to Lincoln. The council at
Hunsley decided to draw up their articles and send them to the
Duke by the hands of four captains, one from each company. But

---

[1] L. and P. xi, 789; copied from the original at the R. O.

before they were fairly written out, a post rode in from Pontefract with word from Aske that the "Lord Steward was about to give him battle." This message must have been despatched on the receipt of some false intelligence, for Shrewsbury was, as a matter of fact, in no position to encounter the Pilgrims; but it checked Stapleton's more peaceful plans. He considered it impossible for any men from Hull to reach Pontefract in time to help Aske. But he ordered all his host to muster at Hunsley at seven o'clock next day to follow up Aske's advance, and he quartered a garrison of two hundred Holderness men in Hull. Sir Ralph Ellerker kept the beacon for that night, though he was only to fire it in case of urgent need[1]. The irony of events, so triumphant when news travelled slowly, decreed that the King should write thanking Sir Ralph Ellerker for his gallant defence of Hull on the day after it was occupied by the Pilgrims[2].

---

[1] L. and P. xi (1), 392; printed in full, Coxe, op. cit.
[2] L. and P. xi, 819 and 820.

CHAPTER VIII

THE PILGRIMS' ADVANCE

Hull did not fall until 20 October 1536, but its siege was merely an incident in the Yorkshire rising. We must go back to 13 October to follow the main course of the insurrection, the advance of the Pilgrims under Aske to York. Before describing this, it will be convenient to take a general survey of the disturbed counties and to note the attitude of those in authority. All through the week the King's commanders were too much occupied with Lincolnshire to realise how much more serious was the trouble in Yorkshire. The news of the rising there does not seem to have reached Shrewsbury's camp at Nottingham until Thursday, 12 October[1]. Lord Darcy and Sir Brian Hastings, the sheriff, were left for a week without instructions or aid to cope with the flowing tide of insurrection as best they might.

On Tuesday, 10 October, Lord Darcy, at Pontefract, heard of the summons sent from Beverley to York, and wrote to the lord mayor of York "as a man of substance, having the rule of the second city of the realm." He informed the mayor that the commons of the East Riding were likely to "invade" York and try to seize the King's treasure. The mayor must put the citizens in readiness to resist the rebels and must summon the gentlemen of the Ainstey to his aid. He need have no fear in opposing the rebels, as, though "men of high experience in war," they had no artillery nor ordnance[2].

At the same time Darcy sent his son Sir George into Marshland to capture Aske; that night Sir George "laid in wait and would have taken him if he had kept the appointments he made with gentlemen to lie in their houses."[3] Nevertheless Aske escaped.

---

[1] L. and P. xi, 658, 672.   [2] Ibid. 627.
[3] Ibid. 1086; see above, chap. vii.

Sir Brian Hastings wrote to Darcy on 10 October from Hatfield, where he was lying with 300 men. The rebels of Howdenshire and Marshland intended to march on York and he advised Darcy to send a force at once "to overawe their faction in that city." Meanwhile he would join Darcy and they might together intercept the rebels on the march and cut them off from York[1]. In a letter to Fitzwilliam dated the next day (Wednesday 11 October) Hastings said that "though the common people murmur" he was keeping "Hatfield, Doncaster and all other places under your rule in good order"; but the people of "all the north are so confederated that they will not be stayed without great policy." He thought that the men who were serving the King should have wages[2].

Darcy answered Sir Brian's letter of the 10th on Wednesday 11 October. He wrote that he knew the extent of the rising and was "putting all the gentlemen within my room in readiness at an hour's warning, when I shall know the King's pleasure." But neither the King nor the Lord Steward (Shrewsbury) had answered his letters. "If you have any certainty from above let me share it."[3]

Darcy was kept well informed about the spread of the movement not only in Yorkshire but in the neighbouring counties. He had many friends who favoured the rebels and acted as spies for him. Darcy used their information just as it suited him at the moment, sometimes sending it on to the King, sometimes keeping it for private ends. About the time that he received Sir Brian Hastings' letter, full of sturdy loyalty, two other letters arrived, one from Lancashire, the other from Wakefield, which, though they contained nothing positively treasonable, were in tone a marked contrast to Sir Brian's. The first was from Thomas Stanley, a priest, who was a kinsman and follower of the Earl of Derby. He reported that the people of Lancashire "say those that are up are for the maintenance of church and faith and they will not strike against them." There had been some local disturbances, but the Earl of Derby "attends the King's command." The writer concluded "your lordship may trust the bearer; he is a tall man if need be."[4] The second letter was from Thomas Gryce, Darcy's steward at Wakefield. He described the general discontent in the country and the sympathy felt for the rebels. The commissioners were afraid to sit lest their meeting should prove a signal for a general rising, and weapons were being sent from York, some of them to the Earl of Derby[5].

---

[1] L. and P. xi, 646.   [2] Ibid. 663.   [3] Ibid. 664.
[4] Ibid. 635; see below, chap. ix.   [5] L. and P. xi, 678; see below, chap. ix.

The Earl was believed to favour the rebels' cause, but, after some wavering, he declared for the King.

Another of Darcy's informants was Thomas Maunsell, the vicar of Brayton. Maunsell had been in Howdenshire on Tuesday 10 October, where he was captured by the commons and accused of being a spy of Sir George Darcy; this was probably in connection with the attempt to seize Aske. It is curious that Darcy should have known from the very beginning of the rising that Aske was the leading spirit; perhaps he owed both this and his minute knowledge of the captain's movements to Maunsell. The vicar was released on Wednesday morning after taking an oath to attend the muster on Skipwith Moor[1]. He went first to Sir George Darcy and then to Lord Darcy at Pontefract, who bade him attend the muster and bring a report of it next day. He returned on Thursday 12 October with the news that the "commons intended to come over the water to Darcy's house (Templehurst) and the (Arch)-bishop's" (Cawood). Darcy told him to go home to Brayton, and if the Howdenshire men "did press to come over the water" (the Ouse) he was to raise all the people on Darcy's lands, for, if the commons on the south-west bank of the Ouse were up, the Howden-shire men would have no motive for crossing, and there would be less likelihood of damage to property. "Darcy said he would thus do the King service."

On Friday 13 October twenty-four men came over the Ouse from Howden to persuade the West Riding to take part with the rest of the county. The parts about Brayton, that is the whole west bank of the Ouse from Cawood to Templehurst, were very willing. The Howden men first "raised the town" (Brayton or Selby) and the vicar promised to do the rest. On Sunday 15 October he was at the head of all the force in "Darcy's room."[2]

Meanwhile not only the Archbishop and Archdeacon Magnus[3] but many gentlemen who found their tenants out of hand fled to Pontefract Castle to escape the rebels. Sir Robert Constable had captured "Philypis a captain of the commons in Lincolnshire," and had taken him to the lords at Nottingham. He was ordered to return home and pacify the east coast if possible, but if the insurrection had gone too far for conciliation, he must turn back to Pontefract and put himself under Darcy's orders. Finding that all the East

---

[1] See above, chap. VII.

[2] L. and P. XI, 1402; see note A at end of chapter.

[3] See above, chap. VII.

Riding was up, Constable went to Pontefract, where he found his friend in a desperate state[1].

On Friday 13 October Darcy answered Henry's gushing letter of thanks[2] with a long expostulation. He said that the King thanked him more than he deserved, but only partially answered his previous letters. The King made no reference to Darcy's repeated appeals for ordnance and money. All the East Riding, part of the West, and nearly all the North, were now up, "in effect all the commons of Yorkshire; and the city of York favours them." The host of the East Riding was advancing on York to seize the King's treasure, and though Darcy had written to the lord mayor to "look to the safety of the city" the people were said to be "lightly disposed." The loyal gentlemen "cannot trust any but their household servants." The Lancashire commons were "of the same mind as the others," and were buying arms. Darcy expected the rebels to visit him shortly, and there was "not one gun in Pontefract Castle ready to shoot. There is no powder, arrows and bows are few and bad, money and gunners none, the well, the bridge, houses of office etc. for defence, much out of frame." This is the refrain of the letter— send money and "in any wise haste to the laying of posts," or the messengers will be cut off[3].

On the very same day Henry was writing severely to Darcy. He marvelled that the unlawful assemblies were not yet put down. He had written to the gentlemen of Yorkshire to muster their forces, and Sir Arthur Darcy, if Darcy himself was too feeble to take the field, was "to repress the traitors as he hopes to be reported a loyal servant."[4] It is easy to imagine the irritation this letter must have caused at Pontefract. It was all very well for the King to marvel, but raising men was not only useless but dangerous, for, though they often only refused to attend the musters, or stole away to the rebels, if a considerable force was collected they would probably desert in a body, and carry their leaders captive to the host of the Pilgrims. General orders were easy to send, but when they were accompanied by neither money nor particular instructions, it was impossible to carry them out. Perhaps if Darcy had taken entire command of the situation without orders, and had spent unstintingly all the money he had left after keeping his garrison of thirteen score men entirely at his own expense[5], something more might have been

[1] L. and P. xii (1), 1225.   [2] See above, chap. vi.
[3] L. and P. xi, 692; see note B at end of chapter.
[4] Ibid. 687.   [5] Ibid. 1086.

achieved or at least attempted. For instance, about 14 October the men of Wakefield declared themselves ready to follow Sir Richard Tempest on the King's part, but Thomas Tempest, who informed his father, Sir Richard, of the fact, added that if the rebels arrived first Wakefield would join them, and they were within ten miles of the town[1]. Sir Richard wrote to Darcy, offering to come to him at Pontefract, but Darcy replied that he had no orders, and that Tempest would be of more use at Wakefield[2].

On Friday, 13 October, Shrewsbury and the other lords at Nottingham sent Darcy the following letter:

"My very god lorde in our right hartie maner we comende us unto you signyfying unto the same that we sent oon Lancaster the kingis harraude of armys unto the rebellious in Lincoln shire with a proclamacion, the copie whereof we sende unto you hereinclosed. And upon the hering thereof they were contented to departe home to their houses, albeit they stayed and taried upon annswere frome my lorde of suffolke; and as sone as they here frome hym we think they woll right gladly repayre home unto their houses according unto the tenore purport and true meanyng of the said proclamacion without any let or stay to the contrary. Also whereas the said rebellious had comfort oute of yorkshire, for ayde and assistance of those there, Insomyche as they have knowledged divers to have come over the watirs of Humber owis and Trent they have nowe promysed to staye the botis there, so that none shall come over, but be glad to retorn again homewards like foolis. And if they dooo come the said rebellious here will (as they affirme) be redy to fyght against them as they mynd themselves (*illegible*) the Kingis true and faithful subiectis." (*About eight lines at the end are mutilated and illegible.*)[3]

There is no sign in this letter that Shrewsbury distrusted Darcy, but according to Sir Henry Saville, when Sir Arthur Darcy was in Shrewsbury's camp[4], the Earl asked how many men Darcy could raise. Sir Arthur replied, five thousand "if the abbeys might stand." This aroused suspicions of Darcy's loyalty, though the words applied more to the disposition of the country than to Darcy's private views. Shrewsbury bade Sir Arthur, "Go and bid your father stay his country, or I will turn my back upon yonder traitors and my face upon them."[5]

Rumour whispered that when Darcy first heard of the rising in Lincolnshire, he said "Ah, they are up in Lincolnshire. God speed them well. I would they had done this three years ago, for the world should have been the better for it."[6] If this was really his opinion, he would not be very well pleased with the news of the

---

[1] L. and P. xi, 702. [2] Ibid. 695.

[3] Ibid. 694; copied from the original at the R. O. [4] See above, chap. vi.

[5] L. and P. xii (1), 783. [6] Ibid. 1087 (p. 497); see note C at end of chapter.

rebels' collapse, but his feelings are not recorded. One of his spies informed him on 14 October that the Lincolnshire host had dispersed, but the writer gave no hint as to whether the news would be thought good or bad[1]. If, as seems probable, Darcy had not yet determined which side to take, the failure of the Lincolnshire rebels would incline him to loyalty.

Darcy's letter of 13 October arrived in London on the 15th, and as anxiety about Lincolnshire was almost over, some notice was at last taken of the Yorkshire trouble. The King wrote to Shrewsbury ordering him to turn his face towards Yorkshire. If he considered his force sufficient to strike "without danger to our honour," he was to "give them (the rebels) a buffet with all diligence and extremity." If he could not venture on this alone, he must wait for the Duke of Norfolk, who was at Ampthill, and a joint commission of lieutenancy would be sent to Norfolk and Shrewsbury to go north together[2]. "This matter hangeth like a fever, one day good, another bad," wrote Wriothesley from Windsor to Cromwell in London[3]. The news must have been doubly unwelcome because when the Lincolnshire revolt collapsed the government had believed the trouble was over.

On the same day (15 October) the gentlemen in Pontefract Castle wrote to the lords at Nottingham that, following their advice, they were lying still; indeed they doubted if they could move with safety, as the commons were before York with 20,000 men, and the country round was rapidly taking up arms. However, they relied on certain gentlemen, their fellows and friends, who were ready to come to the aid of Pontefract with their servants at an hour's warning. The rebels, "notwithstanding your proclamation," were expected at Pontefract on Tuesday 17 October, and, as the King had taken no notice of Darcy's letters about the weakness of the castle, its defenders were in extreme danger unless speedy succour were sent. They had heard that terms had been made with the men of Lincolnshire, and they begged that the same might be offered to the Yorkshire rebels, as there was even more need of such comfort here. In a postscript they sent news of the rising of Durham[4].

It was immediately after the despatch of this appeal that the King's letter of the 13th arrived. Next morning (16 October) Darcy wrote to Shrewsbury with a bitterness easy to understand. The King had sent him letters missive to the neighbouring

---

[1] L. and P. xi, 706.
[2] Ibid. 715.
[3] Ibid. 723; printed in full, St. P. i, 468.
[4] L. and P. xi, 729; see below, chap. ix.

gentlemen which he had forwarded, but he doubted if they could be delivered without falling into the rebels' hands. The King commanded him to "stay or distress the commons who are up in the north and commit the heads to sure ward," but it was totally out of his power to enter upon any such extensive operations. He had succeeded in checking the rising in his own neighbourhood for fourteen days, and had prevented the rebels from joining the Lincolnshire men, but now their forces in the north and west had increased so much that it passed his power to meddle with them, for he was without weapons or money. He dated his letter from "the King's strong castle of Pontefract, even the most simply furnished that ever I think was any to defend."[1]

While Shrewsbury was waiting for orders at Nottingham and Darcy was appealing for help at Pontefract, there was nothing to oppose the advance of the Pilgrims.

On Saturday 14 October Aske's host reached the Derwent, and seized the bridges of Kexby and Sutton. A rumour had reached them that Sir Oswald Wolsthrope and the lord mayor of York had raised the gentlemen of the Ainstey and the burgesses of the city, and that they were about to pull down the bridges and hold the river bank against the rebels; but no such drastic steps had been taken, and the host crossed unmolested at their leisure. Aske wrote to Stapleton after the crossing to inform him of their progress, and to ask for a written copy of the Lincolnshire articles, as he wished to explain by an open proclamation why he "raised the country between the rivers of Ouse and Derwent." Stapleton, however, was unable to satisfy his desire, as the articles brought by Kyme had disappeared, and no other written copy could be found among the host at Hull[2].

The Pilgrims were rapidly appoaching York, where the authorities had neither the will nor the power to stand a siege for the King. The mayor and Sir George Lawson, the treasurer of Berwick who lived at York, wrote to Henry describing the force "assembled to enter the city contrary to their allegiance."[3] Richard Bowyer, a burgess of York and "the King's sworn servant," had acted as a messenger between Darcy and the lords at Nottingham. He brought the King's letters missive of 13 October from Pontefract to William Harrington, the lord mayor of York, and Sir George Lawson, killing a horse on the way. On receiving these orders to put the town into

[1] L. and P. xi, 739.   [2] L. and P. xii (1), 392; printed in full, Coxe, op. cit.
[3] L. and P. xi, 749.

a state of defence, they "determined to send for the gentlemen of the Ainstey to come and help keep the city after the old custom. Captains were appointed to every ward and bar." Bowyer was captain of Botham Bar, and put on his white coat with the red cross of St George back and front[1]. But the burgesses took no great interest in the matter, and the common people, inflamed partly by literature from the busy pens of the friars of Knaresborough, partly by the flight of the Archbishop, had declared for the Pilgrims as early as Wednesday 11 October[2].

On Sunday 15 October the rebel host held a great muster at the very gates of the city. They were believed to be 20,000 strong, and were arrayed in good order, the men of every wapentake forming a separate company which carried as its ensign a cross from one of its parish churches[3]. The horsemen were four or five thousand strong[4], and consisted chiefly of gentlemen with their servants, and of well-to-do yeomen and burgesses. They were therefore better armed and better disciplined than the foot soldiers. All the neighbouring districts had been summoned to join the army at York as soon as possible, and men poured in hourly[5].

From his position before the gates Aske despatched three petty captains and a messenger with a summons to the lord mayor and aldermen to give the Pilgrims a "free passage through the city at their peril."[6] Aske's second proclamation was probably sent with the summons. It was certainly written about this time and circulated all through the country. It ran as follows:

"Lordes, knyghtes, maisters, kynnesmen, and frendes. We perceyve that you be infurmyd that thys assemble or pylgrymage that we, by the favour and mercy of allmyghty god, do entend to procede in is by cause the kynge oure soveragne lord hathe had many imposicyons of us; we dowte not but ye do rizte well knowe that to oure power we have ben all weys redy in paymentes and pryces to hys hyghnes as eny of hys subgettes; and therfor to asserteyne you of the cause of thys oure assemble and pylgrymage is thys. For as muche that shuche symple and evyll dysposyd persones, beynge of the kynges cownsell, hathe nott onely ensensyd hys grace with many and sundry new invencyons, whyche be contrary (to) the faythe of God and honour to the kynges mayeste and the comyn welthe of thys realme, and thereby entendythe to destroy the churche of England and the mynysters of the same as ye do well knowe as well as we: but also the seyd counsell hathe spoylyd and robbid, and farthyr entendynge utterly to spoyle and robbe, the hole body

---

[1] L. and P. XII (1), 306.
[2] Ibid. 1018.
[3] L. and P. XI, 729.
[4] L. and P. XII (1), 1018.
[5] L. and P. XI, 729.
[6] L. and P. XII (1), 6; printed in full, Eng. Hist. Rev. v, 331.

of thys realme and that as well you as us, yffe God of hys infynyte mercye had not causyd shuche as hathe taken, or hereafter shall tacke thys pylgrymage uppon theym, to procede in the same, and whethyr all thys aforeseyde be trewe or not we put it to youre concynes; and yff none thyncke it be trewe, and do fyght agaynst us that entendythe the comyn welthe of this realme and no thynge elles, we truste, with the grace of God, ye shall have smale spede; for thys pylgrymage we have taken hyt for the preservacyon of crystes churche, of thys realme of england, the kynge our soverayne lord, the nobylytie and comyns of the same, and to the entent to macke petycion to the kynges highnes for the reformacyon of that whyche is amysse within thys hys realme and for the punnyshement of the herytykes and subverters of the lawes; and we nother for money malys dysplesure to noo persons but shuche as be not worthy to remayne nyghe abowte the kynge oure soverayne lordes persone. And furthur you knowe, yff you shall obtayne, as we truste in God you shall nott, ye put bothe us and you and youre heyres and oures in bondage for ever; and further, ye are sure of entensyon of Crystes churche curse, and we clere oute of the same; and yff we overcum you, then you shalbe in oure wylles. Wherfore, for a conclusyon, yff ye wyll not cum on with us for reformacyon of the premyssis, we certyfy you by thys oure wrytynge that we wyll fyght and dye agaynst both you and all those that shalbe abowte towardes to stope us in the seyd pylgremage; and God shalbe juge whych shall have hys grace and mercy theryn; and then you shalbe jugyd hereafter to be shedders of crystyn blode, and destroers of your evyne crystens (*i.e. equal Christians*). from Robert Aske chefe capytayne off the conventyall assembly on pylgrymage for the same, barony and comynality of the same."[1]

With the summons Aske sent a promise that if the burgesses would admit his army " in so doing they should not find themselves grieved, but that they should truly be paid for all such things as they (the rebels) took there."[2]

The details of the city's surrender have not been preserved. Aske, who was as careful to put the most loyal complexion on the actions of other people as on his own, said that being " neither fortified with artillary nor gunpowder the same city was contented to receive them."[3] The lord mayor yielded at once to Aske's summons, but the entry of the Pilgrims was postponed until the next day. Aske now sent to the mayor a copy of the Pilgrims' Articles. According to Bowyer his messenger was " a Lincolnshire fellow,"[4] but as Stapleton had been unable to send the Lincolnshire articles, it is probable that Aske drew up a version of his own for the occasion. The document has been preserved and bears the endorsement of the lord mayor, Harrington. The handwriting is

---

[1] L. and P. xi, 705 (3); copied from the original at the R. O., T. R. Misc. Bk. 118, p. 41 ; St. P. i, 466.

[2] L. and P. xii (1), 6; printed in full, Eng. Hist. Rev. v, 334.

[3] Ibid.　　　　　　　　　　[4] L. and P. xii (1), 306.

very bad, probably because the writer was on horseback, and the document is so much faded and defaced that it is in parts illegible, but the general drift of it is clear. It is a mixture of a list of grievances and a petition to the King, some of the articles being cast in one form and others in the other:

(1) By the suppression of so many religious houses the service of God is not well performed and the poor are unrelieved.

(2) We humbly beseech your grace that the act of uses may be suppressed, because it restrains the liberty of the people in the declaration of their wills concerning their lands, as well in payment of their debts, doing the King service, and helping their children.

(3) The tax or "quindezine" payable next year is leviable of sheep and cattle; but the sheep and cattle of your subjects near "the said shire" (Yorkshire) are now at this instant time in manner utterly decayed. The people will be obliged to pay 4*d*. for a beast and 12*d*. for twenty sheep, which will be an importunate charge, considering their poverty and losses these two years past.

(4) The King takes of his Council, and has about him, persons of low birth and small reputation, who have procured these things for their advantage, whom we suspect to be lord Cromwell and Sir Richard Riche, Chancellor of the Augmentations.

(5) There are bishops of the King's late promotion who have subverted the faith of Christ, viz. the bishops of Canterbury, Rochester, Worcester, Salisbury, St David's and Dublin. We think that the beginning of all this trouble was the bishop of Lincoln[1].

The demands of the rebels will be discussed at length hereafter, but as these are the first Yorkshire articles, a few comments may be made on them. The first article was really the root of the whole matter; Aske invariably declared that the religious troubles alone would have caused the insurrection. As to the second it was of much less importance, and he thought that if it had not been in the petitions of Lincolnshire, it would not have been remembered. The third article is rather difficult to understand, but it seems to be a protest against the basis on which the subsidy was assessed. The fourth and fifth are closely allied to the first. The people blamed Cromwell and the heretic bishops for the suppression of the abbeys and all the other unpopular measures. The protest against " base blood " was made chiefly on account of the mere chance that several of the unpopular ministers happened to be men of low birth. It is not necessarily a sign of aristocratic influence. No one resents the success of an upstart more than members of the class from which he sprang, and besides this, the people connected the rise in rents with

---

[1] L. and P. xi, 705; see note D at end of chapter.

the acquisition of lands by the new families, though the old families had for the most part become fully as grasping as their neighbours. As to the bishops, they had consented to the divorce of Queen Katharine, the separation from Rome, and the dissolution of the monasteries, while in the opinion of the conservatives they should have protested against all these measures. Several of them were also personally unpopular and were suspected of favouring the New Learning. These were the articles which the commons of Yorkshire were determined to lay at the King's feet with a humble prayer for redress, and if they "could not so obtain, to get them reformed by sword and battle."[1]

On Sunday night Aske's host encamped before York. On Monday 16 October the Pilgrims entered the city. The morning was spent in making arrangements for their peaceful entry. A proclamation was issued that there must be no spoiling, and that everything must be paid for honestly. It was determined that the soldiers should pay 2*d.* a meal, and the prices of food and horsemeat were declared both to the host and to the citizens[2]. As a precaution against disorder, no footmen were allowed to enter the city, because they were poorer and less easy to control than the horsemen[3].

At five o'clock in the afternoon Aske at the head of four or five thousand horsemen entered the city in state[4]. The rebel cavalry rode through the streets to the Cathedral square. It was "about evensong"; the Minster doors were thrown open and a long procession came forth—all the ecclesiastics attached to the Cathedral in full vestments and due order, from the Treasurer of the See of York to the smallest chorister. The Treasurer, at the head, welcomed the captain of the faithful commons who came to defend Christ's Holy Church, and solemnly led him up the aisle of the great Cathedral to the High Altar "where he made his oblation."[5] The early darkness of mid-autumn must have been falling when Aske came out after the service. He stopped to post on the Minster door an order for religious houses suppressed:

"The religious persons to enter into their houses again and view all the goods there or elsewhere, and thereupon a bill made and indented, the one party to be kept by the cedant; And there to do divine service as the King's bedemen to such times our petition be granted; And to have both victuals, corn and

---

[1] L. and P. xii (1), 901 (21); printed in full, Eng. Hist. Rev. v, 551 et seq.

[2] L. and P. xii (1), 306.

[3] Ibid. 6; printed in full, Eng. Hist. Rev. v, 334.

[4] L. and P. xi, 759.   [5] L. and P. xii (1), 1018.

all other things necessary of the farmers by bill indented, or else record what they take during the time of our Pilgrimage and the time they do divine service of God.   And we trust in God, that we shall have the right intent of our prayer granted of our most dread sovereign lord, plenteously and mercifully. And that no person nor persons do move no farmer nor alienate nor take away any manner of goods of the aforesaid houses, upon pain of death.

By all the whole consent of all the herdmen
of this our Pilgrimage of Grace."[1]

Aske's account of the order is—"First, that the prior and convent should enter into their monasteries suppressed and by bill indented view how much goods were there remaining which before were theirs, and to keep the one part and deliver the other part to the King's farmer, and to have necessary "victum and vestitum" of the delivery of the said farmer during the time of our petition to the King's highness, and to do divine service of God there, as the King's bedemen and women.   And in case the farmer refused this to do, then the said convent to take of the same goods, by the delivery of two indifferent neighbours, by bill indent, their necessaries for their living during the said time."[2]

Besides the great monastery of St Mary's there were many smaller religious communities in York, and while the great house escaped for the present, the others had fallen under the Act of Suppression.   There was general rejoicing among the citizens at the restoration of the religious to their homes, where they had been wont to serve God and succour the poor for so many long centuries. "The commons would needs put them in," and followed them with cheering and torchlight to the doors from which they had been cast out not many months before.   Wilfred Holme describes the scene in his peculiar manner:

> "To the Abbeys suppressed the people they restaurate,
> Rudent incessantly, with clamour excessive,
> Faith and commonwealth, and in the way obviate
> They were with procession and ringing insaciate,
> And the Sacrament Christes body called Eucharistia,
> Was born by Prelates with the crucifix associate,
> With pipes, Drums, Tabrels and Fidlers alway."[3]

Wherever the religious were restored, "though it were never so late they sang matins the same night."[4]

---

[1] L. and P. xi, 784 (ii); printed in full, Correspondence of the 3rd Earl of Derby (Chetham Soc.), p. 51.

[2] L. and P. xii (1), 6; printed in full, Eng. Hist. Rev. v, 335.

[3] Wilfred Holme, The Downfall of Rebellion.   [4] L. and P. xi, 1319.

After leaving the Cathedral Aske went to the house of Sir George Lawson, who was his host, having no choice, as he was sick in bed[1]. Lawson was supposed to be loyal to the King, but it seems unlikely that his house should have been the headquarters of a rebel army[2], even for a few days, unless his sympathies were with the rebels.   Aske need not have gone there if he knew himself unwelcome, for he had many friends in York.

Robert Aske was now in command of an army of about 20,000 men[3], horse and foot, without arquebusses or guns, but efficiently equipped and armed with the ordinary weapons of the period.   He was in possession of the second city of the kingdom and in the heart of a friendly country.   Whatever may be the advantages of such a situation, leisure and sleep are not among them.   He had hardly reached his lodging before Maunsell, the vicar of Brayton and captain of the commons of Selby, came to speak with him; and he had not lain down to sleep when about midnight a messenger arrived from the lords at Pontefract in the person of Thomas Strangways, Lord Darcy's steward.

The vicar of Brayton, after raising most of the country between Selby and Pontefract, on Sunday received a summons to attend the muster before York next day.   He replied that his company was too small, and sent to Darcy for orders.   Strangways came to him from Pontefract and told him to lie at Bilborough with his company.   He was at this village on Monday afternoon, when he heard that his brother was in danger at York for refusing to take the Pilgrims' oath.   The vicar set out for the city with all speed, and managed to see Aske soon after he arrived.   He obtained leave to administer the oath to his brother himself, but that violent loyalist "on seeing him smote him and drove him from the house."   Nevertheless the vicar gave out that his brother had taken the oath and returned to his men at Bilborough.   There he found Strangways and another of Darcy's gentlemen in harness and on their way to York.   They ordered him to raise Pontefract, Wakefield, and the "towns towards Doncaster"; he rode forth on this mission and they pursued their way to York[4].   Darcy had given Strangways minute instructions as to his proceedings at York.   He was to obtain from Aske the Pilgrims' oath and the "articles of their griefs" for the members of the King's Council at Pontefract.   He was also to discover the strength of the rebels and the names of their leaders; finally " if he met any sure friend " he was " to get him to move the captain and commons to pass by Pontefract Castle, or else delay their coming. This to give time for succour to arrive."[1]

It must have been after midnight when Strangways reached York, but he went straight to Sir George Lawson's house and found the captain with his three followers Rudston, Monketon and Gervase Cawood. Strangways asked for a copy of the oath and articles in the name of his master. The captain answered that a nobleman of the King's Council was more likely to send a spy to discover their numbers than a true messenger to know their purposes. Darcy's carefully calculated policy of running with the hare and hunting with the hounds resulted, as usual, in suspicion on both sides. But whatever doubt there might be about Darcy, Strangways himself was at heart with the Pilgrims. He inquired " whether they would agree to a head captain if the articles pleased him ? "[2] and he must have described the unprepared state of the castle and the disaffection of the garrison, for Aske was well informed on these points[3]. It is probable that Strangways offered, in the name of the garrison, to yield the castle to the rebels, whatever attitude the gentlemen adopted. It was well known that the latter would be ready to enter upon the Pilgrimage if a sufficient show of force were made. Darcy would probably be the 'head captain' proposed by his steward. When this was the attitude of the confidential servant, the inference was that his lord's sympathies pointed in the same direction. Aske hastily wrote out " the oath of Lincolnshire," and sent it early next morning to Strangways[4], with orders that he was to leave the city at once, for a great muster was about to be held, and Aske was determined that no accurate account of his army should filter through to the King's headquarters[5].

On Tuesday 17 October, as soon as the city was awake, all the gentlemen in York who had joined the Pilgrimage assembled to take counsel with Aske's officers in obedience to the captain's summons. Sir Oswald Wolsthrope, a man of great influence in York, Plumpton, young Metham, and Saltmarsh were among the members of the council. They decided that each gentleman should go to his own friends in the Ainstey and offer them the oath. Those who accepted it were to come to York at the head of the men of their own district.

---

[1] L. and P. xi, 762.   [2] Ibid. 1402 ; xii (1), 852 (iii).

[3] L. and P. xii (1), 6 ; printed in full, Eng. Hist. Rev. v, 335.

[4] L. and P. xii (1), 852 (iii).   [5] L. and P. xi, 762.

Those who refused were to be given twenty-four hours' warning, and if at the end of that time they had not taken the oath, their goods would be seized. There was no need to call out the commons, as they had armed and mustered not only round York but " in all parts of Yorkshire and the Bishopric " (Durham)[1]. From Richmond came the news that the Earl of Westmorland, Lord Latimer, and Lord Lumley were at the head of the insurgents there[2].

Aske " made and devised the Oath...without any other man's advice," before this council, at which it was first issued[3]. It was administered to the gentlemen and was written down for the convenience of those who carried it about the country.

"The Oath of the Honourable Men
Ye shall not enter into this our Pilgrimage of Grace for the Commonwealth, but only for the love that ye do bear unto Almighty God his faith, and to Holy Church militant and the maintenance thereof, to the preservation of the King's person and his issue, to the purifying of the nobility, and to expulse all villein blood and evil councillors against the commonwealth from his Grace and his Privy Council of the same. And that ye shall not enter into our said Pilgrimage for no particular profit to your self, nor to do any displeasure to any private person, but by counsel of the commonwealth, nor slay nor murder for no envy, but in your hearts put away all fear and dread, and take afore you the Cross of Christ, and in your hearts His faith, the Restitution of the Church, the suppression of these Heretics and their opinions, by all the holy contents of this book."[4]

There is a loftiness in the call—a ring in the words that, even to-day, sets a calm Protestant heart beating to the tune of the Pilgrims' March. It is very different from the impressive vagueness of the Lincolnshire oath. The captain was anxious that the chief reason and aim of the rising should be made plain to all; though perhaps the first phrase, disclaiming any desire to shirk the citizen's duty of paying the taxes, expressed rather what the gentlemen ought to have felt than what they did feel. This oath and Aske's second proclamation were sent out to all parts of the northern counties. They were posted up in Wensleydale and Swaledale next day. Wherever they appeared, the people were prepared and expected them[5].

---

[1] L. and P. xii (1), 6 and 901 (28); printed in full, Eng. Hist. Rev. v, 336 and 560.
[2] See below chap. ix.   [3] L. and P. xii (1), 945 (68).
[4] L. and P. xi, 705 (4); printed in full, Correspondence of the 3rd Earl of Derby (Chetham Soc.), p. 50; Tierney, Dodd's Church Hist. of Eng. i, Append. no. xliii; Stowe, Chron. ann. 1536; Speed, Hist. of Gt Britain, Bk ix, chap. xxi.
[5] L. and P. xii (1), 1021, 1034.

Round York the gentlemen accepted the oath "very willingly when they were once taken and brought in."[1] Only a few refused it, and Aske gave strict orders against any violence being offered to these loyalists. Their houses and goods were not to be seized until the twenty-four hours of grace had fully elapsed, and then only by written authority under the hands of two of the council[2]. Generally the person to whom warning was given fled at once to friends, or to Skipton, Scarborough, or Newcastle, where the loyalists were holding out for the King[3]. Part of the goods of these obdurate ones seems to have gone to the general fund of the Pilgrimage, but most were simply distributed among those who were lucky enough to be on the spot. Aske did what he could to enforce his orders, sending all offenders against them to the siege of Hull, where Stapleton had discovered an effective method of dealing with "pickers."

On Tuesday Aske dined with Lancelot Colins, the Treasurer of York, who had received him in the Cathedral the night before. This dignitary's house was always open to the captains of the Pilgrimage, and they were welcome to break their fast, dine or sup with him during the whole time of the rising. He afterwards explained to the King that "for fear he made them what cheer he could," but he may be given credit for more whole-hearted hospitality than he could be expected to acknowledge afterwards. He admitted that he had given a good deal of money to Aske and other captains, but added the saving clause that it was only "that he might tarry at home."

Lancelot Colins gives several glimpses of life in York while the host was there. On Wednesday morning, 18 October, he heard that "certain gentlemen" were threatening to burn down his house simply because, among the arms on an ornamental tablet over his door, were those of Thomas Cromwell. Cromwell, of course, was not entitled by birth to bear arms, and the gentlemen bitterly resented his assumption of their privilege. Colins had the obnoxious tablet removed, but as the royal arms were also upon it, this simple action might be construed by his enemies into high treason[4]. Within the next few days, Colins was involved in the plundering of a house belonging to William Blytheman[5], who had been clerk to Legh and Layton during the visitation of the monasteries. He fled to Newcastle early in October[6]. Colins

---

[1] L. and P. xii (1), 945 (65).   [2] Ibid. 6, 945 (67).
[3] See below chap. ix.   [4] L. and P. xii (1), 1018.
[5] Ibid. 1264.   [6] L. and P. xi, 1372.

heard that Blytheman's country house had been gutted and hastened to his house in the city to see if he could save anything for the absent owner[1]. Rudston was in command of the spoiling party, and Colins secured some papers, the "best bed, a coat of plate, and what more God knows."[2] He restored most of these things on Blytheman's return home after the rising, and was thanked for his good offices[3].

While the main body of the Pilgrims lay at York, the vicar of Brayton was busy about Pontefract. He spent Monday night at Ferrybridge, and on Tuesday 17 October he made his way to Pontefract and ordered the mayor to raise the town. He then went to the Priory and received a message from Darcy, bidding him go on to "Wakefield and the towns towards Doncaster"; and another message from the Earl of Northumberland at Wressell, begging him "to come himself to take him, because he would be taken with no villeins." The vicar rode on towards Doncaster, passing through St Oswald's and Wakefield, which mustered at his summons. A mile out of Doncaster he was welcomed by six men (aldermen) who took the oath on the spot, and escorted him into the town, where the mayor and commons took the oath amidst much enthusiasm. "Never sheep ran faster in a morning out of their fold than they did to receive the said oath."[4] Another of Northumberland's servants met Maunsell here, and asked him to give the Earl a passport to go to Topcliff, as the Earl was "crazed" and could do no harm. In his deposition the vicar said that he granted the passport, but it is more probable that he refused it, for the Earl, though very anxious to go to Topcliff, remained at Wressell[5]. Maunsell returned to Ferrybridge on Tuesday night[6].

The garrison of Pontefract Castle had been cut off by the rising of the town on 17 October. The last messenger who contrived to go southwards was Sir Arthur Darcy, who carried his father's final remonstrance to the King. The "good old lord" bluntly declared that "we in the castle must in a few days either yield or lose our lives," and that there was "no liklihood of vanquishing the commons with any power here."[7]

The town of Pontefract had from the first refused to supply the castle with provisions, "after the vicar of Brayton came amongst

[1] L. and P. xii (1), 1018. [2] Ibid. 1264.
[3] Ibid. 1018. [4] L. and P. xi, 774.
[5] Ibid. 1402.
[6] See note A at end of chapter. [7] L. and P. xi, 760.

them they durst not[1];" but now the townsfolk captured all the supplies which were being sent in from other places[2], and kept such a close watch about the castle that Shrewsbury's messengers found it impossible to deliver the King's despatches[3].

All accounts of Darcy's conduct give evidence of a divided mind. He could not decide between the claims of loyalty to the Faith and to the King. "He practised much with the commons to know their intention, and often said if he had ordnance they should not have the castle while there was victual in it. Sometimes he would say he trusted to get the commons to pass by and that their grudge against the castle was due to Dr Magnus and the Archbishop." Before he was so closely beleaguered, he had received a message from Shrewsbury, which said that the royal troops were about to advance to Pontefract, and "Darcy seemed glad to hear it, and afterwards sorry when the Lord Steward (Shrewsbury) came not."[4] Perhaps, like the men of Wakefield, he was leaving the decision to chance, and was prepared to join the party which first came to his gates. Sir Brian Hastings, who still lay at Hatfield, trusting no one, not even his own forces, wrote to Shrewsbury at Nottingham on 17 October that Darcy would probably surrender, as the rebels had taken Pontefract Priory, and there were above 40,000 of them at York, their captains being "the worship of the whole shires from Doncaster to Newcastle," including Lords Latimer and Scrope, and only excepting the Earls of Cumberland and Westmorland[5]. The vicar of Brayton was of the same opinion as Sir Brian, and had good grounds for his belief, as on Wednesday 18 October, when he was at Pontefract, Strangways came to him and "showed him how to assault the castle if it were not given up." The vicar promptly set out for York, and was the first to bring news of the rising in Pontefract and Doncaster to the host there. On receiving his assurances that the castle could not possibly stand a siege[6], Aske proposed to march to Pontefract immediately, but there was some dissension in his council. Metham and Saltmarsh, "disdaining that he should be above them," opposed the intended advance. Aske, however, would not give way, but set out with only 300 men for Pontefract[7], where he found the company raised by Maunsell, of unknown numbers.

---

[1] L. and P. xii (1), 1022.   [2] L. and P. xi, 1086.
[3] Ibid. 774.   [4] L. and P. xii (1), 1022.
[5] L. and P. xi, 759.
[6] L. and P. xii (1), 852 (iii); L. and P. xi, 1402.
[7] L. and P. xii (1), 392; printed in full, Coxe, op. cit.

It is not certain when the rest of his forces followed him to Ponte-fract, perhaps not until after the castle was taken. This was the only occasion on which anyone disputed his dangerous pre-eminence with the grand captain.

As soon as Aske arrived at Pontefract, knowing that the soldiers in the castle favoured him, he sent a letter to the lords with a threat that, if they did not surrender, he would make an assault the same night. He rehearsed how the commons were " gnawn in their conscience" with the spreading of heresy, the suppression of monasteries and other troubles, and desired that the lords would be mediators to set forth their grievances to the King. This letter was carried to Darcy by the vicar of Brayton and William Acclom. Both sides desired a personal interview, and it was soon arranged that Sir George Darcy's eldest son should be handed over to the Pilgrims in pledge for Aske's safety, while Aske went to speak with the lords in the castle.

On the morning of Thursday 19 October, 1536, Lord Darcy, constable of the royal castle of Pontefract, Edward Lee, Archbishop of York, Dr Magnus, a learned member of the King's Council, Sir Robert Constable of Flamborough, and all the knights and gentle-men in the castle, including Sir George Darcy, Sir Robert Neville, Sir John Dawnye, Sir Henry Everingham, Sir John Wentworth, Sir Robert Oughtred, Henry Ryder, William Babthorpe, John Acclom and above forty more[1], assembled in the state chamber to meet Robert Aske, captain of the commons, and to hear him plead the cause of the Pilgrimage of Grace[2]. There is something extremely dramatic in this picture of the single man, who spoke for thousands, opposed to the crowd of lords and knights, apparently so much stronger, actually at his mercy. He came, he said, to declare the griefs of the commons, for the redress of which they had entered on that holy pilgrimage,—

" And how, first, that the lords spiritual had not done their duty, in that they had not been plain with the King's highness for the speedy remedy and quenching of the said heresies, and the preachers thereof, and for the suffering of the same, and for the ornaments of the churches and abbeys suppressed, and the violating of relics by the suppressors, with the unreverent demeanour of the doers thereof, with abuse of the visitors, and their impositions taken extra-ordinary, and other their negligences in not doing their duty, as well to their sovereign as to the commons. And to the lords temporal, the said Aske declared they had misused themselves, in that they, semblable, had not so providently ordered and declared to his said highness the poverty of his realm, and that

---

[1] L. and P. xi, Append. 11.   [2] See note F at end of chapter.

part specially, and wherein their griefs might ensue, whereby all dangers might have been avoided ; for insomuch as in the north parts much of the relief of the commons was by succour of abbeys, and that before this last statute thereof made, the King's highness had no money out of that shire in a manner yearly, for his grace's revenues there yearly went to the finding of Berwick. And that now the profits of abbeys suppressed, tenths and first fruits, went out of those parts. By occasion whereof, within short space or (*of*) years, there should be no money nor treasure in those parts, neither the tenant to have to pay his rents to the lord, nor the lord to have money to do the King service withal, for so much as in those parts was neither the presence of his grace, execution of his laws, nor yet but little recourse of merchandise, so that of necessity the said country should either 'patyssh' (*make terms*) with the Scots, or of very poverty enforced to make commotions or rebellions ; and that the lords knew the same to be true and had not done their duty, for that they had not declared the said poverty of the said country to the King's highness, and the danger that otherwise his grace would ensue, alleging the whole blame to them the nobility therein, with other like reasons."[1]

Finally he "required those present to join them and deliver the castle," adding, says Archbishop Lee, "that if we refused he had ways to constrain us, and we should find them people without mercy."[2]

After a brief discussion, in which the Archbishop firmly refused Darcy's polite desire that he would answer first, Darcy replied "that he neither could nor would deliver the King's castle"; as to the commons' grievances, he would consult with his friends and then answer them, but if the castle had only been well furnished with provisions and weapons, Aske should have had neither "the tone ne the toodre" (the one nor the other—that is, neither castle nor answer) "but to his pain."

Lee asked the captain what the Pilgrims wanted him to do. Aske replied that he and Darcy must use their influence with the King to persuade him to grant their petition, and in the meanwhile must give them help and advice. Lee suggested that if he was to be a mediator he had better not join the host but remain neutral. As for advising them "they must first consider whether the enterprise were lawful," but if he might have a safe conduct, he said that he would go and tell the Pilgrims his opinion on that point. He probably hoped to get through to Shrewsbury's camp, for he was well aware that among the host his life would hardly be safe. Aske refused him the safe conduct, indignantly "upbraiding him and the other bishops for not dealing plainly." Lee afterwards declared that

[1] L. and P. xii (1), 6; printed in full, Eng. Hist. Rev. v, 335–6.
[2] L. and P. xii (1), 1022.

he replied "they might have his body by constraint, but never his heart in that cause," but perhaps he did not say the words very loudly.

Darcy gave no opinion on the justice of the Pilgrims' demands. He merely begged for time to take counsel before making his reply. But Aske knew as well as he did that Shrewsbury had promised to relieve Pontefract and might possibly do so. Aske felt sure that he could take the castle by force, but he was anxious to avoid bloodshed and to secure at the same time influential allies; for these reasons he consented to a truce till Friday night, though Darcy pressed for a day longer.

When Aske had returned to his own quarters, the garrison held a council. They had already determined that if no rescue came their only course was to yield. "Out of 300 men not 140 remained and these were not all sound; there was only victual for eight or ten days."[1] "Every day," said Darcy later, "the captain wrote to me charging me on my life to yield the castle or they would burn my house (Templehurst) and kill my son's children."[2] The insurgents were always full of terrifying threats, but were marvellously slow in executing them. On Friday night Darcy again begged for more time. At first he was refused, but when he "bade them £20 for respite till 9 o'clock next morning," Aske, who needed every penny he could collect, gave them till 8 a.m., "against which hour he prepared for his assault." From Aske's own statement it appears that, in spite of exaggerated reports, the rebels at the siege of Pontefract were not a very numerous force[3]. It is interesting, though useless, to consider the question whether Darcy might have held the castle longer. No doubt the government was right in believing that he yielded willingly. Aske himself admitted, under examination, that the Pilgrims' attack might have been beaten off for a few days, if the soldiers of the garrison had remained loyal, but he had been assured that they would turn their coats as soon as the assault was made. He swore "to try to the death," that he had entered into no secret agreement with Darcy, whom he had never seen before he came to Pontefract on Thursday 19 October. Aske's explanation is simple and straightforward, and fits in with the statement of Maunsell, the vicar of Brayton. Thomas Strangways probably first told Aske that Darcy's soldiers favoured the Pilgrims. Later Strangways revealed to Maunsell how to take the castle.

---

[1] L. and P. xii (1), 6, 1022.　　　　[2] L. and P. xi, 1086.
[3] L. and P. xii (1), 392; printed in full, Coxe, op. cit.

Maunsell admitted that he had received Strangways' information, but he omitted the fact, which Aske mentions, that he (Maunsell) went to York and told Aske that if the Pilgrims attacked Pontefract the castle would surrender. In short, Aske was in secret communication with the serving-men, and was sure of their support. He was not in secret communication with Darcy or any of the other gentlemen in the castle, and did not believe that Darcy was responsible for Strangways' offers.

The King's conviction that there had been a definite arrangement made in Darcy's own name to yield the castle to Aske was mistaken, though not impossible. All Darcy's conduct bears out the theory that he did not decide which side to take until the day on which he surrendered the castle. At the beginning of the rebellion he sent his son to capture Aske; his steward was received with suspicion by the Pilgrims; he offered them £20, a large sum of money at that time, for only a few hours' delay. If the garrison had really resolved to join the Pilgrims, further resistance on Darcy's part was impossible, but perhaps the soldiers would have been ready to obey Darcy, even though they were unwilling to fight for the King. If Darcy could have forgotten the fall of the abbeys, the death of the faithful monks, his own unheeded protests and galling detention in London,—if he had rallied his failing strength sufficiently to put on harness and appear himself on the walls of Pontefract—he might have inspired his wavering followers and Pontefract Castle might have been held for the King while provisions lasted. But Darcy had not been persuaded, either by fear of anarchy or by Henry's strong personal fascination, to accept despotism as a necessary form of government, to which he was bound to render implicit obedience. On the contrary he "set more by the King of Heaven than twenty kings."[1] Henry's despotic government was, in Darcy's opinion, dragging the country to ruin and he believed himself called upon as a Christian, as a patriot and as a statesman, to oppose the King's progress on the road which he had chosen. He was deterred from joining the Pilgrims only by fear of the ugly name of traitor and by a soldier's reluctance to yield his post. But he was able to avoid the first by the theory of ministerial responsibility, which was accepted by the Pilgrims, though not by the King. Darcy argued that for twenty years Henry had ruled in an orthodox manner, before he fell under the baleful influence of Cromwell. Let that archtraitor be removed,—

[1] L. and P. XII (1), 853.

let suitable councillors be placed about the King by parliament, and Henry would rule beneficently again. The Pilgrimage was directed not against the King but against his ministers. As for Darcy's willingness to yield, his position was now desperate enough to afford him a good excuse. The rumoured help was no nearer now than a week before; the King's distrust had withheld the money and ammunition which would have enabled him to hold his post. He saw the "fuel and victuals coming in to him being eaten and drunken in the street before his face."[1] Lee describes the final council; "considering the danger of resistance they determined with sorrow to yield, and repented that they ever came there where they had expected to be as safe as if in London."[2]

At 7 o'clock on the morning of Saturday, 21 October, Darcy made his last request for more time, which was refused. The castle was then formally surrendered to Aske, whereupon "the lords spiritual and temporal, knights and esquires," solemnly took the Pilgrims' oath[3].

NOTES TO CHAPTER VIII

Note A. The vicar of Brayton is not a very reliable witness. There is no proof that the earlier part of his evidence is false, but he was one of the most zealous leaders of the Pilgrimage and in his confession, of course, tried to insinuate that he was really devoted to the King, laying all his misdemeanour at Darcy's door. In his account of the week from 15 October to 22 October he never mentioned his second visit to Aske at York, when he told the captain that Pontefract Castle could not hold out.

Note B. As Darcy was the keeper of Pontefract Castle, the blame for its defenceless condition may be laid on his own shoulders. But it must be remembered that he had been detained in London for several years, and had returned home only a few months before the rebellion. All the royal castles in the north were out of repair at this time; the walls of Berwick were falling, Carlisle was scarcely defensible, Barnard Castle was not in good governance[4]. When fortresses so near the Border were neglected, it was not likely that any money would be spent over Pontefract, which lay beyond the area of Scots' raids. After the Pilgrimage of Grace, Henry devoted a good deal of attention to the repair of the northern defences, on which some of the monastic spoils were spent[5].

Note C. Sir Henry Saville reported these words to Cromwell, but it does not appear whether he heard them himself. He was on bad terms with Darcy, who was Sir Richard Tempest's friend.

[1] L. and P. xi, 1086.   [2] L. and P. xii (1), 1022.
[3] Ibid. 6; printed in full, Eng. Hist. Rev. v, 336.   [4] See below chap. ix.
[5] Bates, Border Holds, Introduction, pt v; Arch. Ael. (new ser.) i, 87; Gasquet, op. cit. ii, chap. x.

Note D. A note is appended to these articles in "The Letters and Papers of Henry VIII," Vol. XI, stating that they are some of the articles printed by Speed in his "History of Great Britain." This is a mistake, as the articles printed by Speed are those which the Pilgrims' Council drew up at Pontefract at the beginning of December. They are printed in the same volume of "The Letters and Papers," No. 1246. Speed says nothing about the York articles, which are the germ from which the others grew, but have no further connection with them[1].

Note E. It is impossible to estimate the strength of the Pilgrims' host with any accuracy, though it seems certain that rumour exaggerated their numbers very much. For instance, it was said that the rebels at York numbered 40,000 ; Wilfred Holme puts their number at 25,000 and Darcy at 20,000.

Note F. Two accounts of the first meeting between Aske and Darcy are preserved, Aske's and Archbishop Lee's. Aske's account has been followed in preference to Lee's when they differ for the following reasons :

(1) Archbishop Lee wrote his account when he knew himself to be in danger and desired above everything to vindicate his loyalty ; naturally his testimony is more an explanation and excuse for his own conduct than a simple statement of fact.

(2) Aske prepared his narrative for the King when he believed himself to be pardoned and taken into favour. As he wrote it in London, far away from his authorities, he was obliged to omit many details, but this does not lay him open to the charge that he failed to state the whole truth.

(3) Aske's answers when he was examined in the Tower are fuller and bear out his earlier statement. He knew that he was in fact a condemned criminal, and to lie was alike useless, dishonourable, and certain to be discovered.

(4) When his accounts are checked by a score of miscellaneous depositions drawn up by all sorts of men, he is seldom, if ever, found to have misstated a fact. The other evidence either corresponds to his, or dovetails with his statements. There is only one exception to this, which will be discussed later[2].

(5) Archbishop Lee has clearly perverted the truth in one or two cases in order to put a more loyal complexion on his actions. This is not a very serious charge to bring against a weak old gentleman in peril of his life. It is difficult to believe that Lee made the frequent loyal speeches and defiances which he puts into his own mouth, to the confusion of the rebel leaders, for the Pilgrims, on his own showing, continued to think that he sympathised with them.

(6) With one notable exception, hereafter to be mentioned, Lee did absolutely nothing either for King or commons. In contrast to this indecision, Aske was entirely devoted to his cause. The captain never admitted himself to be in the wrong ; to the end he justified the Pilgrimage as a desperate remedy for a desperate disease. Obviously the man who is not ashamed of the truth is less likely to lie than the man who deplores it.

---

[1] See below chap. XIV. [2] See below chap. XX.

CHAPTER IX

THE EXTENT OF THE INSURRECTION

The main body of the Pilgrims' army was at Pontefract on 21 October, 1536; leaving them there for the present, we will now follow the history of the rising in the northern counties from the outbreak of the insurrection. It will be convenient to carry this account on beyond the date which has been reached, up to the truce of 27 October, in order that the narrative may not be broken a second time.

In tracing the course of the rebellion in the far north, it must be remembered that Northumberland, Durham, Cumberland, Westmorland and the towns of Berwick and Newcastle-upon-Tyne were exempted from the subsidy,—in fact, taking into consideration the remissions which were granted to them on account of their sufferings at the hands of the Scots, it may be said that these places were scarcely taxed at all[1]. Consequently the insurgents lacked one of the bonds which united the subsidy men in Lincolnshire and Yorkshire.

In Cumberland and Westmorland the rising was almost entirely directed against enclosures and unpopular landlords, and received little support from the gentlemen or, with a few exceptions, from the clergy. In Durham and Northumberland, on the other hand, the gentry seem to have been more deeply involved than the commons, owing to the influence of the disinherited Percys. In the Yorkshire dales, as in Cumberland and Westmorland, the movement was chiefly social, and was directed against the Earl of Cumberland, while the gentlemen, who imitated the Earl on a small scale, naturally supported him against the rabble.

It would be incorrect to say that after the rising of Howdenshire and Beverley the rebellion spread northwards, as Hexham and the northern dales had been astir since the end of September, but these

---

[1] Dowell, op. cit. I, Bk III, chap. I, pt II, section 2.

minor disturbances gained significance from the wide-spread movement further south.

The only monastery which offered any determined resistance to the Act for the Dissolution of the Smaller Monasteries was the priory of Augustinian canons at Hexham. Their house did not really come within the scope of the Act, as its yearly value was over £200, but for some reason or other it was included among those to be suppressed[1]. The house had suffered in the Scots' wars, and there is reason to believe that its condition was not very good, either financially or morally, but it was of great importance as a centre of hospitality in the barren region between England and Scotland. On 23 April, 1536, Archbishop Lee wrote to Cromwell begging that it might be spared because "wise men that know the Borders think that the lands thereof, although they were ten times as much, can not countervail the damage that is like to ensue if it be suppressed; and some way there is never a house between Scotland and the lordship of Hexham; and men fear if the monastery go down, that in process all shall be waste much within the land."[2] It seems probable that the canons received a royal exemption from the Act, or that the monastery was immediately refounded, but later in the year they must have heard that they were again in danger, whereupon the prior, Edward Jay, went up to London to try to make terms with Cromwell. He was unsuccessful, however, and returned sadly home by way of York. There he waited on the Archbishop, who received him in his barge, and in the presence of his chaplains and servants warned Jay to submit to the King's will without attempting any resistance[3].

The date of this interview is uncertain, but it seems to have been at the end of September, and when the prior returned home he found that the Archbishop's advice had come too late. In his absence the sub-prior and the master of the dependent cell of Ovingham (two separate persons, not the same man) had laid in weapons for the defence of the monastery and had roused the people, who were the more easily moved as the hated Sir Reynold Carnaby had received the grant of its lands[4].

On 28 September, before the prior's return, the four commissioners for the dissolution were warned at Dilston that they

---

[1] Raine, Mem. of Hexham Priory (Surtees Soc.) preface p. cxxii.

[2] Ibid. Append. p. cxxvi; Wright, Suppression of the Monasteries (Camden Soc.), 123; Burnet, Hist. of Reformation, vi, 139; L. and P. x, 716.

[3] L. and P. xi, 689.   [4] Ibid. 449.

would be resisted. Two of them who were local men, Robert Collingwood and Lionel Gray, rode on with a few servants to reconnoitre. They found the streets of Hexham full of armed men, the alarm bells ringing, and the gates of the Priory shut. The commissioners took up their stand outside, and parleyed with the master of Ovingham, who appeared on the leads of the monastery in harness, accompanied by servants in arms. His first words were, "We be twenty brethren in this house, and we shall die all, or that ye shall have this house." The commissioners advised him to consult with his brethren before rejecting the royal commission, and the master withdrew to do so, commanding the hostile crowd which had gathered about the commissioners to do them no harm. After a space he returned with the sub-prior in canon's robes. They brought the royal confirmation, delivered to the house under the great seal, showed it to the commissioners, and gave them their answer; "We think it not the king's honour to give forth one seal contrary to another, and afore any either of our lands, goods or houses be taken from us we shall all die, and that is our full answer." Gray and Collingwood returned with this reply to the other commissioners who were waiting for them at a little distance. They left behind in Hexham three of their servants, who rejoined them next day, and reported that as soon as their masters had withdrawn the monastery gates were thrown open, and the canons, all in harness, accompanied by some sixty armed men, marched out two by two to a place called the Green, from which they watched the meeting of the commissioners and their departure. When they were out of sight the canons returned to the Priory again. Such was the news that greeted Prior Jay on his return, and he despatched a canon to report it to Archbishop Lee[1]. Other messengers were hastening from Hexham with the same news, one from the commissioners to the King[2], and two from "old Carnaby" of Halton, who sent to his son Sir Reynold, and to the Archbishop, asking the latter to order the canons to submit[3]. To each of the messengers the Archbishop replied by bidding the canons surrender, and Sir Reynold appealed to the Earl of Northumberland who wrote to Cromwell on 4 October[4]. After receiving the report of the commissioners on 5 October the King sent orders that Hexham was to be taken and dissolved by force if necessary. The letter seems to have been

---

[1] L. and P. xi, 689. [2] Ibid. 504; printed in full, Raine, op. cit. i, p. cxxvii.
[3] L. and P. xi, 689. [4] Ibid. 535.

meant for the Earl of Cumberland[1], but the outbreak of the rebellion in Yorkshire prevented him from executing the order[2].

The King also wrote to Archbishop Lee, whom he suspected of encouraging the canons, and Lee replied with one of his long, rambling letters of excuse[3]; his writing is much faded, and difficult to decipher, but the letter shows that the Prior of Hexham was with him at York at the time of the commissioners' visit, and therefore could not have taken part in the resistance which was offered to them at Hexham. Meanwhile in Hexhamshire matters were at a deadlock. No one in the neighbourhood would help the Carnabys against the canons, and no troops could advance from the south on account of the insurrection in Yorkshire. One of the local freebooters, little John Heron of Chipchase[4], who was a follower of Sir Thomas Percy, determined to make use of this state of affairs for his own advantage. Accordingly on the morning of Sunday 15 October he appeared at Halton, and suggested to old William Carnaby that he should act as mediator between the two parties. Carnaby, at his wits' end, accepted the offer, and Heron then rode over to Hexham, where he said nothing of his negotiations with the opposite party, but warned the canons that their only chance of saving their lives was to purchase the help of himself and his friends by granting them certain fees and then "he doubted not but by the help of his son-in-law Cuthbert Charleton—and of one Edward Charleton his uncle—with other such friends as they would make, but all the whole country of Tynedale would die and live in the quarrel." The documents granting the fees were drawn up, but not signed, for the canons were honourably reluctant to join themselves with thieves, and begged Heron to carry a message to William Carnaby that they would deliver up the monastery to the commissioners if Sir Reynold would intercede for their lives and if "they might there serve God and remain." Heron returned to Halton, where he passed the night, but merely said that he was to receive the canons' final answer on the morrow. During the night he secretly summoned the men of Tynedale to assemble next day. In the morning, 16 October, he went again to Hexham, and told the canons that Sir Reynold would make no terms,—he was resolved to have the heads of four canons and of four townsmen to send to the King. Whereupon the canons declared that it was better to defend their lives while they could than wilfully to kill themselves, and

---

[1] L. and P. xi, 544, 760 (2). [2] See below.
[3] Ibid. 689. [4] Bates, Border Holds, 316.

they definitely threw in their lot with the Tynedale men[1]. It was
a fatal though natural mistake on their part. The rebels' cause in
Northumberland was as much injured by the alliance with the
thieves of Tynedale and Reedsdale as the King's was in Cumberland
by the loyalty of the thieves of the "Black Lands," the valleys of the
Esk and Line. When Tynedale and Reedsdale "broke" no man
of substance in Northumberland cared for either church or King
until order was restored. If any power could prevent the mosstroopers from spoiling and killing up to the very walls of Newcastle,
that power would be welcome though it came directly from Satan,
and since the government was at present opposed to the canons and
their allies, it followed that all honest men in Northumberland
supported the government.

As soon as he had made sure of the canons, on Monday, 16 October, John Heron rode back to Halton, and sat down cheerfully to
dinner, with the remark that "It is a good sight to see a man
eat when he is hungry." He knew that he had done a good
morning's work and that in a few hours his friends of Tynedale
would be there, with whose help he proposed to plunder Halton and
carry off Carnaby to Sir Ingram Percy. So far his plans had been
successful, but now his good luck began to leave him, for dinner was
only half done when Archie Robson of Tynedale arrived and began
to talk to John Robson his cousin. Heron guessed what that meant,
and at once drew Carnaby aside and told him that "he could not
find them of Hexham to will to make any stay, but they would
do their worst," and he therefore advised Carnaby to "defend
himself as well as he would for he knew well they would be at
his house straightway, and that Tynedale was part taken with
them." Carnaby reproached him for giving such short notice, saying
that it was "not like a friend of him done to know such a purpose,
and not to declare it till he had half dined," but he still trusted
Heron and agreed to ride with him to Chipchase, to avoid the
attack of the Tynedale men, as Heron declared they were in irre-
sistible force and were resolved to take Carnaby's life. It was now
that Heron's luck failed altogether, for it happened that a servant of
Sir Reynold Carnaby's was riding by St John Ley near Hexham
when he saw the men of Hexhamshire and Tynedale mustering
there. By fair words he managed both to learn their purpose
and to escape from their hands, and set off to carry the news to

---

[1] L. and P. xii (1), 1090; printed in full in Raine, op. cit. i, Append. p cxl
et seq.

Halton, taking a short cut in order to arrive before the host. By chance he saw Heron and Carnaby as they rode towards Chipchase, and managed to tell Carnaby secretly, "That traitor thief that rideth with you hath betrayed you, and it will cost you your life yet; if ye follow counsel I shall warrant you." Apparently their pursuers were now in sight, and by his servant's advice Carnaby begged Heron to stop and parley with them "because he was of their acquaintance and allied amongst them," while he himself rode on to Chipchase. Heron consented, but sent his son George to watch his victim's movements. Carnaby however managed to get rid of George, and as soon as he was out of sight of the Tynedale men, changed his direction and rode to Langley Castle. There he was safe, as it was one of Northumberland's castles, and apparently held by the Earl's own men. Meanwhile Heron, seeing that his prey had escaped, rode back to Halton, which was being plundered by the .Tynedale men. He told Carnaby's son Thomas that his father commanded him to leave the house, and persuaded Carnaby's wife to give him a casket containing her husband's money and plate, but at the last moment, when the casket was actually in Heron's hands, Arthur Errington, a kinsman of the Carnabys, seized it from him and galloped off, accompanied by seven Tynedale men whom he had won to his part. John Heron pursued them "and put a kerchief as a pensell upon his spear point" to lead his followers in the chase, but Errington made his escape. The next day, Tuesday 17 October, Heron returned to Halton, but found it occupied by Lewis Ogle, brother of Lord Ogle, who was an ally of the Carnabys. Heron vainly endeavoured to make him desert Halton "saying he would not tarry there till night, if he knew and perceived as much as he knew, for ten thousand pounds," but Ogle was resolute, and at last Heron "rode home, and never came thither after."[1]

It is now time to look a little into the matter of dates. The canons had defied the commissioners on Thursday 28 September, but John Heron did not make his first move until Sunday 15 October, more than a fortnight later. On the very day that he rode to Halton the commons of Durham rose, and at some time during the week Heron's brother-in-law, John Lumley, brought him a letter from them containing their articles and oath[2]. It seems more than likely that he had been in touch with them from an earlier date, and knew what their movements were to be. The

---

[1] L. and P. xii (1), 1090; printed in full, Raine, loc. cit.
[2] Ibid.; printed in full, Raine, op. cit. p. cxxxvi.

situation in Northumberland was favourable, as the Earl, who was the warden of the East Marches, was lying ill at Wressell Castle in Yorkshire. It is true that Sir Thomas Percy was also in Yorkshire, but Sir Ingram was at Alnwick[1]. He had been deprived of his office of vice-warden by the Earl's command about midsummer, but no new vice-warden had been appointed[2], and Northumberland had made him constable of Alnwick Castle in July[3]. In the circumstances it was natural that he should assume authority and no one seems to have known what his attitude would be. On hearing of the rising in Tynedale and Reedsdale he sent out a summons which bore a suspicious resemblance to the Lincolnshire oath: "It is ordained and appointed that all the gentlemen of Northumberland shall meet at Alnwick upon Sunday 22 October at eleven of the clock, for to take an order by all their advices and consents, what is best for them to do that may be pleasure to Almighty God and most acceptable service to the King's highness and for the common weal of this country and the safeguard of the Marches."[4] The gentlemen of Northumberland, knowing nothing of the oath to God, the King and the Common Weal obeyed the summons readily. Robert Collingwood, the commissioner who was baffled at Hexham, drew up a list of agenda for the assembly in amusing contrast to the actual proceedings. It would be necessary, he wrote, to see that all the gentlemen of Northumberland and their dependants took one way in the King's service, and to take measures against a Scots invasion. As the warden was absent and no vice-warden had been appointed, two gentlemen must be chosen to act as lieutenants of the East and Middle Marches, they must be provided with counsel and support, and all the gentlemen must wait on them as diligently as if they were each receiving a £20 fee. The two lieutenants must at once join with the keepers of Tynedale and Reedsdale to take "a substantial order" to restore peace there, "as ill disposed men rob the King's true subjects every night." Finally everything that was determined must be written out and signed by all the gentlemen present[5]. As it turned out Collingwood would have been very much alarmed if his last suggestion had been enforced.

Sir Ingram Percy in the meanwhile was as politic as the King himself could have been. He did nothing to alarm the gentlemen before the meeting, and sent the Abbot of Alnwick and "other

---

[1] L. and P. xii (1), 1090; printed in full, Raine, op. cit. p. cxlv.
[2] Ibid.; printed in full, Raine, op. cit. p. cxxxvi.   [3] L. and P. xi, 68.
[4] Ibid. 736.   [5] Ibid.

friends that he made" to his brother the Earl of Northumberland at Wressell with a message that he was true to the King and would repress any disturbances in Northumberland if he was restored to his office. The Earl believed his professions and made him sheriff of Northumberland, vice-warden, and lieutenant of the East Marches "with the fees accustomed."[1] After Sir Ingram had sent out the summons to the gentlemen, John Lumley, the messenger from Durham, arrived at Alnwick, whither he had been sent by John Heron. He brought the letter of the commons of Durham, signed by "Captain Poverty," commanding Sir Ingram to take the oath and to remain in Northumberland as a protection against the Scots[2]. Sir Ingram could not put forward the common excuse that he had been forced to take the oath when it was brought by a single messenger from rebels more than fifty miles away; in fact, as soon as the gentlemen had assembled on Sunday 22 October, he attempted no further concealment. Instead of entering into the business of curbing the mosstroopers, as Collingwood and the rest expected, he caused the commons' letter and articles to be read aloud and then ordered all present to take the oath. A few ventured to protest, but as they were "enclosed in the said Castle of Alnwick" with "no remedy but all must swear or else do worse," they all submitted and "will they or not, sworn they were." Having now declared himself, Sir Ingram did not let the grass grow under his feet. He used all possible means to induce the gentlemen of Northumberland to join him, and devoted himself to revenging his own and his brother's wrongs on the Carnabys. Accompanied by Sir Humphry Lisle, Robert Swinhoe and John Roddam with all the forces of Alnwick, he rode to Adderstone by Bamborough, where he believed that Sir Reynold Carnaby was hiding under the protection of his wife's brother Thomas Forster. As a matter of fact Sir Reynold was at Chillingham Castle with Sir Robert Ellerker and others of the King's party, and when Sir Ingram had searched Adderstone unsuccessfully, he departed swearing "By God's heart, he would be revenged of" Sir Reynold Carnaby. Thomas Forster asked what offence Sir Reynold had done him, and Sir Ingram turned upon him,—"Sir Reynold Carnaby hath been the destruction of all our blood, for by his means the king shall be my lord's heir; and now he thinketh a sport, and to ride up and down in the

---

[1] L. and P. XII (1), 1090; Raine, op. cit. p. cxxxvi. Also printed by De Fonblanque, Annals of the House of Percy I, App. lii.

[2] L. and P. XII (1), 351, 467; printed by De Fonblanque, op. cit. I, App. liv.

country, all we being sworn and he unsworn, and this I pray you show him, for surely I will be revenged of him." On the way back to Alnwick he wished to attack Sir Thomas Grey's house at Newstead, but his men dissuaded him. During the same expedition he took possession of Sir Reynold's lands at North Charlton, for the use of his brother Sir Thomas Percy. He afterwards seized all Sir Reynold's possessions in Northumberland. Edward Bradford, Sir Reynold's steward, refused to give up his master's rents. Sir Ingram sent out eighteen of his servants who took him by force "betwixt his parish church and his house," and carried him to Alnwick, where he was "laid in the stocks two nights and a day and kept in hold three days longer," because Sir Ingram would have him forswear his master. Bradford probably submitted or his imprisonment would have been longer.

Sir Ingram now sent to Lionel Gray, porter of Berwick, the other Hexham commissioner, to Sir Roger Gray and to Sir Robert Ellerker bidding them come in and take the oath. They all refused, and Lionel Gray was so closely harried that "the most part of his cattle, by driving and removing from one place to another for fear of the said Sir Ingram, was in point of utter loss and destruction." Hearing that Carnaby, Sir Robert Ellerker and others had taken refuge in Chillingham Castle, Sir Ingram was reported to have sent to Berwick for ordnance in order that he might besiege them, but no actual siege seems ever to have been attempted[1]. Sir Thomas Clifford, the captain of Berwick[2], was a friend of Sir Thomas Percy, and although he was the Earl of Cumberland's brother, he does not seem to have been so much opposed to the rebels as the rest of his family. He received messages from the Percys, and when Lionel Gray begged that his over-driven cattle might be protected in the fields of Berwick, the captain refused his permission. On St Katharine's Day (25 November) Sir Robert Ellerker was told that the Percys were about to attack Chillingham and sent to Berwick for help. Clifford turned out the garrison on the alarm, but said that he did not believe the Percys would attack him, as he was harbouring no fugitives. He asked Sir Robert Ellerker, "Have ye any of the Carnabys in your house?" Sir Robert replied, "I believe as well yea as nay, but they or any of the King's true subjects shall be welcome to me or to my house." He then rode away, hoping that Clifford and his men would follow him, but

---

[1] L. and P. xii (1), 1090; Raine and De Fonblanque, loc. cit.
[2] L. and P. viii, 1143 (1).

instead of this, Clifford ordered the gates to be shut, and only ten men went with Ellerker[1]. This was in the time of the truce, and the alarm of an attack on Chillingham came to nothing. Sir Thomas Clifford was perhaps only anxious to avoid local feuds, because he feared an attack from Scotland which Berwick was hardly able to resist, as the walls were out of repair and parts of them had fallen[2].

For the rest of October, until the truce of Doncaster, Sir Ingram in the exercise of his office as sheriff was busy holding sheriff's tourns at Alnwick, where he appointed Sir Humphry Lisle and others as his officers; as vice-warden he made musters and assemblies "all for the annoyance of the King's true subjects that would not be sworn."[3]

Such was the state of affairs in Northumberland during the first month of the insurrection; practically the whole country, except a few castles such as Halton, Chillingham and Langley, were in the Percys' hands, and Berwick seems to have been in no position to resist them.

It has already been pointed out that there was probably communication between the freebooters of Northumberland and the insurgents in Durham and North Yorkshire. The movement in Mashamshire and Richmond which spread to Durham began as soon as news reached Ripon of the Lincolnshire rising; the message came from Archbishop Lee, with orders to his steward, Lord Latimer, to stay his tenants, but the news had more effect than the orders[4]. On Thursday 12 October Lord Scrope wrote to the Earl of Cumberland that the commons of Mashamshire and Nidderdale had risen the day before (Wednesday 11 October), had occupied Coverham Abbey and Middleham, and were advancing on Bolton to capture himself; he had fled into hiding and begged Cumberland to send help to his wife[5]. Lord Latimer and Sir Christopher Danby were taken and sworn by the commons on the 14th or 15th[6]. John Dakyn, vicar-general of the diocese of York, had hastened from the city of York to his parish of Kirkby Ravensworth in Richmond on hearing of the rising at Beverley, but no sooner had he reached Kirkby Ravensworth than he heard that Richmondshire had also risen on Friday 13 October. This news

[1] L. and P. xiii (1), 1253.   [2] L. and P. xii (1), 85, 219.
[3] Ibid. 1090; printed in full, Raine, loc. cit.
[4] L. and P. xii (1), 1022.   [5] L. and P. xi, 677.
[6] Ibid. 729.

made him fly to a great moor, but he returned to his house and took the oath when he was told that the commons were about to destroy his goods[1]. His parishioners then set out to seize Bowes and other gentlemen at Barnard Castle, and they ordered Dakyn to go to "Galowbaughen" in Richmond to meet the host of Mashamshire, which was advancing under Lord Latimer and Sir Christopher Danby. He obeyed their orders for fear of his life, "for ever the chancellor of Lincoln's death moved his mind." All that day he spent with the Mashamshire men, not daring to say anything displeasing to them. He believed that Latimer and Danby were equally afraid of their men[2]. The brothers Robert, George and Richard Bowes and Thomas Rokeby were the captains in Barnard Castle. They were afterwards accused of not having the town and castle "in good governance"; at any rate they surrendered without a stroke on Sunday 15 October, and took over the command of the rebels[3]. All gentlemen were forced to join, even Sir Henry Gascoigne, whose mother-in-law had just died and lay unburied, but the people willingly submitted to Robert Bowes' authority. He ordered them to divide into parishes, and to choose four men out of each parish to command the rest. A letter was despatched to Cleveland, requiring the people there "with sore comminations" to meet the Richmondshire host at Oxneyfield by Darlington. Dakyn rejoined the Richmond host on Sunday the 15th, and there in the field one Thomlynson of Bedall, against whom he had given judgment in a matrimonial case, threatened him with a great bow, and accused him of being "a maker of the new laws and putter down of holidays" until with the help of his friends Dakyn quieted him by a gift of over forty marks[4].

The summons, spread through the countryside, quickly took effect. On the previous Wednesday, 11 October[5], between two and three hundred men of Mashamshire and Kirkbyshire assembled in the evening round Jervaux Abbey and clamoured for the abbot, Adam Sedbarr, to come out to them. The abbot slipped out by a back door, and took refuge on Witton Fell, with no companions but his own father and a young boy. He remained in hiding for four days, only venturing back to the abbey at night, when the commons had dispersed to their homes. But when Robert Bowes' summons was

---

[1] L. and P. xii (1), 788. [2] Ibid. 789.
[3] Ibid. 775. [4] Ibid. 789.
[5] Ibid. 1035. The Abbot says "the Wednesday after Michaelmas," i.e. 4 October, but he seems to have made a week's error in his reckoning.

received on Sunday 15 October, the rebels returned to Jervaux and declared that they would burn it down if the abbot were not delivered up to them for forbidding his tenants to join them. The terrified monks sent a messenger to the fell, who found the abbot "in a great crag" and told him of the commons' threats, saying that all the brethren cried "Wo" by him. This message caused him to return, though the risk was great, and his friends had difficulty in saving him from the commons, who nearly tore him in pieces, crying "Down with the traitor"! and "Whoreson traitor, where hast thou been?" "Get a block to strike off his head upon." No gentlemen were with them; they had leaders chosen from among themselves, of whom the abbot names Stavely, Middleton, Leonard Burgh and Aslaby. They forced the abbot to take the oath, and carried him off with them, mounted on a barebacked horse, to the meeting at Oxneyfield on Monday 16 October[1]. Assembled there were Bowes with the Richmondshire men, Lord Latimer and Sir Christopher Danby with Mashamshire, and the men of Jervaux with the abbot. Bowes was, as usual, obliged to "stay old grudges" among his followers, in order to induce them to act together. They intended to compel all priests who were "young and able" to join them, and the priests themselves were quite willing in many cases[2]. The chantry priest of Lartington and the parish priest of Romaldkirk were particularly active[3]. Dakyn, however, persuaded Bowes to excuse them all in consideration of their vows, and afterwards ventured to rebuke the cantarist, when he came to his house to demand money, saying that his was not the office of a priest[4].

From Oxneyfield the host advanced to Bishop Auckland on Tuesday 17 October with the object of capturing the Bishop of Durham there. But the bishop had been warned and had fled at midnight[5]. He made his way to his own castle of Norham[6], but even there he seems to have found some difficulty in gaining admittance, for William Franklin, Archdeacon of Durham, was afterwards praised for his "service in taking Norham Castle." Perhaps this means that at the outbreak of the insurrection he had occupied the castle and prepared to defend it. Franklin afterwards endeavoured to go south, but was stopped by Darcy[7]. Thomas Parry, one of the

<hr />

[1] L. and P. xii (1), 1035.   [2] Ibid. 369, 789.
[3] Ibid. 786 (11).   [4] L. and P. xi, 1284.
[5] L. and P. xii (1), 369; printed in full by Milner and Benham, Records of the House of Lumley, 32–45.
[6] L. and P. xii (1), 22.   [7] L. and P. xi, Append. 14.

commissioners[1] for suppressing monasteries was more fortunate. He fled to Norfolk and kept up communications with Franklin, urging him to try to capture Aske[2]. In the end Franklin escaped and went to the King[3]. The Bishop of Durham remained at Norham for several months[4]. For his desertion the commons spoiled his palace at Bishop Auckland "contrary to their own proclamation."[5] The plundering perhaps took place when Bowes had gone to Brancepeth to take the Earl of Westmorland[6]. Westmorland did not join the rebels himself, but he took the oath and sent them a friendly answer[7]. What seems nowadays more extraordinary is that he allowed his son, a boy not much over 13 years, to ride with the rebels[8]. There is nothing to indicate that young Lord Neville was captured or that his presence in the Pilgrim host caused any alarm to his parents.

Sir Thomas Hilton, the sheriff of Durham, was probably at Bishop Auckland with the bishop. On Monday, after the bishop's flight, he sent news of the rising to his cousin John Lord Lumley, who was hunting the hare at his manor of the Isle[9]. On receiving the warning that "as he regarded his honour and safeguard of his substance that he should remove and get him to some sure place for fear of the commons lest he should be taken of them," he packed up his plate and jewels and set out to deposit them in the Maison Dieu at Newcastle-upon-Tyne, which was the strongest house he knew. Arriving at Lumley Castle that night, he stopped to rest there, but sent on his son George with the valuables to place them in safety at Newcastle without delay. On Tuesday 17 October Lord Lumley joined his son at Newcastle, and on Wednesday the 18th Sir Thomas Hilton arrived there and persuaded him to leave the town by telling him that the townsfolk would rise if the commons came that way. Hilton and Lumley went to Hilton Castle, and George Lumley returned to the Isle[10], which shows that he was not at heart opposed to the rebels, as they were in possession of all that district, and mustered that day at Spennymoor[11], some five or six miles away. No sooner had George Lumley arrived than "certain soldiers out of Richmondshire" came

---

[1] L. and P. xi, 381 (B).
[2] Ibid. Append. 14.
[3] Ibid. 1271.
[4] L. and P. xii (1), 22.
[5] Ibid. 789.
[6] Ibid. 29.
[7] Ibid. 369; xi, 945.
[8] D.N.B.
[9] L. and P. xii (1), 369; see note A at end of chapter.
[10] Ibid. 369; printed in full, Milner and Benham, op. cit. 43.
[11] L. and P. xii (1), 1035.

to summon him to Lord Latimer's muster, under pain of burning
the house.   He accompanied them back to Auckland, when he
found, in addition to Lord Latimer and his men, Sir James
Strangways with a thousand men, young Bowes with a thousand
more, Sir Ralph Bulmer and another knight (Sir Christopher
Danby?) each with a company.   Lord Latimer administered the
oath to him and asked him where his father was.   Lumley replied
"feignedly" that he was in Northumberland, whereupon Latimer bade
him send word that if Lord Lumley did not "come in" the rebels
would spoil his house.   They allowed him to return to the Isle,
where he received a message from his wife that his own house
at Thweng was in danger.   Next day, Thursday 19 October, he
set out for Yorkshire, remained two days at Thweng, and then
led his tenants to York[1].

George Lumley did not see his father again until they met
"on the heath before Doncaster," and he denied most emphatically
that he had received any message from him or knew anything of his
movements in the interval.   His reticence is highly honourable
in a son, but very exasperating to an historian, for very little is
known of the rising in the Bishopric until on Friday 20 October
the Lords Neville, Latimer and Lumley rode into York at the head
of 10,000 men, bearing before them the banner of St Cuthbert.
It seems probable that as soon as they were satisfied as to the
disposition of the citizens of Newcastle, Lumley and Hilton set
out and raised Durham without even going through the formality
of being taken by the commons.   It would be extremely interesting
to know how they obtained possession of St Cuthbert's banner,
which was in the charge of the feretrar of Durham Cathedral.
The monks seem to have given it up willingly, as they paid sixteen
pence to Thomas Merlay the standard bearer, but somehow or other
it was injured and five shillings were spent on its repairs[2].   The
bishop's chancery in Durham was spoiled by the commons[3].
Sir Francis Bigod endeavoured to escape from Mulgrave to London
by sea, but his ship was driven back up the coast of Durham and he
landed at Hartlepool.   He was passing the night at the house
of a former mayor of the town when he was warned that the
commons were coming to take him and fled back to his ship.

---

[1] L. and P. xii (1), 369; printed in full, Milner and Benham, op. cit. 33, 43.
[2] Fowler, Dur. Acct Rolls (Surtees Soc.), ii, 483.
[3] L. and P. xii (2), 536; Greenwell, Boldon Buke (Surtees Soc.), vii–viii; Lapsley,
Co. Pal. of Durham, App. iii, 327.

Keeping now the waters and now the woods he returned to Mulgrave and was captured by the commons, who took him to York[1].

The date of these events is uncertain, but Hilton and Lumley must have joined Latimer not later than Thursday 19 October. Meanwhile at Spennymoor on Wednesday 18 October the host had been divided into two parts, the one to advance to York, the other to Skipton. Dakyn and two other aged gentlemen were sent to Jervaux to despatch the posts with letters from host to host[2], and the Abbot of Jervaux was permitted to return home with them. His attitude towards the rising seems to have altered a good deal now that he had discovered it was not a mere riot among the peasants of his own neighbourhood. At Auckland he was attended by his chaplain with a bow and sheaf of arrows, and was heard to say "The King doth cry eighteen pence a day. And I trust we shall have as many men for eight pence a day."[3]

The great fortress of Newcastle could play a decisive part in the success or failure of any northern rising. As has been seen, Lumley and Hilton endeavoured to make sure of it before setting out for York. The mayor and corporation were loyal to the King, and had begun to provision the town and to lay guns on the walls, but they represented only a narrow oligarchy of wealthy merchants who earlier in Henry's reign had won a victory in the Court of Star Chamber over the artisan gilds of the town[4]. The defeated party naturally inclined to the insurgents. Sir Thomas Hilton sent two servants about the town to discover the attitude of the common people, and their report was that no resistance would be made to the rebels. When the guns were laid on the walls the people said "that they might lay the guns where they would but they would turn them when the commons came whither they would."[5] Thus reassured the rebel leaders set out on their march, but Robert Brandling the mayor was a politic man, who set himself to conciliate the commons. His exertions were encouraged by the arrival of William Blytheman, one of Cromwell's commissioners for the suppression of monasteries, who had fled from York to Newcastle. On his way through Richmondshire he had been helped by Dakyn, much to the indignation of the commons[6]. When he reached Newcastle

---

[1] L. and P. xii (1), 578.   [2] Ibid. 789.

[3] Ibid. 369; printed in full, Milner and Benham, op. cit. 34, 35.

[4] Leadam, Select Cases from the Court of Star Chamber (Selden Soc.), pref. p. xcv; p. 75 et seq.

[5] L. and P. xii (1), 369; printed in full, Milner and Benham, op. cit. 43.

[6] Ibid. 788.

safely he sent in an enthusiastic report of Brandling's proceedings[1].
Sadler wrote in a subsequent letter that the mayor "did so
fully reconcile them (the commons) and so handle them that, in
fine, they were determined to live and die with the mayor and his
brethren in the defence and keeping of the town to the King's
use against all his enemies and rebels."[2]   One of the mayor's
measures of conciliation was to punish the only heretic in the town,
Roger Dachant[3], who had been obliged to abjure his opinions before
the Bishop of Durham on 24 November 1531[4].   Among other
heresies he held that every priest might be and ought to be married
and that monasteries ought to be pulled down.   This view had
commended him to the royal visitors, and he was Blytheman's friend,
so that probably his punishment was not very severe.

To sum up, the whole of the county of Durham, including the
fortresses of Barnard Castle, Brancepeth, and Durham itself, was
in the hands of the commons, but Newcastle, after wavering, had
returned to its loyalty.

It is now time to follow out the history of the siege of Skipton
Castle, to which half the Durham host were despatched on 19 October.   The dales of Yorkshire had never been really settled since the
Craven riots of 1535[5].   Dent, Sedbergh and Wensleydale were
the regions where hatred of the government was strongest.   About
the middle of September William Breyar the sanctuary man arrived
at Dent wearing the livery of the Queen's sumpter men.   A smith,
seeing his coat, said "Thy master is a thief, for he pulleth down
all our churches in the country."   The bystanders objected to the
smith's disloyalty and said : "It is not the King's deed, but the deed
of Cromwell, and if we had him here we would crum him and crum
him that he was never so crumwed, and if thy master were here
we would new crown him."   Breyar fled for his life, and complained
to the magistrates of Kirkby Lonsdale, who replied "Alas, man !
what didst thou there ? for they of Dent and of three other parishes
thereabouts were sworn on Monday last past;" but they did not
say to whom they were sworn, nor what the oath was.   About
a week later Breyar heard that the insurrection in Lincolnshire
had just broken out[6].   Darcy wrote from Templehurst on Friday
6 October to warn the King and the Earl of Cumberland of stirrings
in the dales[7], but Cumberland did not take the matter seriously.

---

[1] L. and P. xi, 1207, 1372.   [2] L. and P. xii (1), 259.   [3] L. and P. xi, 1372.
[4] Dep. and Eccles. Pro. at York Castle (Surtees Soc.), 45.
[5] See above, chap. iv.   [6] L. and P. xi, 841.   [7] Ibid. 563, 742.

He was at Skipton Castle preparing to advance against Hexham Priory[1], and was sending his son Lord Clifford to join Shrewsbury on his march to Lincoln. He therefore contented himself by writing on the 8th to Sir James Metcalf and other local gentlemen to keep order in the dales[2]. On the evening of Tuesday 10 October Christopher Aske brought him the news of the Beverley rising[3], and on the 12th came Scrope's letter about the rising of Masham and Nidderdale[4]. On the same day the Earl wrote to Henry to explain his delay in setting out for Hexham[5]. The King sent another peremptory command that he should go to Northumberland in spite of the unsettled state of Yorkshire[6], and on Monday 16 October he set out for Carlisle on his way northward[7]. He had scarcely started when he was forced to retreat into Skipton Castle again, for on Tuesday the 17th Darcy wrote from Pontefract to the King that "My lord of Cumberland on his way to Hexham returned for safety to Skipton Castle." He added that Lord Scrope was with the Earl[8], but this was a mistake. On the same day Sir Brian Hastings told Shrewsbury that Scrope had been taken, and that next day the rebels would muster at Barnsdale and Barnsley[9].

Up to this point the rising had shown all the features of an agricultural riot such as had occurred in Craven the year before. The commons wandered about the county in aimless bands, returning home at night. They had no particular respect for the church, as their treatment of the Abbot of Jervaux showed, and they directed their operations against unpopular landlords. When the abbot was in the Tower he told Cromwell, "My Lord, ye be greatly deceived thinking that the monks and canons were the chief doers of this insurrection, for there were other of more reputation." He believed that one of the chief grievances was the lordship of Middleham, for the commons of Piercebridge said they would make new lords of Middleham and restore divers who were put from their offices by wrong, and the commons of Masham used similar language[10]. He had also heard a serving-man say that the commons had offered to put his master in possession of Sheriffhutton Castle. The abbot, however, did not know the names of either the master or the man. He believed that if he told all he knew the King might pardon him,

---

[1] See above.   [2] L. and P. xi, 604.
[3] L. and P. xii (1), 1186.
[4] See above.   [5] L. and P. xi, 712.
[6] Ibid.   [7] Ibid. 927.
[8] Ibid. 760.   [9] Ibid. 759.
[10] L. and P. xii (1), 1269.

but yet it would cost him his life if it were known that he had
spoken.   Cromwell promised that his revelations should be con-
cealed, and commanded that he should write down what he knew[1],
but nothing more remains about his secrets.   In this district therefore the rising appeared to men of property as a peasant revolt
which threatened their lives and lands, and must be put down as
quickly as possible.

The names of the leaders at the siege of Skipton Castle show
the character of the movement,—they were "Merlione," evidently
a peasant who took the name from the prophecies, and John Norton
of Norton Conyers, with his two sons Richard and Thomas[2], who
were captains in the Rising of the North thirty-three years later[3].
John Norton took up arms not only in defence of his religious
principles, but also to avenge the private wrongs that he had
suffered at the hands of the Earl of Cumberland in the feud which
has already been described[4].   When the Earl of Cumberland retreated
to Skipton Castle on Tuesday 17 October, the forces which he had
collected dispersed to save their houses, and only about eighty men
remained with him.   From these Christopher Aske "tried out" forty
young men, who were sufficient to defend the whole castle except
the barmkyn[5].

Meanwhile the commons at Skipton established communications
with the main body at York, and on the church doors of Swaledale,
Wensleydale and elsewhere was posted Aske's summons to those
who would rescue the commonwealth from the heresies into which
it was falling[6].   The summons contained no expressions of hostility
to the King, and it was now that some of the gentlemen began to
join the commons.   Sir Stephen Hamerton was told that there was
such a bill on Giggleswick church door, probably on Wednesday
18 October.   On Thursday he went to see it, but the commons had
taken it down and gone to a muster at Neales Yng.   Sir Stephen
was warned by some wives as he returned from hunting that the
commons were searching for him, and he was presently surrounded
by three hundred men "who said he had ruled them, but now they
would rule him."   Their leaders, Jakes and Fawcett, administered
the oath to him, and he was sent with eight others to Skipton
Castle to request Cumberland to join them.   The Earl asked them

[1] L. and P. xii (1), 1269.   [2] Ibid. 698 (3).
[3] Sharp, Mem. of the Reb. of 1569, pp. 275, 277.
[4] See above, chap. iii.   [5] L. and P. xii (1), 1186.
[6] L. and P. xi, 892; Hist. MSS. Com. Report vi, 446; Correspondence of the
3rd Earl of Derby (Chetham Soc.), 47 et seq.

why they rose, and they replied that it was for fear of Bishopdale, Wensleydale and the other wild regions. He promised to see them recompensed if they were robbed, but they answered, "Nay, my lord, but this will not serve us." The Earl however was firm, and sent back the message: "I defy you, and do your worst, for I will not meddle with you."

On Saturday 21 October Hammerton and his companions returned to Monubent, the appointed rendezvous, where they were kept waiting, as the commons had gone to take Nicholas Tempest, the brother of Sir Richard Tempest[1]. His home was at Bashall in Bolland and he himself had gone into hiding, but the commons plundered his goods and seized his son John, a child. They threatened to strike off the boy's head if his father would not join them, whereupon Tempest returned and took the oath[2]; after this he was always earnest for the commons' cause[3]. On hearing Cumberland's answer the commons were very angry, "and swore they would have my lord of Cumberland or die," but they received letters from Sawley Abbey asking for help against the Earl of Derby, and in consequence set out thither on Sunday, 22 October, taking no further part in the attack on Skipton[4]. Nevertheless the besiegers at this time were reinforced by half the forces of Richmond and Durham[5]. After two or three days' siege, finding the castle impregnable without ordnance, the commons resolved to capture Elinor Lady Clifford, the daughter of the Duke of Suffolk and of the King's sister Mary, together with Lady Clifford's young son and the Earl's two daughters, who were all staying at Bolton Priory. The besiegers threatened to lead them before the host at the assault next day, and if it was unsuccessful, "to violate and enforce them with knaves unto my Lord's great discomfort." But before the commons could secure the ladies, Christopher Aske, with the help only of the vicar of Skipton, a groom and a boy, contrived to bring them by night over the moors from Bolton and right through the rebel host into the castle without being detected[6]. Fearing for their safety, he then wrote Robert Aske "an unkind letter," telling him that the Earl would never yield while he lived, and that if Robert assaulted the castle it "should be a double death, once to see the said Earl his master slain, and the ladies then being within the castle, which

---

[1] L. and P. xii (1), 1034.

[2] Ibid. 1014; printed in Yorks. Arch. Journ. xi, 251.

[3] Yorks. Arch. Journ. xi, 261–2.

[4] L. and P. xii (1), 1034.   [5] See above.

[6] L. and P. xii (1), 1186; printed in part by Froude, op. cit. chap. xiii.

should be death also to them." Robert replied in a "like letter of unkindness," saying that he would not himself assault the castle but that the Earl's enemies would certainly take it if he did not yield. He was led to believe this by a letter from the Duke of Suffolk to the Earl which he had intercepted, but he found out afterwards that this letter referred to Carlisle and not to Skipton[1]. The siege lasted for about ten days, but the castle was not taken. While it was in progress the commons robbed the Earl's parks, and pulled down his houses at Bardon and Carleton, "which were so strong as to take three days in breaking."[2]

Communications were maintained between the besiegers and the other bodies of the rebels by Dakyn and the elderly gentlemen who had been placed for that purpose at Jervaux Abbey. The post-masters received some unsigned letters from Sir Christopher Danby, which they requested him to sign, and others from William Conyers, and on one occasion Dakyn wrote to the Abbot of Fountains for post-horses. Copies were taken of all the letters which passed through their hands, but the copies were left at the abbey and probably destroyed. One of the gentlemen, Mr Siggiswick, being aged and sick, returned home, and his place was taken by another aged man, Mr Catherick[3]. When the two hosts joined at Pontefract, Dakyn and the others returned home[4], but the siege of Skipton lasted until Norton was summoned to take part in the first conference at Doncaster[5]. As soon as the truce was proclaimed Aske wrote to the commons forbidding them to molest the Earl until the King's answer was received, and to the Earl begging him to observe the truce. His orders were obeyed, although the commons maintained a very hostile attitude[6].

The only other stronghold in Yorkshire which held out for the King was Scarborough Castle. It was a royal castle, and the constable was Sir Ralph Evers[7] the younger, afterwards Ralph first lord Evers. After a career of some distinction on the border he was killed at the battle of Ancrum Moor 1545, where it was said that Annan, the general of the Scots, on seeing his body, burst into tears exclaiming, "God have mercy on him, for he was a fell cruel man, and over cruel. And welaway that ever such slaughter and bloodshed

---

[1] L. and P. xii (1), 698 (3). [2] L. and P. xi, 927.
[3] L. and P. xii (1), 787, 789. [4] See below, chap. x.
[5] L. and P. xii (1), 6 ; printed in full, Eng. Hist. Rev. v, 331 et seq.
[6] See below, chap. xi.
[7] Eure, Ewer, Ewers, Evers, Ewry, Ivers, Yevars, and many other forms.

should be among Christian men."[1] Evers has even his modest niche in literature, for the moody Baron of Smailholm

> "...came not from where Ancrum Moor,
>   Ran red with English blood ;
> Where the Douglas true and the bold Buccleuch,
>   'Gainst keen Lord Evers stood."[2]

Like most keepers of royal castles, he made his profit out of his charge. He was accused of having taken the lead roofs off the towers and turrets to make into brewing vessels for himself, and to exchange for French wines[3]. But in spite of these peccadillos he was true to his post, and on 17 October Darcy reported that Scarborough was besieged by the commons[4]. Some of Archbishop Lee's servants, flying thither from York, were captured by the besiegers, but rescued and brought into the castle by Sir Ralph[5]. The commons had seized the town[6], and it was only the castle which held out.

Very little is known about this early stage of the siege, but it seems to have been closely maintained. There was afterwards a story that Sir Ralph and his company had "no sustenance but bread and water for the space of twenty days,"[7] and his appeals for help to the royal generals show that he was hard pressed[8]. The rebels had some ordnance, which they had probably taken from ships in the harbour, and they knew how to use it, for Sir Ralph reported "of late part of the wall and the ground of Scarborough Castle is shot down in the outer ward betwixt the gatehouse and the castle."[9] Nevertheless the rebels were baffled and failed to take the castle.

The sieges of Skipton and Scarborough occupied the men of the northern dales so completely that their contingent had not reached Pontefract on 21 October. Aske reckoned that they would be twelve thousand men, armed and mounted, under the leadership of Lord Scrope, Sir Christopher Danby, Sir William Mallory, the Nortons, the Markenfields and others[10].

In contrast to the rising in the Dales, the insurrection in Lancashire seems to have been caused chiefly by discontent at the royal supremacy and the suppression of the monasteries.

---

[1] Hamilton Papers (Scot. Rec. Soc.), II, 565.
[2] Sir Walter Scott, The Eve of St John.
[3] L. and P. XII (1), 535.   [4] L. and P. XI, 760 (2).
[5] L. and P. XII (1), 1022.   [6] L. and P. XII (2), 1212 (vi).
[7] Lord Herbert of Cherbury, Reign of Henry VIII (ed. 1672), 478.
[8] L. and P. XI, 989.   [9] L. and P. XIII (1), 45.
[10] L. and P. XII (1), 6 ; printed in full, Eng. Hist. Rev. V, 331 et seq.

The principal leader was one Atkinson, probably the same John Atkinson alias Brotton who had escaped after preventing the vicar of Gisburn from reading the Act of Supremacy in the parish church on 11 July 1535[1]. The centre of the insurrection was St Mary's Abbey, Sawley[2], a monastery which was beloved by the commons, "being the charitable relief of those parts, and standing in a mountain country and amongst three forests."[3] It contained an abbot and twenty-one monks and, as one of the lesser monasteries, had been dissolved by the commissioners; but on Thursday 12 October the commons reinstated the brethren[4], who naturally threw themselves heart and soul into the pilgrims' cause. One of them probably composed the famous song of the Pilgrimage:

> "Christ Crucified,
> For thy wounds wide,
> Us commons guide,
> That pilgrims be."[5]

Among their papers are notes for a sermon maintaining that it is lawful for a man to fight for the Faith and to resent injuries done to God and his neighbours[6].

In several other places the commissioners for the suppression of the monasteries encountered opposition. The Priory of Conishead had been threatened in 1525 when Wolsey dissolved a few of the smaller monasteries, but it was spared at the intercession of the Duke of Suffolk, who reported it to be "a great help to the people."[7] On Monday 16 October 1536, the prior wrote to William Collins, bailiff of Kendal, begging him to make proclamation that help should be sent to the priory, or else all they had would be taken from them[8]. About this time or a little earlier, in an undated letter, news was sent to Darcy that "this week past Manchester College should have been pulled down, and there would have been a rising, but the commissioners recoiled."[9]

In the neighbouring county of Cheshire the commissioners were actively resisted. The Abbot of Norton had been deposed and imprisoned, apparently on a charge of treason[10]. A servant of Cromwell

---

[1] See above, chap. IV.   [2] Also spelt Salley.
[3] L. and P. XII (1), 6.   [4] L. and P. XI, 784.
[5] Ibid. 786 (3); printed in full, Eng. Hist. Rev. V, 331; J. Horsfall Turner, Yorkshire Anthology, 143; The Antiquary, November 1880.
[6] L. and P. XI, 786 (2); cf. 1421.
[7] Gasquet, Hen. VIII and the Eng. Mon. I, chap. III; L. and P. IV (1), 1253.
[8] L. and P. XII (1), 849 (29).   [9] L. and P. XI, 635.
[10] See note B at end of chapter; cf. L. and P. XI, 486.

was put in his place to effect the surrender of the monastery, which took place at the beginning of October 1536. On Sunday 8 October when the commissioners had packed up the jewels and movable property, and were ready to leave, they were attacked by the former abbot, who had escaped from prison, and was now at the head of two or three hundred country people. The commissioners fled, and took refuge in a tower, but they contrived to send a message to the sheriff, who set out at once, and came upon the abbot and his followers at 2 o'clock in the morning, feasting on an ox and other victuals by the light of great fires which were burning within and without the monastery. They were taken by surprise and could make no effective resistance. The abbot and three of his canons were captured, but most of his followers fled under cover of the darkness. The sheriff reported that the abbot was expecting reinforcements and "it was thought if it had not been quickly handled the matter would have grown to further inconvenience." As it was, the King's farmer was restored, and the abbot and canons were imprisoned in Halton Castle. The King sent orders for their execution, but they were not carried out at once, and on 30 November the abbot was still living. His fate is uncertain, but he was taken to Chester Castle for safer keeping during the insurrection, and it is unlikely that he escaped[1].

The commons of Lancashire expressed sympathy with the Lincolnshire rebels, and there was a widespread belief that the young Earl of Derby inclined to the same side. His servants were so bitter against Cromwell that a spy in the household wrote "or your lordship (Cromwell) should be there as they would have you to be I had liefer to be in Jerusalem to come home upon my bare feet."[2]

Thomas Stanley, a priest who was related to Derby, corresponded with Lord Darcy, and used all his influence to persuade the Earl to join the rebels[3]. For a time it was believed that he had been successful. Aske showed Bigod a letter from the Earl, and said that he would be with them in time of need. Afterwards a servant of Bigod's who was sent with a letter to Derby, told him that in the rebel host he was "cried traitor." The Earl replied that "there was no man in England save the King who should say such a thing of him but he would lay his sword on his face," and he trusted the King would let him "boulte out" the occasion of this

---

[1] L. and P. xi, 681, 787, 1019, 1212; Gasquet, op. cit. ii, chap. ii.
[2] L. and P. xi, 859.   [3] Ibid. 635.

slander[1]. Perhaps his indignation was so great because there were some grounds for the rebels' confidence in his sympathy. Nicholas Tempest had heard that Derby "had written such a letter to the lord Darcy that he knew the said lord of Derby would do little in the matter [on behalf of the King] when it should come to the point." He believed that the gentlemen who trusted to Derby to protect them against the rebels would find themselves deceived in him[2]. It was said that Aske called him "false flattering boy" who ran away from the commons[3], for when it came to the point he chose to serve the King.

On Tuesday 10 October Derby received a summons to prepare his men in case the rebellion should spread from Lincolnshire into those parts[4]. The monks of Sawley were restored on the 12th, and on the 19th, Thursday, news of this having reached the King, further orders were sent to Derby, that instead of joining Shrewsbury on his advance northwards, as had been intended, he must suppress the rising in Lancashire, send up the ringleaders and hang the brethren in their monks' apparel. A commission under the Privy Seal was sent to him to authorise his proceedings[5]. He was given authority over all Lancashire, Cheshire, North Wales and Staffordshire, excepting the parts already committed to Shrewsbury. This liberal commission delighted Derby so much that his previous inclination was overcome and he resolved to oppose the rebels. He showed the commission to Thomas Stanley, saying that no ancestor of his had ever had the like, to which Stanley retorted that "no more should he neither have had" if it had not been to support Cromwell. A heated argument followed, but Derby was now quite determined on his course[6]. The King's judicious display of confidence had made an ally of a man who might have been a most dangerous enemy. Derby might have avenged his ancestor Sir William Stanley by overmatching Henry VIII if he had thrown his powerful influence into the scale against the King. But on the other hand, the Earl's love of ruling and his commanding position as by far the most important man among the Pilgrims would have made it necessary for them to acknowledge him their leader, if he had joined them, and as he was not very wise

---

[1] L. and P. xii (1), 578.

[2] Ibid. 518; printed in Yorks. Arch. Journ. xi, 261–2; see note D at end of chapter.

[3] L. and P. xii (1), 853.

[4] L. and P. xi, 634; printed in full, Correspondence of the 3rd Earl of Derby (Chetham Soc.), 18.

[5] L. and P. xi, 783; printed in full, Correspondence of the 3rd Earl of Derby, 28.

[6] L. and P. xi, 807.

it may be doubted whether he had sufficient tact and ability for the position. He would have been but a doubtful acquisition if he had introduced fresh divisions into their council. This, however, is only speculation, as Derby prepared to fight for the King. Nevertheless the commons of Lancashire were wholly in favour of the rebels, and Stanley believed that if one quarter rose the rest would. He reported to Darcy that Derby and Lord Monteagle his cousin would not be able to set out before the following Wednesday, 25 October[1], and meanwhile the commons were rising in response to a summons from "Mr Captain" (Aske or Atkinson?). An example of this summons is preserved in an unsigned letter to "Cousin Townley." Its date seems to be Saturday 14 October. The writer had received a letter from "Mr Captain in this our Pilgrimage of Grace," containing the order "that on sight thereof ye fail not with all your company to be on (blank) Thewseday (Tuesday 17th?) next by (blank) of the clock in all your best array, as ye will avoid displeasure of the contrary doing." The writer was sure that his cousin would be glad to hear this. He had sent orders to the commons of Lancaster side to take the gentlemen who were favourable to the Pilgrimage, and was sorry that "Cousin Townley's" brother had not taken the oath, as he was inclined to it at one time[2]. Sir John Townley and his brother, who was also called John, are afterwards mentioned as being active on behalf of the commons[3].

Such a summons was brought by George Willen and William Gaunt from Dent to Kendal on Saturday 14 October. The men from Dent had come, as they said, to ask Sir James Leyborne what they should do about the summons, which they had received from Richmondshire. All the advice they received from Leyborne the steward and William Collins the bailiff was "not to meddle." Next day (Sunday 15 October) the commons under the leadership of Tom Dockwray and Brian Jobson assembled at daybreak in the North Street of Kendal, and took all the chief men of the town, rousing them from their beds and making them swear to be true to God, the King and their ancient laudable customs. "Mr Leyborne" had fled, but his friends promised that he would do as the other gentlemen did, and his brother Nicholas "sealed to a book which was read concerning their customs" in his name. The complaint that their ancient customs were being violated was the

---

[1] L. and P. xi, 807.   [2] Ibid. 804.

[3] Ibid. 1155 (1), 1251; printed in full, Correspondence of the 3rd Earl of Derby (Chetham Soc.), 67.

characteristic grievance of Cumberland and Westmorland, and will be discussed more fully hereafter. Beyond visiting Mr Leyborne's house again on Friday 20 October the commons of Kendal did not do much until on Saturday 21 October they received a summons from the men of Dent to muster with them on Monday 23 October at ten o'clock on Ennesmore. Here a local quarrel broke out, for the Kendal men answered that they "would have nought to do" with Dent. The reply of the latter was that if Kendal did not attend the muster, the town should be spoiled by ten thousand men. For a moment the citizens of Kendal thought of resistance, but in the end some five hundred of them went to Ennesmore. There they found that the captains were Atkinson, James Cowper, John Middleton, John Hebyllthwayte of Sedbergh, James Bushell of Middleton and the vicar of Clapham, who "was the common swearer and counsellor in all that business and persuaded the people that they should go to heaven if they died in that quarrel." The men of Kendal told the captains that they were sworn, but that their gentlemen would not come in, to which the others answered, "If ye cannot rule them, we shall rule them." A muster was appointed at Kendal next day at 8 a.m., when they would have spoiled Mr Leyborne's house but for the bad weather. On Friday 27 October Leyborne and the other gentlemen at last came in and were sworn at Kendal Tollbooth, and on Saturday 28 October they mustered on Kelet Moor and marched to Lancaster[1].

It was this rising which prevented Derby from marching on Sawley when he received the King's first orders, dated 19 October[2]. The delay annoyed Henry so much that on the 28th he wrote repeating his instructions[3], but Derby was doing his best. He occupied Preston in order to lie within striking distance of both the rebel hosts, the one lying near Kendal, which was said to number five or six thousand men, but was probably under three thousand, and the other defending Sawley Abbey. His attitude alarmed the monks of Sawley, who sent into Yorkshire for help on Saturday 21 October[4], but his attention was at first occupied by the Kendal rising. Many fugitives hurried to his protection, among the first being the abbot and deputy steward of Furness, who came by water to Lathom before the Earl occupied Preston[5]. From Lathom

---

[1] L. and P. xii (1), 914.   [2] L. and P. xi, 783.
[3] Ibid. 894.   [4] See above.
[5] L. and P. xi, 947 (2); printed in full, Correspondence of the 3rd Earl of Derby, 38.

the abbot wrote to his monastery that he had taken a way to be sure both from King and commons[1], and while he remained with Derby the monks levied men for the rebels and sent them money, telling their recruits "Now must they stick to it or else never, for if they sit down both you and Holy Church is undone; and if they lack company we will go with them and live and die with them to defend their most godly pilgrimage." They gave out that the King was not right heir to the crown because his father came in by the sword, and they maintained the papal authority so earnestly that some of their tenants were willing to wager that the new laws would be annulled in three years. Four of the monks of Sawley had been sent to Furness, and three of them, who had capacities[2], returned to Sawley when the commons restored it[3].

The Prior of Cartmell, who had been restored against his will, fled to the Earl at Preston, where he was joined by Lord Monteagle and Sir Marmaduke Tunstall, whose houses lay between Lancashire and Westmorland in the district where the rising took place[4]. Sir Robert Bellingham, Aske's brother-in-law, and other gentlemen were taken and sworn by the commons but afterwards escaped to Preston. It must have been for this desertion that the commons threatened to spoil the house of Aske's sister Margaret, Sir Robert's wife, but Aske prevented them from doing so[5].

Atkinson entered Lancaster at the head of the host from Dent and Kendal on Saturday 28 October[6]. He administered the oath to the mayor and all the burgesses, but the mayor escaped to his master the Earl of Derby. The commons threatened to plunder his house if he did not return, and Derby sent two of his servants to Atkinson to explain that he was detaining the mayor, and to order the commons to depart in the King's name. Atkinson declared that as the mayor would not come, his friends, who had been his sureties "were forfeitures," and he gave the servants a list of their names. As for the rest of the message, the commons had a pilgrimage for the commonwealth to do, which they would accomplish or die. The servants replied that if twelve of their chiefs would sign a promise to fight on Bentham Moor, the Earl would undertake to meet them there and determine the quarrel by battle. Atkinson answered that they would not fight unless the Earl hindered their pilgrimage, or attempted to join the Lord Lieutenant. If they had

---

[1] L. and P. xii (1), 652.
[2] See above, chap. v, note B.
[3] L. and P. xii (1), 841 (3).
[4] L. and P. xi, 947 (2).
[5] L. and P. xii (1), 698 (3).
[6] Ibid. 914.

agreed to fight, Derby had resolved to wait for help from Cheshire, as he could not trust his men[1]. It was probably the report of these messengers which convinced him that the rebels at Lancaster were not very formidable, and he therefore turned his attention to Sawley. It was known in Lancaster on the 28th that the reinforcements from Yorkshire had arrived there[2].

After the resolution at Monubent on Saturday 21 October Sir Stephen Hamerton had gone to Colne and Burnley, marching down one bank of the Ribble, and Nicholas Tempest had gone to Whalley, marching down the other bank. The latter reached Whalley on Monday 23 October. For more than two hours the monks refused to admit him and his three or four hundred men, but at last they opened their doors for fear of burning. Tempest administered the oath to the abbot and eight of the brethren. Sir Stephen Hamerton and his men arrived the same night and the two leaders recounted their experiences to each other[3].

Hearing that Derby was doing his best to raise forces against them, they sent to Walter Strickland to come to their aid, but received no reply[4]. Then definite news was brought that Derby intended to set out from Preston on Monday 30 October and would spend that night with his forces at Whalley Abbey, which was some four miles from Sawley. The rebels at once occupied a hill by the abbey, prepared to fall on Derby, who did not know of their movements[5]. An encounter between the rebels and Derby's forces seemed inevitable, and the situation was on the whole in favour of the former. It is true that Derby had levied over eight thousand men, but their loyalty was doubtful[6]; the Pilgrims at Sawley, unknown to Derby, had occupied a strong position, and those at Lancaster were preparing to take him in the rear[7]. Derby himself admitted that the roads were very difficult and that there would have been a great fray "though no doubt the traitors would have been overthrown."[8] Just at this critical moment, at nine o'clock in the morning on Monday 30 October, Berwick Herald-at-Arms rode into Preston and delivered to the Earl a letter from Shrewsbury and the other lords, informing him of the first appointment at Doncaster, and directing

[1] L. and P. xi, 947 (2); printed in full, Correspondence, 38.
[2] L. and P. xii (1), 914.
[3] Yorks. Arch. Journ. xi, 253 and L. and P. xii (1), 1034.
[4] Yorks. Arch. Journ. xi, 256.   [5] L. and P. xii (1), 1034.
[6] L. and P. xi, 947 (2).   [7] L. and P. xii (1), 914.
[8] L. and P. xi, 947.

him to "sparple his force and do no hurt."[1] After a formal consultation with the gentlemen present, he disbanded his men and returned to Lathom, probably with a very thankful heart[2]. The same news had reached Whalley in a letter from Aske, forbidding the Pilgrims to meddle with Derby even if he attacked them, and directing them to withdraw into the mountains, unless he (Derby) "raised fire," in which case they must send by post to Aske. Hearing that the Earl had withdrawn, they also broke up their forces, and "kept every man his own house, ready to be up and come together at an hour's warning."[3]

From Lancashire[4] we turn to Cumberland and Westmorland, where there had been considerably more enclosing of common land by the landlords than in the other counties. This was the principal grievance of the commons in those parts. On 17 August 1536 Sir Thomas Wharton reported to Cromwell that there had been divers riots in Cumberland, probably against the enclosures, although one riot was traced to the Bishop of Carlisle[5], and was most likely a private feud.

On Sunday 15 October the curate of Kirkby Stephen did not "bid St Luke's day (Wednesday 18 October) as a holyday," which exasperated his parishioners so much that they threatened to kill him; to pacify them he was forced to announce the holiday as usual[6]. Probably it was on the same day that Robert Thompson, vicar of Brough-under-Stainmore, received a letter from the commons of Richmondshire which he read aloud to his parishioners, perhaps in the parish church. The contents of the letter ran: "Wellbeloved brethren in God, we greet you well, signifying unto you that we your brethren in Christ have assembled us together and put us in readiness for the maintenance of the faith of God, His laws and His Church, and where abbeys was suppressed we have restored them again and put the religious men into their houses: wherefore we exhort you to do the same."[7] This letter seems to have been signed "Captain Poverty," as was the one sent to Sir Ingram Percy[8].

---

[1] L. and P. xi, 900, 901, 922; nos. 901 and 922 are printed in full in Correspondence of the 3rd Earl of Derby, 36 and 37.

[2] L. and P. xi, 947.

[3] Yorks. Arch. Journ. xi, 256.   [4] See note C at end of chapter.

[5] L. and P. xi, 319; printed in full, Raine, Priory of Hexham, i Append. p. clvi n.

[6] L. and P. xii (1), 687 (2); printed in full, Wilson, The Monasteries of Cumberland and Westmorland, no. xxii.

[7] L. and P. xii (1), 687 (1); printed in full, Wilson, op. cit. no. xxi.

[8] See above.

Next day the men of Kirkby Stephen held a muster on Sandforth Moor in response to the summons from Richmond, and chose as their captains Robert Pullen, Nicholas Musgrave, Christopher Blenkinsop and Robert Hilton. Vicar Thompson went to Penrith that night, to escape from the commons as he said, but it seems more likely that his object was to spread the news of the rising. He rejoined the muster next day, Tuesday 17 October, when the commons went to take Sir Thomas Wharton. As he had fled, they captured his eldest son instead. On Wednesday 18 October they went to Lamerside Hall, believing that Sir Thomas and other gentlemen had taken refuge there, but they found only servants. Pullen then issued an order that the gentlemen should come in by a certain day or their houses would be plundered, and appointed men bound by oath to collect the goods which the captains declared forfeit. The leaders agreed that next day, Thursday 19 October, Pullen and his men should march down one side of the Eden and Musgrave with his down the other. Pullen's company set out and arrived at Penrith the same day, but Musgrave's band spent the night at Lowther, where they had in vain hoped to take Sir John Lowther. Penrith had already risen in response to the summons from Richmondshire, which had probably been brought by Thompson. Four captains had been chosen, Anthony Hutton, John Beck, Gilbert Whelpdale or Whelton, and Thomas Burbeck, who took the names of Charity Faith, Poverty and Pity. Gilbert Whelpdale, Captain Poverty, was Robert Thompson's brother-in-law, and appointed him his chaplain and secretary. Pullen's company spent Thursday night in Penrith and on Friday 20 October set out again. Thompson accompanied them as far as Eamont Bridge, where the oath was administered to Dudley and other gentlemen, but he turned back to Penrith at the request of the commons there, in order that he might help them with his counsel. On the same day they held a muster on Penrith Fell, where Thompson and the captains organised their forces as well as they could. "Sir" Edward Perith, who must have been a priest, was appointed the crossbearer, to carry the cross before the host. George Corney, another priest, wrote letters to the neighbouring gentlemen at the dictation of the captains, and Thompson taught Thomas Berwick, the town-crier, a proclamation to be uttered before every meeting "to the effect that, as the rulers did not defend them from thieves and Scots, they had chosen the four captains, who commanded all to live in peace and to say five *aves*, five *paters* and a creed." The letters were sent to Sir

Edward Musgrave, who came in and took the oath with all the parish of Edenhall and the country round Penrith. Another muster was held on Saturday 21 October, when the commons beyond Eden were sworn, and a meeting was appointed on Monday 23 October at Cartlogan Thorns. On Monday the commons of Caldbeck, Greystoke, Hutton, Shewlton and Sowerby rose and came to Cartlogan Thorns, bringing with them Bernard Towneley, the chancellor of the diocese, Richard Bewley, Richard Vachell and other gentlemen. Sir John Lowther also came to the meeting, "to summon certain men of Sowerby to keep the day of march," i.e. the day appointed for a meeting with the Scots warden. Sir John's attitude is doubtful; he does not seem to have been brought in by force, and the commons looked upon him as their friend[1].

The next muster was appointed to be held on Wednesday 25 October at Kilwatling How[2]. A new actor now comes on the scene—Abbot Carter of Holm Cultram. The Priory of Carlisle and the Abbey of Holm Cultram were the only two monasteries in Cumberland wealthy enough to escape the Act of Suppression. There had been several scandals in connection with Holm Cultram in recent years, and the abbot seems to have realised from the first that without a revolution his house was doomed[3]. Consequently when the news of the rising reached him he sent orders to all his tenants to attend the muster at Kilwatling How under pain of hanging[4].

There on Wednesday 25 October the gentlemen and commons of the neighbourhood were sworn, and four clergymen, the parson of Melmerby, Dr Towneley, the vicar of Sowerby and the vicar of Edenhall, were appointed Chaplains of Poverty to instruct the commons in the Faith, a lesson which was much needed, as those who attended the muster announced that if the other clergymen of the district did not come in they would strike off the heads of those already in their hands, and set Towneley's head on the highest tree of the diocese[5].

On Wednesday and Thursday a picturesque ceremony took place in Penrith chapel, when the four captains followed Thompson in procession round the building with their swords drawn. They then put up their swords and the vicar said mass, and expounded

---

[1] L. and P. XII (1), 687 (2); printed in full, Wilson, op. cit. no. XXII.
[2] Ibid.   [3] V. C. H. Cumberland, II, 48.
[4] L. and P. XII (1), 1259; printed in full, Wilson, op. cit. nos. XXIV—XXVII and Raine, op. cit. I, p. cliv.
[5] L. and P. XII (1), 687 (1).

the Ten Commandments, showing how all the present troubles had arisen from breaking them. This was called the captains' mass. A priest objected that swords should not be drawn in church, and the ceremony was given up[1].

The chief problem now before the rebels was the attitude of Carlisle. This was determined almost by accident. On Monday 16 October the Earl of Cumberland intended to send his son Henry Lord Clifford to join Shrewsbury[2]. Finding that he could not go directly southwards by land without a considerable risk of falling into the rebels' hands, Lord Clifford conceived the ingenious idea of travelling north to his uncle Sir Thomas Clifford at Berwick and taking ship to Lincolnshire[3]. The general rising, however, forced him to seek refuge in Carlisle Castle, and there he lay four days in hiding. Meanwhile on Friday 27 October the citizens of Carlisle sent messengers to the commons of Penrith under safe conduct. The commons were mustered on Sanderdale Hill, and the messengers reported that the burgesses of Carlisle would take no oath, but otherwise would be with them. All the people who lived in that neighbourhood thought that they would be ruined if Carlisle were not secured, for the mosstroopers of the Black Quarters, the valleys of Esk and Line, had already begun to plunder them. By Thompson's advice they proclaimed that no one should take provisions into the town, hoping that it might be reduced by starvation, as Hull had been[4]. The threat would have been sufficient for the townspeople, as they had neither ordnance nor powder and the walls were in ruins, but Lord Clifford came out of his hiding-place, and said that as his father's deputy he would be their captain and jeopardy his life with them. They were so far encouraged that they promised not to give over the town[5], especially as the commons had withdrawn for the moment to Cockermouth, where they passed the night of Friday 27 October. The Abbot of Holm Cultram joined them in person at Cockermouth on Saturday 28 October, and the rebels' council ordered Sir John Lowther, "who was at Carlisle," the abbot, Towneley, Richard Blenkhow and Thomas Dalston to go to Carlisle with orders to the mayor to meet the commons and take the oath for himself and his brethren on the following Monday at Burford (Brunfelde) Oak. The priests were very unwilling to go and one

[1] L. and P. xii (1), 687 (2).   [2] L. and P. xi, 742; see above.
[3] Ibid. 927.
[4] L. and P. xii (1), 687 (1), (2); printed in full, Wilson, op. cit. nos. xxi and xxii.
[5] L. and P. xi, 927.

Percy Simpson exclaimed that "they would never be well till they had stricken off all the priests' heads, saying they would but deceive them." The appointed messengers went no further than Dalston, but they sent "Sir" William Robin to Carlisle and he brought back word "there was a proclamation that no man should make any unlawful assembly," which was evidently news of the first truce of Doncaster. The abbot and Towneley told Thompson of this, but he and the other captains believed that it was only a trick to gain time and mustered next day. Towneley and other messengers were again sent to Carlisle, where they were shown the proclamation of the truce, and sent it back to the host at once. They do not seem to have believed that it would pacify the commons, and delivered their message to the mayor, who asked for a day's respite. When Towneley and the others returned to Burford Oak, however, they found that the commons had agreed to disperse until Friday 3 November, when they were to assemble again. Thompson went back to Penrith and took no further part in the proceedings[1].

All this time Lord Dacre had been lying quiet at Naworth Castle. By reason of his feud with the Cliffords and his late trial for treason it had been hoped that he would join the commons, but his recent experience had been enough for him, and Sir Ingram Percy called him "first a traitor to the king and after to the commons" for remaining loyal[2]. He was in occasional communication with Shrewsbury[3], and on 30 October he sent to Lord Clifford, offering to come to his aid if the commons besieged Carlisle, and asking Clifford to come to him if they besieged Naworth. Clifford willingly agreed[4]. When the commons mustered at Burford Oak on Friday 3 November Sir Christopher Dacre came to them from Carlisle under safe conduct[5], and with the help of Towneley and the gentlemen and priests who were with them he persuaded them to accept the truce and to disperse[6]. It was agreed that they should bring their wares to market as before, and that Lord Clifford should prevent his soldiers from "riding on the commons."[7] After this Lord Dacre went secretly up to London[8], thinking that he would

---

[1] L. and P. xii (1), 687 (1), (2).

[2] Ibid. 1090; printed in full, Raine, op. cit. i, Append. p. cxxx et seq.; De Fonblanque, op. cit. i, Append. lii.

[3] L. and P. xi, 647, 846.

[4] Ibid. 1331.   [5] Ibid.

[6] L. and P. xii (1), 687 (1).

[7] L. and P. xi, 993; xii (1), 687 (1); printed in full, Wilson, op. cit. no. xxi.

[8] L. and P. xi, 1096, 1331.

be less liable to misrepresentation if he were actually under the King's eye.

The movement in Cumberland and Westmorland was essentially a rising of the poor against the rich. The rebels wanted to abolish rents, tithes and enclosures[1]. In spite of the exhortations of the enthusiast, Robert Thompson, and the Abbot of Holm Cultram, the commons showed no particular zeal for the Church and treated the clergy with little respect. In consequence the gentlemen and clergy stood aloof, and the mass of eager but undisciplined commons were as great an anxiety to the leaders of the rebellion as they could be to their opponents.

From this brief sketch of the state of the northern counties up to the first truce of Doncaster two points stand out. In the first place the discontent was very strong and very widespread. The gentlemen who were usually equal to keeping order were reduced to a few isolated fortresses, Chillingham, Scarborough and Skipton; even the large towns, such as Carlisle, Newcastle and Berwick, were wavering. The progress of the insurrection may be described in the words which a German historian uses with regard to the Peasants' War of 1525: "the peasant revolts were, in general, less of the nature of campaigns, or even of an uninterrupted series of minor military operations, than of a slow process of mobilisation interrupted and accompanied by continual negociations with the lords and princes—a mobilisation which was rendered possible by the standing right of assembly and of carrying arms possessed by the peasants."[2] The widespread character of the rebellion was in its favour, but the second point is against it. In consequence of the great extent of the district affected it was inevitable that there should be many conflicting interests, which only genius could unite in a common cause. In one place the course of the rising was determined by local feuds, in another by religious enthusiasm, in another by agricultural grievances.

Though such a mass of discontent was very dangerous to the King, it was almost equally dangerous to those who were attempting to control and guide it to a definite object. It will be noticed that there were two distinct sets of agitators, whose aims were sometimes almost antagonistic. First, there was the religious movement which usually centred in some monastery—Hexham, Sawley, Furness or Holm Cultram. Its motives and object have already been described,

[1] L. and P. xi, 1080; xii (1), 687 (2).
[2] Lamprecht, *Deutsche Geschichte*, v, 343, quoted by Bax, op. cit. 109.

and it was the cause with which the gentlemen sympathised. Second there was the social movement directed chiefly against raised rents and enclosures. Its centre seems to have been Richmondshire, and it was this cause which was most influential in Cumberland and Westmorland. The leaders had adopted the name of Captain Poverty as a symbol of their intention. The commons, they meant, were led by Poverty. There was, of course, no one definite Captain Poverty, though individual leaders might assume the name, as at Penrith, but wherever that name is used the rising was directed primarily against the gentlemen, and no particular devotion was shown to the Church as an institution. It was this second movement which resembled in many particulars the Peasants' Revolt in Germany in 1525. There, as in England, the first demands of the peasants were social, not religious[1]. In Germany they soon became combined with a reforming campaign against the Church, while in England the religious movement was reactionary, but the ideals of the peasants had something in common with both tendencies, for while on the one hand they wanted reform of abuses, on the other their social programme was reactionary, looking back to the primitive form of the village community[2]. This may be observed in the English as well as in the German movement. The leaders of the religious insurrection in England, Aske and Darcy and the friars, seem originally to have had little or nothing to do with the social movement, and though they tried to direct it to their own ends they were rather alarmed by it.

NOTES TO CHAPTER IX

Note A.   The Isle was not Holy Island in Northumberland, as stated in the Index of the "Letters and Papers." It was the name of a country house in the parish of Sedgefield, Durham, which was built on an island formed by the river Skerne and its tributaries.

Note B.   An attempt was made in 1535 to involve the Abbot of Norton in a charge of issuing counterfeit coin[3].

Note C.   Kendal is now in Westmorland, but in early times it was included in Lancashire, and even in Henry VIII's reign the boundary between the two counties was still unsettled[4].

Note D.   The summary of Nicholas Tempest's confession which is given in the "Letters and Papers," XII (1), no. 1014 is so brief that it gives no idea of the contents of the document. The subsequent references are therefore given to the "Yorkshire Archaeological Journal," vol. XI, where the confession is printed in full.

Bax, op. cit. 61.   [2] Ibid. 88.   [3] L. and P. IX, 183; XII (2) 597.
    [4] Nicholson and Burn, Westmorland and Cumberland, I, 11–12.

CHAPTER X

THE MUSTERS AT PONTEFRACT

It was a strange kind of warfare in which the garrison of a surrendered castle immediately went over to the enemy—joined in their counsels and became their leaders. When all the gentlemen at Pontefract had taken the oath Aske "would have yielded up his white rod and name of captain to the nobility there, which refused, but willed him to continue as captain because otherwise amongst the nobility there were parte [likely] to be disdain, if any of them would have taken this office upon them." A council was held at once[1]. Every man was willing and earnest, excepting the Archbishop and his friend Dr Magnus, who did not attend the councils[2]. Darcy and Sir Robert Constable became acknowledged heads of the Pilgrimage. Constable and Aske had some time before been "in displeasure" with one another, but, true to their oath, they set aside all private disputes[3]. They worked loyally together to muster and drill the bands of Pilgrims which marched in every hour. At the councils all the worshipful men "commoned" together "for the setting forth of the battles and company towards Doncaster, for the preparation for victuals, scoutwatches and for the orders of the field, and who should be in the van-ward and middle-ward, and for the answers of the heralds, and good espials, and search the fords of Don for passage with the host." Copies of the oath and Aske's proclamations were sent out with the messengers who carried orders and advice to companies on Pilgrimage in all parts of Yorkshire, in Durham, and in all the north. Darcy had received trustworthy information from Lancashire, that the people were about to rise though the Earl of Derby was obstinate in loyalty[4]. Aske still had

---

[1] L. and P. xii (1), 6; printed in full, Eng. Hist. Rev. v, 343.
[2] L. and P. xii (1), 1022.
[3] Ibid. 901 (41); printed in full, Eng. Hist. Rev. v, 568. See above, chap. iii.
[4] L. and P. xi, 807.

hopes of the young nobleman, and he sent the servant who brought the news back again, with a letter to the Earl, and a copy of the oath to be "spread abroad" on his way through the country[1].

While the leaders of the Pilgrimage were holding counsel, word was brought to them that a herald in the King's coat of arms was riding into the town. This was Thomas Miller, Lancaster Herald, sent from Scrooby by the Earl of Shrewsbury to read to the Pilgrims the same proclamation which had dispersed the men of Lincolnshire. He was a man of parts and conduct, as became the honourable bearer of the messages of a King. As he approached Pontefract, he fell in with troops of countrymen on their way to the musters. They treated him respectfully and listened to his assurances that the King had never even thought of levying taxes on burials, christenings, etc. Several hundred, as he said, even promised him to go home, though it does not appear that they turned back at once. As he was making his way to the market cross to read his proclamation in due form, he was stopped and told that the captain of the host, Robert Aske, had sent for him. He was taken up to the castle, and passed through the three wards; at the gate of every ward was a porter with a white rod and "many in harness of very cruel fellows." He was brought into a hall full of people and told to wait till the captain's pleasure was known. Unappalled by this show of strength and order, the herald made his way to the high table and boldly began to declare the King's will. He was interrupted by a summons to the castle chamber. Here he found himself before the Archbishop, Darcy, Sir Robert Constable, Sir Christopher Danby, with other knights and gentlemen. In the midst was Aske himself, "keeping his port and countenance as though he had been a great prince with great rigour and like a tyrant," said Lancaster afterwards, shocked at such assurance in a traitor. Not deigning to address a mere gentleman when lords spiritual and temporal were present, the herald, with due regard for precedence, first offered to deliver his message to the Archbishop and then to Darcy. Both bade him give it to the captain, who "with an inestimable proud countenance, stretched himself and took a hearing of my tale." On understanding his mission the captain asked to see the proclamation. The herald drew it from his purse and Aske "read it openly without reverence to any person[2], and

---

[1] L. and P. xii (1), 901 (1), (28); printed in full, Eng. Hist. Rev. v, 560. See above, chap. ix.

[2] See note A at end of chapter.

said...he would of his own wit give me the answer. He, standing up in the highest place of the chamber, taking the high estate upon him, said: Herald, as a messenger you are welcome to me and all my company, intending as I do; and as for this proclamation sent from the lords, from whence ye come, it shall not be read at the Market Cross nor in no place amongst my people, which be all under my guiding, nor for fear of loss of lands, life or goods, nor for the power which is against us doth not enter into our hearts with fear; but are all of one accord with the points of our articles, clearly intending to see a reformation or else to die in those causes." Miller asked what the articles might be; the captain answered that they were going "to London, upon pilgrimage to the King's Highness" to petition him for "full restitution of Christ's Church of all wrongs done to it" and the putting down of vile blood from the Council. At Miller's request, Aske gave him a copy of the oath and offered to sign it. The herald "prayed him to put his hand to the said bill and so he did, and with a proud voice said: This is mine act who so ever says to the contrary." The herald again begged that he might read the proclamation to the commons, and even fell on his knees in his anxiety to do his errand truly. But Aske was determined. "He clearly answered me that of my life I should not, for he would have nothing put in his people's heads that should sound contrary to his intent." He dared not let Lancaster proclaim openly that the Lincolnshire Rebellion was over. It was already rumoured in the Pilgrims' host, and roused such fury among the commons that Aske doubted whether he could save the herald's life if he declared the news to be true[1]. The Pilgrimage must not be stained with the murder of a messenger. Moreover the proclamation itself was unsatisfactory, containing no offer of pardon, nor as much as demanding the Pilgrims' reasons for rising in arms. These the King persisted in assuming that he knew—they were the false rumours of new taxes[2]. Indeed the proclamation, though couched in the most sonorous English, contained so little to the point that it was no wonder a serious leader of the Pilgrimage should treat it with scorn.

Miller naturally thought that had he been allowed to accomplish his mission the effect would have been great. All the ploughmen and farm hands, he believed, "would have gone home,...for they say that they be weary of that life they lead, and if (any) say to

[1] L. and P. xii (1), 6; printed in full, Eng. Hist. Rev. v, 336.
[2] L. and P. xi, 826 (2).

the contrary of the captain's will he shall die." He must have heard the commons grumbling at the strict orders against spoils.

Aske ended the interview by promising Lancaster perfect safety whenever he brought messages in the King's coat, and "if my Lord Shrewsbury or other lords of the King's army would come and speak with him, they should have of him their safe conduct to come safe and go safe. And also said: Herald, commend me to the lords from whence you come, and say to them, it were meet they were with me, for it is for all their wealths I do....Then he commanded Lord Darcy to give me two crowns of five shillings to reward whether I would or no, then took me by the arm and brought me forth of the castle and there made a proclamation that I should go safe and come safe wearing the King's coat, on pain of death; and so took his leave of me and returned into the castle, in high honour of the people as a traitor may. And I missed my horse, and I called to him again for to have my horse, and then he made a proclamation that whoso held my horse and brought him not again immediately, bade kill him without mercy. And then both my horse was delivered unto me; and then he commanded that twenty or forty men should bring me out of the town, where I should least see his people."[1]

On this same Saturday 21 October 1536, Sir Thomas Percy arrived at Pontefract at the head of nearly ten thousand men from the north-east. To describe the raising of this company we must go back a week or more. Sir Thomas was at Seamer in the North Riding, his mother's house, when the first news of trouble in Lincolnshire came. Three days later a servant arrived from Wressell Castle, bringing venison for the Dowager Countess from the Earl. He brought word that Aske had raised the commons of Howden-shire, and the tenants of Wressell cried before the Earl's gates "Thousands for a Percy!" The country round was much disturbed, and Sir Thomas grew anxious to return home to Prudhoe Castle in Tynedale where his wife and children were. It must have been about 14 or 15 October that he attempted to go north secretly, disguised in one of his servant's coats, leading his own mail horse, and accompanied only by his page and a couple of men. They presently fell in with two rebel leaders. One of them "a man with a red face" was William Percehay of Ryton; he seems to have recognised Sir Thomas or at least to have suspected who he was. Seeing the Percy livery he asked where Sir Thomas might be. They replied

---

[1] See notes B and C at end of chapter.

he was at Seamer. Percehay of Ryton told them the commons had mustered at Malton and were determined to have Sir Thomas for their captain. They had set watch to take him, and if he did not join them by noon they would "leave my lady his mother never a penny or pennyworth of goods." Sir Thomas went back to Seamer and told the old Countess that he could not make his way home "whereupon she wept and sore lamented." About two o'clock in the afternoon a large company of commons led by several gentlemen came to summon him to join the Pilgrimage. The captains entered the house without any resistance being offered and Sir Thomas "came forth to them to the great chamber." They told him they were assembled for the weal of all; and Lord Latimer, Lord Neville, Danby, Bowes and many more had already joined them. Sir Thomas willingly took the Pilgrims' oath and agreed to attend the muster next day "at the Wold beyond Spittel." He went with a dozen or more followers, but "within a while" four or five thousand commons assembled there. Next day they spoiled the house of Mr Chamley, who had refused to come in, crying "Strike off his head," when Sir Thomas protested. He returned that night to Seamer to comfort his mother and assure her of his safety, staying there two nights before leaving for a large muster at Malton. From there he sent for Sir Nicholas Fairfax and together they took command of about ten thousand men; they received orders from Aske to march to York, but in a day or two they were counter-manded to the siege of Hull, and, when news came that Hull had surrendered, to Pontefract[1].

They passed through York on the 20th and their entry was attended with some pomp. Sir Oswald Wolsthrope had been raising the people west of the city in the triangle of country between the rivers Ouse, Nidd and Wharf, holding musters at Bilborough and Acomb. He joined forces with Percy and made the Abbot of St Mary's, much against his will, walk at the head of the troops as they marched through York carrying his finest cross; "at the town's end" Sir Thomas allowed the abbot to steal away "leaving his cross behind him." He supposed "Sir Oswald had not been pleased with the abbot" from whom they had all been getting money[2]. Sir Thomas Percy himself was especially splendid. He had sent for "a great trotting bay gelding" from the sub-prior of

---

[1] L. and P. XII (1), 393; printed in full, De Fonblanque, op. cit. I, chap. IX; L. and P. XII (1), 392; printed in full, Coxe, op. cit.

[2] L. and P. XII (1), 393.

Watton, who was under obligations to his family[1]; and he had bought in the city (not at his own cost, but at that of the kindly Treasurer, Colins) four pounds worth of velvet[2]. "Gorgeously he rode through the King's highness' city of York in complete harness with feathers trimmed as well as he might deck himself at that time."[3] His servants must have worn the Percy livery, scarlet and black, with the silver crescent on the breast. He must have looked a worthy son of the Magnificent Earl, and no wonder the commons greeted him joyfully. They "showed such affection towards him as they showed towards none other," and called him "Lord Percy,"—for was he not "the best of the Percys that were left next to my lord of Northumberland?" The King could rob him of his inheritance, never of his blood. But Sir Thomas was honourably loyal to his brother. "He lighted off his horse and took off his cap and desired them that they would not so say, for...the same would turn him but to displeasure."[4]

At Sir George Lawson's house Sir Thomas, Sir Nicholas Fairfax, Sir Oswald Wolsthrope and the rest of his party met George Lumley, Lord Lumley's heir, who had ridden in from Thwing with his tenants. They discussed the attitude of the religious from whom Percy had received help in money, provisions and men. He especially praised the Prior of Bridlington who had sent two brethren "the tallest men that he saw."[5] The prior was a good friend to the Pilgrims though he had troubles of his own. He was threatened by the commons recruiting for Percy, but they were satisfied when, besides the two brethren, eleven horsed tenants of his joined them. Later Aske gave him "a writing for the assurance of his goods" and in return he contributed twenty nobles to the Pilgrimage treasury. In spite of his paper he gave £4 to the men of Holderness "not to drive away his cattle there."[6] But this last may have been a voluntary gift, in spite of the saving clause. The religious were being heavily taxed. Sir Nicholas Fairfax said that as it was a spiritual matter "he thought meet that the priors and abbots and other men of the Church should...go forth in their own person." He went himself to the unfortunate Abbot of St Mary, who had

---

[1] L. and P. xi, 792.

[2] L. and P. xii (1), 1018.

[3] Ibid. 1090; printed in full, De Fonblanque, op. cit., i, App. lii.

[4] L. and P. xii (1), 369; printed in full, Milner and Bentham, *Records of the House of Lumley*, chap. v.

[5] L. and P. xii (1), 393, printed in full, De Fonblanque, op. cit. i, chap. ix.

[6] L. and P. xii (1), 1019.

already done his best to satisfy Percy and Wolsthrope. Sir Thomas sent Lumley on a round of religious houses, to St Saviour's of Newburgh, Byland, Rievaux, Whitby, Malton and Kirkham, while John Lambeth, his servant, went to Mountgrace, Bridlington, and Guisborough: "to move the abbots or priors and two monks of every of those houses with the best cross to come forwards in their best array." Byland, Newburgh and Whitby contributed forty shillings each, but all had given Percy help before. The abbot of Rievaux and the prior of Guisborough were ready to come in person, but Aske countermanded Percy's orders, bidding Lumley obtain such "benevolence" as he could, but let the religious themselves tarry at home[1]. The money which the Pilgrims collected would be spent by the captains on food and lodging for their men. Each of the commons "found" by his township was given twenty shillings to begin with: the ordinary rate of pay for soldiers was eight pence a day, so this would last at least a month and with presents, spoils, etc. might be made to go further, as the Pilgrims were on a kind of volunteer service. The townships had taxed themselves to raise this money. Gentlemen went at their own cost.

After Lancaster Herald had left Pontefract, Aske and Sir Robert Constable held musters on St Thomas' hill near Pontefract where they "tried out the men." "No man there but was willing to do his best and prepare for battle."[2] News came that the Earl of Shrewsbury had mustered his army on Blythe Law. As the lords and captains sat at supper in the castle hall that night, a messenger came in with a letter for Darcy. He read it through and dropped it on the board with a sigh[3]. Aske, who was sitting opposite, reached across for the paper, which was to this purpose: "Son Thomas, the Earl of Shrewsbury entendeth to take you sleeper." It was unsigned. The captain assured Darcy that there was "scorage (scouts) enough out to give him warning." Darcy advised that Ferrybridge (now Wentbridge) should be watched for the night; and Aske sent a company accordingly. Who was the spy in Shrewsbury's ranks? If Darcy ever revealed his name it was to Aske alone; and Aske never betrayed him. The question was more interesting to Henry than to us, but there can be no doubt that a considerable party in the royal army secretly favoured the Pilgrims and were ready to desert if the latter gained a victory.

---

[1] L. and P. xii (1), 369; Milner and Bentham, op. cit. chap. v.
[2] L. and P. xii (1), 901 (41); printed in full, Eng. Hist. Rev. v, 568.
[3] L. and P. xii (1), 852 (iv).

Blythe, where Shrewsbury mustered, is close to Scrooby in Nottinghamshire about twelve miles south of Doncaster and at least twenty-five, as the crow flies, from Pontefract. There was not, therefore, any immediate danger of surprise. Ferrybridge is on the Aire, hardly two miles north of Pontefract on the direct road from York—an essential joint in the Great North Road. But at that time this important passage was called Ferrybridges, and Wentbridge, also on the main road, but two miles south of Pontefract, was known as Ferrybridge[1]. This naturally causes some confusion on a first reading of the documents concerned. It was Wentbridge that Darcy advised Aske to hold in case of Shrewsbury's sudden advance. The Went is a far smaller stream than the Aire, but when the waters were swollen it would probably be impracticable for an army to ford it. Ferrybridge on the Aire was also guarded; but for different reasons. It was in the rear of the Pilgrims' host and out of reach of attack. Nevertheless no one was allowed to cross northwards without a passport from Aske: this served the double purpose of checking spies or suspicious letters and preventing the retreat of "those who were faint-hearted."[2] An instance of the keeping of Ferrybridge is given by the adventures of Harry Sais. He was a servant of Christopher Askew, the gentleman of the King's Chamber whom Cromwell had sent to Lincolnshire[3]. He came north early in October to bring home three of his master's horses which were "with one Mr Knevet at grass." By the time he reached his destination the country was up, and he dared not take the horses lest they should be stolen. He set out southwards without them, accompanied by a gentlewoman, Mrs Beckwith, perhaps one of Leonard Beckwith's family. When they came to Ferrybridge they were stopped by the guards and told to swear to be true to God and the King; Sais said he was willing. "And not to us?" asked another. "If ye be true to the King, or else I would be loath to swear." He was told: "If ye do not swear thus, to be true to God and to the King and to the commons, thou shalt lose thy head." So he took the oath "upon a little book that one of them brought forth of his sleeve." He was taken to Pontefract during the siege and saw the rebel host, which he thought was about ten thousand, the most part horsed but without much harness. When the castle was taken it was said the Pilgrims would go forward to London. He was allowed to go southwards and at Wentbridge he found the

---

[1] L. and P. xi, 879.   [2] L. and P. xii (1), 1175.
[3] See above, chap. vi.

lady waiting; they continued their journey together and passed
through Shrewsbury's host at Doncaster[1].

On Sunday 22 October at nine o'clock in the morning William
Stapleton brought to Pontefract the host of Beverley which had
been besieging Hull.   They had set out for York on Saturday
morning, leaving a garrison in Hull.   Stapleton, Rudston and
Sir Ralph Ellerker rode in advance, and presently met a post from
Aske with a letter announcing the surrender of Pontefract Castle
and the capture of the Earl of Northumberland by a party of the
commons.   At York they heard the equally welcome news that
Sir Thomas Percy "had gone towards Pontefract with a goodly
band the same day."[2]   Sir Ralph, two of the Rudstons and young
Robert Aske dined at Sir George Lawson's where they heartily
abused Cromwell, Sir Ralph saying that he "was a traitor and he
would prove it if the King would hear him."[3]

After passing through York the companies parted, no doubt for
convenience in foraging.   Sir Ralph and Rudston spent the night
at Shirburn, while the Stapletons rode home to Wighill, "and lodged
their folk a mile off at Tadcaster."   The night was full of flying
rumours carried from company to company by posts spurring through
the muddy lanes.   One cried in passing that every man must go
forward for Doncaster Bridge was down; another came to Wighill
from his master Sir James Strangways, who lay at Wetherby with
Lord Latimer, Lord Neville and their northern host.   About midnight, William and his nephew were roused from their beds by a
messenger from Shirburn, sent on by Ellerker with orders for them
to be at Pontefract by nine o'clock in the morning, and there they
arrived at the appointed hour on Sunday 22 October[4].

Besides bands from different parts of the shire, all the country
round Pontefract was taking up arms.   As soon as news of the
surrender of Pontefract Castle came to Wakefield no one there was
in any doubt as to which side he would take.   Thomas Grice, Darcy's
steward, who put his master first and his religion second, was
overjoyed to find duty and inclination point the same path.   At
Halifax the Tempests and their faction declared for the Pilgrimage;
it immediately appeared that Sir Henry Saville was loyal.   The
old feud divided the district into two violent parties.   At first both
sides hoped to turn the insurrection to good account against their
enemies.   John Lacy, the bailiff of Halifax under Sir Richard

[1] L. and P. xi, 879.   [2] L. and P. xii (1), 392; printed in full, Coxe, op. cit.
[3] L. and P. xii (1), 1320.   [4] Ibid. 392.

Tempest whose son-in-law he was, declared for the Pilgrims "before any of those parts went to Aske." He ordered the men of the town to harness themselves and to take the church cross and carry it before them into Lancashire where they would raise the commons; and this he commanded in the name of Sir Richard Tempest. Henry Farrore, a partisan of Saville's, refused to go and the expedition seems to have been given up. Lacy had made a political rhyme "touching the King very sore." The only verse preserved does not scan very well: "that as for the King a nappyll and a fair wench to dally with all would please him very well." This embodies the popular conception of Henry at that time. The people believed him a bluff jolly King Hal, who cared not who ruled his kingdom as long as he had his pleasures. The rhyme was repeated to the vicar, Holdsworth, by a yeoman named Middleton, and they went together to Sir Henry Saville, who was sick in bed, and told him of the matter. But Middleton was somewhat alarmed by the serious way it was taken and said his wife had reminded him that the rhyme was not about the King but about the "Bishop of Canterbury." Holdsworth sent a servant to "make good cheer" with Middleton and his wife and "spy a time" to get to the bottom of the matter. He asked the woman if the rhyme were not about the Bishop. "Nay, Marry!" said she, "it was made against the King and my lord Privy Seal." Her husband contradicted her, but she answered "Marry! it is so, for it was so indeed against the King and my lord Privy Seal, by God! without fail." In this way the vicar and Saville collected accusations against their enemies[1].

Aske's advance and the general success of the movement soon changed the face of things. Sir Henry Saville, in spite of his sickness, found it advisable to fly to Shrewsbury. Dr Holdsworth made his way to London, in the happy belief that his gold was safely hidden[2] and the rebels would find in his vicarage only such goods as he did not mind losing. The Lacys instantly seized his house and seem to have made it their headquarters; they took all the locks off the doors, and divided everything they could get amongst themselves. Thomas Lacy was given the fire-wood that was stored under the stairs; he carried it off, and seeing the earth below he remembered it was said that the vicar hid money in the ground. " He

---

[1] L. and P. XII (1), 784. See above, chap. v, for the message from Halifax to Lincoln.

[2] See above, chap. IV.

took a piked staff and struck into the ground and at the first stroke hit the pot." He told nobody of his find but took the money home in his sleeve, presumably by little and little. He stored it "in a pepper poke of canvas which would hold a pound of pepper, but the gold did not fill it by two fingers' breadth." He used some of it for himself though he never counted the whole amount[1].

Meanwhile most of the gentlemen of the country-side joined the insurgents. Sir William Fairfax, the stingy farmer of Ferriby Priory was an exception. As he was riding through the town of Wakefield about 22 October the commons demanded that he should take the oath. They received no favourable answer, the knight putting spurs to his horse and riding for home. Immediately the whole town assembled in arms, six hundred men and more, led by Thomas Grice who was proclaimed their captain, a canon of York, and the bailiff. They pursued the fugitive, who in the meantime had reached Millthrop Hall and gone to bed. A party of commons rushed to his room, tore him out of bed "and him evil entreated to the great fear and danger of his life." They haled him before Thomas Grice, "then sitting on horseback in the street," and he was compelled to swear instantly; Grice gave him into the charge of the bailiff of Wakefield and a guard of commons, commanding them to carry him to Aske. He was "in most cruel manner conveyed...to the said town of Wakefield as though he had been a felon"; there they kept him all night, and at eight next morning brought him before Captain Grice again. A guard of two hundred men or more was told off to take him to Pontefract Castle. At length he was carried before Aske, who was holding a great muster on St Thomas' Hill, and "delivered to the said traitor Aske and other detestable villains of his company as a prisoner taken by the said Grice."[2] As usual, it is here at the most interesting place that Sir William's complaint ends. Once out of the hands of his private enemies he seems to have submitted to fate and gone quietly forward with the Pilgrims[3].

Next came in the band of the Bishopric of Durham, five thousand strong, under the leadership of Lords Latimer, Lumley and Neville Westmorland's son and heir, Sir Robert Bowes of Barnard Castle and his sons, Sir John and Sir William Bulmer[4]. Part of Richmond-shire was with them, and the rest of it, with Wensleydale, Craven,

---

[1] L. and P. xii (2), 369 (4).

[2] Star Chamber Cases, vol. xx, fol. 9.

[3] L. and P. xii (1), 6, printed in full, Eng. Hist. Rev. vol. v, p. 340.

[4] L. and P. xii (1), 392; printed in full, Coxe, op. cit.

and Ripon, was besieging Skipton Castle under the Nortons and others. Orders had been despatched for this second host to attend the Pontefract musters, and they were about to obey, bringing Cumberland and Lord Scrope if they could catch them[1]. The Haliewer folk brought with them the famous banner of St Cuthbert[2], which was preserved in the monastery of Durham and only brought forth on high feast days and in time of war. It was of white and crimson velvet, richly embroidered in gold and silk, with St Cuthbert's cross in the midst. Often as it had been borne in the field against the Scots it was "never carried or showed at any battle, but, by the especial grace of God Almighty, and the mediation of holy St Cuthbert, it brought home the victory."[3] The Bishopric host wore badges embroidered with a black cross and with the insignia of the Five Wounds of Christ[4], a wounded Heart in the centre, from which drops of blood are falling into a Chalice, two pierced Hands above, and two pierced Feet below. They were the first to use this device as a badge; it was blazoned on the Pilgrims' banner[5].

When they marched into Pontefract Lord Darcy was at dinner[6], —a meal which began at eleven and commonly lasted two hours, though in "busy times" it must often have been cut short. Aske brought in the lords and gentlemen of the county Palatine and presented them to Darcy in the castle chamber. The two chiefs called a select number aside into a deep window. The three lords, Sir Robert Constable, Sir Thomas Percy, Sir Ralph Ellerker, Rudston, Roger Lassells, Robert Bowes, Sir John Dawnye, Sir William Fairfax, Sir Oswald Wolsthrope, Sir Robert Neville, Robert Challoner, Thomas Grice and William Babthorpe were among the councillors[7]. It must have been a very large window.

Darcy gave them the latest news, that Shrewsbury, supported by Norfolk, had reached Doncaster: it was determined to advance to the Don next day and oppose his crossing[8]. The formation of the army was then discussed. The Bishopric men as the bearers of St Cuthbert's sacred banner[9] must lead the vanguard in battle, and Darcy advised that they should lie that night at Wentbridge where they might guard against a night attack while at the same time

---

[1] L. and P. xii (1), 698 (3).   [2] Ibid. 946 (118).
[3] Fowler, Rites and Monuments of Durham (Surtees Soc.), 26.
[4] L. and P. xii (1), 901 (73); printed in full, Eng. Hist. Rev. v, 571.
[5] Hall, Chronicle, ann. 1536; see note D at end of chapter.
[6] L. and P. xii (1), 393; printed in full, De Fonblanque, op. cit. i, chap. ix.
[7] L. and P. xii (1), 392.   [8] Ibid., see below, chap. xiii.
[9] L. and P. xii (1), 946 (118).

they would be a couple of miles on their way to Doncaster. But Robert Bowes objected to this arrangement; his men and horses were in no fit state to go further that night. Finally it was agreed that Sir Thomas Percy should command the vanguard, until the host had re-mustered on the banks of the Don. He was to have under him Sir Ralph Ellerker, Sir William Constable, Rudston and the Stapletons with the whole of the East Riding, which having come in early had rested through the day. The rest of the host was to follow next day—the middle ward composed of the West Riding under Darcy and Sir Richard Tempest, the rear ward of the Bishopric with their own leaders and Aske[1].

Darcy on seeing the badge of the Five Wounds worn by the Bishopric gentlemen, was reminded that the same device had been used on his Spanish Expedition against the Moors[2]. Somewhere in the castle a store of the badges was found, and promptly distributed among the Pilgrims. Darcy himself gave one to Aske[3] and through the whole host it was gladly worn as the true symbol of their pilgrimage for the Faith. Why Darcy had kept these old badges so long, and how there chanced to be so many; whether they were really old, and if not, who had made them, were questions which afterwards excited Henry's curiosity. But, if they were ever answered, the answers are lost.

Proclamation was made to the host "for every man of the east parts to void the town on pain of death, and to draw to Wentbridge to wait upon" Sir Thomas Percy. Stapleton and the other captains mustered the men and marched them down to the Went, where they passed the night[4].

To summarise the position of the Pilgrims—on the night of Sunday 22 October they had advanced as far as Wentbridge, which was occupied by a strong force. The main body lay at Pontefract while a host of unknown strength was expected from Mashamshire and the Dales, but had not yet arrived. They had captured Hull, York, Pontefract, Barnard Castle, Durham and Lancaster, but still had in their rear the loyal towns of Newcastle-upon-Tyne, Berwick and Carlisle (which, however, was not able to offer much resistance), and also some isolated castles, Skipton, Scarborough, Chillingham

---

[1] L. and P. xii (1), 393; printed in full, De Fonblanque, op. cit. chap. ix.
[2] L. and P. xii (1), 900 (73–87); printed in full, Eng. Hist. Rev. v, 554–5. See above, chap. ii, and note D at end of chapter.
[3] L. and P. xii (1), 901 (73).
[4] Ibid. 392'; printed in full, Coxe, op. cit.

and Norham. At this point the fortunes of the Pilgrims may be left for a time, in order to consider the forces with which the King was preparing to oppose them.

NOTES TO CHAPTER X

Note A. The proper "reverence" on receiving a letter from the King was to take off the hat, kneel down, and kiss the seal.

Note B. It is not clear which of two extant proclamations to the rebels Lancaster Herald had with him on this occasion. The one indicated in the "Letters and Papers" does contain an offer of pardon, if the rebels will disperse and give up ten leaders. The other is very similar but contains no promise of pardon, so this was probably the one used[1].

Note C. An abstract of Lancaster Herald's account of his mission is given in L. and P. xi, 826, but the account is printed in full in "State Papers," I, p. 485; in a Newcastle-upon-Tyne Tract by Longstaff, "A Leaf from the Pilgrimage of Grace"; and in "Archaeologia," xvi, p. 331; Froude also makes considerable quotations from it. Lancaster Herald represents himself as acting boldly and with dignity, and Aske with considerably more dignity than the Herald thought became a captain of rebels. In marked contrast with this account is Archbishop Lee's version of the same affair. According to the Archbishop "Robert Aske so blustered and spake so terrible words that the poor man fell down upon his knees for fear and said he was but a messanger." Lee raised him, saying, "it beseemed not that coat armour to kneel before any man there." This is hard to reconcile with the earlier account. The Archbishop must have been good-naturedly trying to befriend Miller, who was afterwards accused of shaming the King's coat by kneeling to a traitor. At the same time Lee's little perversion enabled him to exhibit himself in a nobly loyal attitude. In Lee's narrative Aske always appears as a ferocious captain of banditti, but this portrait is not confirmed by the other evidence.

Note D. For a full discussion of this symbol see "The Western Rebellion of 1549" by Frances Rose-Troup, Append. A, and "Notes and Queries," 11th ser., VIII, 107, 176, 217, 236, 258. A badge, said to be that worn by Sir Robert Constable during the Pilgrimage, is preserved at Everingham, Yorks. An excellent photograph of this badge forms the frontispiece of "The Western Rebellion of 1549"; there is another in "The Yorkshire Archaeological Journal," pt. LXXXI, and a sketch in "The Transactions of the East Riding Antiquarian Society," VI, 47.

Antonio Guaras, a Spaniard who lived in England under Edward VI and wrote a chronicle of Henry VIII's reign, says that the Pilgrims wore as their badge "The Five Plagues of Egypt"! His mistake arose from the similarity between the Spanish phrases "cinco plagas de Egipto," the five plagues of Egypt, and "cinco llagas de Cristo," the Five Wounds of Christ[2]. But although this is some excuse, he might have known that the Plagues of Egypt were not five but twelve.

[1] L. and P. xi, 826 (2), (4).
[2] Spanish Chron. of King Henry VIII (ed. M. A. S. Hume), chap. XVII.

CHAPTER XI

THE FIRST APPOINTMENT AT DONCASTER

The Duke of Norfolk was the most experienced general whose services were available to Henry at this crisis, but the King was very reluctant to trust him, as he was suspected of sympathy with the rebels. At the first alarm Henry had sent for Norfolk, but it has already been shown how he was superseded at the last moment by Suffolk[1]. When the danger again became pressing, however, Henry was obliged to face the risk of employing him.

In order to understand how this came about, it is necessary to go back to 9 October, when Norfolk was at Woolpit, mustering the men of Norfolk and Suffolk. He was anxiously awaiting orders to go northward, and wrote to Henry that he was willing to serve under the Duke of Suffolk. He expected to have 2500 men under him in the course of a few days. As to artillery, "I have my own five fawcons and twenty brass hakbushes, but want gunners." He was badly in need of bows and arrows, and begged that they might be sent at once[2]. Three hours after his letter was despatched he received orders to ride to the King at Windsor, and he set out the same night by moonlight[3]. He had hardly reached Colchester next morning, after a fifty mile ride, when despatches arrived ordering him to be at Ampthill on 16 October with the troops which he had just mustered. He was overjoyed at being ordered to the front at last, but in spite of his professed willingness to serve under Suffolk he wrote to Cromwell asking that his right as Marshal of England to command the vanguard, should be recognised. For the rest he was all obedience and loyalty; he would not fail; he himself would be at Ampthill, as such was the King's pleasure[4]. But the troops would be obliged to go round by Cambridge and Huntingdon. Ampthill was thirty miles south of Huntingdon, and Norfolk knew that

---

[1] See above, chap. v. [2] L. and P. xi, 625.
[3] Ibid. 626. [4] Ibid. 642.

it was impossible for them to be there on the appointed day[1], but he was determined not to risk Henry's displeasure, and said nothing of his difficulties to the King. He sent an account of his precautions for the quiet of the country, where he left his son Thomas with 300 men, and begged that his eldest son the Earl of Surrey might go with him[2]. The beautiful and accomplished Surrey seems to have been the only living creature whom the cold-blooded old warrior really loved.

On Thursday 12 October the Duke of Norfolk was at home at Kenninghall, and wrote to Cromwell that though the men could not be at Ampthill on the 17th, he hoped to have them as far as Cambridge. From Cambridge to Huntingdon was only twelve miles and "it were pity with ill-horsed men" to go back thirty miles to Ampthill. If the King, whom he still expected in person, would consent, Norfolk would meet him at Huntingdon on the 18th "with a company meet to be a pretty wing to a battle." In spite of his boast of their efficiency, Norfolk did not dare to ride to the King until his men were well on their way, and if Surrey did not go with them they were likely to dwindle in numbers[3].

Norfolk was rather aggrieved that the King had commanded fewer gentlemen to join his company than had gone with Suffolk[4]. The reason of this was that when the King received good news from Lincolnshire, he believed that the rebellion was over[5], and orders were actually sent out on the 12th and 15th to countermand the Ampthill musters[6]. In spite of Norfolk's complaint, the knights and abbots who had received the King's orders to join Norfolk were able to provide plenty of men, though they lacked means to equip them. "If I had harness and time to carry footmen I could bring three times as many," Norfolk declared, and every letter ends with an urgent request for "at least 400 bows and 500 sheaves of arrows. This were better than gold or silver, for, for money, I cannot get bows nor arrows."[7] He hoped these stores would be at Cambridge when his men arrived there[8].

On Sunday 15 October Norfolk was with the King at Windsor[9]. On the same day, Henry sent long instructions to Shrewsbury and Suffolk about the arrangements to be made in Lincolnshire[10]. If the rebellion in Holderness was already pacified, they were to work

[1] L. & P. xi, 671.   [2] Ibid. 659.   [3] Ibid. 671.
[4] Ibid. 642.   [5] See above, ch. vi.
[6] L. and P. xi, 670, 720, 721.   [7] Ibid. 642.
[8] Ibid. 659.   [9] Ibid. 726.
[10] Ibid. 715, 717.

together; if not, Suffolk must advance to Lincoln, while Shrewsbury marched against the Yorkshire insurgents. The King seems to have had no doubt that his force would be large enough to settle their business[1].

When Norfolk arrived at Windsor, he found that the Ampthill musters had been countermanded, and that the King had given up all intention of going north. There seemed nothing for him to do but to arrange for the laying of posts[2]. But on leaving Windsor that night he met a messenger on the road with letters from Lord Darcy[3]. These were the letters dated from Pontefract on the 13th, and they proved so alarming that Norfolk returned to Windsor[4].

At last the King realised that the Yorkshire rebellion was not a mere demonstration of sympathy with Lincolnshire, but an entirely distinct and far more serious protest against his policy. He instantly changed his plans. If the worst were true, Norfolk must be given a joint commission with Shrewsbury to proceed against the rebels, and must take command of the troops at Ampthill before they dispersed. The Marquis of Exeter, who was also mustering men, was to be his second in command[5]. A postscript was added to Shrewsbury's instructions to inform him of this arrangment, and to direct him to suppress the Yorkshire rising at once, if he was strong enough,—if not, to wait for Norfolk, who would join him with 5000 men[6].

The King, who had been reassured for a moment by the harmless end of the Lincolnshire rising, was now really alarmed by the news from Yorkshire[7]. On 17 October Leonard Beckwith reached Windsor bringing from York letters from the lord mayor and Sir George Lawson in which they begged for protection against the rebels[8]. Next day another messenger arrived with letters from Darcy describing the serious state of affairs. This man also carried by word of mouth a lengthy account of the rebels and the rumours which circulated among them[9]. Whether because he repeated only what he knew would please the King, or because anything which did not suit the royal mind was omitted in writing down his report, these "bruits" contain no word of the rebels' real demands, but give as their only grievances the imaginary taxes on burials and christenings, white bread and white meat, and so forth[10].

[1] See above, ch. VI.
[2] L. and P. XI. 726.
[3] Ibid. 716.
[4] Ibid. 723; see above, ch. VIII.
[5] L. and P. XI, 726.
[6] Ibid. 716.
[7] Ibid. 749.
[8] Ibid. 704.
[9] Ibid. 768.
[10] See above, chap. IV.

The King "had no great trust in Darcy." He was hard put to it to find money for the troops under Shrewsbury, Suffolk, and Norfolk, and he never seems even to have contemplated sending any money and stores to Pontefract. Cromwell, who was in London, received orders from Windsor "to make shift to the utmost" to get money, and if he could not raise enough, to coin the King's plate in the Jewel House[1].

On 22 October it was known in London that Hull had surrendered, and it was feared that many of the Lincolnshire captains would fly thither. The King sent orders to Cromwell to "taste the fat priests thereabouts;" Dr Chamber had already presented the King with 200 marks, and Dr Lupton had given £200[2].

The arrival of any news from the north was watched for with lynx eyes, less because it was of so much interest to the government than because the King lived in constant fear that the rebellion would spread southward. For instance, when Harry Sais reached London safely without the horses, he related his adventures to his master, Christopher Askew[3]. Askew had some interest in the little Benedictine nunnery at Clementhorpe, York, which had lately been dissolved. The abbess had promised him £30 to be her suitor to the Queen, and had offered to present 300 marks to the Queen herself, if the house might stand. But it had been dissolved in spite of the abbess' efforts, and there the matter had ended for the time. When the Pilgrims restored the scattered sisterhood, the abbess sent word to Askew by Sais that she was again in a position to bribe the Queen, and that if she could by this means legalise her position, her brother-in-law, one of the Ellerkers, would convey the money through the disturbed country. Askew informed the Queen's chancellor of this renewed offer, and through him it came to Cromwell's ears. On 26 October Askew and Sais were examined before the Council. By this time it was "in every man's mouth that Pontefract Castle was given over."[4]

Meanwhile Norfolk set out from Windsor for Ampthill on Monday 16 October, authorised to muster 5000 men[5]. At Amersham he received a letter from his son Surrey, who had reached Cambridge with his forces on Sunday night. About 9 o'clock letters had arrived at Cambridge for the Duke, which Surrey had been instructed to open. They proved to be from Cromwell and the Privy Council, announcing that Lincolnshire was quiet again, and that the advance

---

[1] L. and P. xi, 768.   [2] Ibid. 834.   [3] See above, ch. vii.
[4] L. and P. xi, 879.   [5] Ibid. 738.

of the troops was therefore to be delayed till further orders were received. Surrey dared not make this news public, lest the men should disperse without waiting for definite orders. After consulting only two friends, he decided to hold musters at Cambridge next day, and wrote to his father for advice. Many of the gentlemen in their zeal had sent two or three times as many men as they had been commanded to provide, and Surrey was obliged to send for 1500 extra coats. These "liveries" may have been embroidered with the famous white lion of the Howards, but more probably they were the ordinary English uniform of that day, white tunics with St George's red cross on the back and breast. Food was so dear that the soldiers could not make 3*s*. 4*d*. keep them for two days, although this was an exceptionally high wage, as 8*d*. a day was usual in most parts of the country. In spite of these drawbacks, Surrey boasted that the company was "judged by those here who have seen many musters the finest ever raised on such short warrant."[1]

Many more men had been collected than the 5000 that Norfolk was authorised to muster, for Exeter had at least 2000 and 1000 more were coming from Gloucestershire. All Norfolk's soldierly instincts protested against dismissing men while the extent of the rising was still so uncertain. He wrote to Henry to ask that he might be allowed to keep at least 6000; even then nearly 2000 would have to be sent home[2]. But as no orders came to the contrary, the 2000 were dismissed when Norfolk reached Ampthill[3].

On Tuesday 17 October Suffolk with Fitzwilliam, Russell and the rest of the royal troops entered Lincoln, and by securing the capital placed themselves in a position to keep the county in subjection[4]. The Humber and the lower reaches of the Trent were guarded against the Pilgrims' crossing[5].

On the same day Shrewsbury was at Newark with 7000 men[6]. He had heard from Darcy that the rebels were 40,000 strong. In spite of this he was anxious to advance. He had just received the King's commission to act as his lieutenant in Yorkshire in conjunction with Norfolk[7], and he wrote to the Duke that if the rebels were really too strong to be attacked, he would "keep them in play" until Norfolk could bring up his 5000 men to Doncaster, which Shrewsbury begged him to do as quickly as possible[8].

[1] L. and P. xi, 727; printed in full, E. Bapst, Deux Gentilshommes-poètes de la Cour de Henri VIII, 220 n.

[2] L. and P. xi, 738.   [3] Ibid. 800.   [4] See above, chap. vi.

[5] L. and P. xi, 694.   [6] Ibid. 758.

[7] Ibid. 772.   [8] Ibid. 758.

On Wednesday 18 October Shrewsbury sent Lord Hussey, who had brought him 200 horsemen, to the King[1]. About midnight, when lying at Southwell, the Earl received news that Pontefract Castle was besieged and the Earl of Northumberland taken, and above all that the rebels were before him at Doncaster, which had risen at their instigation. He sent at once to Suffolk for as many horsemen as could be spared, under the command of Fitzwilliam or Brian[2].

Norfolk and Exeter received Shrewsbury's letter of the 17th at 6 o'clock in the evening of Wednesday 18 October. They were together at Ampthill in no very enviable position. The 2000 men mustered there were only waiting for their wages before disbanding. Norfolk's own men were still at Cambridge, Exeter's at Buckingham, and the Gloucestershire gentlemen at Stony Stratford, all obediently awaiting further orders, according to their last instructions. Although there was no great difficulty in ordering them to set out for Doncaster, uniting at various points on the way, it would take them over a week to get there. They could not advance more than 20 miles a day, as they were badly horsed and the roads were deep in autumn mud. It was impossible to preserve order and discipline on the march unless wages were regularly paid, but money was scarce and went fast. The men could not feed their horses and themselves for 8*d.* a day, and the £10,000 which had been sent to the Duke was not enough to pay off the disbanded company and also to provide for those going northward. Norfolk was afraid to set out without money to last as far as Doncaster, as an unpaid army might dissolve in the face of the rebels, or advance only as a disorderly rabble[3]. Shrewsbury had sent for £20,000, and the King, expecting Norfolk and Exeter to reach him much sooner than was practicable, wrote that they should receive their next wages from Gostwick in Shrewsbury's camp. As to the amount per day, the King flatly refused to raise it.

The generals received this despatch early on Thursday 19 October. They could not afford to delay any longer, but money must be obtained at once. In their answer to the King they explained that they could not be with Shrewsbury for a week or more. Let the King only lend them £1000 each and send it to Stamford on Saturday 21 October; they would repay him at the end of the campaign. As it was the King's pleasure that no higher wages should be paid, the men should have only the ordinary amount from the government. But they could not live on 8*d.* a day; they were to be divided into

---

[1] L. and P. xi, 772.   [2] Ibid. 774; see above, chap. viii.
[3] L. and P. xi, 776.

companies (probably of 100 men) under captains, and "if the men grudge upon reasonable ground for lack of money," Norfolk "will cause the captains to give them money out of their own purses." From this it is evident that it was almost as costly to fight for the King as to fight against him[1].

After sending off this despatch, Norfolk rode to his own company at Cambridge, leaving Exeter at Ampthill to discharge the last of the 2000. This was finally done on Friday 20 October, though Sir Anthony Browne, who was collecting men for the Duke of Suffolk, secured 600 of the best mounted. "The rest, being mostly horsed, made haste home to spare their charges." These men were "able and well furnished" and were very much displeased at being dismissed, after all the trouble of attending the musters, without having seen any fighting[2]. But on Friday night Norfolk at Cambridge, and Sir William Paulet and Sir William Kingston at Beaconsfield, received imperative orders from the Council that they should on no account dismiss any men. If some had gone already they must be resummoned and sent to Suffolk under Sir Anthony Browne, with ten pieces of ordnance[3]. Norfolk promptly answered that the Ampthill men could not be recovered. He must have felt a certain satisfaction in making this reply, for he was very angry that the troops which had been refused him should be granted to Suffolk. Sir Anthony Browne had secured 600 horsemen, and Norfolk marvelled that he should need such a large number, unless there was a new outbreak in Lincolnshire. He added bitterly, "I am apt to think that some desire great company more for glory than necessity." As for the munitions he was ordered to send to Suffolk, he could not spare any. He had never even heard of the ten pieces of ordnance he was now ordered to give up. What he had was his own, and so small that it was carried in two carts. As to money, £2000 had been despatched to him, but he had only received £1200. More was promised him in ten days, but "neither I nor my lord Marquis will be able to keep our companies so long without money." If he had not unsparingly spent £1500 of his own "here would have been ill work. The pension of France hath now done no hurt to me nor the King's affairs."[4] Sir William Paulet and Sir William Kingston returned to Ampthill and did their best to produce the missing 2000 men, but evidently they had little hope of success[5]; in the end the attempt

[1] L. and P. xi, 793.
[2] Ibid. 803.
[3] Ibid. 800, 803.
[4] Ibid. 800.
[5] Ibid. 803.

was abandoned, after a brisk correspondence about the men and the munitions for Suffolk had been carried on for some time[1].

On Saturday 21 October "the Lord Privy Seal's band" consisting of 200 horsemen under Richard Cotton joined Norfolk. The leader's letter describes the conditions under which the troops advanced:

"Pleaseth it your lordeship to be advertysed that according to your commandement I have presented your company to my lorde of norffolk and Mr browne the hoole nomber of them was cc. we be all apoynted to attende upon Mr brownen who haith willed me to take like charge of your lordshipes company like as yor lordshipe commanded me at my departing frome you, which god willing there shalbe no defaulte in me for wante of good will to do that thing that the kinges highness may be truley served. And to the advauncement of your honore, by the advice of Mr Browne I have retorned back xl of your company of such as ware worste horsed, so that we ar nowe clx of as well horsed men as any ar in the company and no suche of no one manes brynging. There were dyvers of essex men which ar tall men of person and good archers to the nomber of xii which hade no sadles butt rode uppon panylles after there countre facion which I thought was not to your honour. Soe I have bought them sadles with other apperell for there horses according as in my conceyte was meyte for your honour. Great murmer and gruging there was amonges your lordshipes company by cause thay thought the waiges of viiid by the day was to little to fynde them and there horses. Soe as well as my pore witt will serve me I have pacefied them with fare wordes soe that there is little said thereof nowe emonges any of us. Your lordship haith here many of your houshold servauntes which ar yonger brether and as I am privye unto have no greate store of money; they be at your lordshipes horseyng; ether they shall marre there horses for lacke of meat or elles make suche sheftes for money that shall not stend well with your lordshipes honor. I beseche your lordship to pardon me for wrytting this rudely and pleyne unto you butt I se the thynges that is like to ensue that I can no lesse doe if I shall do according as your lordship put me in trust, but to advertyce you. I beseche your lordship that I may know your pleasure in the premisses if it please you that I shall geve unto every gentilman being a yonger brother asertyn [sum] which in my pore oppenyon ware moche to your honour. Your pleasure knowen therein I shall lay forthe the money of myne owen purse till wee retorne.

This berer William Jonson haith by mysfortune hurte his arme soe that he is not able to goo in this vyage. I assure your lordship we shall have agret lacke of hym in the company for he was a man that toke moche payne in provyding of lodinge for all oure company. I trust your lordshipe will take no displeasure with me for keping one of your cokes here for we may ill spare hym emonges the company. This the holy gost have you in hys costodye. Frome burne the xxi day of october

your dayly orator

Rychard Cotton."[2]

[1] L. and P. xi, 799, 823, 824, 825, 835 etc.
[2] Ibid. 831; copied from the original at the R. O.

On 18 October the King had despatched letters to Shrewsbury by Thomas Miller, Lancaster Herald, with orders that the Earl should advance on the rebels immediately, "not doubting that they will seek to hide themselves at your approach."[1] Shrewsbury was to send the herald to the rebels with an enclosed proclamation. The effect of this mission has already been told[2].

In obedience to his orders, Shrewsbury advanced; but these orders were issued in the mistaken belief that Norfolk would join him in a day or two. On Saturday 21 October when Shrewsbury was as far north as Scrooby[3], Norfolk had only reached Cambridge and Exeter was still further behind[4]. The King was aware of Norfolk's situation, but did not know how far Shrewsbury had advanced. He wrote to Norfolk, commending his intention of sending letters and proclamations to the rebels, in order to pacify them, if possible, without a battle. He bade him forward orders to Shrewsbury to guard the line of the Trent and hold the bridges at Nottingham and Newark. Shrewsbury was to "settle himself in such a strong place as he may keep without danger till Norfolk come to him." As soon as their forces were united, they were to wait together on the Trent until the rebels either attempted a crossing or dispersed[5]. This admirable plan of campaign seems to have been originally Norfolk's own; unfortunately it was frustrated by Shrewsbury's advance. The line of the Don, which Shrewsbury proposed to defend, had none of the advantages of the Trent. The river was smaller and could easily be forded even in winter. The people on both banks favoured the rebels; food was therefore hard to get, and the country was barren, low and unhealthy.

At 6 o'clock in the morning of Monday 23 October Norfolk was at Newark in great uneasiness of mind. Attended only by four servants, he had far outridden his company, which could not be expected until the next day, while Exeter would not arrive till the day after. The distance between Newark and Doncaster was then called thirty miles, but by modern reckoning it is nearer forty. Norfolk had already written to Shrewsbury, imploring him on no account to risk a battle. If Shrewsbury should be forced to fight and were defeated, the only chance of checking the rebels was for Suffolk and himself to hold the bridges over the Trent. He feared the result of Shrewsbury's advance so much that he wrote to ask the King to send

---

[1] L. and P. xi, 771.
[2] Ibid. 826; see above, ch. x.
[3] L. and P. xi, 840.
[4] Ibid. 816, 822; printed in full, St. P. i, 488.
[5] L. and P. xi, 816.

orders that Suffolk must co-operate with him[1]. For two nights
Norfolk had had no rest, but now he indulged in three or four hours'
sleep at Newark Castle.   When he awoke, it was to find that Lord
Talbot had ridden in from his father's camp.   Shrewsbury was lying
on the south bank of a little river called Goole Dyke, about four
miles south of Doncaster, which he intended to enter by Rossington
Bridge.

Lord Talbot's news was good. Shrewsbury had no intention of
fighting until Norfolk joined him on Wednesday or Thursday;
but he hoped he would be able to advance from Doncaster before
that, as his men were dying "very sore of the sickness."   The rebels
had made no attempt to win the bridges at Doncaster and Rossington.
It was "sore bruited" that they would not fight at all.   Many true
subjects had enlisted under the King's banner. Sir Henry Saville
had been among his tenants at Wakefield "and brought much harness
and men from them."   Sir Brian Hastings had left Hatfield and
brought in his "300 tall horsemen," but Suffolk had not yet sent the
detachment which Shrewsbury needed as scouts and skirmishers. So
far Talbot was reporting what he knew to be true; in addition he
had heard rumours that Sir Richard Tempest had captured one of
the rebel leaders, and that Lord Dacre and Lord Scrope were marching south by way of Skipton and Wakefield to join the King's army.
This rumour, however, was unfounded, although Talbot believed it.
Sir Richard Tempest was with the rebels at Pontefract, and Lord
Scrope was riding to their musters at the head of the dalesmen,
while Lord Dacre was lying neutral in Naworth Castle[2].   Lord Talbot
also brought news of the surrender of Pontefract, and hinted at his
suspicions of Darcy's loyalty.   Pontefract Castle, he said, was considered stronger than Newark, and Norfolk agreed that Newark
might be held against any force which had not heavy ordnance,—
"greater pieces than demi-culverins."

Shrewsbury was evidently in as much danger of under-estimating
the rebels' strength as Norfolk had been of over-estimating it.   The
news did not entirely overcome Norfolk's anxiety; he still feared
"only two things,—lack of victual and my lord Steward's fighting
before his coming."   Talbot carried back Norfolk's instructions as to
how Shrewsbury's camp should be fortified and defended in case of a
sudden attack.   Norfolk was in hopes that many of the rebels would
come over to him on hearing the letters and proclamations which
he was about to send, for ever since the victory of Flodden he

---

[1] L. and P. xi, 845.   [2] See above, ch. ix.

had been more beloved in the north than any other nobleman, a circumstance which had not escaped the King's jealous notice[1].

The two armies, that of the Pilgrims and that of the King, were now in touch with one another, and it is possible to follow their movements simultaneously.

On Monday 23 October, when Lord Talbot was with Norfolk at Newark and Shrewsbury's forces lay at Rossington Bridge, the rebels continued their advance from Pontefract. Gostwick, Shrewsbury's treasurer, was at Tickhill, south-west of Rossington, and from there he sent for Lawrence Cook, the Prior of the White Friars at Doncaster, and ordered him to cross the water and ride towards Pontefract to view the Pilgrims' army, bringing back word of their number and equipment. The prior secretly sympathised with the Pilgrims, but, like many of his brethren, he was much more afraid of the King. He went among the rebels in perfect safety and even had an interview with Aske, either at Pontefract or somewhere near it on the road south. The prior easily gathered what information he needed and gave some in return. The captain asked if Shrewsbury's men were in Doncaster, and finding they had not even reached the town, still less prepared it for defence, he said he would be there before them and lie there that night. Perhaps he said this in the heat of the moment, or he may have given a misleading account of his plans in order to hurry Shrewsbury's advance, for he was too able a leader to risk a battle with a swollen river in his rear[2]. Another reason for avoiding Doncaster was the presence of the plague in the town; the Pilgrims seem to have escaped the infection by keeping to the north of the river[3]. The prior told Aske that Gostwick expected a large sum of money from the King. It arrived at Tickhill next day, and Aske sent to know if it had come, but the prior, being then so much nearer the King's forces, assured the messenger untruly that it had not. After his inspection of the rebels on Monday (or possibly the day before, as he gives no dates) he returned quietly to Doncaster, and thence went to Shrewsbury and reported what he had seen[4].

On Monday Sir Thomas Percy and his 4000 men advanced from Wentbridge to Hampole, about six miles away[5], where he was joined by the forces of the Bishopric and Richmondshire, under Lords

[1] L. and P. xi, 846; see note A at end of chapter.
[2] L. and P. xii (1), 854.   [3] L. and P. xi, 846, 909.
[4] L. and P. xii (1), 854.
[5] Ibid. 393; printed in full, De Fonblanque, op. cit. i, chap. ix.

Latimer, Lumley, and Neville, Sir Thomas Hilton, and Robert Bowes[1]. These companies completed the "vaward," which was altogether about 12,000 strong. They encamped near "a little nunnery beside Robin Hood's Cross."[2]

Next morning, Tuesday 24 October, Aske rode into the camp at Hampole, and ordered a muster on the neighbouring heath "above Barnesdale."[3] The men of the North and West Ridings, who had remained at Pontefract, were now coming forward under Sir Robert Constable; they formed the "middle ward." The "rear ward," composed of the men from Mashamshire and the Dales, had not yet reached Pontefract[4], and only the Archbishop and Lord Darcy remained in the town with their own servants[5]. They had been left "for their ease," and indeed Lee's military ardour was not such as to enable him to spend nights in the open among all the discomforts of an autumn campaign; while Darcy was over eighty, and though still vigorous in body and mind, suffered much from his old wound. Nevertheless, when their absence became known at the muster, the commons' suspicion was aroused, and they held them "in great jealousy and despair," for what was considered lack of zeal, if not positive unfaithfulness[6].

It was perhaps at this time that Darcy suggested to Lee that the Pilgrims' oath and articles should be printed, in order that they might circulate more freely and that their principles might be known. Lee protested against this, as he did against every decided step, and the matter was allowed to drop[7]. It is an interesting question where Darcy proposed to have the articles printed. To send them abroad would have taken too long, as the printed copies were wanted at once. There had formerly been a printing-press at York, and possibly one at Beverley, but that was twenty years ago, and the press had long since been removed[8]. This difficulty may have had as much to do with the abandonment of the scheme as the Archbishop's remonstrances.

While the muster was being held at Barnesdale Heath on Tuesday, Lancaster Herald was brought to Aske and delivered a letter to the rebel leaders from Shrewsbury at Doncaster. It was read, and the captains held a brief council before the host. They decided

---

[1] L. and P. xii (1), 29.

[2] Ibid. 393; printed in full, De Fonblanque, op. cit. i, chap. ix.

[3] L. and P. xii (1), 1175.   [4] Ibid. 6; printed in full, Eng. Hist. Rev. v, 337.

[5] L. and P. xii (1), 393.

[6] Ibid. 392; printed in full, Coxe, op. cit.   [7] L. and P. xii (1), 1022.

[8] Duff, Eng. Provincial Printers to 1557, Lecture ii, York.

that Aske should ride to Pontefract and consult Darcy as to their answer, and the captain immediately set out, only pausing to appoint two gentlemen, Robert Delariver and Anthony Brackenbury, to see to Miller's comfort and safety[1]. The letter was one of those brought by Talbot from Norfolk. The Duke suggested that much useless bloodshed might be prevented if "four of the discreetest men of the north parts" came to the lords at Doncaster and explained the causes of the rising. Hostages would be given in pledge of their safety[2].

There is no account of the considerations which affected the decision of Aske and Darcy as to the answer. They were quite willing to treat; this was the first occasion on which the King or his lieutenants had made any inquiry as to the causes of their assembly, and such a tacit admission that they were not in arms from mere wilfulness was a step forward. The Pilgrims had always protested their loyalty to the King's person. They thought that he had been led astray by lowborn favourites, but, if he would grant the petition of his faithful subjects, war was the last thing that they desired. On the other hand, if he refused to redress grievances which were felt by so large a part of his kingdom, his subjects would be justified in using armed force to bring him to a more reasonable frame of mind. Such was the attitude of the Pilgrims, and they could not maintain it if they attacked the King's army before their petition had been presented, and consequently before they knew whether the King would grant it or reject it. The pressing question during the next few days was, were they to sacrifice this conditional loyalty and use their advantage over Norfolk's weakness?

It was a momentous problem which they had to solve. If they gave battle, and failed, their cause was lost for ever; but if they won the immediate result would be a civil war, and that a religious civil war, of all forms of strife the bitterest and most cruel; it might be complicated by a foreign invasion, which, in those days of England's weakness, might conceivably have led to conquest and annexation. The Pilgrims were not blind to these possibilities. They declared that though they had taken up arms to amend their own affairs, they would accept no help from Scotland, and if an invasion was threatened during the time of insurrection, they protested that they were as ready as ever to defend the Borders. To plunge the country into war was a desperate step which they had only

[1] L. and P. xii (1), 6, 392, 1175.
[2] L. and P. xi, 846; xii (1), 6; printed in full, Eng. Hist. Rev. v, 337.

contemplated as a possible last resource in the future. Nevertheless their present situation was tempting; the King's army was before them, barring their road south, but scattered, unprovided, faint-hearted and entirely at their mercy. It was in their power to strike a decisive blow—a blow from which the King's party might never recover. It is easy to guess what would have been the decision of a Caesar or a Cromwell; but the Pilgrims had no such leader in their ranks. Aske and Darcy were not world's wonders, and they made their choice as disinterested men, honestly desiring their country's good, were likely to do.

They determined to accept the Duke's offer of a conference, but they did not altogether trust him. They would not risk four of their leaders in his host, but they proposed that four, six, eight, or twelve lords and gentlemen from each side should meet at some place on neutral ground. The northern gentlemen would then explain the grievances which had forced them to rise, and would discuss these points and the best road to a peaceful conclusion with the Duke and his companions[1].

If this proposal were accepted, it would be well to have a clearer and fuller set of articles than had yet been drawn up, and Aske applied to the Archbishop for help as to the wording of the "spiritual articles." Lee had already been requested by various gentlemen to help them in this matter, but he had not the smallest intention of doing anything so imprudent. He first returned evasive answers, and when pressed said testily, "that they had spun a fine thread if they made so great a business and could not tell why."[2] He was very anxious to go home, and Aske would probably have been glad to give him leave, for, though he expected money and advice from high ecclesiastics, he did not encourage them to march with the army[3]; but the commons were in a suspicious mood[4], and Aske did not dare to return from Pontefract to Hampole without both Darcy and Lee. The Archbishop's servants told him that Aske had threatened to "strike off his head" if Lee did not go to the field, and "from that day he accounted himself a prisoner and went with Lord Darcy."[5] Nevertheless the Pilgrims continued to believe that the Archbishop sympathised with their cause[6].

[1] L. and P. xii (1), 6; printed in full, Eng. Hist. Rev. v, 337.
[2] L. and P. xii (1), 1022.
[3] Ibid. 369; printed in full, Milner and Benham, op. cit. chap. v.
[4] L. and P. xii (1), 946 (117).
[5] Ibid. 1022.   [6] Ibid. 29, (2), (3).

The vanguard returned from the muster to their camp at Hampole for the night of Tuesday 24 October. The weather was bad, and early next morning, as the men crouched over their smoking camp fires, cooking their rations as best they could, a little troop of about thirty horsemen from Doncaster appeared, which hovered round the camp, examining their numbers and position[1]. When no one could strike an enemy beyond longbow range, warfare was a very intimate and personal affair. It does not seem that much notice was taken of the reconnoitring party, until they chanced upon a couple of stragglers from the Pilgrims' camp, doubtless in search of stray poultry; the King's men seized these two, made them fast and began their retreat[2]. The shouts of their captured comrades roused the Pilgrims, "all men ran to their horses," and after a hot pursuit the King's men were obliged to let their prisoners go and hasten their own retreat[3]. The whole camp was in commotion, every man who could get to his horse joining in the chase. Stapleton was among the first, who never paused till they reached the top of Scawby Hill. Before them lay the valley of the Don; the thirty horsemen, undiminished, were making for the bridge at the gallop. Inflamed by the sight of a flying foe, the Pilgrims looked upon Doncaster as absurdly near and unprotected. There was a general cry to surprise the town by a sudden attack. Wild and disordered as the pursuers were, an attempt so utterly unexpected might have perhaps been successful. But Stapleton thought the risk too great, and riding along the ragged front of the company, he succeeded by commands, entreaties and reasonings in turning them from their purpose[4].

Other skirmishes took place in the two or three days during which the armies lay facing one another. One was doubly interesting as it concerned the badge of the Five Wounds, and caused the only known casualty among the Pilgrims. "Mr Bowes scrimmaged with his company with the scoriers (scouts) of the Duke of Norfolk's host, and there one of Mr Bowes' own servants ran at another of his own fellows, because he had a cross on his back, and weened he had been on the party of the Duke of Norfolk's host, and there with a spear killed his own fellow. And for that chance then was there a cry for all men to have the badge of I H S or the Five Wounds on him both before and 'hind them. And there, to his (Aske's) knowledge, was

---

[1] L. and P. XII (1), 393; printed in full, De Fonblanque, op. cit. I, chap. IX.
[2] L. and P. XII (1), 392; printed in full, Coxe, op. cit.
[3] L. and P. XII (1), 393.
[4] Ibid. 392.

all the men that was slain or hurt of either party, during all the time of business."[1] The unlucky Durham man must have put on his white coat with St George's cross, which he would be accustomed to wear at the King's musters.

On Wednesday 25 October Aske, Darcy and the Archbishop left Pontefract, and came to Hampole, overtaking on the way Sir Robert Constable and the middle ward, who had probably lain at Wentbridge the night before. The rear ward seem to have reached Pontefract and taken up their quarters there either this day or Thursday[2]. Lancaster Herald was brought to the captain by the two in whose charge he was left, and he was despatched to Doncaster with the message that the Pilgrims were willing to arrange a conference[3].

The vanguard had gone forward to Pickburn, about a mile nearer to Doncaster than Hampole, where the middle ward now occupied their old camp. The little nunnery had been converted into headquarters for Lord Darcy and the gentlemen of his division. A dry resting-place was very desirable "for there was a sore rain, which raised the waters, especially the Don," and "the people were lodged in woods and villages."[4] Aske sent out only skirmishers on "scout-watch," as it was called; these were Bishopric men, who, like all Borderers, were particularly expert at this open, individual kind of fighting. There were no scouts born and bred to the work in the King's host, and the Pilgrims had the best of it in the various little brushes which took place, the redcross men who showed themselves on the north bank of the river being promptly encountered and forced to take refuge with their own people across the bridge.

While Lord Darcy, the Archbishop and Sir Robert Constable were taking up their quarters at Hampole, Aske rode on to Pickburn to hear the reports of the scouts and spies as they came in, and to take counsel with the commanders of the vanguard. In the evening Lancaster Herald returned to the Pilgrims' camp with further messages from Shrewsbury. He brought, not an answer to their last proposal, but an exhortation to the rebels prepared by Norfolk some days before, which bade them either humbly submit themselves to the King's mercy as ungrateful traitors, or make ready to abide danger by battle, to be given them by the Duke "in place convenient."[5] Shrewsbury must simply have sent it on as soon as it

[1] L. and P. xii (1), 901 (73); printed in full, Eng. Hist. Rev. v, 571–2.
[2] L. and P. xii (1), 29, 393, 946 (118), 1175 (ii) (3).
[3] Ibid. 6; printed in full, Eng. Hist. Rev. v. 337.
[4] L. and P. xii (1), 392, 1175 (ii) (3).
[5] L. and P. xi, 887; printed in full, State Papers, i, 495.

arrived without considering how far the negotiations had already advanced. It was particularly irritating to the Pilgrims, as it appeared to be a deliberate set-back to all schemes for a peaceful settlement.

A long debate followed the reading of the letters. The insurgent leaders knew that their numbers were overwhelming. Shrewsbury could not muster, at the highest estimate, 8000 men at Doncaster. Most of his army were at Scrooby; Norfolk and Exeter at places even further south[1]. Such cavalry as he had were ill-horsed; many, "every third man," according to rumour, were with the Pilgrims at heart[2]; the rest were "faint" and without enthusiasm; such as did not desert outright were not likely to give much trouble if attacked with vigour[3]. Aske's scouts brought him word as to where every company of the enemy was quartered, and how the bridge was defended and guarded; no muster could take place on the south bank without his knowledge. In contrast to Shrewsbury's troops, the Pilgrims were at least thirty thousand strong; they were "as tall men, well-horsed and well appointed, as any men could be." Every witness attests their devotion to their cause. "There were neither gentlemen nor commons willing to depart, but to proceed in the quarrel; yea, and that to the death."[4] In these circumstances the leaders naturally resented Norfolk's haughty and final tone, as if he had command of the situation. The Durham lords were ready to accept the new messages as a sign that all further negotiations were broken off; they advised that the challenge should be accepted, and that the attack should be made at once[5]. There was little to fear as to the issue. Norfolk afterwards declared that Doncaster was in the greatest danger "if the rebels had taken their advantage like men of war." As soon as the rain ceased and the waters of the Don fell, Shrewsbury's position would be quite untenable[6].

Aske, however, headed a party in the council which favoured moderate measures[7]. He pointed out that they had assembled for the very purpose of laying their grievances before the King for remedy. There was no shame in discussing their petition with the King's lieutenant; it was only another step on their Pilgrimage[8].

---

[1] L. and P. xii (1), 1175 (ii) (4).
[2] L. and P. xi, 909; 1319; extracts printed in Froude, op. cit. chap. xiii.
[3] L. and P. xii (1), 1175 (ii) (4).
[4] L. and P. xi, 1319; xii (1), 6, 29, 1175 (ii) (5).
[5] L. and P. xii (1), 6.
[6] L. and P. xi, 1241.   [7] L. and P. xii (1) 1175 (ii) (4).
[8] Ibid. 6.

Norfolk, Shrewsbury, and the other lords of the old noble blood were the very men that the Pilgrims were suggesting as more suitable counsellors for the King than his low-born favourites; the lords had probably more sympathy for the rebels' demands than they dared to show. It was bad policy to attack those most able to further the petition at court, where the Pilgrims had little influence. Whatever the result of a pitched battle, it would make a civil war inevitable. Even though the Pilgrims were successful at first, the King might prove the stronger in the end, and all the nobles and gentlemen of the northern counties would be " attainted, slain and undone, and the country made a waste for the Scots."[1]

Darcy was in favour of negotiating for another reason. In his opinion " it were better (to) have garrison war than hosting war in time of winter."[2] The Pilgrims were not hampered by the bad weather to the same extent as the royal troops. They were advancing at their leisure, without ordnance, and they were well supplied with food and fuel from a base not a dozen miles away. Nevertheless a truce would give them time to organise and develop. They would be able to determine on the best places to hold, and to provide for their defence in case the petitions were refused. They might possibly receive money and encouragement from the Pope. Above all, the leaders could trust the commons not to lose heart during a short truce. All were steadfastly determined to fight if the King would not listen to them[3]. Of course the King would equally be able to strengthen himself; but the Pilgrims trusted a good deal to the secret assurances of sympathy which they received from the midland and southern shires. The King might summon a larger army, he was not likely to raise one any more loyal.

In brief Aske and those who thought with him " feared not the royal troops though they were 40,000," but they did not desire civil war. Their one aim was certain political and religious reforms, and they endeavoured to bring their object to pass in as constitutional a manner as was then possible. They would lose little or nothing by consenting to negotiate for a truce; they might gain much; at least they would preserve their consistency.

These were the chief considerations which Aske laid before the council. The earlier ones are stated in his own writings, while the later may be gathered from the circumstances. His arguments

---

[1] L. and P. xii (1), 1175 (ii) (4).

[2] Ibid. 900 (72); printed in full, Eng. Hist. Rev. v, 554.

[3] L. and P. xii (1), 901 (21); printed in full, Eng. Hist. Rev. v, 559.

convinced the lords and gentlemen. They decided that they were strong enough to treat, and that they would accept Norfolk's first offer, not his second. Lancaster Herald was again despatched with the message that four gentlemen would come, upon due pledges, to speak with the Duke next day. Robert Bowes, who was to be one of the four, set out at once with Aske for Hampole to announce the arrangement to Darcy and Constable[1].

None of the leaders entirely trusted the Duke. They thought that he would not "dishonour himself by making a night attack—a kind of battle seldom heard of, especially at that season, being November,"[2] but they were quite prepared for such an infringement of military etiquette. The first question that Darcy asked Bowes was "who was that night in scoutwatch?" This being satisfactorily answered, they discussed the details of the meeting next day, and also what their tactics should be in case of battle[3]. It was not improbable that no peaceful settlement would be concluded, and in that case they would be able to make the most of their present advantage after having done their best to avoid war.

On the night of Wednesday 25 October Norfolk, with Surrey and about thirty gentlemen and servants, lay at Welbeck. His men, ordnance and artillery, were at Tuxford, while Exeter had reached Nottingham with only part of his company. At midnight Norfolk was roused by the arrival of posts from the north, who brought the news that Shrewsbury had arranged to treat with the rebels, and that the Duke's presence at Doncaster was urgently required.

The letter which he wrote to the King before setting out shows that the Pilgrims did him no injustice when they suspected his intentions:

"Sir havyng this present hour receyved the lettre herin closed and never hard one worde fro my lord steward but this sith Monday last at v in the morning not with standyng dyvers sent fro me to hym to know of his newes, I being in bed and not a slepe accompanyed with suche as be named in a sedul herin closed, I have taken my horse only accompanyd with my brother William and Sir richard page, Sir arthur darcy and iiii of my servants to ryde towards my lord steward accordyng to his desire, not knowyng wher th' enemys be nor of what nomber, nor no thyng more than is conteyned in their letter, wherin I am so far priked that what so ever shalbe the sequell I shall not so spare the litle poure carkes that for any ease or danger other men shall have cause to obiect any lageousnes in me and Sir most humble I besech you to take in gode part what so ever promes I shall make unto the rebells (if any suche I shall by th' advyse of others make) for sewrely I shall observe no part theroff for any

---

[1] L. and P. xii (1), 946 (2), (118).   [2] Ibid. 1175 (ii) (4).
[3] Ibid. 946 (2), (118).

respect of that other myght call myn honour distayned langer than I and my company with my lord marquess may be assembled to gyder, thynkyng and repewting that none oth nor promes made for polecy to serve you myn only master and soverayne can destayne me who shall rather be torne in a myllion of peces then to show one poynt of cowardise or untrouth to your maieste.

Sir I trust the sendyng for me is ment to gode purpose and if it chaunse to me to myscary most noble and gracious Master be gode to my sonnys and to my poure doghter. And if my lord steward had not advansed fro trent unto my comyng and that then I myght have folowed th' effect of my letter wryten you from Cambrige these traytors with ease myght have be[en] subdewed. I pray god that hap torne not to moche hurt. In hast at Welbek xiiii myles fro dancaster at xii at nyght.

Yr most humble servant

T. Norffolk."[1]

At one or two o'clock on the morning of Thursday 26 October Norfolk reached Doncaster in answer to Shrewsbury's summons. He came in the greatest anxiety, offering to sacrifice his honour to his loyalty, but, considering how closely his political aims resembled those of the rebels it is probable that he was only partly sincere in this. He may have intended double-dealing with the King as well as the enemy—soothing Henry's anger by assurances of the pie-crust nature of his promises, while he secretly hoped that the King would not dare to set aside terms made openly in his name. Henry at least suspected this, but however true it might be the state of affairs at Doncaster must have convinced the most eager general that it was wise to treat rather than to fight. Lack of food, fuel and shelter, scanty wages and disease were rapidly sapping the feeble loyalty of Shrewsbury's men. If Norfolk did not really see and believe the position to be desperate, he still reported it so, and eagerly as the King expected and demanded more favourable tidings, none of the royal officers attempted to modify the Duke's gloomy reports[2].

At dawn a great muster was proclaimed in the Pilgrims' host. The vanguard came forward from Pickburn and the middleward from Hampole. After the morning had fully come, "the whole host appeared at the Stowping Sise before Doncaster."[3] Stowping Sise and Scawsby Lease[4], which is also mentioned as the mustering place, are different parts of the plain on the north bank of the Don.

With spirits quite undamped by the wet night, company after company filed past and took its place in the ranks behind St Cuthbert's

---

[1] L. and P. xi, 864 ; copied from the original at the R. O.
[2] Ibid. 884; printed in full, State Papers, i, 493 ; L. and P. xi, 909.
[3] L. and P. xii (1), 1175 (ii) (4).   [4] Ibid. 201 (p. 90).

crimson and silver standard and the Pilgrimage banner of the Five Wounds of Christ, which device every man wore in miniature on his breast and back. All "the flower of the north" were there[1]. The captains spurred up and down, striving to bring their men into good array; and the companies engaged in friendly rivalry, each trying to excel its neighbours in order and discipline. Experience and popularity both proved useful in this matter; Darcy, Sir Robert Constable, Sir Ralph Ellerker, Robert Bowes, and Roger Lassells marshalled the smartest companies[2].

Priests and friars moved along the lines, commending and encouraging the soldiers; no man, they said, should fear to die in defence of the Faith, with the sign of Christ's Passion over his heart[3]. Perhaps the ranks chanted the hymn made for the Pilgrims by the monks of Sawley. It is well fitted for a marching song, and there is a certain charm, between quaintness and wildness, in the irregular lines, which are at least simple and sincere:

"God that rights all
Redress now shall
And what is thrall
   Again make free,
By this voyage
And Pilgrimage
Of young and sage
   In this country.

Whom God grant grace!
And for the space
Of this their trace
   Send them good speed,
     With health, wealth and speed—
Of sins release
And joy endless
   When they be dead[4]."

It is a relief to find that the vicar of Brayton was not with the host. That disreputable person had gone quietly home, after he had secured, at the spoiling of Sir Brian Hastings' house, fifteen head of cattle and at least £3 worth of goods[5].

It is impossible to give the exact number of the Pilgrims. Aske, who was in the best position to know, twice stated that there were 30,000 men or more at the muster, divided into vanguard and middle-

---

[1] L. and P. xi, 909.   [2] L. and P. xii (1), 29, (2), (3).
[3] Ibid. loc. cit.; 900 (74), (87); printed in full, Eng. Hist. Rev. v, 554, 555.
[4] L. and P. xi, 786; printed in full, Eng. Hist. Rev. v, 344.
[5] L. and P. xi, 1402.

ward, and that the rearward at Pontefract were 12,000 strong; but even Aske probably had not very definite information[1]. The only other witness who gave figures was Marmaduke Neville, a captain of the Bishopric, who stated that there were 28,000 at the muster and 12,000 at Pontefract[2].

There is no doubt that, even if the rearward was not 12,000 strong, it was believed to be so in the forward host. Allowing the same number for the vanguard and middleward, there would be 24,000 at the muster, and 36,000 men would be the total number of Pilgrims assembled in arms under Aske's direct command. The numbers are large, considering that only Yorkshire and Durham had sent men, that, as the leaders declared, every man was efficiently if roughly armed and provided with 20s., and that the greater part were horsed. It is possible that their strength was greatly over-estimated.

The vanward was composed of all the men from the Bishopric of Durham, under the command of Lords Lumley, Neville and Latimer and Sir Thomas Hilton, and the men of Cleveland and part of Richmondshire under Sir Thomas Percy and Robert Bowes; in the middleward were the men of the East and West Ridings, and of the Ainstey of York, with almost all the knights and gentlemen or their eldest sons from those parts, under the command of Sir Robert Constable and Lord Darcy. These forces completed the muster at Stowping Sise. The rearward at Pontefract included the western parts of Richmondshire, together with the men from Masham, Ripon, Kirkbyshire, Wensleydale, Fendale and Netherdale, under the command of Lord Scrope, Sir Christopher Danby, Sir William Mallory, the Nortons, the Markenfields and many more knights and gentlemen. Aske moved constantly between the two forward divisions, though his place, in case of an engagement, was with his own Howdenshire men in the middleward[3].

When all were in array, the lords and gentlemen held a council before the host. They agreed that Sir Thomas Hilton, Sir Ralph Ellerker, Robert Bowes, and Robert Challoner should go on the embassy to the Duke. At the head of so splendid an army, with Doncaster lying before them, the war party seem to have made their last suggestion of immediate attack; the town might be taken almost without effort[4]; Shrewsbury and Norfolk might be captured and

---

[1] L. and P. xii (1), 6; 1175 (ii) (3), (4).   [2] Ibid. 29.
[3] Ibid. 6; printed in full, Eng. Hist. Rev. v, 336–7.
[4] L. and P. xii (1), 1175 (ii) (4).

forced to take the Pilgrims' oath.   But the moderate party again prevailed; they argued that the more evident their superiority, the more likely they were to obtain favourable terms.   The leaders resolved on the five essential points which were weighty enough to explain their rising.   The articles were not written down, but Robert Bowes undertook to repeat them to the Duke from memory[1], an easy feat, as they were in substance the original five :

First, that the Faith might be truly maintained.

Second, that the ancient liberties of the Church might be maintained.

Third, that the unpopular statutes might be repealed and that the law might stand as it did at the beginning of the King's reign "when his nobles did order under his Highness."

Fourth that the "villein blood" might be expelled from the Council and noble blood restored.

Fifth, that Cromwell, Richard Riche, and the heretic bishops might be deprived and banished or otherwise punished as subverters of the laws of God and of the commonwealth[2].

On these terms the Pilgrims were willing to accept the King's general pardon and return peaceably to their homes.   The articles are expressed in vague and wide terms, but the messengers who carried them were ready to amplify and explain their provisions. The vagueness may have been adopted deliberately because, in the first place, the Pilgrims did not wholly agree among themselves— some, for instance, were warmly in favour of the papal supremacy, while others were willing to accept the royal supremacy.   In the second place, the general character of the articles would make it easier for the delegates on both sides to come to an agreement. There was no expression used which came within the scope of the Treason Act, and there were no details over which the two parties might haggle and quarrel.   Henry, with his usual adroitness, seized upon this vagueness at once and turned it to his own advantage. He declared that he could make no direct answer to articles which were so general, vague and obscure.   His flatterers borrowed his expressions.   Archbishop Lee declared that the rebels would not write down the articles for "their enterprise could not be avowed."[3] Henry's panegyrist, William Thomas, declared that "when they [the rebels] came to reasoning in very deed they wist not well what to demand except the preservation of their holy mother church, which

---

[1] L. and P. xii, 1022.   [2] L. and P. xi, 902; printed in full, State Papers, i, 496.
[3] L. and P. xii (1), 1022.

their Prelates and Religious did evermore beat into their heads."[1]
Yet when the Pilgrims, in answer to the King's criticism, proceeded
to draw up a detailed list of their grievances, they were told that it
was "a double iniquity to fall into rebellion and also after to procure
matters to be set forth to justify that rebellion."[2] The two statutes
which the Pilgrims most strongly opposed were the Act of Succession,
which declared Princess Mary illegitimate, and the Act of Suppression. The latter was covered by the second article, and they were
afraid to press the other too strongly, lest they should compromise
Mary, who had of late been treated more kindly. The third article
included this statute, besides the Act of Uses, and all the other
unpopular measures of the long parliament, even to the alienation of
the Percy estates to the crown. The Pilgrims probably did not hope
to bring about such an extremely sweeping reaction, but they realised
that in order to obtain a little from Henry they must begin by
demanding a great deal.

Four hostages were delivered to Aske in pledge for the safety of
Sir Thomas Hilton and his companions; the hostages returned with
the Archbishop and Sir Robert Constable to Hampole nunnery for
the night[3]. There was general hope of good results from the meeting,
and both Darcy and Constable were anxious for an agreement[4].
They were encouraged by the gentlemen from Norfolk's camp, "Mr
Herington, Mr Vellers, Mr Litilton" and another whose name is not
known, but may have been Gifford[5]. Villiers and Gifford were afterwards accused of having expressed sympathy with the Pilgrims[6], and
on Gifford's return to Buckinghamshire rumour said that he was
prepared to raise a rebellion if the churches were attacked[7].

If the gentlemen were anxious for a peaceful issue, the commons
were by no means opposed to it. Otherwise the negotiations could
scarcely have proceeded so far. The commons were prepared to
fight if the King refused the petition, but if he granted it without
trouble, so much the better. As to the King's soldiers, the Pilgrims
regarded them rather as friends who were unwillingly forced to take
part against them than as enemies. All the southern men, they said,
"thought as much" as they, but the southrons dared not show it; as
for themselves, they were plain northern fellows, and said what they

[1] Thomas, The Pilgrim (ed. Froude).
[2] L. and P. xii (1), 900 (93); printed in full, Eng. Hist. Rev. v, 555.
[3] L. and P. xii (1), 6; printed in full, Eng. Hist. Rev. v, 337.
[4] L. and P. xi, 1300.
[5] L. and P. xii (1), 6.
[6] Ibid. 1315.		[7] Ibid. 456.

thought. The Pilgrims were so certain of success against the King's reluctant levies that their sporting instincts seem to have revolted against so easy a victory. "They wished the King had sent some younger lords against them than my lord of Norfolk and my lord of Shrewsbury. No lord in England would have stayed them but my lord of Norfolk," whom they honoured as the victor of Flodden, and suspected to be as much opposed to Cromwell and the Suppression as themselves[1].

At noon on Friday 27 October, in due fulfilment of the agreement, Sir Thomas Hilton and his three companions returned across the bridge and were delivered in exchange for the hostages. The result of the meeting was not final. Norfolk, Shrewsbury, Rutland, Huntingdon, Surrey and their council had received the four and listened to their grievances. Finding that they brought no written copy of the articles, Norfolk ordered them to be written down at Bowes' dictation[2]. The King's nobles said that they were willing to meet a party of the Pilgrims' leaders, as the latter had proposed, on Doncaster bridge, where they would discuss the articles in detail. Hilton and the others agreed to a meeting on the same day of about thirty on each side, and hastened to announce the arrangement to their own leaders. The representatives had to be chosen speedily. They were headed by Darcy, Latimer, Lumley, Sir Robert Constable, Sir John Bulmer, and the four who had crossed in the morning. Aske did not go with them, but held a second great muster on the plain. Such a demonstration would remind the southern host of their strength, guard against any attempt to capture their leaders on the bridge, and keep the Pilgrims together in order to hear the result, whatever it might be. Aske "ordered the whole host standing in perfect array to within night."[3] As time went on and still the conference on the bridge did not break up, some murmuring arose in the ranks. The old cry was raised that the gentlemen would make terms for themselves and betray the commons to the King's vengeance[4]. Aske had stayed with them to quiet these fears. Though their suspicion was not justified on this occasion, the commons had grounds for the fear of the gentlemen's desertion. It was that which brought confusion and failure on the Lincolnshire rising.

No complete account remains of the conference on Doncaster bridge. It seems probable, however, that Norfolk attacked the

[1] L. and P. xi, 1319 ; extracts printed in Froude, op. cit. chap. xiii.
[2] L. and P. xii (1), 1022.
[3] Ibid. 6; printed in full, Eng. Hist. Rev. v, 338.
[4] L. and P. xi, 1086.

Pilgrims' representatives on their weak side, in the very way that the commons feared. They were all gentlemen, he may have said, and by their own account they had been forced to take the rebels' oath against their wills. They were now at some distance from their captors, and near the King's troops; let them desert in a body and leave the commons without leaders. The King would doubtless pardon and reward all who took his part at such a crisis. Darcy's retort was to turn to the Earl of Shrewsbury. "Talbot," he said, "hold up thy long clee[1] and promise me the King's favour, and I will come to Doncaster to you." Shrewsbury's honour was not so accommodating as Norfolk's. " Well, my lord Darcy, then ye shall not come [in]," he replied frankly[2].

Failing in this direct attack, Norfolk seems to have betaken himself to treachery, or half-treachery, in an attempt to be on good terms with both sides. The Pilgrims desired a religious reaction, and Norfolk's views were well known to be conservative. It was said that he had persuaded the King to countenance the doctrine of purgatory in the Ten Articles[3].

The Pilgrims required the repeal of certain statutes. Norfolk was reported to have said at Nottingham that the Act of Uses was the worst act that ever was made[4], and on the present occasion he was said to have told the Pilgrims that " it was pity they were on life, so to give over the Act of Uses," which was not mentioned in the articles[5]. Norfolk denied these last words, and the King professed to believe his denial[6], but they were afterwards brought up against him[7].

Darcy and probably others spoke strongly against Cromwell[8]. Norfolk could truthfully assure them that he hated Cromwell as much as they did.

The Earl of Surrey seems to have committed an indiscretion on his way north. At Cambridge and Thetford he had heard and applauded a song against Suffolk, which was sung by a wandering fiddler, John Hogon, to the popular tune of " The Hunt Is Up." The song had as little rhyme or metre as most political songs and ran :

"The hunt is up etc.
The masters of art and doctors of divinity
Have brought this realm out of good unity,
Three noblemen have taken this to stay;
My lord of Norfolk, lord Surrey and my lord of Shrewsbury.
The Duke of Suffolk might a made England merry—"

[1] clee, *claw or hand.*   [2] L. and P. xi, 1086.   [3] L. and P. xii (1), 778.
[4] Herbert, op. cit. 628.   [5] L. and P. xii (1), 1162.
[6] Ibid. 1192.   [7] Herbert, loc. cit.   [8] L. and P. xi, 1086.

No more is preserved[1]. In July 1537 Surrey was in serious danger on account of a charge which Darcy brought against him—probably that he had promised his support to the Pilgrims[2].

How far Norfolk encouraged the Pilgrims was never discovered, but Lord Herbert of Cherbury (1649) relates:

"All this great service of the Duke of Norfolk yet could not exempt him from calumny: For the Lord Darcy during his imprisonment had accused him, as favouring the rebels' articles when they first met at Doncaster: But the Duke denied it, offering the Duel; saying, that Aske (who suffered at York before the said Lord) told him that said Lord's intentions; who (he said) bare him ill will ever since the Duke had solicited the said Lord to deliver Aske into his hands, when he was in chief credit with the rebels; which Darcy denying, some expostulation pass'd between them. Nevertheless I find the King was so well satisfied of the Duke, that those things were pass'd over without further questioning."[3]

Some of these statements are manifestly incorrect. Aske did not suffer before Darcy, but a fortnight after, and this part of the story seems to be a confused memory of Aske's last words concerning Norfolk and Cromwell, not Norfolk and Darcy[4]. On the other hand it is true that the Duke solicited Darcy to kidnap Aske, much to Darcy's indignation, and this is mentioned in no other early printed account of the Pilgrimage. It is possible that Herbert may have had access to some report of Darcy's examination, now lost, and may have found these interesting particulars there.

Assuming that Herbert's story is substantially true, it is easy to understand the meaning of the terms on which a truce was finally arranged. Norfolk was to ride to the King in all haste, accompanied by Sir Ralph Ellerker and Robert Bowes, whose expenses would be paid by the lords and knights of the Pilgrimage[5]. The messengers were to lay the Pilgrims' petition before the King and to return with his answer. Within the next two days, both armies must disperse, and a truce, binding on both sides, was to last until the messengers returned. These terms at first sight appear to be much less favourable than the Pilgrims might have been expected to exact in their commanding position, but Norfolk's friendly attitude makes all clear. So far were the Pilgrims from going over to the King that Norfolk promised to be on their side. He did not yet declare himself openly, because he could be of more use to them while he continued

---

[1] L. and P. xii (1), 424.
[2] E. Bapst, op. cit.; see note B at end of chapter.
[3] Herbert, op. cit. 492.   [4] See below, chap. xx.
[5] L. and P. xii (1), 946 (118).

nominally in the King's service, but his influence at court, backed by their armed demonstration, might reasonably appear a sufficient guarantee for the success of their cause. When at length the thirty returned from the bridge to the impatient Pilgrims they were able to announce the terms on which the formal appointment had been concluded with the King's nobles, but as Norfolk required secrecy to be observed with regard to his own intentions, they could not explain their full grounds for confidence. Nevertheless the Pilgrims seem to have been well enough contented with the results[1].

Norfolk's state of mind is best shown in his letter to the Council, written a couple of days later on his road south. Henry, angry and suspicious, believed that his desperation was assumed or, at least, exaggerated, but the letter bears evident traces of having been composed by a man in great fear and distress of mind and body.

"my gode lordes I came to this towne this nyght late wher I founde the skantest soper I had many yeres as wery a man as can be and with contynewall watche and agony of mynd so tanned [?] that in my liff I never was in that case I have be[en] a bed now iii howrys and ii tymes waked in that tyme the one with lettres fro my lord of Suffolk th' oder fro the Kynges highnes of the xxvii of this moneth the contentes wheroff shuld be not necessary to answer our affaires being in the trade they now be in. alas my god lordes I have served his highnes many tymes without reproch and now inforced to appoynt with the rebelles my hert is nere broken. and notwithstondyng that in every mannes mowth it is sayde in our armye that I never served his grace so well as now as in dissolvyng the army of th' enemy without los of ours yet fearyng how his maiestie shall take the dispeachyng of our bande I am the most unquiet man of mynde lyvyng. all others here joyfull and I only sorowfull. alas that the valiannt hert of my lord steward wold not suffer hym to have taried abouts trent but with his fast hastyng forwardes to bryng us into the most bareyne countre of the realme wheroff hath insewed th' effectes that I saw long afore woll fall Gode my lordes it was not the feare of th' enemys hath caused us to appoynt, but thre other sore poyntes. foulle wether ande no howsing for horse nor man at the most not for the iiid part of the army and no wode to make fiers withall, honger both for men and horsis of suche sort that of trouth I thynk never Inglishe man saw the like. pestilence in the towne mervelous fervent and of suche sort that wher I and my son lay in a fryers x or xii howsis sore infected within ii butts length, on fryday at nyght the mayers wiff and ii of his doghters and one servant died in one howse how many others of the towne I know [not] but of souldyers ix and if ther wer lefte in the towne or within v myles one lode of hey or one lode of ootes, pese or beanys all the purveyors say untrewly. which iii poyntes these ar for an armye I report me to your wisdomes and to have advansed to th' enemys no vitayle for man nor horse but all devasted by th' enemys and not possible to have yeven batayle but upon apparaunt los theroff. and if we shuld have retyred in enemyte assewred rewyn

[1] L. and P. XII (1), 6; printed in full, Eng. Hist. Rev. v, 338.

of our company. havying no horsmen and they all the floure of the north and how at every streyte they shuld at their will have set on the formest part or the hindermost your wisdomes can well consyder. and my lordes accordyng to my dewtie to advertise the trouth. thogh never prince had a company of more trew valiaunt noble men and jantlemen yet right few of souldiers but that thoght and think their quarelles to be gode and godly. the companys that came with my lord marques and me I trust wold have done their partes and the noblemen of the rest. but I feare what th' oders woll. my lords what case we wer in when roger ratclyff[1] and I wept secretly togyders I report me to you neyther of us bothe but with gode will wold have be[en] prisoners in turkey to have had it at the poynt it is now. thogh not as we wold it wer and yet onys agayne my lords wo wo wo worth the tyme that my lord steward went so far forth for and he had not ye shuld have herd other newes. ffy ffy upon the lord darcy the most arraunt traytor that ever was lyvyng and yet both his sonnys trew knightes. old sir roberd constable as ill as he and all his blode trew men fynally my gode lordes if the kynges highnes shuld wright to me to gather the army to gyders it is not possible to be done. and for godds sake help that his highnes cause not my lord of Suffolk to put any man to deth unto my comyng. nor openly to call the lord darcy traytor and also to stay that I be not in his displesure unto the tyme I may be herd and then Judge me accordyng to my desertes scribled at tuxford at v in the mornyng this sonday.

yr owne

T. Norfolk."[2]

Late as it was, Darcy and Aske rode to Pontefract on the evening of the conference, and next morning, Saturday 28 October, they proclaimed the truce and ordered the rearward to go home. It was easier to give the order than to see it obeyed. The dalesmen had come far and were very reluctant to go home empty-handed, without any definite triumph. They had not been represented at the conference, and consequently felt that the appointment need not bind them. Their captains, Lord Scrope, Sir Christopher Danby, and the others, were willing to accept the truce, but the commons were wild and much more difficult to control than those of the forward divisions. Nevertheless in the end the commands, arguments and persuasions of Aske, Darcy and Sir Richard Tempest, seconded by the efforts of their own leaders, prevailed on the aggrieved and disappointed rearward, and they sulkily set out on their homeward march, leaving Pontefract empty for the rest of the army, which lay there that night[3].

On the same day Darcy received a message from Thomas Grice, who had heard from Lancashire that the Earl of Derby intended to

[1] He was an usher of the King's Privy Chamber.
[2] L. and P. xi, 909 ; copied from the original at the R. O.
[3] L. and P. xi, 928, 1045.

attack Sawley Abbey[1]. Aske immediately sent the news of the truce
to the Pilgrims there, and Darcy wrote to request Shrewsbury to
stop Derby's operations. It has already been shown how these
messages prevented a collision between the opposing forces[2]. At the
same time Aske sent messengers to all the places in which there had
been risings with "the most special letters that could be devised"
commanding the Pilgrims to leave the castles they were besieging,
break off their musters and go peaceably home[3]. The reception of
these letters has been described above.

Norfolk despatched a messenger on Saturday to carry the news
of the truce to the King, and set out himself with Ellerker and Bowes
on the same day[4].

On Sunday 29 October the King's heralds, Chester and Carlisle,
watched the last men of the Pilgrims' host "disparple" at Pontefract
and take their way home over Ferrybridge. The heralds were back
at Doncaster before noon, where Shrewsbury's army was also disbanding[5]. Northward went the insurgents, southward the King's
men,—a strangely peaceful parting. At Tadcaster William Stapleton
bade farewell to his men of Beverley, "desiring them to keep good
rule" on the homeward march, and went back to Wighill, returning
to his usual autumn hunting and shooting as though he had never
been the captain of a rebel host[6]. Thus the uneasy quiet of an
armed truce fell on England at the end of October 1536.

Norfolk's anxious letter shows that he expected the King to be
very angry at the news of the truce. Yet all the advantages of it
were on the King's side. It was very unlikely that the Pilgrims
would have another opportunity of striking so crushing a blow as
that which they had deliberately foregone. Henry did not fail to
realise the advantages of his position, although he was furious at the
way in which they were obtained. He felt it a blot on his honour
that his lieutenants should have made terms with the rebels, instead
of scattering them, with or without bloodshed, and selecting a suitable
number for execution; but as the rebels had dispersed, his experience
taught him that they were very unlikely to assemble again in such

---

[1] L. and P. xi, 899; see above, chap. ix.

[2] L. and P. xi, 900, 901; 901 printed in full, Correspondence of the 3rd Earl of
Derby (Chetham Soc.), 36.

[3] L. and P. xi, 928; xii (1), 6; printed in full, Eng. Hist. Rev. v, 338.

[4] L. and P. xi, 902; printed in full, St. P. i, 496.

[5] L. and P. xi, 910, printed in full, St. P. i, 497; xii (1), 6, printed in full, Eng.
Hist. Rev. v, 338.

[6] L. and P. xii (1), 392.

large numbers, and he was convinced that with a little delay, a little diplomacy, and plenty of southern musters, the north might be brought into complete subjection without any concessions being made at all.

When the problem is considered in the light thrown on Henry's character by the later events of his reign, it is surprising that the leaders of the Pilgrimage should have expected him to give way so easily. It is practically certain that while Henry lived and ruled he would never have changed his policy. The rebels did not propose to dethrone him; yet by no other means could his work be undone. This they never realised till too late. It must be remembered that Henry had reigned for twenty years before doing anything that greatly alarmed his most conservative subjects. By making the truce, the Pilgrims preserved their consistency. If the King refused their petition and civil war ensued, he and not they would be responsible. But as a matter of fact, they did not believe that the King was in earnest about the religious changes. In their eyes it was all some devilry of Cromwell's. It was too absurd that the monasteries should be suppressed; they had been there for hundreds of years,—and how could the country do without them? Except for the wandering reformers and their scattered disciples, English people believed the New Learning to be not only wicked but ridiculous. Within two years of his death, Sir Thomas More was busily writing most excellent and amusing little tracts proving that there was not really the slightest danger that Catholic England would be infected with heresy. Although things had now gone so much further, Aske and his followers still believed implicitly in the strength of their cause. It was impossible that the Faith should fail to triumph in the end. Wolsey had suppressed monasteries and countenanced the hated divorce, but he fell. Anne Boleyn had caused the death of More, Fisher, and the Carthusian monks, but she had followed them to the scaffold. Cromwell must go the same way. If once he were dead, and Norfolk, with the other conservative lords, restored to full power, the work of the last four years would disappear without difficulty— so the Pilgrims thought—and all might go on as if no dark-haired coquette and no "Englishman Italianate" had ever crossed the destinies of England. A complete reaction seemed perfectly easy then. Looking back, it is equally easy to talk very wisely of tendencies and inevitable results; but no age can tell whither it is tending. The Pilgrims could not see that there was no going back— that the New Learning was bound to triumph and to regenerate as well as destroy—that despotism had yet a great part to play before it was shaken and dragged down by civil war and revolution. They were so sure of their own strength that they were pathetically willing to behave with chivalrous moderation to the side which they regarded as the weaker.

NOTES TO CHAPTER XI

Note A. North country readers will not need to be told that the commander-in-chief at Flodden was Thomas Howard, Earl of Surrey, afterwards second Duke of Norfolk, and that his eldest son, who appears so frequently in this book as the third Duke of Norfolk, was his second in command. The latter was then simply Lord Thomas Howard, Admiral of England. He played an important part in the campaign. Holinshed gives him the credit of suggesting the strategy which placed the English forces between the Scots army and the Border. In the field he commanded the vanguard, with the centre of which he fought. He was said to have gone into battle loudly challenging the King of Scots to single combat, and to have performed great deeds, slaying the Earl of Crawford with his own hand. At the moment when the issue was most doubtful,—when the dying Marmion cried :—

> "Tunstall lies dead upon the field,
> His life-blood stains the spotless shield :
> Edmund is down :—my life is reft ;
> The Admiral alone is left,"—

Lord Thomas was actually standing firm in the face of the Scottish attack ; taking the Agnus Dei from his neck, he sent it to his father as a token to hasten to his assistance. He was regarded as the hero of the day no less than Surrey[1].

Note B. M. Bapst has shown that the correct date of the letter from Norfolk to Cromwell, printed in L. and P. XI, 21, as belonging to 1536, is really 1537[2].

[1] Arch. Ael. (N. S.) XVI, 351 et seq.
[2] Bapst, op. cit. p. 227 n.

CHAPTER XII

THE FIRST WEEKS OF THE TRUCE

The King was at first as well satisfied with the advantage gained by the appointment at Doncaster, as he was displeased with the means by which it was obtained. "So sudden recess" was a stain on his honour "if the contrary might have been maintained." However, the thing was done, and it only remained to bring the northern men to a sense of their wickedness and graciously grant them a pardon on the same terms as the pardon to Lincolnshire, namely, that they would take and deliver such culprits as the King's vengeance demanded, and submit themselves humbly to his mercy, taking oaths of future obedience[1].

Henry does not seem to have realised at first that there was any danger of another rising. On Sunday 29 October he was summoning an army to meet the rebels, which, he declared, he would lead in person[2]. Next day news of the appointment had come, and these musters were countermanded, with the proviso that the men must be ready again at reasonable warning. General pardons to all rebels dwelling north of Doncaster for offences committed before 1 November were drafted on 2 November, in terms resembling the Lincolnshire pardon. The excepted persons were Robert Aske, Hutton of Snape, Kitchen of Beverley, William Ombler the bailiff, Henry Coke of Durham shoemaker, Maunsell vicar of Brayton, and four others unnamed[3]. Henry considered that to demand only ten culprits after a month of open rebellion was a display of the most princely lenity, and no doubt from his own point of view he was right. It was intended that this pardon, or rather promise of pardon— for each individual was to sue in Chancery for his own—should be proclaimed throughout the north by the King's heralds, who must observe and report on the state of the country, especially noticing

[1] L. and P. xi, 944.
[2] Ibid. 885, 886, 906.
[3] Ibid. 955.

how deep might be the supposed penitence of the commons, and how far they were determined to support the restored monks and nuns. The heralds were also to read long lectures on the folly of the rebels' demands, the wickedness of rebellion, and the beneficence of the King[1].

On Sunday 29 October Latimer preached the sermon at Paul's Cross. His text was "Put on all the armour of God," and he took occasion to refer to the northern men, who wore "the Cross and the Wounds before and behind," in order to "deceive the poor ignorant people, and bring them to fight against both the King, the Church, and the Commonwealth." He compared the rebels to the Devil, who also professed to put on the armour of God to deceive the ignorant, and he exhorted his hearers to be steadfast and loyal, and to assume the true armour of a Christian, with all the elaborate allegories and analogies for which the subject gives scope[2].

All the King's plans were formed between 29 October, when news of the appointment reached London, and 2 November, when Norfolk arrived at court. It may be imagined with what anxious hearts Norfolk, Bowes and Ellerker set out for Windsor on Saturday 28 October[3]. They were followed by Fitzwilliam as the representative of Suffolk and the other lords at Lincoln, who were almost as uneasy as Norfolk with regard to the King's attitude[4]. Norfolk was so much worn out by his exertions that he could not travel more than thirty miles a day[5]. From Grantham on 30 October he wrote to ask whether he should bring Bowes and Ellerker straight to court, or leave them in London until he and Lord Talbot, who had come up with them, had seen the King[6]. The whole party was summoned to Windsor, where they arrived at ten o'clock on the morning of Thursday 2 November, but Norfolk was commanded to come into the royal presence first. After dinner the King sent for the northern gentlemen. On first seeing them, Henry could not repress an outburst of rage, but he allowed himself to be soothed by Norfolk and other members of the Council, and in the end promised to write an answer to the articles with his own hand[7]. He seemed to be taking Norfolk's action so quietly that Fitzwilliam sent a reassuring letter to Suffolk[8].

---

[1] L. and P. xi, 956.

[2] Latimer's Remains (Parker Soc.), p. 29.   The sermon is misdated 1535.

[3] L. and P. xi, 909.   [4] Ibid. 914.

[5] Ibid. 1009.   [6] Ibid. 921.

[7] Ibid. 1009.   [8] Ibid. 979.

Henry's calm was partly due to the fact that he did not yet realise fully the crisis to which affairs had come. He saw that the danger had been very great, and that he was not yet in a position to punish disaffection with severity, but he still believed that the worst was over. The rebels had dispersed, and a temporary show of mildness on his part was all that was required. He could not refuse a very wide pardon, but there was no need to contemplate any concessions to the Pilgrims' impudent demands, which they were no longer able to press upon him. Holding this opinion, he drew up an answer to the articles in his own hand, "and no creature was privy thereto until it was finished."[1] It ran as follows:

"First, as touching the maintenance of the Faith; the terms be so general, that hard they be to be answered; but if they mean the Faith of Christ to which all Christian men be most obliged, we declare and protest ourself to be he that always do and have minded to die and live in the purity of the same, and that no man can or dare set his foot by ours in proving of the contrary; marvelling not a little that ignorant people will go about or take upon them to instruct us, (which something have been noted learned), what the right Faith should be, or that they would be so ingrate and unnatural to us, their most rightful King, without any our desert, upon false reports and surmises, to suspect us of the same, and give rather credence to forged light tales than to the approved truth by us these twenty-eight years used, and by our deeds approved.

To the second, which toucheth the maintenance of the Church, and liberties of the same; this is so general a proposition that without distinctions no man with truth can answer it neither by God's laws nor by the laws of the realm. For first the Church which they mean must be known; secondly, whether they be lawful or unlawful liberties which they require; and these known I doubt not but they shall be answered according to God's law, equity and justice. But yet, for all their generality, this I dare asseever, that (meaning what Church they list) we have done nothing in their prejudice that may not be abidden by, both by God's law and man's; and in our own Church, whereof we be the Supreme Head here in Earth, we have not done so much prejudice as many of our predecessors have done upon much less grounds. Wherefore, since it is a thing which nothing pertaineth to any of you our commons, nor that you bear anything therein, I cannot but reckon a great unkindness and unnaturalness, in that ye had liever a churl or two should enjoy those profits of their monasteries, in supportation of vicious and abominable life, than I your prince for supportation of my extreme charges, done for your defence.

The third toucheth three things; the laws, the common wealth, the directors of the laws under us. Touching the laws, we expressly dare testify that (blind men deeming no colours, nor yet being judges) it shall be duly proved that there were never in any of our predecessors' days so many wholesome, commodious and beneficial acts made for the common wealth, and yet I mean it since their time that would fain have thank without desert. For Our Lord forbid (seeing

---

[1] L. and P. XI, 957, 995.

we have been these twenty-eight years your King) that both we and our Council should have lost so much time as not to know now better than when we came first to our reign, what were the common wealth and what were not. And though outrecuidance of some may chance will not let them to acknowledge it so, yet I trust and doubt not but the most part of our loving subjects (specially those which be not seduced by false reports) do both think it, accept it, and find it so. Now, touching the common wealth; what King hath kept you all his subjects so long in wealth and peace; so long without taking or doing wrong one to the other; so indifferently minister[ed] justice to all, both high and low; so defended you all from outward enemies; so fortified the frontiers of this realm, to his no little and in a manner inestimable charges? and all for your wealths and sureties. What King hath given among you more general or freer pardons? What King hath been loather to punish his subjects, or showed more mercy amongst them? These things being so true as no true man can deny them, it is an unnatural and unkind demeanour of you our subjects to believe or deem the contrary of it, by whose report so ever it should be. As touching the beginning of our reign, where ye say so many noblemen were councillors; who were then councillors I well remember and yet of the temporalty I note none but two worthy calling noble; the one Treasurer of England [*the Earl of Surrey, Norfolk's father*], the other High Steward of our house [*the Earl of Shrewsbury*]; others, as the Lords Marney and Darcy, but scant well born gentlemen; and yet of no great lands till they were promoted by us and so made knights and lords; the rest were lawyers and priests, save two bishops, which were Canterbury and Winchester. If these then be the great number of noblemen that ye speak of and that ye seemed then to be content withal, why then now be ye not much better content with us, which have now so many nobles in deed both of birth and condition? For first of the temporalty, in our Privy Council we have the Duke of Norfolk, the Duke of Suffolk, the Marquis of Exeter, the Lord Steward (when he may come), the Earl of Oxford, the Earl of Sussex, the Lord Sandys our Chamberlain, the Lord Admiral Treasurer of our House, Sir William Poulet Comptroller of our house: and of the spiritualty, the Bishop of Hereford [*Edward Fox*], the Bishop of Chichester [*Richard Sampson*], and the Bishop of Winchester [*Stephen Gardiner*]. Now how far be ye abused to reckon that then there were more noblemen in our Privy Council than now? But yet, though I now do declare the truth to pull you from the blindness that you were led in, yet we ensure you we would ye knew that it appertaineth nothing to any of our subjects to appoint us our Council ne we will take it so at your hands. Wherefore henceforth remember better the duties of subjects to your King and sovereign lord, and meddle no more of those nor such like things as ye have nothing to do in.

To the fourth; where ye the commons do name certain of our Council to be subverters both of God's law and the laws of this realm; we do take and repute them as just and true executors both of God's laws and ours as far as their commissions under us do extend. And if any of our subjects can duly prove the contrary, we shall proceed against them and all other offenders therein according to justice, as to our estate and dignity royal doth appertain. And in case it be but a false and untrue report (as we verily think it is), then it were as meet and standeth as well with justice that they should have the self same punishment which wrongfully hath objected this to them, that they should have had if they deserved it. And one thing amongst others maketh me think that this slander should be untrue; because it proceedeth from that place which is both so far distant from where they inhabit, and also from those people which never heard them preach nor yet knoweth any part of their conversation. Wherefore we exhort you our commons to be no more so light of credit, neither of ill things spoken of your King and sovereign, nor yet of any of his prelates and councillors; but to think that your King, having so long reigned over you, hath as good discretion to elect and choose his councillors as those (whosoever they be) that hath put this in your heads.

Here, in this final point, which ye our commons of Yorkshire do desire and also in the matter of the whole, we verily think that the rest of our whole commons (whereof ye be in manner but an handful) will greatly disdain and not bear it that ye take upon you to set order both to them and us, your both sovereign; and that (though ye be rebels) ye would make them as bearers and partakers of your mischief; willing them to take pardon for insurrections which verily I think and doubt not they never minded; but like true subjects to the contrary hath, both with heart and deed, been ready at our call to defend both us and themself.

And now for our part; as to your demands, We let you wit that pardon of such things as ye demand lieth only in the will and pleasure of the prince; but it seemeth by your lewd proclamations and safe-conducts that there be amongst you which take upon them both the King's and councillor's parts, which neither yet by us nor by consent of the realm hath been admitted to any such room. What arrogancy then is in those wretches (being also of none experience) to presume to raise you our subjects without commission or authority, yea, and against us, under a cloaked colour of your wealth and in our name; and as the success will declare, (we being no more merciful than ye yet hitherto deserve) to your utter confusions? Wherefore we let you wit, ye our subjects of Yorkshire, that were it not that our princely heart cannot reckon this your shameful insurrection and unnatural rebellion to be done of malice or rancour, but rather by a lightness given in a manner by a naughty nature to a commonalty and a wondrous sudden surreption of gentlemen; we must needs have executed another manner of punishment than (ye humbly knowledging your fault and submitting yourselves to our mercy) we intend to do. And to the intent that ye shall all know that our princely heart rather embraceth (of his own disposition) pity and compassion of his offending subjects than will to be revenged of their naughty deeds; we are contented, if we may see and perceive in you all a sorrowfulness for your offences and will henceforth to do no more so, nor to believe so lewd and naughty tales or reports of your most kind and loving prince and his Council, to grant unto you all our letters patent of pardon for this rebellion; so that ye will deliver unto us ten such of the ringleaders and provokers of you in this rebellion, as we shall assign to you and appoint. Now note the benignity of your prince. Now note how easily ye may have pardon, both gentlemen and other if ye list. Now note how effusion of blood may be eschewed. Now note, what this little while of your rebellion hath hindered yourselves and country. Now learn by a little lack to eschew a worse. Now learn, by this small warning, to keep you true men.

Thus I, as your head, pray for you my members, that God may light you with his Grace to knowledge and declare yourselves our true subjects henceforth, and to give more credence to these our benign persuasions than to the perverse instigations of maliciously disposed persons."[1]

Although the tone of this document was on the whole milder than that of the reply to the Lincolnshire rebels, it must have caused dismay to Norfolk, who knew that the Pilgrims would regard it as a declaration of war. It contained no answer to any of their grievances, except the statement that the King was entirely right, and they were entirely wrong. The only hint of conciliation was the promise that if any members of the Council could be proved to be subverters of the laws, they should be punished, and this was qualified by the King's certainty that no one could prove anything of the sort. Even the promised pardon was not general. Norfolk must have learnt enough of the Pilgrims' feelings to know that they would never accept this answer, and they were in a position to attack Suffolk almost as soon as it was received, for their musters were made on the spot, while the King's troops had to be conveyed there from a distance. Yet for the moment there seemed to be no way in which the answer might be altered. The Council did not dare openly to criticise the King's own composition, and on the morning of Sunday 5 November, Bowes and Ellerker set out from Windsor with the King's reply, which they themselves do not seem to have read. But at noon a message was sent to Cromwell commanding him to stop them until the King had consulted his Council again[2]. Such news had been received from the north that Fitzwilliam wrote that the ambassadors must be stopped in London. If they had started, a post must be sent after them[3].

The particular report which had just arrived has not been preserved, but its contents at last convinced the King that the time was not yet ripe for his answer. He must temporise, not threaten. The same news which made him realise this gave him an excuse for delay. It was possible to declare that the Pilgrims had broken the truce, and that the King therefore refused to negotiate with them[4]. A message which Aske had sent to Sir Marmaduke Constable was one of these alleged breaches[5]. It was also said that Leonard Beckwith had been attacked. He was a receiver of the suppressed abbeys' goods and therefore very unpopular. His house was plundered by William

---

[1] L. and P. xi, 957; printed in full, State Papers, i, 506.
[2] L. and P. xi, 985.   [3] Ibid. 986.
[4] Ibid. 995, see below.   [5] L. and P. xi, 1009.

Acclom and sixty commons, and his mother put in such fear that she was ill for the next seven months; but this had happened before the truce[1]. The King also complained that Aske had sent letters into Cumberland, Westmorland and Lancashire[2]. These were the letters which announced the truce and ordered the rebels to disband. On these pretexts Bowes and Ellerker were detained and the King embarked on a new policy.

It must be placed to the credit of Henry's honesty, if not of his generalship, that he was unwilling to drop force and resort to treachery, as Norfolk advised. From the time of the first outbreak in Lincolnshire the King had been urging his lieutenants to proceed to extremities. He frequently ordered them to give battle, and he seems to have felt no doubt as to the result. It was not by his will that the outbreak of hostilities had been delayed so long. The revolt might have been finally crushed by one decisive blow, but on the other hand it was even more likely that the rebels would have been victorious, and that the battle which the King desired would have been the opening of a civil war, the end of which no man could foresee. This may seem too confident a statement to base on the reports of Norfolk, as their gloomy tone was partly due to sympathy with the rebels, but there is positive evidence of the weakness of the royal troops, apart from Norfolk's letters. In the first place, the royal forces were never concentrated at one place; they straggled north in scattered contingents, which could easily have been cut off in detail. In the second place, the King's soldiers did not receive regular and sufficient pay. In the third place, the Duke of Suffolk, whose loyalty was unquestioned, was as unwilling as Norfolk to risk a battle. Jealousy ran so high among Henry's nobles that if Suffolk could safely have made a great show of activity, in contrast to Norfolk's hesitation, or could have sent very cheerful reports, in contrast to Norfolk's desperate letters, there can be no doubt that he would have done so, and won the King's favour. Only the gravity of the situation can have forced him to support Norfolk.

These facts were obvious to Henry when he was cool enough to observe them, and accordingly his blustering was temporarily suspended. He was still absolutely determined that he would make no concessions to the Pilgrims, but he was forced to resort to temporising and treachery, as it was impossible for the moment to compel them to submit to his will. Accordingly he laid his plans anew.

---

[1] L. and P. xii (i), 536, 1163; see above, chap. viii.   [2] L. and P. xi, 1009.

His first object was to delay the northern messengers. All waste of time was time gained. Hot blood would cool, and anger die down, men would settle into their ordinary ways, and hopeful spirits would grow despondent, if time was given them to realise the dangers and difficulties of civil war. The return of Bowes and Ellerker would be watched for less and less eagerly every day they tarried, and the King's answer, however unfavourable, might find the people readier to submit than to rise again. The King's second line of attack was directed against the very citadel of the Pilgrims' position—the loyalty of their leaders. Letters of thanks were sent to all the gentlemen of the north who had taken the King's side, and they were encouraged to return to their own homes, or remain there as the case might be, in order that they might report the arrangements and movements of the Pilgrims, and use their influence with the neighbouring gentlemen, often friends and relatives, to bring them over to the King[1]. Promises of pardon and reward, hints at grants of land, perhaps belonging to the very monasteries they had risen to defend, perhaps the property of men like Darcy and Constable who would not escape unattainted, doubtless had the desired effect on some of the gentlemen[2]. The King might well anticipate that these methods would bring such disunion into the Pilgrims' councils that any concerted action would be rendered impossible and isolated outbreaks would be the worst that need be feared.

The Pilgrims from the first did their utmost to guard against the King's assault on their weak places. They strove to keep the gentlemen banded together by frequent councils and constant communication. With the commons their task was doubly difficult. They must keep unruly members from spoils and other offences against the truce, and at the same time encourage the fervent and patriotic spirit which was the mainstay of their venture. Henry issued sermons and exhortations,—the Pilgrims replied with poems. John Hallam returned home to Watton after the disbanding at Pontefract, and brought with him "certain rhymes made against my lord privy seal, my lord Chancellor, the Chancellor of the Augmentations and divers bishops of the new learning which rhymes had been sung abroad by minstrels."[3] He showed them to Friar John Pickering, one of the Friars Preachers, who had taken refuge at the Priory of Bridlington[4]. Pickering was inspired to write something

---

[1] L. and P. xi, 1002, 1003, 1005, 1032, 1037.
[2] Ibid. 1027, 1077, 1120.
[3] L. and P. xii (1), 1021 (3). 　　　　　[4] Ibid. 1019, 1207 (8).

better than these clumsy verses to encourage the Pilgrims in the good cause. With this intention he composed a long poem in the elaborate Latin style which seems to have been the fashion then in Yorkshire. He "made the said rhyme by rhyme that the hearers might better bear it away, but not that it might be sung by minstrels" and he himself showed it only to a few friends, who all praised it. Nevertheless it soon spread abroad and·"was in every man's mouth about Bridlington and Scarborough." It is difficult to understand how anyone could sing the verses, for they have none of the rugged charm of the Pilgrims' marching song. They are long-winded, involved, and interspersed with scraps of Latin. The Pilgrims are compared first to the Maccabees, afterwards to Mordecai, with Cromwell in the character of Hamon:

> "This cruel Hamon by his false invention
> In the north doth perceive the faithfull commonty,
> By his great expenses intending utterly
> Us to destroy and bring in captivity.
> But great God above that ever doth procure
> For his faithful people all that is necessary,
> And even provide I you do ensure
> His falsehood to be known and eke his policy.
> No fair words we shall trust after my opinion
> But boldly go forward in our peregrination."

The gist of the poem is an exhortation to be loyal to the King, but to fight to the death against Cromwell[1].

Thus both parties were working quietly and effectively to improve their position, and in consequence were constantly accusing each other of breaches of the truce. It cannot be denied that, however honest their intentions, the first appointment at Doncaster was not well kept on either side. The diplomacy of the King and the wildness of the commons—to say nothing of mutual suspicion— were against it. Considering all the circumstances it was perhaps as strictly observed as engagements of the kind ever are.

The presence of Suffolk in Lincolnshire made it absolutely necessary for the Pilgrims to secure their borders. Norfolk, of course, had no power to promise the dispersal of Suffolk's army, even if the rebels demanded anything so unreasonable; but he had undertaken that the King's Lieutenant in Lincolnshire should observe the truce and threaten no invasion of Yorkshire[2]. The Pilgrims had stipulated that none of the prisoners at Lincoln should suffer execution till a

---

[1] L. and P. xii (1), 1021 (5); printed in full, Longstaff, A Leaf from the Pilgrimage of Grace; see note F at end of chapter.

[2] L. and P. xi, 1049, 3 (3), (6), (7); 1058 (4).

final settlement had been reached, which must have been all they could do at the time for their unlucky fellows[1]. But Suffolk, instead of keeping all his host round Lincoln, where he himself lay, sent garrisons to Grimsby, Barton and other towns on Trent and Humber[2]. These places were fortified, the river traffic was controlled by their commanders and every effort was made to collect the boats on their own side. Hull, the most important citadel on the north of Humber, was known to favour the King, partly because of Beverley's devotion to the Pilgrims. Further east, Sir Brian Hastings lay at Hatfield with his tenants and servants about five hundred strong, ready to stand to arms at a word[3]. Even at Wakefield, right in the rebels' country, Sir Henry Saville was bullying and coaxing his neighbours to join the King[4]. These formed the King's first line, pushed right to the frontiers of the rebels. His second was the line of the Trent. The castles at Newark and Nottingham were being garrisoned and re-fortified. Shrewsbury was at his Derbyshire seat, Wingfield, ready to muster all the country at the first warning from the north, and to hold the bridges at Derby and Burton-on-Trent[5]. Nor must it be forgotten that the Pilgrims had also an enemy at their flank. The Earl of Derby had orders to be on the alert. He kept nightly watch along the Pilgrims' borders and ascertained by constant musters the available strength of Lancashire and Cheshire[6].

Such were the King's general defences, the details of which will appear presently, and it remained for the Pilgrims to make themselves equally secure. The defence of the Trent was not fully organised until the middle of November, but the first line was prepared at the beginning of the truce, and Hull was in some danger of falling by a sudden attack.

The Pilgrims' strongest line of defence was along the Humber, Ouse and Aire, and such were its advantages, particularly in the way of scarcity of bridges, that it could be made almost impassable, if properly garrisoned with determined troops. But the commons had risen and joined them through all the country south as far as the Don, Marshland, and the Isle of Axholme, which lay between the Don and the Trent. In order to keep this part of the country, they would be obliged to hold the line of the Trent. The result of this was that the district south of the Ouse became debatable

---

[1] L. and P. xi, 909.   [2] Ibid. 990, 1075, 1077.
[3] Ibid. 966.   [4] Ibid. 960.   [5] See below.
[6] L. and P. xi, 992, 1010, 1022, 1031; printed in full, Correspondence of the third Earl of Derby (Chetham Soc.), pp. 53, 55, 56.

ground, where each party was constantly complaining of breaches of the truce.

The first business of the rebel leaders was to stay the "wild" men of the North Riding. It may be conjectured that the expected arrival of these rough allies had something to do with the making of the truce, for all the well-to-do Pilgrims were very shy of the commons who were more bent on social reform than on religious conservatism. Although Darcy and the captains were able to disband the forces that were at Pontefract and Doncaster[1], it was not to be expected that the remote districts could be quieted at once. The truce was not acknowledged in Cumberland until 3 November, as has been described, and then only in part and with great reluctance[2]. The monks of Furness were giving money to their tenants and encouraging them to attend the musters on Hallowmas Eve, 31 October[3]. On his return from Jervaux to Richmond John Dakyn was obliged to keep the freest hospitality he could, and distributed seven nobles among his parishioners, that they might not rob him as they had done some of the neighbouring clergy[4].

As time went on the unrest became more marked, but for the moment there was an uneasy lull, and the leaders of the Pilgrimage began to strengthen their defences. Orders were given on the 30th that beacons should be laid and that nightly watch should be kept in the church towers of the East Riding, where some attempt might be made from Lincolnshire[5]. Aske spent the night of Sunday 29 October in York, declaring the order and staying the country. Next day, Monday 30 October, he turned his attention to the delicate problem of the Earl of Northumberland's position, and rode to Wressell Castle. On the way he heard that Sir Marmaduke Constable, who had been in hiding, had returned home at the news of the truce, and that the commons were threatening to plunder his house if he would not take the oath. Aske wrote to Sir Marmaduke advising him to come to Wressell for protection, but he fled to Lincolnshire[6]. This was the message of which the King complained on 5 November.

The unfortunate Earl of Northumberland, still lying ill at Wressell Castle, was now besieged by most unwelcome visitors. First came Aske, "to have agreed him and his brother Sir Thomas Percy." The

[1] See above and L. and P. xi, 902.   [2] See above, chap. ix.
[3] L. and P. xii (1), 841 (2), (3).   [4] Ibid. 789 (i).
[5] L. and P. xi, 924, 1048.
[6] L. and P. xii (1), 6; printed in full, Eng. Hist. Rev. v, 338.

Earl refused to have anything whatever to do with his brothers, but towards Aske his attitude was on the whole friendly. The commons at Snaith had seized two coffers of the Earl's clothes, which had been sent from London. Aske saved them from destruction and made a bill of the contents, "a gown and doublet of crimson satin and the rest of small value." He had sent word to the Earl that he could have his coffers on sending for them, but he made Aske a present of them, and now affirmed that if there had been more Aske should have had it for saving his life from the commons[1].

Failing in his principal object that day, Aske seems to have returned to York for the night to take counsel with Sir Thomas. Next day, Tuesday 31 October, Hallowmas Eve, they dined together at St Mary's Abbey, York, and then received news of the arrival of William Stapleton, who sent word to Aske that he was about to ride to Wressell to pay his duty to the Earl his master, and would be glad to be allowed to ride in Aske's company. But Aske and Sir Thomas Percy set off without him, and when Stapleton reached the Castle Aske was with the Earl, trying in vain to persuade him to make Sir Thomas lieutenant of one March and Sir Ingram of the other. Afterwards Stapleton himself visited the Earl, whom he found in bed "weeping, ever wishing himself out of the world, which the said William was sore to see." That night Sir Thomas, Aske and Stapleton all slept at Wressell.

Next day, Wednesday 1 November, Aske went to the Earl again, and they came to terms. The Earl, under compulsion, consented to what Aske and the lords had resolved upon, but he absolutely refused to make any concessions to his brothers, or even to see Sir Thomas. It may be imagined that he would not find it easy to face the brother whom he had disinherited. Stapleton added his persuasions to those of Aske. He really feared for the Earl's life, as he had heard the commons say in the field, "Strike off the head of the Earl and make Sir Thomas earl," and Sir Thomas Hilton had exclaimed, "He is now crept into a corner and dare not show himself, he hath made a many of knaves gentlemen to whom he has disposed much of his living and all now to do nought himself." The Earl's obstinacy made Stapleton half-angry, but nothing could move him to see his brother. The Earl was very earnest on behalf of the King and Cromwell against the commons, and when Stapleton warned him that he was actually in danger he only replied that "he cared not, he could die but once, let them strike off his head and rid him of much pain."

[1] L. and P. xii (1), 698.

The upshot was that the Earl went to York, leaving Wressell in Aske's hands. Aske set out for Hull, Sir Thomas went to Seamer, and Stapleton went home[1].

Northumberland found no peace at York, for there he was visited by Sir Ingram Percy, who had come up to demand seven hundred marks salary as vice-warden of the East Marches and one hundred marks for the lieutenancy. His brother consented to see him, but was shocked by the language he used about Cromwell, " wishing him, being of the King's most honourable Council, to be hanged as they and he might look unto ; and if he were there present, as he wished to God he were, he would put his sword in his belly."[2] Northumberland promptly deprived him of the offices which he had obtained by his trick[3], and appointed Robert Lord Ogle vice-warden, and Sir Roger Grey and Sir John Widdrington lieutenants, all three being of the Carnaby faction[4]. After this both Sir Thomas and Sir Ingram set out for the north.

On or about Sunday 5 November, Shrewsbury sent his chaplain John Moreton to discover the Earl's state, and to try to obtain payment of her allowance to his daughter the Countess, as she was now living with him. The messenger went to Wressell, and was there taken by Aske's men, who were holding the castle[5]. On 10 November Aske visited the Earl again at Selby[6]. Now that his brothers were gone he was more tractable, and made over to Aske his castle of Wressell and his tenants, for so long as Aske should lie in garrison there, and also his " spice plate " which was at Watton Priory[7]. By this formal deed he obtained power to remove his " evidences " from the castle, and as he was very anxious about them, he sent two servants, who brought them away at midnight[8].

Thus the Pilgrims received Wressell Castle, but before the negotiation was completed Aske had been busy in a great many other places. After his interview with Northumberland he rode to Watton, to arrange the affairs of Watton Priory. The prior, a creature of Cromwell's, had fled south with all the money he could lay hands on, leaving " three or four score brethren and sisters of the same house without forty shillings to succour them." They wished

---

[1] L. and P. xii, 392; printed in full, De Fonblanque, op. cit. i, chap. ix ; and Coxe, op. cit.

[2] L. and P. xii (1), 1090; printed in full, Raine, op. cit. i, App. p. cxxxvii; see note A at end of chapter.

[3] See above, chap. ix.   [4] Raine, op. cit. i, App. p. cxxxiv n.

[5] L. and P. xi, 1048.   [6] Ibid. 1039.

[7] L. and P. xii (1), 849 (53) ; printed in full, De Fonblanque, i, App. no. liii.

[8] L. and P. xii (1), 1062.

to elect a new prior, but Aske persuaded them to accept the sub-prior as the defaulter's deputy. This affair of the Prior of Watton should not be overlooked, for it had a part in bringing about the final tragedy. Next day Thursday 2 November Aske went on to Hull[1].

The Duke of Suffolk had caused considerable alarm to the Pilgrims by occupying Grimsby and the neighbouring country[2] in force as soon as the truce was made. They considered that this was "contrary to the appointment,"[3] although of course the agreement did not include Suffolk. Aske made Sir Robert Constable governor of Hull, and under his directions the walls were put in a state of defence and a garrison of two hundred soldiers was maintained there[4]. Shipping was also prepared, which alarmed the royalists in their turn. They thought that the rebels' object must be either to escape by sea, or to send for powder and ordnance from abroad, and watch was kept to prevent communications with Flanders; but as a matter of fact the preparations were made partly in fear of an attack on Hull by sea, and partly to intercept any succour which might be sent to Scarborough or Berwick[5].

The Pilgrims employed various methods to obtain the money needed for their garrisons. Sir Robert Constable paid most of the expenses of Hull; he "borrowed" the money, perhaps rather vigorously, from John Lambart, who tried unsuccessfully to recover £165. 8s. 3d. from Sir Robert's brother Sir William Constable[6]. Lambart had however received sufficient security from Sir Robert[7]. Dr Holdsworth the vicar of Halifax had fled to his patron Sir Henry Saville. His goods were confiscated and £10 of the money went to the defence of Hull[8]. The collector of customs attempted to fly to the King with three hundred marks in his possession, but Sir Robert Constable seized him and swore that that money should be spent first[9]. The lead of Marton Priory, which had already been removed from the building, was seized by the rebels and assigned to Edmund (?) Copendale for sale. He paid over to Aske for it in all £9. 13s. 4d.[10] Aske also obtained on 10 November the Earl of Northumberland's sign manual to use his "spice plate" lying at Watton Priory, for the

---

[1] L. and P. xii (1), 6; printed in full, Eng. Hist. Rev. v, 338–9.
[2] L. and P. xi, 966, 990, 998.
[3] L. and P. xii (1), 6; printed in full, Eng. Hist. Rev. v, 339.
[4] L. and P. xi, 990; xii (1), 6.
[5] L. and P. xi, 998; xii (1), 6.
[6] L. and P. xi, 1070.　　　　　　　　[7] L. and P. xii (1), 698 (2).
[8] Ibid. cf. xi, 997.　　　[9] L. and P. xi, 1169.　　　[10] L. and P. xii (1), 698 (2).

purposes of the rebellion. The Prior of Ellerton was now in charge of the house during the absence of the Prior of Watton[1], and on the first summons refused to give the plate up. Aske wrote again severely, saying that "it is pity to do anything for that house that so unkindly orders me, who have done more for religion than they can ever deserve," and threatened that if he complained of the prior's conduct to the commons the house would be plundered[2]. Alarmed by this, the prior took the plate to Aske himself, and the convent of Watton received Aske's thanks four days later[3]. Some money may have been obtained by plundering the houses of those who had fled to the King, but this was a very uncertain source of revenue, as the plunder was usually divided among the spoilers who carried out the work. Finally gifts were received from well-wishers, particularly from the monasteries[4].

In this connection may be mentioned the curious story of Harry Osborne of Gloucester. He was serving with his father in the King's army under Sir Charles Trowen, and obtained leave "to go among the northern host to know the fashion of them." When he came back he seems to have drawn freely upon his imagination; parts of his story are obviously untrue, and the rest is very suspicious. He asserted in the first place that Lord Stafford had joined the rebels with one thousand men[5]. This was not true, but it seems to have been widely rumoured. Wilfred Holme thus enumerated the allies on whom the rebels depended:

> "They noised the Emperor with them was participate,
> And the Bishop of Rome with the Scottish king commixed,
> With them to commilitare they were clearly fundate,
> And Ireland and Wales of their part was fixed,
> The Earl of Derby outlawed, and of their part mixed,
> And the Duke of Norfolk every cause accounted,
> All commoners commoned with the Earl Staffort enixed,
> And as for they of Lincolnshire a great sum surmounted."[6]

Speed gives a list of the lords who were present at the second appointment at Doncaster, among whom is Lord Streffre, which may stand for Lord Stafford. All the names in this list are wildly misprinted, e.g. Romemer for Bulmer and Clayer for Ellerker[7]. Osborne also said that "Lady Rysse," i.e. Katherine Howard widow of Rice (Richard) ap Griffith had joined them with three thousand men and

---

[1] See below, chap. XVII. [2] L. and P. XI, 1039.
[3] Ibid. 1069. [4] L. and P. XII (1), 853.
[5] L. and P. XI, 1195. [6] Holme, The Downfall of Rebellion.
[7] Speed, Hist. of Great Britain, Book IX, chap. 21.

had brought half a cartload of plate, which was being coined for their use. Osborne produced a groat which he asserted to be of their coinage, "and it is a fay (true?) king Harry groat." This story had an air of probability, for Richard ap Griffith had been executed for treason in 1531, and his widow might very well sympathise with the rebels[1]. Also they would have no difficulty in coining money, as there were mints at York and Durham, and Hastings reported on 8 November that the rebels had made posts from Hull by Temple-hurst, York and Durham to Newcastle "to prepare new money."[2] These posts are mentioned again on 13 November[3]. But as nothing more is ever heard of "Lady Rysse" and her groats they may have only existed in the vigorous imagination of Harry Osborne.

Darcy depended for money on a cess regularly levied on the parishes. He set to work to collect one as soon as the truce was proclaimed, and it is a sign of the commons' earnestness that they assisted in gathering it. Sir Henry Saville seized the collectors at Dewsbury and forced them to give up the money under pain of hanging as traitors, conduct which caused much indignation among the Pilgrims[4].

Meanwhile Aske left Hull for Wressell Castle, which he made his headquarters, before Monday 6 November[5]. On that day Suffolk wrote to the Mayor of Hull requiring him to deliver up Antony Curtis, William his servant, Robert Horncliff and Christopher Blaunde, who were lying in prison in the town. The mayor and Sir Robert Constable refused to give them up without a special order from the grand captain, who cannot therefore have been in Hull that day[6]. Curtis and Horncliff were two of the messengers who had been sent by the Lincolnshire rebels to Beverley. They had been cast into prison as liars on bringing news of the failure of Lin-colnshire[7]. When this proved true they must have been detained in revenge for the betrayal of Woodmancy who seems to have been given up to Suffolk by the Lincolnshire men; for Morland, on flying to Yorkshire, was driven out of Beverley because the magistrates said, "Ye are worthy to have no favour here, nor ye may not tarry here, for our messenger called Woodmancy, whom we sent into Lincoln-shire, hath been ill-entreated with you there and was cast into

---

[1] Froude, op. cit. II, chap. IX.
[2] L. and P. XI, 1017.   [3] Ibid. 1059.
[4] Ibid. 960, cf. 1139.
[5] L. and P. XII (1), 6; printed in full, Eng. Hist. Rev. V, 339.
[6] L. and P. XI, 996.
[7] See above, chap. VII.

prison[1]." On Tuesday 7 November Suffolk sent the Mayor's refusal to the King, with the incorrect assertion that it came from Aske[2]. On or before Sunday 12 November, Horncliff and Curtis "brake the prison" and threw themselves on the mercy of Sir Anthony Browne[3] at Barton[4]. He sent them on to Suffolk at Lincoln, when they found that they had escaped out of the frying-pan into the fire[5]. A spy of Sir Francis Brian's reported that these two were said to have been "the beginners of the mischief" and that Aske himself had told him that they "were the first that sware him in Lincolnshire," and afterwards raised Yorkshire[6]. After this information they were practically dead men, and Suffolk at once petitioned the King that their property might be bestowed on his own kinsmen[7]. Yet even Suffolk seems to have realised that the accusation was probably false, for Aske always said, in authentic documents, that Hudswell first gave him the oath[8]. Nevertheless, Suffolk considered the story good enough to hang Curtis, and he repeated it to him. Curtis was so indignant at the accusation that he offered to go and kill Aske, although he was his kinsman. Suffolk had the assassination of Aske a good deal at heart just then (20 November), but he seems to have suspected that Curtis' wrath was merely an excuse for escaping back to the Pilgrims. At any rate he did not accept the offer, though he reported it to the King. He also sent up Curtis' confession, but unfortunately it has not been preserved[9].

Such was the position at the seat of war from Friday 27 October until Sunday 5 November. Although Henry had resolved to suspend his answer to the Pilgrims' petition, Bowes and Ellerker were allowed to send a letter to Pontefract by their servants. They described the progress of their embassy and gave the reason for the delay in their return. Several copies of this letter were sent for distribution among the northern gentlemen, in order to test their temper towards the King. The servants set out from Windsor for the north on Tuesday 7 November[10]. At the same time the King was preparing a swifter means of ending his difficulty.

On Tuesday the Duke of Norfolk sent for Percival Cresswell, a servant of Lord Hussey, and ordered him to prepare to ride north. Next day Hussey directed Cresswell to write in his (Hussey's) name

---

[1] L. and P. xii (1), 481.
[2] L. and P. xi, 1004.
[3] Ibid. 1075.
[4] Ibid. 1095.
[5] Ibid. 1075.
[6] Ibid. 1103.
[7] Ibid. 1104–5.
[8] Ibid. 1120; see above, chap. vi.
[9] L. and P. xi, 1120.
[10] Ibid. 1009.

a certain letter to Lord Darcy and to show it to the Council. After the Council had approved of the letter Lord Hussey signed it, and Cresswell took it back to Norfolk and the Bishop of Hereford. They sealed it up and gave it to him with another letter from Norfolk to Darcy and also certain instructions by word of mouth. His further orders were to ride post after the servants of Bowes and Ellerker, and to pass through the rebels with them: if he did not do this he must obtain a safeconduct, for on no account must the letters be taken by the commons.

Cresswell reached Doncaster before the servants and sent to Darcy for a safeconduct, but before it came the other messengers arrived, and they all went on towards Templehurst. One of Lord Darcy's servants met them and they arrived there on Friday 10 November. Darcy was in the garden with about half a dozen of the commons and his servants. Cresswell paid his respects to him, saying aloud that he trusted all should be well, and secretly that he brought a private message from Norfolk and the King. Darcy led him into the house, and on the way Cresswell managed to pass the letters into his hands unobserved. Darcy went into an inner room to read them, leaving Cresswell among the commons in an outer chamber. They began to abuse Cromwell, and asked Cresswell whether he had been dismissed from the King's Council. Cresswell answered that he had not seen Cromwell at court for the last two days, and that the principal noblemen about the King were Norfolk, Oxford, Sussex, Fitzwilliam, Paulet, and Kingston. Thereupon the commons exclaimed, "God save the King and them all! for as long as such noblemen of the true noble blood may reign and rule about the King all shall be well." They discussed the question of Cromwell's dismissal a little longer, and then told Cresswell that whatever answer Darcy and the gentlemen might make, "If ye speak with the King's highness ye shall show him, or else ye shall show my lord's Grace your master and other the foresaid true noblemen of the Council, that if the King's Grace do not send and grant unto us our petitions, which we sent unto his Highness by the Duke's Grace your master, whatsoever letter, bill or pardon shall be sent on to us we will not accept or receive the same, but send it to his Highness again." Cresswell remonstrated with them, but they replied, "if ye be a true man ye will report the same, for that thing that moves us to this is the faith we bear unto God, to the King's person, and all his true noble blood and the commonwealth."[1]

[1] L. and P. xii (1), 1013.

Meanwhile Darcy had read the letters and had sent a messenger to summon Aske[1], who was at Selby that day[2]. The letter to Darcy from Norfolk was dated 6 November. It informed him that the King had written answers to the articles "which be of such sort that in mine opinion there is nothing to be amended therein." Norfolk went on to complain of the breaches of the truce. He then dropped into a confidential vein,—people were saying unpleasant things about Darcy,—it was whispered that he might have defended Pontefract longer,—that he was in an agreement with Aske. Norfolk defended him as well as he could, and always maintained, like a true friend, that Darcy had been constrained by force; but what a splendid disproof of all these slanders it would be if Darcy should capture Aske and send him up to Windsor "dead or alive, but alive if possible, which will extinct the ill bruit and raise you in the favour of his Highness."[3] Hussey's letter was dated 7 November and was much shorter. He had been in great trouble and danger, he said, partly because he was accused of being Darcy's confederate. The Duke of Norfolk had delivered him, and now said that he would also befriend Darcy if he would send up Aske "quick or dead." Hussey therefore begged him to accomplish the King's pleasure[4].

After reading these letters, Darcy sent for Cresswell. There were several other gentlemen in the room, who were not very willing that Darcy should speak to the messenger apart, but he promised to tell them all that passed. Then he bade Cresswell declare his credence. Cresswell replied that it was the same as the letters, in that Darcy would win the King's confidence and a great reward if he sent up Aske. Darcy's answer is rather refreshing reading: "I cannot do it in no wise, for I have made promise to the contrary, and my coat was never hitherto stained with any such blot. And my lord's Grace your master knoweth well enough what a nobleman's promise is, and therefore I think that this thing cometh not of his Grace's device, nor of none other nobleman, and if I might have two dukedoms for my labour I would not consent to have such a spot in my coat." Darcy evidently suspected that Norfolk's message was inspired by Cromwell, as Hussey's letter undoubtedly had been. He did not realise what a nobleman "of the true noble blood" was capable of doing. Cresswell had nothing to say in reply, and they all went to dinner. During the meal Aske arrived, and after dinner the captains of the Pilgrimage held a council. On Saturday

---

[1] L. and P. xii (1), 6; printed in full, Eng. Hist. Rev. v, 339.
[2] L. and P. xi, 1039.   [3] Ibid. 995.   [4] Ibid. 1007.

11 November, after mass, Darcy sent for Cresswell, and bade him tell the King that Darcy was now doing him better service than he had ever done. As for Pontefract Castle, he called the Archbishop and Archdeacon Magnus to witness that there was neither powder, ordnance nor artillery in it, that the King sent no reply to his letters, and that he had used all means to defend it while he could. He begged the King to excuse him if he and the other gentlemen "spake somewhat largely" against Cromwell, as that pleased the commons best. To Hussey, Darcy sent no letter, but he bade Cresswell to "have him recommended to him," and to say that he was sorry for his trouble[1].

On Saturday at six o'clock in the evening Cresswell set out for Windsor with letters from Darcy to Norfolk and to the ambassadors, and Aske's explanation of the alleged breaches of the truce. The captain stated that he wrote to Sir Marmaduke Constable in Lancashire and Sir Thomas Wharton in Westmorland only for their own protection. His other letters were to stay the country. As for spoils, if there had been any since the truce he was willing to make restitution, but he doubted if they could be proved[2]. Darcy's letters are highly characteristic. To Bowes and Ellerker he wrote that their delay was a far greater violation of the agreement than anything that had happened in the north, and that their letter was "taken but for a persuasion." If they would bring back the King's answer themselves, it would do more good than twenty letters[3]. To Norfolk he expressed his joy that the King had been graciously pleased to answer the articles in person. He denied that the truce had been broken; on the contrary, he and the other gentlemen had stayed Lancashire, Cumberland and Westmorland, although those counties were not included in the appointment at Doncaster, because it was not then known that they had risen. As for his surrender of Pontefract, he had declared the whole circumstances to Cresswell, and again protested his loyalty and his ill-treatment. Coming to the most important part of the letter, the suggested capture of Aske, Darcy was as emphatic as he had been to Cresswell. He was ready to serve the King as a scullion "without a penny rent from his lands" but "alas, my good lord that ever ye being a man of so much honour and great experience should advise or choose me a man to be of any such sort or fashion to betray or disserve any living man,

---

[1] L. and P. xii (1), 1013.
[2] L. and P. xi, 1046 (3); cf. L. and P. xii (1), 392 (p. 193).
[3] L. and P. xi, 1046 (1).

Frenchman, Scot, yea, or a Turk; of my faith, to get and win to me and mine heirs four of the best duke's lands in France, or to be king there, I would not do it to no living person." Finally he declared "roundly and truly" that there would be no satisfactory "stay" until Bowes and Ellerker were sent back with the King's full answer, and in particular the promise of a free parliament and a full pardon, for their letters were looked upon as mere persuasions[1]. In writing this letter Darcy, as perhaps he knew, signed his own death warrant. No past service, no future pardon, could protect a man who so boldly exalted his own honour above the King's pleasure.

After making his reply, Aske returned to Wressell Castle and sent out a summons to all the gentlemen and leaders of the Pilgrimage to attend a general council at York on Tuesday 21 November[2]. It was hoped that the messengers would have returned from London by that time; if they had not, their letter would be shown and further steps would have to be taken to bring the King to terms[3]. No sooner had Aske and Darcy disposed of one set of accusations than another sprang up. On Wednesday 8 November, the day that Cresswell left London, Sir Brian Hastings wrote to tell Suffolk of a rumour that Darcy was about to march on Doncaster, while Aske and Constable would transport the men of the East Riding, Howden and Marshland by water to Gainsborough and Stockwith, and both hosts would meet at Lincoln, where they intended to capture the weapons collected there by Suffolk[4]. On the same day Suffolk sent a force from Lincoln to occupy Newark, led by Richard Cromwell, Sir John Russell and Sir Francis Brian[5]. This however was not in consequence of Hastings' report, for on Thursday 9 November Hastings received two letters from Suffolk asking for news of the rebels. Hastings wrote back the same day, referring to his earlier letter. He mentioned the arrival of Percival Cresswell at Doncaster, and declared that if he had two guns and ordnance he could keep the bridges there with his own men. He did not think that the occupation of Newark was necessary, but there was danger in north Lincolnshire. The rest of the letter was taken up with his private grievances against Sir Arthur Darcy[6]. Meanwhile he was furthering the King's cause in another way by acting as go-between from the

---

[1] L. and P. xi, 1045.
[2] See note B at end of chapter.
[3] L. and P. xii (1) 6; printed in full, Eng. Hist. Rev. v, 339.
[4] L. and P. xi, 1017.   [5] Ibid. 1016.
[6] Ibid. 1026.

Earl of Shrewsbury to Sir George Darcy[1]. Lord Darcy's sons had no sympathy with their father's views. Sir George had joined the commons only on compulsion, and was now eager to obtain a pardon and make his peace with the King.

Henry seems to have calculated a good deal on the effect that the letters sent by Cresswell would have. If Darcy should kill or capture Aske, there would certainly be another rising; leaderless and disorganised by treachery, it would be easily suppressed. The King therefore laid plans to deal with the situation which he hoped to produce. Shrewsbury's son Lord Talbot returned from court to Wingfield on Thursday 9 November, bearing instructions that if the commons rose again, Shrewsbury must advance to Derby and there hold the bridges. The old Earl seems to have been quite tired of the whole business. He wrote back that the water at Derby and the Trent four miles away at Burton-on-Trent could not be held, there were so many fords and bridges, and it would take ten thousand men or more to hold the Trent between Newark and Burton. The rest of his letter contained better news for the King; he mentioned the rumour that Darcy would seize Doncaster, which gave an excuse for further delay of the messengers, and enclosed a letter, which if revealed would endanger the life of the sender,—probably one from Sir George Darcy[2]. At the same time Shrewsbury wrote to Cromwell begging to be excused from the chief command on account of his age and feebleness[3]. Of course the King would not excuse Shrewsbury[4]; his age, his great reputation, and his well-known devotion to the Church of Rome made him too valuable to be spared.

Letters were sent on the 9th and 10th to the Earl of Derby and the gentlemen of Cheshire and Lancashire, warning them to be ready to join Shrewsbury at an hour's notice[5]. At the same time orders were sent to the Earl of Rutland to occupy Nottingham, and he wrote to the King that he had done so on Friday 10 November. His report was little more encouraging than Shrewsbury's. He had provisioned the castle and inspected the river, but there were four bridges and nine fords. It would require a great force to defend the castle and so much of the river, but lying there was very chargeable. He had little money of his own, as his rents from Yorkshire were stopped, and of the £500 that Norfolk had sent him only £300 remained.

[1] L. and P. xi, 1027.
[2] Ibid. 1028.   [3] Ibid. 1029.   [4] Ibid. 1063.
[5] Ibid. 1022, 1031; printed in full, Correspondence of the 3rd Earl of Derby (Chetham Soc.), p. 56.

The rest had been spent on bringing up gunners, on posts and on fortifying the fords at Doncaster. Moreover he had "no great experience in the war" and begged that some expert man might be sent to help him[1].

The news of these movements on the part of the royal troops shortly reached the headquarters of the rebels. Roger Ratcliff was with Rutland at Nottingham on Thursday 9 November. He was sent with letters from Rutland to Derby, and returned with fresh letters from Derby to Fitzwilliam, but as he passed through Wakefield he was captured by Grice, who set him naked in the stocks and read his letters. News of this reached Nottingham and was sent on Saturday 11 November in a letter to one of Derby's servants, which was also intercepted[2].

The King now issued the proclamation and reply to the rebels which he had drawn up as early as 2 November before seeing their articles[3]. This is the most probable explanation of a letter from the Council dated 11 November, which notified that the King had pardoned all the rebels of Yorkshire except ten, and that the proclamation of this, with the King's answer to the rebels' demands, was to be read in all market-towns[4]. Although the date of this letter is Saturday 11 November, it must really have been issued earlier, for it was received that day at Nottingham[5], and what is more extraordinary at Skipton, where Christopher Aske read it in Skipton market-place, to the great indignation of the commons[6].

All these proceedings on the King's part show that he believed the rising in Yorkshire to have collapsed as that in Lincolnshire had done. He expected that by this time most of the commons would have gone quietly home again and that the gentlemen would be ready and anxious to make their peace. Only a few of the wilder spirits were still holding out, and they could easily be dealt with, particularly if Darcy, as he expected, captured or killed Aske. By acting on these assumptions Henry nearly precipitated an outbreak. The commons were by no means pacified; on the contrary they were with difficulty induced by the gentlemen to observe the truce. The gentlemen realised that it was too late for submission and that their only chance of safety lay in treating with the King on equal terms.

---

[1] L. and P. xi, 1037, 1038.
[2] Ibid. 1042. The letter is endorsed in Darcy's hand. See note C at end of chapter.
[3] See above.
[4] L. and P. xi, 1040.
[5] Ibid. 1042.
[6] L. and P. xii (1), 1186.

Finally Darcy indignantly rejected the suggestion that he should betray Aske. Henry's manœuvres set the whole of the north simmering with irritation. Suffolk and the royal generals were very much offended that messengers had been sent direct to the rebels, instead of communicating first with themselves[1]. Rutland, Shrewsbury and Derby were grumbling at being ordered to carry out expensive operations without money[2]. Newark proved as difficult to defend as Nottingham and Derby[3]. Among the rebels the utmost suspicion was aroused by the delay in the return of Bowes and Ellerker, by the vagueness of their letter, and by the King's proclamation, which seemed to throw back the negotiations to the very beginning again. Darcy had his own reasons for believing that the King did not intend to come to terms, and the movements of the royal troops caused great uneasiness.

The result of all this was an alarm which took place on the night of Saturday 11 November. Men " in white coats " (the royal uniform) were observed mustering secretly in a wood near Snaith. When Darcy was informed of this he wrote to warn the honour of Pontefract[4]. Beacons were burned and the whole country-side rose[5]. It was said that Fitzwilliam had come " up the water to Thorne " with five thousand men, and that he and Hastings intended to capture Darcy[6]. To Darcy this seemed the natural result of his reply to Norfolk's letter. He threatened that if Hastings burnt his house at Snaith he would " light him with a candle to all the houses he had," and prepared to go himself to encounter the royal troops. His servant William Talbot saw him take off his cap, saying that he set more by the King of Heaven than by twenty kings, and though he might not ride he could go where he would if he had a horse litter, and " the highest hill he could find there would he be "; they might shoot at him as much as they pleased, for he would kneel by his litter and say a prayer that would preserve both him and all his servants. Then he caught Talbot " by the head and wrestled with him and cast him down and swore by the (*illegible*) he waxed more cant than he was of many day before."[7] In short Darcy was in high spirits at the prospect of a fight at last. The alarm however was quickly appeased. Hastings declared that he had only summoned his neighbours because he heard that the rebels

---

[1] L. and P. xi, 1006, 1035, 1036. [2] Ibid. 1066, and see above.
[3] L. and P. xi, 1087, 1094. [4] Ibid. 1048.
[5] Ibid. 1056. [6] Ibid. 1059.
[7] L. and P. xii (1), 853.

were going to raid his cattle, as they had done before. The same night and next day letters were despatched to Suffolk explaining the commotion and assuring him that it was pacified[1].

Nevertheless Darcy had many grounds for anxiety. Sir George Darcy's negotiations with Hastings and Shrewsbury, in which Sir Arthur Darcy and William Maunsell, the vicar of Brayton's brother, had also taken part, were discovered by an intercepted letter, and the commons brought both the letter and Sir George to his father[2]. Darcy must also have known that it was more than probable that his assassination had been proposed as a test of loyalty to some other rebel, as Aske's had been to him. On Sunday 12 November he wrote to Shrewsbury, his old friend, in whom he placed more confidence than in any of the other royalists[3]. The letter was sent by his servant Thomas Wentworth, who was instructed to show openly a copy of the letter from Bowes and Ellerker, and to Shrewsbury alone a copy of Darcy's answer to Norfolk's letter, " which answer recites the effect of the whole letter, else I would have sent both." The other contents of the letter fall naturally into three parts. First and most important, would Suffolk observe the truce or would he not? Must the leaders of the Pilgrimage be constantly prepared for a surprise attack, for capture or for assassination? Or would he lie quiet until Bowes and Ellerker returned? On this point Darcy earnestly begged that he might be told the whole truth.

In the second place Darcy assured Shrewsbury that there could be no permanent settlement until the messengers returned from the King with a definite answer, and he begged him to use his influence to bring that about.

In the third place Darcy set forth his own grievances, for the Pilgrims also had plenty of complaints to make about breaches of the truce. Sir Henry Saville had prevented the levying of cesses, and now proposed to go to the King[4]. Sir Brian Hastings had caused the alarm the day before; he was persuading gentlemen to forsake the commons, and had arrested a load of corn at Doncaster[5]. The Duke of Suffolk had sent a herald with messages and had demanded prisoners from Hull[6]. He had also stopped the Duke of Norfolk's servant and was making threatening movements[7]. Finally

---

[1] L. and P. xi, 1044, 1050, 1056.
[2] Ibid. 1059.
[3] Ibid. 1049.
[4] Ibid. 960, 1051.
[5] Ibid. 1117.
[6] Ibid. 1049.
[7] Ibid. 1050.

it was a great breach of the truce that Bowes and Ellerker had not returned; the commons were very wild, particularly in Cumberland, which was not really included in the appointment; the gentlemen were doing their very best to stay them[1].

Shrewsbury replied to this letter on Monday 13 November. He assured Darcy that the truce was being strictly observed by the royal troops, and that Bowes and Ellerker would return shortly. Hastings had acted only in self-defence, and if Saville had offended he should make restitution. According to the terms of the truce all prisoners were to be released; he for his part had sent back those that he had taken, and he thought that Suffolk might fairly demand his. He concluded by thanking Darcy for staying the commons[2]. After Darcy's servant had returned, Shrewsbury received from Sir Brian Hastings his account of the disturbance on Saturday night, and the capture of Sir George Darcy's letter[3]. In other respects Hastings reported that the rebels were "more gentle," and that when they had examined a man and found nothing against him they gave him "certain articles" which contained the oath to be true to the King, his issue and the commonwealth, for the reformation of heresies, the restoration of abbeys, the punishment of the subverters of the law, and the re-appointment of noblemen to rule under the King[4]. Shrewsbury sent on all these documents and his own replies to the King on Tuesday 14 November, at the same time expressing his anxiety as to the fate of Sir George Darcy, and his hope that the King would be satisfied with his answer to Darcy, as he had "not been accustomed to make answer in any such causes."[5] This was as far as Shrewsbury, who was an honourable man, dared go in condemnation of the King's plot against Aske.

The alarm at Pontefract was only the beginning of further disturbances. On Sunday 12 November there was an attempt to provoke a rising at Beverley[6]. On Thursday 16 November there were rumours of riots and deer-slaying at Rawcliffe, Goole and Howden, and it was also said that Scarborough was again besieged[7]. The Earl of Derby heard on Monday the 13th that Dent and Sedbergh were stirring again[8], and shortly afterwards there was a report in London that he had been attacked by his own men, who were

---

[1] L. and P. xi, 1049.
[2] Ibid. 1058, 1068.
[3] Ibid. 1067.
[4] Ibid. 1059.
[5] Ibid. 1067.
[6] Ibid. 1078.
[7] Ibid. 1088.
[8] Ibid. 1060, 1092; printed in full, Correspondence of the 3rd Earl of Derby (Chetham Soc.), pp. 59, 61.

mutinous for want of pay[1]. The Percys had proclaimed the truce in Northumberland for twenty days, as soon as they arrived there, at a county meeting which they summoned at Rothbury. But they continued to plunder and hunt down the Carnabys; and the thieves of Tynedale, especially little John Heron, were with Sir Thomas "as familiar as they had been his own household servants." Sir Thomas "took upon him as lieutenant," and even tried to hold the warden court with the Scots wardens, but they suspected his authority and refused to meet him[2].

In Cumberland a muster was held on Wednesday 15 November at the summons of Richard Dacre, who "took upon him to be grand captain of all Cumberland," and appointed as petty captains Christopher Lee a servant of Dacre, William Pater and Alexander Appleby[3]. The commons of Westmorland wrote to Lord Darcy on the same day. They explained that they would admit no gentlemen to their council, as they were afraid of them, but they "had more trust in Darcy than any other" and they laid their grievances before him[4]. The questions raised by this list of grievances will be considered later. The point at present is that Cumberland and Westmorland were preparing to rise again.

Meanwhile the royalists in Lincolnshire received some slight encouragement. Gonson, who was lying with the royal forces at Grimsby, sent out a "crayer" on 11 November, which captured two other "crayers," coming the one from York and the other from Hull, but as they were harmlessly laden with salt they were set free on the 17th[5]. By means of a pursuivant communications were established with Hull on Wednesday 15 November, and the King's officers were able to buy wine and sugar there[6]. More important still was the fact that two gentlemen of Marshland had contrived to convey professions of their loyalty to John Cavendish at Burton; but as that part of the country was greatly under Darcy's influence, and as the commons were very suspicious, the negotiations proceeded but slowly[7].

The whole situation is best represented in the report which Thomas Treheyron, Somerset herald, drew up of two interviews which he had with Darcy on Tuesday 14 November. He had been

---

[1] L. and P. xi, 1097, cf. 1178; printed in full, loc. cit. p. 65.

[2] L. and P. xii (1), 1090; printed in full, Raine, op. cit. i, pp. cxxxi–cxxxiv; De Fonblanque, op. cit. i, App. no. lii.

[3] L. and P. xi, 1331.   [4] Ibid. 1080.

[5] Ibid. 1095.   [6] Ibid. 1075, 1078, 1095.

[7] Ibid. 1077.

sent to Templehurst by Suffolk, nominally to inquire into the alarm of Martinmas day, but actually to see what news he could pick up. His account is as follows:

"The effect of the comynicacon betwene Thomas lord Darcy and Thomas Treheyron[1] otherwyse called Somerset herauld of arms and his seyng etc.

Apon Monday the xiii day of november Charles duc of Suffolk the kynges lieu tenante in the countie of Lyncoln commanded Somerset the kynges herauld of armes to goo from lyncoln in to the north to the lord Darcy. And on tweysday the xiiii day he aryved at templehurst a goodly place of the lord Darcys stondyng nygh the Ryver of ayre in the countie of York. And at his comyng thyther, he was honorable reseyved by the lordes offecers, and they brought hym through the hall in to a fayre parler and Immedyatly that he was in the parlor the lord Darcy sente one of his servants to hym prayng hym to take the payne to come to the chamber to the lord his master and he went with hym were the lord Darcy was; and whan he sawe hym he welcomed hym with his cappe off and toke hym by the hande sayng Sir I thinkke ye have brought me sum newys from the kyng our soverayn lord. and the herauld answered that he came not from the Kyng but from the duc of suffolk lord lieu tenante of the Kynges armye in the countie of lyncoln with certayn messages from his Grace to [your *crossed out*] his [*written over it*] lordshipe. than sayd the lord Darcy my felowe herauld I pray you shewe me your messages   sir sayd the herauld with a good wyll.

The herauld. Sir my lord undrestondeth that apon Saterday last paste a great nomber of the Kynges peple ded aryse abowght Pomfryte and this partyes and sette bekyns on fyer. Sir his grace merueleth what they do meane in so doyng, seyng that the entreate that was made betwene the Duc of Norfolk, the erll of Shreysbury yow and other at Doncastre is not it [*sic, probably* yet] ended. Were-fore he desyeryth yow to cause them to be in peax, and if they will not, his grace muste nedes of necessite provyde for them of his parte, Whych he wold be vayrey lothe to doo.

The lord Darcy. my felowe herauld, my lord of Suffolk hath don lyke a wyse prynce to send yow to me for this cause and I wyll Informe yow of all the truyth thereof. it is true that on Saturday last paste, my cossyn sir bryan hastynges sent xx of his men abowght his affayres to a howse that he has on the other syde of the watter of don, and beffore that tyme it was bruted amonges the comens, that he wold come over the water in to this parties to th' entent to take the goods of the Inhabitance here In satisfacion for spollyngs and robyries don to hym beffore that tyme, and after this Rumor [went? *word obliterated*] amonges the peple, a folyshe woman perseyvyng his servantes in whyte cotes nygh on to the water thinking verely they wold have come Indede, to have Robbed them as it was beffore spokyn, Cryed owt alarum. and other heryng this crye gyvyng therto to [*too*] lyght credens aryse, and sett certayn bekins on fyer. but as sone as I hard thereof what with love and fayre wordes I caused them to go home to ther howses in peax and sythenz they haue ben all in peax, and to th' entent that ye may perseyve that this is true that I have sweed [*shewed* ?] yow see here a letter that my cossyn sir bryan hastynges sente

---

[1] See note D at end of chapter.

to me, and by that ye may perseyue the truyth[1]. and he toke the letter and rede it and the tenor thereof agreed with the wordes of the lord Darcy.

The lord Darcy. my felowe nowe wyll I demand a questyon of yow, and if your comyssion be so large I pray yow answere thereto beffore this gentellman my cossyn and other that be here Sir it is comenly spokyn amongest us that my lord of Suffolk is myndcd to lay sege beffore the town of hull and if he so do he shuld not do well as I think for it is within our compossision What his grace plisure is therin I pray ye swee us.

The herauld. Sir by the fethe of a herauld my lord of Suffolk neuer mynded to ley any sege to hull, ne to breke any poynte of the compossicion made betwene the lordes and yow at Doncastre, nor hath not stoped any of the passages, but suffreth every man as well on our parties as of this to come [*and*] go with vytalle and to do any other thinges at ther plesures, without any agen sayng of any man; but Sir I am sure that suche speche cometh by cause that part of our armye lyeth at barton apon Hombre and Grymsby, whyche ar nygh on to thos costes, and you know my lord that so great a nomber of men as wee be can not be vytalled and loged if they shuld lye all in one place and therfore they do not remayn only in the townes affore named but also in the Citie of lyncoln and all other townes and vyllages abowght the same, to th' entent they may be well vytalled and loged at ther ese, and not for no other cause, and this my lordes grace commanded me to swee yowr lordssip.

The lord Darcy my felowe I am veray glade to here yow this say, and I pray god thanke my lord of Suffolk for sending yow hyther to us with this newys. and sirs I am glade yow ar here to here my felowes mesage pray yow report it to our cappteyn and to other the comons for they wylbe veryray glade to here it. for before they were in great dowght thereof.

The herauld sir my lord of Suffolks Grace understondeth that a lettre that he wrotte to the lord of cumberland in comfortyng hym to kepe hym self agenst the rebellyous[2], for the whych name sum be angrye therwith, he trusteth that yowr lordship: whych he hath hard ever speke of so muche honor, ne no other man of nobillitie substance or honest reputacion: will take hym self, in the lien of that name, but they that be other and taketh them self for rebellyous his grace thinkith he can not gyve them a fayrer name.

The lord Darcy my felowe of truyth suche a letter came to our cappteynes handes, and as toychyng rebellyous if ther be any suche I wold to god, they were with my lord of Suffolk at lyncoln, and as for me I trust to declare my self for non of them but for the Kynges true servante, and I have don hym good servyce, I wyll shewe yow howe. Sir at the first tyme that Aske reysed the peple here abowghtes [*noted in margin*] I sayd to my ffryndes and servantz sirs wee can not do the Kyng a hygher servyce, than take this felowe, and I layd suche wayte for hym, that if he had kept the appoyntmentz that he made with gentelmen to come and lye with them at ther howses at iii or iiii nyghtes one after the other I had taken hym, but whan he appoynted to be with ony of them at one nyght he wold not come in ii or iii nyghts after, and whan I sawe I could not gett hym, and that the peple ded aryse on every parte, ye and fother that I myghte not trust my own tenantz, than I wente with as monye as

---

[1] L. and P. XI, 1059.   [2] Ibid. 1005.

I myght gett to the kynges castell of pomifrytte to kepe and defende the same and I had with me xiii^{xx} men at my own coste xiiii days, and put the kyng not to one halfpenye of charge, and thyther came to me the archibussop of Yorke, and master magnus thinkyng by cause I was an old man of warre, that by my polycie they might have escaped. they can bere me record of all this that I shew yow, and thair I sent lettres to the Kyng for yede what answer I had from hys hyghnes I have redy to shewe, and also I sent lettres to our lord lieu tenante and his answere I have in lyke case to shewe, and every day the cappteyn wrytt letters charging me apon payne of my lyff, that I shuld yeld the castell and do as they wold do, and if I wold not, if they myght take me by fforce they wold slee me, and all they that was with me, and ferther they wold born my howses, and kylle my sons childern, than I beyng in this myschif seyng no other remyde wold have made with them compossion, and this was on the fryday at nyght, and I bade them xx li to spare me tell the morowe ix of the cloke, and for all that I could doo with all the fryndes I could make, they wold not respyte me but tell vii of the cloke, than could I not hyere ne see no sucker come and I had not in the castell so muche gowne-powdre as wold fylle a whalnot shell no nor I had not so muche fuell as to dresse our supper, and ferther my vytalles that shuld have come to me was eten and dronkyn in the strete beffore my face, I than beyng an old man of warre and knowyng the feates therof, perseyvyng my self in that danger and could escappe no otherwyse with my lyff, for savegard of the same ded yelde my self, and I promysse yow if I had not wrought politykly, it had cost me my lyff.

The herauld my lord I think well that this is true that yow say, and at that tyme ye could not have esscapped with yowr lyff no otherwyse than ye dede, but whan yow were at the entreatie with the lordes beffore dancastre, I am sure ye were a great dystance from the hoste, I mervell than that yowr lordship had not gone from them with the lordes for ye myght have esscapped ther handes at that tyme if it had plesed yowr lordship.

The lord Darcy my felowe I wyll shewe yow a taylle for that whan Thomas fitz Garrard ded rebelle in Irelande he sente word to the duc of Rychemonde howse [*whose*] sole god pardon that if he wold reseyve hym he wold yeld hym to hym, and the duc answered full wysely and sayd by my fethe if I were sure to gett hym his pardon, I wold be glade to reseyve hym, but he that wyll ley his hed on the bloke, may haue it sone stryken of [*note in the margin:* What he menyth by this and how he knew that fizgarrard offred himself to my lorde of Rychmond].

and my felow I spake to my lord of Shryesbury with thes wordes Talbot hold up thy longe clee and promyse me that I shall have the Kynges favor and shalbe Indeferently hard, and I wyll come to dancastre to yow, and th' erll of Shryesbury sayd to me well lord Darcy, than ye shall not come it [*sic*], and ferther if I had thought any treason I myght have foughten with the duc of norfolk and th' erll of Shryesbury, on the othersyde of dancastre with ther own men and brought never a man of our hoste with me.

[*Note in margin:* how he knew that the duke of Norfolkes men woold have fought agaynst hym.]

The herauld my lord I think that muche that yow say is true but sir were yow say that ye myght have foughten with the duc of Norfolk and th' erll of

Shreysbury with ther own men by my truyth I thinke if ther men ded promyse to tak your parte if ye wold come and fyght with them they ded it to dysseve yow to the entent to haue gotten therby sum pyllage or other profith, for they had not a subtillier meane to dysseve ther enymys than to promyse them to fyght with them, and whan it cometh to the poynt to fight agenst them, and so I think they wold have proved yow and if you had proved them, and one thing I am sure of that ther was never men more desyros to fyght with men than our men be to fyght with yow and if it pleased the Kyng to suffre them.

The lord Darcy   well I pray god they be all as true as yow think they be, but let that passe. if it please the Kynges highnes to send me my pardon, although I have no nede of it if I myght be Indeferently hard, onles they wyll say it is treason that I was amonges them, whych was for savegard of my lyfe, as I have sayd, I wyll come to his highnes were it will pleas hys grace to have me, and I hyere say that manye persuacions be made by Cromwell and other to the gentillmen here to come from hence to the kyng whome I pray god longe to preserve in proprius helth hys highnes may well have them so that he pardon them, but it is not so muche suerty for his own person to have them with hym in brydwell as to have them here; for I can prove that wee have done his highnes as good servyce as though wee had byn in hys pryvye chamber and as for my part I have byn and ever wylbe true both to kyng henry the vii and to the kyng our soverayn lord and I defye hym that wyll say the contrary, for as I have ever sayd one god one feth and one kyng.

The herauld. my lord ye say truyth wee can have but one god one feth and one kyng, and my lord ye say that ye were true servant to kyng henry vii and to the kyng our soverayn lord sir I think ye were true to the kyng hys father and to his grace at ther coronacons whan yow did your homage and fealty, my lord I pray yow pardon me that I am so playn with your lordshipe, for ye I thinke may well say that ye were ever true to kyng henry the vii, and by my feth I never hard the contrary but my lord as to the kyng: howe can yow say that yow have byn ever true to hym: seyng that yow have borne harnys agenst his lieu tenante whych represented his own person for that tyme.

The lord Darcy   that that I ded was by constraynte for to save my lyf, and that myght welbe perseyved whan we were at the entreatie at dancastre, for by cause the lordes and wee tarried a whyll abowght the entreatie our own hoste wold have ronned apon us to have kylled us sayng that wee wold bytray them.

The herauld well my lord of truyth in tymes paste whan I have byn with your lordship at mortlake and at Westmynster I have hard yow always speke of so muche honor truthe and fethfulnes, that if yow shuld be falty in any of them ye were worthye beffore all other to suffre for it. I trust yowr lordship will not be angrye with me that I shewe yow as my hert thinkes.

The lord Darcy   no my felowe for yow say truth for I had rather have my hed stryken of than I wold defyle my cote armor, for it shall never be sayd that old Thome shall have one treators tothe in his hed, but the King nor no other alyve: shall make me do any unlaufull acte, as to stryke of your hed, and to send it hym in a sake, whych thing myght be a rebuke to me and to my heyres for ever.

[*Note in margin*   no. the strykyng off the hede]

The herauld my lord yow speke this as though sum mocyon hath byn made to yow, to take your capptayn, and send hym to the Kyng, thinke yow my lord that it were a unlaufull acte, to tak or kylle hym and send hym to the Kyng, if he be a rebellyon as sum do take hym.

The lord Darcy my felowe peraventure it were lawfull for yow and not for me, for he that promysseth to be true to one, and deseyveth hym, may be called a treator : whych shall never be seyd in me [*note in margin*: no. the promise of the lord Darcy] for what is a man but is [*his*] promysse, but for all laufull thinges whych is not agenst our feth, he is not lyving that shalbe more redy to do his grace comandement than I, for if his highness would comand me to go with yow his herauld to defie the great Turk, by the fethe that I owe to god and hym I wold do it with a good wyll as old as I am.

The herauld my lord by cause ye speke of our feth howe say yow to the excludyng of bushope [*sic*] of Rome, and his auctorytie, do yow thinke that that is agenst our feth.

The lord Darcy by my truth I think that is not agenst our feth, and what I spake therin to Cromwell, he knoweth hym self well Inough

The herauld my lord I pray yow gyve me leve to aske other questyones of yowr lordship. sir hyere yow that any other be upe ferther north.

The lord Darcy my felowe is [*sic*] I hyer say that ther is a huge nomber upe in Westmerland comberland and lancashyre, and have mustered, and abowght the bushoppryche of Durem they begyn to spoylle, and by cause yow shall hyere the truyth, ye shall hyere one of my seruantz an honest hardy man, I wold the kyng had x m suche, and he hath byn amongst them, and sawe ther musters, and than his seruante whas called upe, and when he came, the lord Darcy commanded hym to shewe the herauld what he had seen in Westmerland comberland and lancashyre, than sayd his seruante that he had byn amongst them and that he had seen them mustering and by ther report they were to the nomber of vii^{xx} thowsaud [140,000] men.

The herauld I mervell not muche to hyre of that grete nomber that yowr servante speketh of for I thinke well ther may be so many tage and rage but truly of chosyn men of warre ther be not so many as I think in al the north and half Scotland.

The lord Darcy sir ye knowe not this countrey, for it is a countrey greatly pepled Well I wyll speke no more thereof, but by my fethe [*word obliterated*] letter that cometh nowe to my remembrance that was sente to our cappteyn causeth my hert to blede, for it was wrytten to hym out of thos parties that he shuld not shrynk in this busynes and they wold send hym xxx,m men with a moneth wages in ther pursses and ever that were don they wold send an other moneth wages and the thcrd if nede shuld be, and besydes this they have xxx m men moo to defend agenst the Scotts if they wylbe busie, for they have mustered, and shewed ther selfes aginst the coste and all this is besydes our companye.

The herauld my lord if it be so it [*yet*] thanked be god the kyng hath men Inough to meat with them all and one thing wee be sure of, wee have the ryght if god be god, for I knowe that it is agenst the lawe of god to be periured and ther is non that can fyght agenst the King ther naturall soverayn lord ne agenst anie of his true subiectes what quarell so ever it be with owt his grace comyssion, that can excuse ther selves from periury

The lord Darcy   ye say true if they were resonable men, but I wold to Christ the King knowe the Jeobardy that is in it for as ferre as I can perseyve by any thing that I can hyre the kyng is so encensed, that he knoweth not the truyth, therefore I wold I myght speke with my son bryan or my son Russell for I knowe that they dare and wyll speke to the King the truyth   I pray god all may be well, now my felowe by cause it is cold, I pray yow take the payne to go with my servante ther, and he shall brynge yow to a fyer to ese your self.

And his servante brought hym into a fayre parlor were was a good fyer, and brought hym a pasty of veneson brede wyne and bere, and made hym good chere and after he had well esed hym self, the lord sent for hym agen, and sayd My felowe have yow any thing els to say to me from my lord of Suffolk.

The herauld   Sir ye, my lordes grace understondeth that it is comenly noyssed here amonge yow, that our armye shuld Robe spoylle and vyolate euery manes wyf doughter and servante and that ther shuld be put to execution manye of the comons that hath submytted ther selfes, sir, the truyth is that ther was never no suche actz comytted amongest us except one Robyrie that was don on a preste for the whych one of our own armye sir frances bryan servante was putt to execucion.

The lord Darcy   Sir shewe my lordes grace that wee hyre full well that he doth good Justice, and specyally at Stamford by hym that cryed a newe kyng[1], for if he had byn amongest us in all our Rage he shuld never have come to execusion, but wee wold have hewen hym in a thowsande pees, wee love so our kyng, therefor it I say agen I wold he were hanged by the neck that wyll refuce his pardon, for if his grace wyll send it me not with stondyng I have no nede to have it if I myght be Indeferently hard I wyll come to his grace let them burn this house, and kyll my sons chyldern yf they wyll, so that I myght scappe with my lyff from them, let this passe, sir I have reseyved a lettre syns yow were here, I pray yow rede this artycle in it and the herauld ded rede it, were in was wryten by hym that sent it after this maner, My Lord I hard the Lord Cromwell say that yow were a notaryus treator, and I answered that he was a false knave and yowr lordship shuld prove your self a true man to the kyng, then sayd the lord Darcy, I beshrewe hym for his labor, for I knowe I spak folyshe wordes of hym my self at dancastre the whych nowe I am sorye for, for to say truth every man had a begynyng and he that the kyng will have honored wee must all honor and god forbyde that any subiect shuld goo abought to rule the kyng in his owne realme or be agenst his plesure in any lawfull thing, and my felow ther was sent me a ryme owt of Westmerland lancashyre and comberland that makith me to lawgh, for by my truth I mervell how they can make it, and yow shall have it with yow[2], and he toke it to the herauld whych brought it to the kyng, and ferther he sayd to the herauld

shewe my lord of Suffolk that the comens have beseged carlyell, and the mayer hath proffered to be sorne [*sworn*] to them, and they wyll not reseyve hym, but that they wyll have the towne, and the castell at ther plesures, and also shew hym that my lord of comberland is in great parell of his lyf for if the comens myght gette hym, they would kylle hym for he is the worst beloved that ever I hard of, and specially with his own tenants, and if ther be no remyde founde I thinke he can not escappe, it the cappteyn ['is his' *crossed out*]

---

[1] See note E at end of chapter.   [2] See note F at end of chapter.

and he be come of ii sustres [*written in*] [son *crossed out*] and he hath wrytten dyvers lettres for hym, I feth I wold he were in this howse, than I wold trust to ryde hym out of ther haundes.

The herauld   my lord I pray you what means suld be founde to helpe hym.

The lord Darcy   well my lord of Suffolk is wyse Inough and can devyse a meane for hym full well, I pray yow have me humble recomended onto his grace, and shewe hym that I pray god the kyng have not as muche nede to tak side nerar home as here for and he sawe the lettres that cometh dayly to our capteyn from all parties of this realme he wold mervell.   I pray god save the kyng.   [*Note in margin:* An Interogatory upon this.]

and than the lord Darcy tok hym by the hand and gave hym a dowble duket and to barwyk persyvante an angell and so wee tok our leve of his lordship.

NOTES TO CHAPTER XII

Note A.   The date at which Sir Ingram Percy came to York is not known with certainty, but his visit appears to have taken place about this time.

Note B.   Sir Brian Hastings misrepresented the summons in his letter of 13 November.   "The rebels intended to have had a general council or parliament at York on Saturday last but the posts from my Lord of Norfolk, Sir Ralph Ellerker and Mr Bowes stayed them."[1]   As a matter of fact it was the posts which caused the Council to be summoned.   Hastings' information was often inaccurate.

Note C.   It seems that Ratcliff was either going to or returning from Lancashire when he was captured, for otherwise he had no reason to go near Wakefield, and as he was carrying letters to the Lord Admiral [Fitzwilliam] it was probably his return journey.   The letter containing the news of his capture was written by Gervis Clyfton to Mr Bankes.   Robert Bankes gave evidence against the rebels before the Earl of Derby on 2 December[2].   He may have been the person to whom the letter is addressed.

Note D.   Thomas Treheyron, Somerset Herald, was murdered in Scotland by two of the Lincolnshire refugees in November 1542[3].

Note E.   The only other reference to this incident, which seems to have been the appearance of the usual Yorkist pretender, is made by Wilfred Holme, who says that

...."the commons before Doncaster
Ascribed a Carter to a king coequal in degree."[4]

[1] L. and P. xi, 1059.
[2] Ibid. 1230; printed in full, Correspondence of the 3rd Earl of Derby (Chetham Soc.), p. 70.
[3] Hamilton Papers, i, no. 242.
[4] Wilfred Holme, The Downfall of Rebellion.

Note F. There were a great many rhymes flying about and it is impossible to identify this one. Many of the rebel manifestoes were roughly metrical. The following is part of one which circulated in Westmorland and Lancashire:

"Gentle commons, have this in your mind,
    Every man take his lands' lord and ye have need,
    As we did in Kendalland
    Then shall ye speed.
Make your writings, command
    Them to seal to grant you your petitions as your desire.
Lords spiritual and temporal, have it in your mind,
    The world as it waveth,
And to your tenants be ye kind,
    Then may you go on pilgrimage
Nothing you withstand,
    And commons to you be true through all Christen land,
To maintain the faith of Holy Church
    As ye have take on hand.
Adieu, gentle commons, thus I make an end.
Maker of this letter, pray Jesu be his speed,
    He shall be your captain
    When that ye have need."

This proclamation is printed twice in the Letters and Papers, vol. XI, 892 (3) and vol. XII (1), 163 (2).

There was a song against Cromwell called Crummock, which was sung in Westmorland in the time of the rebellion. It may have contained some local allusion to Crummock Water[1], but the commons of Yorkshire also sang

"Cosh, Crummock, cosh, I would we had thee here,"[2]

which must have likened the Lord Privy Seal to a bad-tempered cow.

In the summer of 1538 Isaac Dickson commanded a minstrel who was singing in an ale-house by Windermere to give the song called Crummock which he had sung at Crossthwaite during the rebellion. The minstrel, who had to adapt his wares to the party in power, did not dare to sing the song. Dickson passed from threats to blows, but still the minstrel refused, fearing the halter more than Dickson's dagger. There was a brawl, and both Dickson and the minstrel were arrested[3].

In connection with Friar Pickering's poem comparing Cromwell to Haman, it may be noted that in the anonymous play of "Godly Queen Hester," which is attributed to Skelton, a similar parallel is drawn between Haman and Wolsey, the suppression of monasteries by the latter being likened to Haman's persecution of the Jews. See "The Library" October 1913 "Early Political Plays" by M. H. Dodds.

[1] Froude, op. cit. II, chap. XIV.   [2] Wilfred Holme, op. cit.
[3] L. and P. XIII (1), 1346, 1370.

CHAPTER XIII

THE COUNCIL AT YORK

On Tuesday 14 November 1536 the King decided that the Pilgrims' ambassadors must be sent back with some sort of answer, as the reports from the north showed that delay was not producing so good an effect as he had hoped[1].

On Thursday 16 November Sir Brian Hastings sent to Lord Darcy a complaint that the commons were killing the King's deer[2]. Darcy wrote back next day in very good spirits, for he had heard that Sir Ralph Ellerker and Robert Bowes were returning and would be at Doncaster next day[3]. Now that they were on their way home down the road over which they had travelled with such anxious hearts three weeks before, the two northern gentlemen made all the haste they could, and seem to have reached Templehurst late on Friday 17 November[4]. A post was despatched on their arrival to summon Aske from Wressell, but rumour had preceded it. Aske was told that Bowes and Ellerker had returned with orders to arrest him, and he wrote to Darcy to inquire into the meaning of this warning. Darcy replied with a most emphatic assurance that "neither Sir Ralph Ellerker nor Robert Bowes, my cousins, nor myself would for none earthly goods send to have you come hither but after a just and true sort." Darcy begged Aske to come at once, as his presence was urgently required. A post must be sent to London that day, and measures must be taken for the meeting at York and other matters. Darcy advised him to bring William Babthorpe with him[5].

The letter and credence of Bowes and Ellerker were laid before the small council of the chief captains of the Pilgrimage at Templehurst on Saturday 18 November[6]. Darcy, Sir Robert Constable,

---

[1] L. and P. xi, 1061.   [2] Ibid. 1088, cf. 1168.
[3] Ibid. 1096.   [4] Ibid. 1103.   [5] Ibid. 1107.
[6] L. and P. xii (1), 901 (42—3); printed in full, Eng. Hist. Rev. v, 569.

Aske and Babthorpe were present, and there may have been others. The report of the messengers was not very satisfactory. The King's reply to the articles, written in his own hand, was not forthcoming. There was only a verbal message, and when it was divested of Henry's complaints about the unnatural conduct of his subjects, reproaches for breaches of the truce, and professions of clemency, all that remained was the statement that he found their articles "general, dark, and obscure," but that he would send the Duke of Norfolk to Doncaster to make a full reply to them. The rebels were to appoint three hundred representatives to meet the Duke, and if they insisted they might have a safe-conduct[1]. Norfolk's letter was a little more explicit, as he suggested that the meeting should take place on 29 November; he added that as a special compliment to Darcy his kinsman Fitzwilliam had been appointed to attend the meeting. As the letter was intended to be read openly, Norfolk made no allusion to the capture of Aske, and merely replied to Darcy's remonstrance, "I have lived too long to think otherwise than truly and honestly," which was rather a doubtful argument[2].

Darcy was very anxious that the King's offer should be accepted at once. He was better acquainted with Henry than the other gentlemen, and knew that what appeared at first sight vague and unsatisfactory was really an extraordinary condescension. He wanted to despatch a message of acceptance immediately[3], but the other captains were not so well pleased and insisted on referring the letter and message, with the whole question of peace or war, to the great council which had already been summoned to meet at York[4]. As it was to be held on Tuesday 21 November, this meant only three days delay in the answer, which did not seem an unreasonable length of time after the King had kept them waiting for three weeks. The gentlemen had begun to assemble at York as early as 15 November[5], and all would be ready on the appointed day.

As the negotiations might come to nothing, the captains at Templehurst debated as to what they should do if the treaty fell through and war was declared. They made arrangements for garrisoning Hull, Pontefract, and other places, and discussed the difficulties of obtaining provisions and ammunition[6]. It was decided that on the outbreak of hostilities they must divide their forces into

[1] L. and P. xi, 1064 (2).   [2] Ibid. 1065.
[3] Ibid. 1107, cf. xii (1), 901 (44), printed in full, Eng. Hist. Rev. v, 570.
[4] L. and P. xi, 1115, 1116.   [5] Ibid. 1077.
[6] L. and P. xii (1), 901 (43); printed in full, Eng. Hist. Rev. v, 569.

three armies to cross the Trent at three different points, and a rendezvous was appointed on the south of the river[1]. They considered the question of opening communications with the Emperor, who, they believed, would help them. Dr Marmaduke Walby, vicar of Kirk Deighton and prebendary of Carlisle, had come to Templehurst with Sir Robert Constable[2]. It was resolved that he should sail for the Netherlands to ask the Regent to send money, 2000 arquebuses and 2000 horsemen, and to open communications with the Pope on behalf of the Pilgrims. Darcy said that he would inform the Imperial ambassador in London that Walby was going on this mission[3]. Walby was selected because he knew noblemen at the Regent's court who had formerly been ambassadors in England. He was given £20 for his expenses and went to Hull, but before he embarked Darcy sent word that he was to delay his journey; on hearing this he returned home and never took the message[4].

The captains who had met at Templehurst seem to have remained there until it was time to go to York. Aske was at Templehurst on Sunday 19 November[5]. That night a warning was sent to Pontefract that Sir Henry Saville had ordered all his men to muster at Rotherham on the following day. Saville knew that "all the great men" were now "forth of their business," and it was feared that he was secretly cooperating with the royal troops to capture Wakefield or Pontefract, possibly even Templehurst and the captains there[6]. This news was sent on from Pontefract to Wakefield, where the energetic Thomas Grice seized Sir Henry Saville's men before they could set out, and compelled Brian Bradford and others to take the Pilgrims' oath before witnesses[7].

Shrewsbury was told on 19 November that Thomas Grice was harassing Sir Henry's loyal tenants so that they were forced to fly to Rotherham and elsewhere[8]. On this report Shrewsbury wrote to Darcy to complain of his steward's conduct, and Darcy, after receiving Grice's explanation, wrote back to ask Shrewsbury to keep Sir Henry Saville in order[9]. It is possible that this was an actual attempt to capture the leaders of the Pilgrimage when they were all together at Templehurst. Several points suggest this explanation, as for instance

[1] L. and P. xii (1), 1186.

[2] Ibid. 1081; ibid. (2), 268; see above, chap. ii.

[3] L. and P. xii (1), 1080; cf. ibid. xii (2), 292 (iii).

[4] L. and P. xii (1), 1080.   [5] L. and P. xi, 1115.

[6] Ibid. 1114.   [7] Ibid. 1113.

[8] Ibid. 1112.   [9] Ibid. 1122, 1123, 1141.

the rumour which Aske heard before he came to Templehurst[1], the fact that no excuse for Sir Henry Saville's conduct was offered, although the previous alarm caused by Sir Brian Hastings had been explained, Sir Henry Saville's prompt flight to Shrewsbury at Wingfield[2], and Suffolk's letter to the King on Monday 20 November, the day after the supposed attempt had been baffled by Grice's vigilance. In this letter Suffolk wrote that the apprehension of Aske and Constable was a very doubtful matter, which he would not attempt unless he was sure that it could not come to their knowledge until it was accomplished, as if suspected it would only cause more mischief[3]. This suggests that Suffolk had recently tried to carry out the King's request, but, having failed, wished to hide his failure and to excuse himself from any further endeavour.

Norfolk and Fitzwilliam had already set out from London, and had advanced as far as "the house of Sir Robert a Lee," at Quarrendon in Buckinghamshire[4], when they were met by a messenger from Bowes and Ellerker sent to tell them that the Pilgrims had not yet decided to treat with them[5]. Norfolk wrote to Darcy on Monday 20 November, complaining bitterly of the alarm on Martinmas day, which he attributed to false persons who desired to prevent a peaceful settlement of the trouble. He begged Darcy to use all his influence on behalf of peace, and assured him that on the King's side nothing was "thought or meant to impeach the same our good purpose."[6] The Pilgrims' suspicion had naturally been awakened by the network of royal plots which they discovered or half-discovered. They were no longer so sure as they had been in the beginning that the King was the fountain of honour, and that Norfolk was as straightforward as they were themselves. It was unfortunate that they were cheated again by Norfolk's fair words.

In spite of the delay in the Pilgrims' answer, Norfolk and Fitzwilliam decided to continue their journey in order to review the royal troops, inspect the fortifications at Nottingham and Derby, and consult with Suffolk at Newark[7].

On Tuesday 21 November the great council of the Pilgrims assembled at York. The building where they held their meetings is never named. Darcy was not present; the captains agreed to excuse him on account of the difficulty which he had in travelling, and he

---

[1] See above.
[2] L. and P. xi, 1139.
[3] Ibid. 1120.
[4] M. A. Everett-Green, op. cit. iii, no. lxxi.
[5] L. and P. xi, 1126.
[6] Ibid. 1121.
[7] Ibid. 1126.

remained at home until the second great meeting which they had already determined to hold at Pontefract[1]. The captains who are named as being present at York were Robert Aske, Sir Robert Constable, Sir Stephen Hamerton[2], Nicholas Tempest, Lord Latimer, Sir James Strangways, Robert Chaloner, Sir Ralph Ellerker, Robert Bowes, William Babthorpe, William Stapleton, Lord Scrope, Sir Nicholas Fairfax, and Sir Richard Tempest[3]. There were in addition about 800 of the lesser gentlemen and commons, as a certain number had been chosen out of every wapentake or parish to attend the meeting[4]. The Abbot of Holm Cultram gave 40s. to the representatives from Penrith[5]. Among these less important persons were Marmaduke Neville, a younger brother of the Earl of Westmorland[6], one Walker, John Fowbery, William Aclom, and Robert Pullen[7]. There were also some royal spies, for instance Hugh Hilton, a servant of the Earl of Huntingdon[8]. The most interesting of these spies was Christopher Aske. He had arrived at Wressell Castle on Friday 17 November, under safe-conduct, to lay before Robert Aske the injuries that the Earl of Cumberland had received from the commons. On his arrival the two brothers fell into an argument as to whether Robert could have taken Skipton Castle or not. Robert said that though it was strong the defenders wanted artillery and powder, and he could have taken it easily. Christopher replied that it was impregnable, and should never be taken while the Earl and he himself were alive. In describing this conversation to Norfolk months afterwards, Robert acknowledged that he had been misled by an intercepted letter from Cumberland which really related to the weakness of Carlisle, and consequently perhaps he could not have taken Skipton. While the brothers were discussing this interesting point, Darcy's letter announcing the arrival of Bowes and Ellerker was brought to Robert, who hastily prepared to ride to Templehurst with about sixty of his men. His followers grumbled at the sudden summons because they had not yet had their dinner, and said "a man was worthy his meat, or else his service was ill." Christopher took the opportunity to assure his brother that the commons would turn against him and either kill

---

[1] L. and P. xi, 1116.   [2] Ibid. 1115.

[3] Ibid. 1135; Yorks. Arch. Jour. xi, 260; L. and P. xi, 1127; xii (1), 392, 698 (3).

[4] Ibid. 466, 687 (2); printed in full, Wilson, op. cit. no. xxii.

[5] L. and P. xii (1), 1259 (2), (3).   [6] Ibid. 29.

[7] Ibid. 466, 536, 687; printed in full, Raine, Hexham Priory (Surtees Soc.) i, Append. p. cliv.

[8] L. and P. xi, 1171.

him themselves or give him up to his enemies "like Jacques Dartnell, William Wallas and others." Much the wisest and safest course for Robert would be to go and make his peace with the King.   Robert, however, was no fine gentleman; he thoroughly understood his rough followers, and paid not the smallest attention to Christopher's prognostications.   His Yorkshiremen never betrayed him,—that was reserved for the King.   While Robert was away Christopher contrived to go through his brother's private papers, and found the scheme for invading the south which had been drawn up in case the negotiations at Doncaster should fail.   Christopher afterwards went to York and there "demeaned himself so covertly that he returned to Cumberland knowing all their purposes."[1]

The first business of the great council at York was to appoint two hundred representatives to deal with the questions before them[2].   Robert Bowes gave an account of his mission to this body, telling them everything that had been said and done before the King and his Council, mentioning the proposed conference at Doncaster, and reciting "the goodness of my lord Privy Seal to the commons promised by his word—and therewith he stayed."   Henry and Cromwell had made good use of the time that the ambassadors spent at court by winning them entirely to the King's side.   Bowes and Ellerker were not influenced in any dishonourable way, but they came back quite convinced of the King's good faith and mercy, and satisfied that the Pilgrims might safely disband, since their purposes were accomplished.   As far as they were personally concerned they were right to believe in Henry's goodwill, for they were both trusted and employed by him after the rebellion.

When Bowes had finished his speech Sir Robert Constable requested him to withdraw while the council debated on it. Constable then laid before them a very different matter[3].

Young Sir Ralph Evers had been besieged in Scarborough Castle as early as 17 October[4].   Supplies had been sent to him about 27 October, rather against the King's will, as he was afraid the rebels would capture them[5].   They arrived safely, and after the truce, when the siege was raised, Evers wrote to ask Suffolk for more[6].   His request was sent up to London on 5 November, and on 10 November Cromwell himself wrote to Evers[7] and sent the letter

[1] L. and P. xii (1), 698 (3), 1186.   [2] Ibid. 466.
[3] Ibid. 392 ; printed in full, Coxe, op. cit.
[4] L. and P. xi, 760 (2).   [5] Ibid. 883.
[6] Ibid. 989.
[7] Ibid. 1032 ; printed in full, Merriman, op. cit. ii, no. 169.

to Thomas Hatcliff at Lincoln. Hatcliff despatched a trusty messenger with £100 and the letter to Grimsby, where they were entrusted to Edward Waters to be conveyed to Scarborough[1]. On Wednesday 15 November he embarked in a "crayer," and for some days no further news was heard of him by his comrades[2]. He was, however, almost immediately captured by the commons of Beverley and the Wold under the leadership of John Hallam, and the siege of Scarborough Castle was at once renewed. Hallam "wrung Waters by the beard" and threatened to cut his head off. By this violence he extracted from him the confession that Cromwell had sent him[3]. To save himself Waters produced Cromwell's letter. The commons divided all the loose cash on the ship among them, receiving 3s. each, but they sent to Aske the £100, Edward Waters, and Cromwell's letter. Waters remained with Aske, but his troubles were now over and he was not treated like a prisoner. He had a servant, a chamber and a feather bed of his own, and spent his time in hunting and shooting[4].

It was the letter which had been captured on this occasion that Sir Robert Constable now read to the council of the Pilgrims at York, in order that they might compare it with "the goodness of my lord Privy Seal to the commons, promised by his word." On 10 November Cromwell had written that if the Pilgrims continued longer in rebellion they should be so subdued that "their example shall be fearful to all subjects whiles the world doth endure."[5] The reading of this letter naturally made a great impression on the assembly. The flat contradiction between the two messages confirmed the suspicion that the King's conduct had awakened. The Pilgrims doubted whether it would be safe to treat with the King while he was under the influence of a man so unscrupulous as Cromwell. Sir Robert Constable gave his advice most decidedly, "as he had broken one point in the tables with the King he would break another, and have no meeting, but have all the country made sure from Trent northwards, and then he had no doubt all Lancashire, Cheshire, Derbyshire and the parts thereabout would join with them. Then, he said, he would condescend to a meeting."[6] But there were strong influences on the other side. Darcy was known to be in favour of the conference[7]. Babthorpe spoke on the side of

---

[1] L. and P. xi, 1106, 1162.   [2] Ibid. 1103, 1106.

[3] Ibid. 1088, 1116; xii (1), 201 (ii) (iv), 202.   [4] L. and P. xi, 1128.

[5] Ibid. 1032; printed in full, Merriman, op. cit. ii, no. 169.

[6] L. and P. xii (1), 466.   [7] See above.

peace[1]. Aske adhered steadily to his policy of trying every means
to obtain peaceful redress of their grievances before they resorted to
force. The King had replied to the articles, although the Pilgrims
had not yet received his answer. It would be the height of incon-
sistency to present a petition and then refuse to receive the reply.
They would commit themselves to nothing by agreeing to confer with
the Duke of Norfolk, and much good might result from the conference. The treachery which they all resented so bitterly must be
due to the evil influence of Cromwell, but Cromwell's power, as they
hoped, was waning. They were going to treat, not with Cromwell,
but with Norfolk, and Norfolk was faithful and honourable. He
would perform his promises, and once he was restored to his place at
court he would bring the King back to a better frame of mind.
Such seem to have been the arguments employed by the advocates of
the conference, but no further record of the debate remains. In the
end the peace party prevailed, and it was decided that three hundred
representatives should be sent to Doncaster to meet Norfolk and to
hear the King's reply on St Nicholas' Eve, Tuesday 5 December[2].
This date was fixed upon in order to give time for sending messages
into distant parts of the country[3].

The next point to be discussed was the King's complaint that
the articles which had been sent to him were vague and obscure.
To remove this difficulty it was resolved that another general council
should be held at Pontefract two days before the conference at
Doncaster. Every shire or wapentake would be desired to send
the discreetest men to represent it, and the representatives must
bring up a list of the grievances of their own district[4]. This order
resembles the "cahiers" of the Third Estate at the meeting of the
States General in 1789. All the grievances were to be laid before
the general council and digested into a set of articles explanatory
of the first, and this new set of articles would be sent to Norfolk.
At the same time the Archbishop of York and other learned men
were to be requested to draw up spiritual articles setting forth all
the grievances connected with religion[5]. It was further resolved
that Lord Darcy should be instructed to have everything prepared at
Pontefract for the meeting, and a list was drawn up of the districts

[1] L. and P. xii (1), 392; printed in full, Coxe, op. cit.
[2] L. and P. xi, 1127; xii (1), 29.	[3] L. and P. xi, 1139.
[4] L. and P. xii (1), 6; printed in full, Eng. Hist. Rev. v, 339.
[5] L. and P. xii (1), 901 (25); and 945 (88–90); printed in full, Eng. Hist. Rev. v,
570, 573; cf. L. and P. xi, 1127; xii (1), 1175 (ii).

from which the three hundred were to be summoned, with the names of the principal gentlemen and the number of commons who were to appear from each place[1].

After the most important business of the meeting was completed, minor points were considered. Complaints were made of the behaviour of Sir Henry Saville, and it was decided that the whole matter should be entrusted to Darcy, as he was already in communication with Shrewsbury about it[2]. A letter was drawn up requesting the Earl of Cumberland to surrender Skipton Castle; Lord Scrope, Sir Richard Tempest and others were appointed to carry it, but in the end it seems to have been sent by Christopher Aske[3]. All the resolutions of the meeting were written down, and a report of them was sent to Darcy[4].

This seems to have been all the business which was transacted that day, and at the end of the afternoon sitting all dispersed to their lodgings[5], Constable and Bowes being at the house of Sir George Lawson[6].

Next morning Wednesday 22 November the council met again. Another obstacle in the way of peace was laid before them. There were disturbances in Lancashire, and in Dent and Sedbergh[7]. Derby had written to Fitzwilliam on 19 November to say that he was under an obligation to melt down the lead and bells of the suppressed priory of Burscough before 30 November, but he was afraid to do so as it might provoke a fresh rising. He therefore asked the King to grant him respite. As the letter was not despatched before Sunday 19 November, he probably had received no answer and the rumour that he was going to fulfil the obligation was causing fresh unrest[8]. When the matter was laid before the council at York, Sir Robert Constable again took the side of resistance, and advised that nothing should be done to discourage their allies in those parts. William Babthorpe spoke on the other side, and in the end a compromise was reached[9]. Darcy was requested to communicate with Shrewsbury in order that the Earl of Derby might be restrained[10]. In the meantime, orders were sent to Craven, Kendal, Dent, Sedbergh and

---

[1] L. and P. xi, 1155, (1), (2), (4). [2] Ibid. 1127.
[3] L. and P. xii (1), 698 (3). [4] L. and P. xi, 1127.
[5] L. and P. xii (1), 29. [6] Ibid. 946 (118).
[7] Yorks. Arch. Journ. xi, 260–1.
[8] L. and P. xi, 1118; printed in full, Correspondence of the 3rd Earl of Derby (Chetham Soc.), p. 128.
[9] L. and P. xii (1), 392; printed in full, Coxe, op. cit.
[10] L. and P. xi, 1134, 1140, 1153, 1154.

Lonsdale that if Lancashire mustered they were to muster also and send word to the captain[1]. The council felt justified in giving this order by Cromwell's letter and the attempted relief of Scarborough, which were "contrary to the appointment."[2]

A letter was drawn up and sent to Norfolk to suggest arrangements for the conference at Doncaster. This letter has been lost,—may we imagine that Henry tore it up in a fit of rage?—but its contents seem to have been as follows :—

(1) The Pilgrims complained that Waters' expedition to Scarborough was a breach of the truce[3].

(2) The meeting at Doncaster was to take place on St Nicholas Eve, 5 December[4].

(3) It was requested that there might be a truce for fourteen days after that date[5].

(4) The Pilgrims required safe conducts for those who were to meet Norfolk, and hostages for Aske, as he ran the greatest risk[6].

(5) They desired that the meeting might take place on neutral ground[7].

The other business which came before the council that day related to the restored monasteries; as the rebels had put the monks in again the latter turned to the leaders for help in the difficulties of their new position. In reply to one of these appeals the council ordered that Robert, Prior of Guisborough, should enjoy his office, and Sir John Bulmer was required to see that the order was executed[8]. The Prior of Sawley had sent his chaplain to Aske to desire counsel touching the house. The chaplain spoke to Nicholas Tempest, who advised him to find friends to plead his cause at the great council at Pontefract[9].

There remains no record of the business which the council at York transacted on Thursday 23 November. There was probably some discussion of the grievances which were to be considered more fully at Pontefract. It was commonly said that the statute empowering the King to appoint his successor by will had been framed in order that Cromwell himself might be made the King's heir. Earlier in the year it had been said that he was plotting to marry the Lady Mary[10]. Now the story went that he was to have married Lady Margaret Douglas, the King's niece, and that

[1] L. and P. xi, 1135.
[2] L. and P. xii (1), 901 (28); printed in full, Eng. Hist. Rev. v, 560.
[3] L. and P. xi, 1162. [4] Ibid. 1127.
[5] Ibid. 1174. [6] Ibid.
[7] Ibid. 1175. [8] Ibid. 1135 (2).
[9] Yorks. Arch. Journ. xi, 261. [10] L. and P. xi, 41.

when her secret marriage with Lord Thomas Howard was discovered, the act of attainder against Lord Thomas had been procured so that it might still be possible for Cromwell to marry Lady Margaret. When John Hallam returned to Scarborough from the council at York, he reported that the council had resolved that the statute must be repealed and that the Lady Mary must be acknowledged as the King's heir, for if these measures were not taken the King would make Cromwell his heir[1].

The commons stated very emphatically that they would have no pardon but by Act of Parliament, and that Parliament must be held at some place where all could come and go safely. On this point one of the petty captains named Walker said to Aske at the council, "Look you well upon this matter, for it is your charge, for if you do not you shall repent it,"[2] a prophecy which was sadly fulfilled. The commons of Westmorland had already delivered a list of their grievances, and Aske sent back instructions that they must inquire into the visitation of Legh and Layton, and take the opinion of the clergy of Cumberland and Westmorland on matters of faith[3]. Altogether the sitting seems to have been a stormy one, and a spy reported that he thought the Pilgrims would come to no agreement with Norfolk at Doncaster[4].

On Friday 24 November an order was made, by the advice of Bowes[5], that there should be no plundering, musters nor casting down of enclosures until the meeting at Doncaster, unless "commanded by our captain general or else warned by burning of beacons and ringing of bells awkward," which alarm would only be given on sufficient grounds[6]. There is no record of any other business, and the council seems to have broken up on Saturday 25 November.

The break-up of the council at York was followed by an uneasy movement through all the rebel country. Suffolk was alarmed by a report that the beacons of Holderness, Howden and Marshland were burned on Thursday and Friday, 23 and 24 November, and that musters were being held there[7]. Sir Ralph Ellerker returned to Hull on or before Sunday 26 November, and the garrison tried to stop the communication which had been established between Hull and Grimsby[8]. On the night of 28 November armed men with their

---

[1] L. and P. xii (1), 533.   [2] L. and P. xi, 1170.

[3] L. and P. xii (1), 687 (2); printed in full, Wilson, op. cit. no. xxii.

[4] L. and P. xi, 1171.

[5] L. and P. xii (1), 901 (107); printed in full, Eng. Hist. Rev. v, 570.

[6] L. and P. xi, 1155, (1) (ii), (2) (ii).   [7] Ibid. 1166.

[8] Ibid. 1169.

faces blackened went round the parish of Chorley in Lancashire, under the leadership of John the Piper, and forced the inhabitants to take the oath to God, the King and the commons[1]. Lord Monteagle could not collect his rents in Kendal, and arrested a vicar who spoke in favour of the rebellion[2].

While the council at York was sitting Norfolk and Fitzwilliam were inspecting the lines of defence prepared by the royal troops. Their arrangement was as follows:

Gonson was in command at Grimsby, and Sir Anthony Browne at Barton, with his men disposed along the Trent from Barton to Gainsborough[3]. Sir Brian Hastings held Doncaster, and had fortified the bridge, while on 22 November the Earl of Rutland sent Sir Nicholas Sturley with six pieces of ordnance, 100 men and gunners to occupy Tickhill Castle, five miles south of Doncaster. Shrewsbury had made sure of Rotherham, as the idea of fortifying Derby had been given up[4].

Suffolk and his staff were at Lincoln. The Duke occupied the Dean's house, and in the Cathedral was the harness which had been collected from the Lincolnshire rebels. In the castle were about 140 prisoners, several of whom had been saved from execution by the truce. The villages along the Humber and the Trent were occupied, and the boats had been collected so that they might be instantly destroyed if there was an alarm. The council, that is probably Suffolk's council, had resolved to build a tower on a hill between Lincoln and the Trent[5].

The captains at Newark were Sir Francis Brian and Sir John Russell with 700 men. This was also Richard Cromwell's post, but he had been sent up to the King. The castle was supplied with ordnance, and the people of the neighbourhood had been ordered to bring in a certain quantity of grain from each township. They were submissive and feared Lord Borough and the Lincolnshire captains. The bridge was being fortified, and a drawbridge over the Trent was being built at Muskham, a village to the south of Newark, but the river was very shallow and difficult to defend, except when the floods were out[6]. After the wet October, the weather was better about the middle of November and the water fell. The castle would only hold 100 men and had no supply of water[7].

[1] L. and P. xi, 1230; printed in full, Correspondence of the 3rd Earl of Derby (Chetham Soc.) 70–75.
[2] L. and P. xi, 1232.   [3] Ibid. 1095.
[4] Ibid. 1136.   [5] Ibid. 1155, (5) (ii).
[6] Ibid.   [7] Ibid. 1087, 1094, 1103.

At Nottingham the castle was held by the Earl of Rutland with four or five hundred men, and the gentlemen of the neighbourhood, who sat in council with him weekly. It was provisioned and supplied with corn in the same way as Newark. Rutland had built a new drawbridge and fortifications. The country people were loyal[1]. The castle was well supplied with ordnance, but more gunners and powder were needed, as Suffolk and Shrewsbury were always sending for powder, which Rutland could ill spare[2].

All the royal commanders were constantly writing for money, but a fairly adequate supply was now forthcoming[3], though the King was so anxious to be economical that John Henneage received orders to pay none of the monastic pensions or debts in Lincolnshire except in very urgent cases. On 27 November Suffolk remonstrated warmly against such an impolitic means of saving. He would rather pay the pensions out of his own pocket, he declared, if he had the money, than that the men of Lincolnshire should be made to remember their late folly, and to suspect that the charges of the suppressed houses would not be paid[4]. Half the debt was paid and the other half held over[5].

When he despatched Ellerker and Bowes to the north, the King wrote to Suffolk on 14 November that a free pardon might be proclaimed to all Lincolnshire men except those who were in prison. Henry stated that he was moved to this clemency by comparing the repentant demeanour of Lincolnshire with the continued rebellion of Yorkshire. Part of the weapons which had been collected might be restored to the most trustworthy gentlemen, to distribute among men of approved loyalty, but great care must be exercised in this. If Norfolk summoned Suffolk to be present at Doncaster, he must leave Sir Francis Brian and Sir William Parre as his deputies at Lincoln[6]. Suffolk received these orders on the 16th, and wrote back to report the position on the 18th. He begged the King to appoint some place for storing the weapons which were not given back; the orders as to fortifying Doncaster, Newark and other places had been carried out, but Suffolk reminded the King that he had only 3600 men to hold a river line of fifty miles[7].

Such was the general disposition of the royal troops while the Pilgrims were holding their council at York.

---

[1] L. and P. xi, 1155, (5), (ii). [2] Ibid. 1136.
[3] Ibid. 958, 1093, 1124, 1152, 1163. [4] Ibid. 1180.
[5] Ibid. 1268. [6] Ibid. 1061.
[7] Ibid. 1103.

Norfolk and Fitzwilliam approached slowly. On Wednesday 22 November they had reached Towcester and received news of the alarm caused by Sir Henry Saville on the 19th. Norfolk wrote Darcy a letter of reproof for "innovations attempted," which he forgot to sign[1], and it must have given Darcy some small satisfaction to be able to point this out in his reply of Sunday 26 November to "your letter, as I think by the seal, but it is unsigned." His reply contained only an assurance that the disturbance was entirely due to Saville, and that he desired peace as much as Norfolk[2]. Darcy had written to Sir Brian Hastings as early as 20 November to arrange for lodgings in Doncaster for the conference[3], but the King's captains were surprised to hear a rumour that he intended to bring 10,000 men there on Thursday 30 November and that 10,000 more were summoned to meet at Wakefield on the following Monday[4].

Norfolk and Fitzwilliam reached Leicester on Friday 24 November, where they received the letter which had been drawn up by the council at York on the 22nd[5]. They despatched a copy of it to Suffolk[6] and sent the original to the King, who replied to it on Monday 27 November[7].

Henry's answer is one of those documents which fill the reader with reluctant admiration and reveal the secret of his constant success. It shows the attitude which the King had deliberately assumed towards the rebellion. According to his version of the event, a few unscrupulous persons had misled the commons of Yorkshire by false stories about the acts of the King's parliament. The ignorant commons had thereupon risen and forced the gentlemen to join them by threatening their lives. The gentlemen, however, although they had taken the treasonable oath, had succeeded in staying the commons, and after inducing them to disperse quietly had sent two gentlemen to the King to explain their unwilling treason and to sue for pardon. This the King was willing to grant to them, in consideration of the ignorance of the commons and the force used to the gentlemen, on condition that the seditious persons who had first stirred up the tumult were taken and surrendered to the royal justice. The chief of these seditious persons of course was Aske. Henry put forward this account of the rising so consistently and so firmly that he convinced not only his contemporaries but also his historians, and it has been so universally accepted

[1] L. and P. xi, 1139.   [2] Ibid. 1167.
[3] Ibid. 1147.   [4] Ibid. 1170.
[5] Ibid. 1174.   [6] Ibid. 1162.
[7] Ibid. 1174.

that it is necessary to consider whether it is really true, and all the foregoing history a mere exaggeration. The answer to this question is given by the preparations against the rebels which have just been described. Henry was the last man in the world to garrison a chain of forts from Grimsby to Nottingham and to spend thousands of pounds on keeping an army under arms for two months merely to suppress a trivial rising of discontented labourers. The gravity of the situation was perfectly apparent to the King, but he knew the value of telling a consistent and dignified story, not only to foreign courts and to the south, where news came so slowly and uncertainly that the King's account was sure to be accepted, but even to the rebels themselves. It is difficult at all times to believe that a clear, firm statement is a deliberate lie, and it was particularly difficult for the northern gentlemen to believe that the King was lying. The whole tone of the King's letter was such as to make the gentlemen feel small and ashamed of themselves, and yet to suggest that if only they would be sensible and come up to the King, as any reasonable person would do, they might still be safe and recover their self-respect.

Henry began by marvelling at the expressions used in their last letter, which sounded almost as if they made themselves a party with the commons. As for their complaint that he had broken the truce by attempting to send letters and money to Scarborough, he did not even condescend to reply to it directly. Of course the King must be at full liberty to send anything he pleased to any of his subjects at any time or place.

He went on to declare that he would not send Norfolk and Fitzwilliam to the Pilgrims until he was better assured of their loyalty. Now the Pilgrims did not want Norfolk to come before 5 December; until then they would have been much better pleased if he had stayed with the King. But Henry contrived to put his threat in such a way that the readers of the letter would probably never think of that, and would feel that Norfolk really must be allowed to continue his journey if possible.

In the third place Henry remonstrated against the suggestion that his own subjects, resorting to the man appointed as his deputy, should require a safe-conduct, a neutral meeting place, a special truce and hostages. It was not like subjects petitioning their king, but like a war between princes. They were perfectly mad to make such a demand, and if they were not careful he would take measures to cut them off as corrupt members.

In the fourth place, Henry "thought no little shame" that the northern gentlemen allowed "such a villain as Aske" to subscribe their letter before them all. Aske was "a common pedlar in the law," whose "filed tongue and false surmises have...brought him in this unfitting estimation among you." In the opinion of Henry and all his nobles the honour of the gentlemen was greatly touched in that they had allowed such a thing.

This was the boldest and cleverest stroke in the whole letter. The gentlemen complained that the King's minister Cromwell was base-born and not fit to sit on the royal council. The King retorted that their leader was a villain, that is, not a scoundrel in the modern sense, but a villein or serf, a man born unfree. Henry's accusation was quite groundless; Aske's family was armigerous, and he was cousin to half the gentlemen in Yorkshire. Nevertheless the King's assertion was likely to do almost as much harm as if it had been true. The grand captain was regarded with jealousy by many gentlemen who had not the courage to hold his post, and if the King told them that their honour was touched in following him, then it must be touched; the King must know best.

Finally Henry closed his letter by declaring that in spite of everything he would still be merciful. If the Pilgrims would permit free recourse to the King on the part of his subjects, withdraw from the castles and towns they were holding, send the ship that they had taken to Evers, and "show their submission by deeds," *i.e.* by surrendering Aske to the King, he would perhaps be graciously pleased to pardon them, though he did not actually promise to do so, but if they did not do all this immediately then he did not intend that Norfolk should "common with them further."[1]

Though he took this high tone in writing to the Pilgrims themselves, Henry did not neglect other precautions. He instructed Norfolk to make sure of Doncaster and Rotherham[2], and told Suffolk that he might promise pardons to the gentlemen of Marshland who had entered into communication with him[3]. On receiving a copy of the Pilgrims' letter, Suffolk had written to the King in great alarm to excuse himself from any complicity in the despatch of Waters to Scarborough[4], but Henry was quite prepared to pass over that incident and did not even refer to it. As he believed that Sir Robert Constable was still at York, he ordered Suffolk to practise with the

---

[1] L. and P. xi, 1175.   [2] Ibid. 1174.
[3] Ibid. 1176; see above, chap. xi.   [4] L. and P. xi, 1162.

townsfolk of Hull, in order that the town might be seized at the first favourable opportunity[1].

Other measures were also taken. The royal spies in the north endeavoured to frighten the commons by spreading reports that the Emperor and the King of France were coming to help Henry, each with 40,000 men, and by exaggerating the number of the musters at Ampthill. They reported that the commons were in great dread of the King's ordnance, having little of their own[2].

As it was the religious grievances which made the rising so threatening, the King proceeded to demonstrate his orthodoxy in the usual way, by persecuting the heretics. "This year, 12 November, being Sunday, there was a priest bore a faggot at Paul's Cross standing in his surplice for heresy, which priest did celebrate at his mass with ale."[3] On 17 November Barnes was imprisoned in the Tower, and Field, Marshall, Goodall and "another of that sort of learning," probably Rastell, were all arrested[4]. John Bale was examined on 19 November concerning certain heretical doctrines which he was accused of preaching. The interrogatories put to him have not been preserved, but one of his answers might have been laid to heart by the inquisitors of all religious parties; he said that "he would fain know of his accusers who is so familiar with God as may know that secret point?"[5] Field and Rastell appear to have been examined at the same time[6].

On 19 November Henry issued a circular to his bishops. It was drawn up in two forms, one for heretical bishops, reproving them for their offences, the other, for those who had not gone so far, cautioning them as to their behaviour. The bishops were ordered to explain personally the King's Articles to their flocks, to preach passive obedience to the King, to observe and maintain all laudable ceremonies, and to prevent all unlicensed preaching and contemptuous words about usages and ceremonies[7]. Several little tracts on the advantages of peace and the duty of obeying the King were also circulated, and the King's reply to the Lincolnshire rebels was printed and issued[8].

An allusion has already been made to the report that Henry would receive help from abroad. A marriage between Mary and the

---

[1] L. and P. xi, 1176.   [2] Ibid. 1170.
[3] Wriothesley, op. cit. i, 58; cf. L. and P. xii (1), 876.
[4] L. and P. xi, 1097, and note p. 718; cf. 1424.
[5] Ibid. 1111.   [6] Ibid. and 1487.
[7] Ibid. 1110 (1), (2); (3) printed in full, Halliwell-Phillipps, op. cit. i, 354.
[8] L. and P. xi, 780 (2), 936, 987, 988, 1215, 1405–6, 1409, 1420, 1422–3.

Duke of Angoulême, now Orleans, had long been hinted at by the French and English ambassadors at the respective courts. On 11 October 1536 Henry wrote to Gardiner and Wallop, his ambassadors in France, that they were not to allow it to appear that he desired the match, but were to induce the French to make all the advances[1].

In the same letter he mentioned the rising in Lincolnshire, but treated it very lightly[2]. On 5 November he wrote again to declare that the reports of the insurrection were very much exaggerated, that it was all over, and the two shires of York and Lincoln lay entirely at his mercy. Pomeroy had arrived from France to treat of the marriage of Mary and Angoulême, but Henry was not satisfied with the form of his credentials, which he considered too unceremonious. He had referred the ambassador to the Council, and intended to give him no certain answer[3].

On 10 November the Imperial ambassador was informed that the Council was considering the French match and that Francis was so anxious to bring it about that he was willing to consent if Mary were only declared the King's heir in default of legitimate issue, and given a title and an income. The Emperor had been proposing a marriage between Mary and Don Luis of Portugal, which Mary herself would have preferred. The negotiations with France were used to bring the Imperial ambassador to the point of making a formal proposal for her hand, and on 23 November Chapuys wrote to ask for instructions, as Mary informed him that Francis had offered to settle an income of 80,000 ducats on her marriage with Angoulême, but her father still made little of the proposal[4]. So long as Henry could tantalize both monarchs with the offer of Mary's hand, he knew he need not fear that either of them would help the rebels.

Such were the King's measures of precaution; to which may be added the vigilant watch kept upon the southern counties, to repress the first signs of disaffection. William Constable, Sir Robert's son, who was wandering about the country with his schoolmaster, was arrested at Stowe in November[5], and afterwards detained at Ross in the Christmas holidays[6]. Two men were arrested and examined in

---

[1] L. and P. xi, preface, p. x.

[2] Ibid. 656; printed in full, Tierney, ed. Dodd, Church Hist. of Eng. vol. i, Append. no. xlii.

[3] L. and P. xi, 984; extracts printed by Tierney, op. cit. i, Append. no. xliv.

[4] L. and P. xi, 1143; Cal. S. P. Spanish, v (2), 114, 116.

[5] L. and P. xi, 1008.   [6] L. and P. xii (1), 30.

London because they came from Louth[1], and information was received against another Lincolnshire man, who was said to have used seditious language at Fittleworth in Sussex[2]. Norfolk's complaint that he could not trust his soldiers receives some confirmation from reports of the musters in Kent and in Suffolk, where some of the men were heard to declare that the northern men had right on their side and that they themselves would not fight against the rebels[3]. On 22 November a pedlar was committed to Canterbury gaol for spreading sedition[4]. From time to time a bold parish priest ventured to express his sympathy with the rebels. On 26 October the parson of Wimborne, Dorset, "preached purgatory."[5] In the Isle of Wight on 11 November the vicar of Thorley denied the royal supremacy[6], and the parson of Wickham in Hampshire fled from an accusation of sedition[7]. The parson of Radwell in Hertford preached against the suppression of the abbeys in November[8].

On 19 October Bishop Latimer sent to Cromwell copies of some ancient Latin verses, containing a lament over the oppression of the Church, and also some fantastic prophecies. The Bishop remarked that he sent them because he knew that Cromwell loved antiquities, and that the bearer would explain how some people expounded the lines[9]. These were no doubt some of the prophecies which were being circulated by Cromwell's opponents[10]. A man was imprisoned at Bath on 20 October for repeating a prophecy, although he protested that he did not know its meaning[11], and another was accused in December of speaking against Cromwell at the Antelope inn in Worcester[12].

During the time of the insurrection Cromwell kept himself a good deal in the background, for the hatred he inspired was as strong a bond between gentlemen and commons as religious enthusiasm. He was as much in favour with the King as ever, and was always within reach of the court, but he did not reside there[13]. He was in London when Bowes and Ellerker were with the King at Windsor, and Cresswell had not seen him at court for two days together[14]. On

---

[1] L. and P. xi, 1177; printed in full, Merriman, op. cit. ii, no. 171.
[2] L. and P. xi, 920.
[3] Ibid. 841 (iv); 1111; cf. xii (1), 1318.   [4] L. and P. xi, 1133.
[5] Ibid. 876.   [6] L. and P. xii (1), 275.
[7] L. and P. xi, 1265.   [8] L. and P. xii (1), 572.
[9] L. and P. xi, 790; printed in full, Latimer's Remains (Parker Soc.), ii, 375; cf. Merriman, op. cit. ii, no. 168.
[10] See above, chap. iv.   [11] L. and P. xi, 809.
[12] Ibid. 1328; xii (2), 515.   [13] L. and P. xi, 879.
[14] See above, chap. xii.

21 November the King was at Richmond, and Cromwell still was not with him[1], but his absence did not deceive the watchful eyes which were upon him. The Pilgrims had friends in the south who were able to send them information on such points. One of these secret friends came to Aske after the council at York. He found the captain sick of a "severe colic," which prevented him from riding to Templehurst, as he had intended to do after the council. The secret friend, whose name is unknown, reported that the King was at Richmond, and "Cromwell only the ruler about him." Cromwell was more bitterly hated than ever, and the south parts longed for the coming of the Pilgrims, but they must be on their guard, for on Thursday 23 November ten ships of war took ordnance from the Tower, and it was said that Suffolk was advancing with 20,000 men. Aske was not sure whether to believe the last news, but he considered it a suspicious circumstance that Sir Anthony Browne had occupied Doncaster. He wrote to ask Darcy to remonstrate about the fortification of Doncaster Bridge and to watch Ferrybridge and Pontefract[2].

Not only did the rebels receive news from the south but in spite of all precautions on the part of the government the rebel manifestoes found their way southward, and even one copy could travel far and quickly. Richard Fletcher, the gaoler of Norwich, was at Lynn on Sunday 29 October, and there met some of Norfolk's disbanded troops. One of these men, who was the clerk of Mr Fermor, son and heir of Sir Harry Fermor, gave Fletcher a bill to deliver to John Manne of Norwich; his story was that his master had been given this bill by the Duke of Norfolk. Fletcher supped at the Bell at Lynn, and by the desire of the company the bill was read aloud. The goodman of the inn, George Wharton, was so much struck by its contents that he caused one of Fletcher's prisoners to make two copies of it. It seems in fact to have been Aske's second manifesto. When Fletcher reached Norwich he showed the bill to several people including the Mayor, Mr Fermor, who "marvelled that such a bill should be suffered to go abroad," but did not attempt to suppress it. Fletcher delivered the original to John Manne, but kept a copy for himself, which he continued to show to his friends. At length he went up to London, and while there Leonard Stanger, servant to Mr Willoughby, saw the bill and "said it was naught and took it away to burn it." Meanwhile George Wharton of the Bell at Lynn gave one of his copies of the bill to some Cornish soldiers who were

---

[1] L. and P. xi, 1124; printed in full, State Papers, i, 510.
[2] L. and P. xi, 1128.

coming from the north on a pilgrimage to Walsingham. This gift may have had curious results[1]. His other copy he lent out among his neighbours[2]. At Templehurst on 18 November Aske was heard to say that he had given a copy of the oath to a gentleman of Norfolk, who would forward the matter in the south[3].

Another manifesto which had probably been going about the country for some time was taken at Bromsgrove, Worcester, on 12 December[4]. A fourth was circulating in a higher rank of society. On Sunday 19 November Sir George Throgmorton attended the morning sermon at St Paul's, and there met his friend Sir John Clarke. After the sermon they dined together at the Horse Head in Cheapside, and when the goodman and his wife had left the room the two gentlemen began to discuss the rising in the north. Sir George had read the King's printed reply to the Lincolnshire rebels, but he did not know what the Yorkshiremen demanded. Sir John promised to let him see a copy of their articles[5]. They walked back to St Paul's together and parted, and that night Sir John's servant brought Throgmorton a copy of the Pilgrims' oath, the five articles, and one of Aske's proclamations[6].

A few nights later Sir George Throgmorton supped at the Queen's Head in Fleet Street betwixt the Temple gates[7]. At this inn there was an informal club of lawyers and members of parliament, who, if they had dared to say so, were in opposition to the government[8]. On this particular evening Sir George met another frequenter of the Queen's Head, Sir William Essex, and again the conversation turned on the northern rebellion. Sir William was curious about the demands of the Pilgrims, and Sir George sent his servant to find and bring back his copy of the oath, etc., which he had " thrown into a window," *i.e.* put into the box under the window-seat. Sir William kept the papers for several days, caused his servant to copy them, and returned them to Throgmorton. After this Essex returned to his home near Reading. His own copy of the papers he kept carefully put away, but his chamber-boy, Geoffrey Gunter, who had copied them for him, had also made another copy for himself[9]. Geoffrey Gunter was not discreet. He lent his copy to William Wyre, the host of the Cardinal's Inn at Reading, and within a week there were several copies circulating in the town. Richard Snow,

1 See below, chap. xix. 2 L. and P. xi, 1260.
3 L. and P. xii (1), 369; printed in full, Milner and Benham, op. cit. chap. v.
4 L. and P. xi, 1286, 1292. 5 Ibid. 1406.
6 Ibid. 1405. 7 Ibid. 1406.
8 L. and P. xii (2), 952. 9 L. and P. xi, 1406.

vicar of St Giles, obtained one and Richard Turner another, but they were uneasy about the matter, and on 30 November they gave their copies to the bailiff and the serjeant of Reading, to be laid before the magistrates of the town. The justices on 2 December examined all the parties in Reading, and sent their replies to Cromwell[1]. They were all summoned to London immediately. On their way they met Sir George Throgmorton, who was going to visit Sir William Essex. He was told about the affair, and although he tried to make light of it, saying that everybody in London was reading the rebels' articles and Aske's letters, yet secretly he was very much disturbed, and burnt his copy. Sir William Essex, who had burnt his also, was almost ill with anxiety, and on receiving orders to examine Gunter and send him up to London, Essex set out to throw himself upon the King's mercy. Throgmorton, hearing nothing from him, followed him up to London, only to find that Essex was in the Tower and that he himself must join him there[2]. In January 1537 they were still prisoners, and it was thought that the charges against them were very grave[3], but towards the end of the month they were released[4]. It does not appear whether Sir John Clarke was ever called to account for his share of the business.

The presence of secret friends of the Pilgrims in the south was more alarming than the mutterings of discontent among the peasantry. They might be found anywhere, in the army, at court, in the King's Council. Henry never more than half believed Norfolk's reports of the rebels' strength, because he knew that the Duke secretly sympathised with the enemy. But though that altered the direction of Henry's fears, it did not allay them, for a king is in a dangerous position when he cannot trust his own commander-in-chief. There were continual rumours that Norfolk had either gone over to the Pilgrims or allowed himself to be taken by them[5]. He himself said that he could not trust his men[6], and there was even a story that one of the soldiers had attacked him with a dagger[7]. The loyalty of the Marquis of Exeter, who was sent with Norfolk and Shrewsbury against the rebels[8], was still more doubtful than that of Norfolk. He held his command, however, until the first appointment

---

[1] L. and P. xi, 1231.

[2] Ibid. 1406.   [3] L. and P. xii (1), 86.

[4] Ibid. 237.

[5] Cal. S. P. Spanish, v (2), 114, 116, 122; L. and P. xi, 1143, 1159; Cal. Venetian S. P. v, 125, 126.

[6] L. and P. xi, 909.   [7] Ibid. 1195.

[8] Ibid. 726; see above, chap. xi.

at Doncaster[1], and offered to advance the King money for the payment of his men[2]. As soon as he was ready to set out in the first instance, he was stopped by a countermand[3], and when he did start, on 18 October, he was behind Norfolk, who contrived to obtain all the money sent down from the Treasury. On 21 October Exeter had "not a penny to convey himself and his train toward my lord Steward."[4] Money was sent to him at Ampthill on 23 October[5]. He joined Norfolk in the end[6], but he took very little part in the campaign[7]. When the truce was made he returned to court, where his wife had been in waiting on the Queen since the middle of October[8]. As a reward for his services he received a grant of the dissolved priory of Breamore on 9 November[9]. Reginald Pole's brothers, Lord Montague and Sir Geoffrey Pole, were ordered to provide men at the beginning of the rebellion, and Montague was to attend on the King's own person[10].

A little more light is thrown on the mystery of the Pilgrims' southern correspondents by a letter from Chapuys to Charles V, which was despatched on 22 November. It is in the form of a journal, written from day to day from the beginning of the month. His earliest news was that the Duke of Norfolk, the Marquis and others had gone to confer with the rebels, and that if they had not wisely resolved on this step, the King would have been in great danger. The ambassador's informant was "one of the principal gentlemen in the King's army." Chapuys next heard that Norfolk had come up to court, both to justify his own action and to forward the petitions of the northern men. Norfolk was bringing with him two ambassadors from the rebels "Master Raphael Endecherche and Master Dos." Norfolk and the other noblemen "were all good Christians"; they did not wish for a battle, and showed as openly as they dared that they thought the rebels had right on their side.

Chapuys gave a brief account of the rebels' position. They were reported to be 40,000 strong, and among them were 10,000 cavalry. They were in good order, but required money and musketeers. Their banner was a crucifix, and Lord Darcy and the Archbishop of York were with them. Their numbers would probably increase, as the south parts sympathised with them, and presently news came that

---

[1] L. and P. xi, 737, 750, 751, 769, 776, 788, 803, 825, 834, 845, 850.
[2] Ibid. 793.   [3] Ibid. 776.
[4] Ibid. 822.   [5] Ibid. 842.
[6] Ibid. 887.   [7] Ibid. 1143.
[8] Ibid. 860.   [9] Ibid. 1217 (6).
[10] Ibid. 580 (1), (2).

another province (Cumberland and Westmorland) had risen because the return of the ambassadors was delayed. The lack of money might ruin everything, but this would be remedied if the Pope sent Reginald Pole with supplies, and want of money was not felt on one side only, for Henry had complained to Mary that the insurrection had cost him £200,000.

When Ellerker and Bowes first arrived Chapuys heard that their articles were:

(1) that their petition might be authorised by Parliament,

(2) that Parliaments might be held in the ancient way, and that all pensioners and government servants might be excluded,

(3) that the Princess' (Mary's) affairs might be dealt with by Parliament,

(4) that the King might not take money from his people except in time of war.

These articles were said to be signed by all the gentlemen. In the third particular Chapuys was mistaken, but (1), (2), and (4) were all points on which the rebels insisted, and later in the letter he mentioned that he had been mistaken about (3); the rebels had not ventured to name Mary, for fear the King did her harm.

Chapuys believed that the King would not give way, as he boasted that the Duke of Orleans (Angoulême) was willing to marry Mary although she was not legitimate, and that the King of France would help him with four or five thousand men. Later Chapuys found that his conjecture was correct. The King would not change anything that had been determined by Parliament, and told the rebels that they had no right to meddle with his Privy Council. Nevertheless the news of the fresh rising might force him to alter his decision, and Norfolk was using his influence on the Pilgrims' side. Finally Bowes and Ellerker were sent back with no better answer. "The King said he would rather lose his crown than be so limited by his vassals." Five or six ships were being prepared, and Henry boasted that he would go against the rebels in person, but first he had despatched Norfolk and Fitzwilliam to corrupt them by secret means if possible. Chapuys, however, thought that it was more likely that the King's emissaries would go over to the rebels themselves.

Chapuys heard that Lord *Hussey* had sent a message to the King that the rebels were ready to fight, for they were a third more numerous than the King's troops, with provisions and money, and they expected the Emperor to help them. "Hussey" is probably a mistake for "Darcy"; Chapuys had great difficulty with English names, and his account of the message seems to be derived from Darcy's interview with Somerset Herald.

In a very interesting passage, Chapuys says that "among fifteen or twenty articles which the northern ambassadors have proposed" there were two which he thought unreasonable,—(1) that the King should give an account of his expenditure, showing what had become of his father's treasure and of all the money he had obtained from the Church and by taxation, and (2) that in cases of treason the criminal's property should not be confiscated, but should be restored to his heir, and that the lands of Buckingham and others who had been executed should be thus restored. Chapuys feared that if the King yielded on the main points, the rebels might lose all by insisting on these or similar minor details[1]. The interesting point is that no detailed list of demands had yet been drawn up by the rebels. They had only sent in the five general articles, and did not think of going into particulars until the King replied that their demands were "general, dark and obscure." The resolution to draw up a detailed list of grievances was taken at York on 21 November, and the list was not compiled until the council met at Pontefract. Moreover, the complete articles do not contain either of the two demands which Chapuys mentions.

Where then did the ambassador hear of the fifteen or twenty articles of which these were two? The reference to the Duke of Buckingham suggests that his informant was one of the Poles. The northern Pilgrims had no particular interest in Buckingham, and the clause is not likely to have been inserted in a northern petition, but if, as is possible, the Poles were the secret friends who communicated with Aske, they may have drawn up a list of their own complaints, shown it to Chapuys, and then sent it north. There is one letter which may possibly be connected with this. John Heliar, the vicar of East Meon in Hampshire, and rector of Warblington, had fled to France some time before. Warblington was the home of the Poles, and Heliar was their friend and dependent; Sir Geoffrey Pole was accused of having aided his escape[2]. On 21 December 1536, after the second conference at Doncaster, Richard Langgrische, a priest, wrote from Havant, a town near Warblington, to Mr Heliar beyond the seas: "I have been so far north since your being beyond sea that I lacked messengers, but now having your servant ready to bear my letters, I could no longer use unkind silence. I trust to settle in my own country among my friends within a few years. Not that

---

[1] L. and P. xi, 1143. [2] L. and P. xiii (2), 797.

I like the north so ill, but mine own country so well. Everyone desires your prosperous return."[1] There is not much in this, only the fact that a priest who lived in the same neighbourhood as the Poles, and knew a self-exiled friend of theirs, had been in the north at the time of the Pilgrimage, and was in hopes that better times were at hand. Still the circumstances suggest that he may have been the messenger to the rebels. This, however, is only a conjecture. Chapuys derived his information partly from Mary, partly from a gentleman in the royal army, and partly from someone at court who had good, but not first-hand, information. For instance the informant cannot have had direct communication with Bowes and Ellerker, or he would have known that their articles were not signed, and that Mary was not mentioned; on the other hand, he reported the general tone of the articles rightly, and corrected the mistake about Mary. The identity of this informant, however, cannot be discovered.

The Pilgrims were firmly convinced that they had the sympathy of Europe, and in particular of the Emperor, who was very popular in England. In order to trace the impression which the news of the rising made abroad, it may be as well to recapitulate the various letters to and from the ambassadors.

Henry was nominally the ally of Francis I, but relations between them were strained at this time, as James V of Scotland had arrived in France on 27 August 1536[2] with the avowed intention of marrying a French princess, although Henry was bitterly opposed to such a marriage. In his letter of 11 October Henry instructed Gardiner and Wallop to make themselves fully acquainted with the nature and qualities of the young King[3].

On 23 October the Bishop of Faenza, the papal nuncio in France, wrote to Rome that the rising in England against the suppression of abbeys was so serious that the King would probably be forced to yield. The passages from England had been closed, and it was difficult to get news, but this showed how grave the situation must be. James V was winning favourable opinions everywhere, and was to marry Francis' daughter Madeleine. Cardinal du Bellay suggested that by means of this marriage Francis might be influenced to act against Henry, who was very unpopular among the French nobles[4]. Du Bellay had a correspondent in London who on 24 October sent

---

[1] L. and P. xi, 1350.   [2] Ibid. 631.

[3] Ibid. 656; printed in full, Tierney, ed. Dodd, Church Hist. of Eng. i, Append. no. xlii.

[4] L. and P. xi, 848.

news that the Lincolnshire rebels had dispersed, but that there was a much more serious rising in Yorkshire[1]. After this no further news reached France for some time. The Bishop of Faenza believed that Henry was purposely preventing communications for fear the King of Scotland should learn the extent of the insurrection[2]. On 3 November there was a rumour that Henry himself was besieged in a castle[3]. The Pope wrote to Francis I on 7 November to congratulate him on the Scots marriage and to exhort him not to help Henry against the rebels[4]. It was known in France on 19 November that Henry was negotiating with the rebels, and James V sent civil messages to the Pope, promising to serve him if possible[5].

The betrothal of Madeleine de Valois to James V took place on 26 November[6]. The papal nuncio was delighted. He reported that Francis and James were both ready and even anxious to act against Henry. Francis, however, said that the disturbances in England were now at an end; nevertheless he would let Faenza know when the time came to move[7]. James was very affable to the nuncio, but treated the English ambassadors with marked coldness. Du Bellay was in hopes that the time had almost arrived to strike at Henry. The movement in England had been premature and without a leader, but though it was now pacified, the malcontents would rise again at the summons of the King of Scotland[8]. On 28 November Faenza sent to the Pope further professions of James' goodwill, and his readiness to act against his uncle[9], and on 29 November he reported that James was entering into negotiations for a treaty with Denmark which would be very prejudicial to Henry[10].

From all this it appears that Francis was ready to turn against Henry if he dared, but he was afraid of precipitating an alliance between England and the Emperor. Faenza suggested that to prevent this the Pope might excommunicate Henry, and make it impossible for anyone to become his ally openly[11]. The party in the French court which was hostile to Henry and the papal nuncio himself built great hopes on James. They did not realise that there was no other prince in Christendom whose interference in English affairs would not have been preferred by the most ardent Pilgrim to that of James V. Of all Henry's reproaches to the rebels the one which had most effect was that they were exposing their country

---

[1] L. and P. xi, 860.   [2] Ibid. 953.
[3] Ibid. 976.   [4] Ibid. 1012.   [5] Ibid. 1119.
[6] Ibid. 1172, 1183.   [7] Ibid. 1173.   [8] Ibid. 1183.
[9] Ibid. 1194.   [10] Ibid. 1203.   [11] Ibid. 1173.

to the danger of a Scots invasion[1], and reports were spread by the royalists that the Scots were mustering on the borders[2]. The Pilgrims professed themselves willing to help the King against the Scots at any time[3], and an attempt on James' part would have strengthened Henry by rallying the whole kingdom to his side against their ancient enemies.

The Imperial ambassador in England watched the progress of events with no less interest than the French. His reports have already been quoted, and need only be mentioned briefly. In his despatch on 7 October Chapuys alluded to the Lincolnshire rising, which he believed to be more threatening than the King would admit[4]. His despatch was sent to the Emperor at Genoa[5]. Next day he wrote to the Count of Cifuentes, the Imperial ambassador at Rome, chiefly about Mary's affairs; at the end of his letter he alluded to the rising, but thought it might turn out to be nothing after all[6]. On 14 October he reported to the Empress that there was certainly a rebellion, and from the King's preparations it seemed to be a great one, but he still had no certain information[7]. The next day, apparently, he had obtained information, and sent his nephew with an elaborate account of the whole affair to the Regent of the Netherlands, advising her to help the rebels[8]. By this time negotiations for peace had been opened between Charles and Francis, but the project proceeded slowly, though the Pope was very anxious to reconcile them, in order that they might unite against Henry[9].

The Regent of the Netherlands sent to Calais for news on 24 October, and professed her willingness to help Henry against the rebels[10]. Lord Lisle, as in duty bound, replied before 28 October that the disturbances were ended[11], and on 6 November received congratulations from the Netherlands on the restoration of peace in England[12]. These professions of friendship did not receive much credit in England. John Hutton, the English agent at Brussels, wrote to Cromwell on 9 December that "there is large talking of the rebellions in England."[13] Cromwell ordered him to buy "500 pair of Almain rivets," but the Regent's Council refused to

---

[1] L. and P. xi, 826 (2), 955, 1064 (2); xii (1) 1175 (ii).
[2] L. and P. xi, 1044, 1170.   [3] Ibid. 1086, see above, chap. ix.
[4] L. and P. xi, 576; see Cal. S. P. Spanish, v (2), 104.   [5] L. and P. xi, 779.
[6] Ibid. 597; Cal. S. P. Spanish, v (2), 105.
[7] L. and P. xi, 698; Cal. S. P. Spanish, v (2), 110.
[8] L. and P. xi, 713, 714; Froude, "The Pilgrim," p. 113.
[9] L. and P. xi, 744, 779.   [10] Ibid. 861.
[11] Ibid. 905.   [12] Ibid. 1000.
[13] Ibid. 1275.

license the export of harness, giving the excuse that the Emperor needed all that could be procured. Cromwell was afraid that the rebels were procuring arms from the Low Countries, but Hutton assured him that they could not obtain much, as the Regent was favourable to Henry, and the customs officers were so strict that it would be difficult to smuggle weapons. Three ships had sailed from Zeeland for Newcastle-upon-Tyne in November which might have carried arms, but there was only one Newcastle vessel at Antwerp on 13 December, with some men from Newcastle and York, and one from Hull. Hutton promised to take care that she carried nothing for the rebels[1]. There is no evidence to prove that the Pilgrims obtained any armour from the Netherlands, but when William Morland entered Sir Robert Constable's service at Hull his master gave him a pair of Almain rivets, which he wore when he carried Sir Robert's banner[2].

On 22 November Chapuys despatched from England the full account of the Pilgrimage which has been described above[3], and on 24 November it was noted on one of the Emperor's despatches that the rebels in England had dispersed only after obtaining terms which were disgraceful to the King[4]. Charles V, however, refused to move at all in the matter, either for or against the Pilgrims[5].

The persons to whom the rising was of the greatest importance were the Pope and Reginald Pole. At the beginning of October Paul III summoned Pole to Rome, and, in spite of Henry's positive prohibition, Pole obeyed. He was at Sienna on his way there on 10 October[6]. On his arrival he was lodged at the Vatican, and was treated most kindly by the Pope[7]. It is exceedingly difficult to calculate how long it took for news to travel from England to Rome, but it seems probable that when Pole arrived some account of the Lincolnshire insurrection had been received there, as the Bishop of Faenza wrote on 1 November to Ambrogio, the Pope's secretary, alluding to the rising as something of which they both had knowledge[8], and on 6 November Dr Pedro Ortiz reported to the Empress that a letter had come from the Regent of the Netherlands with news that the rebels numbered 30,000 to 40,000 men[9]. This was probably taken from Eustace Chapuys' letter of 15 October[10].

[1] L. and P. xi, 1296.   [2] L. and P. xii (1), 380.

[3] L. and P. xi, 1143; Cal. S. P. Spanish, v (2), 114, 116.

[4] L. and P. xi, 1159 n.   [5] Ibid. 1159.

[6] Ibid. 654.   [7] Ibid. 1100.

[8] Ibid. 953.

[9] Ibid. 1001; Cal. S. P. Spanish, v (2), 115.   [10] See above, chap. vi.

When he heard this news, Reginald Pole cannot have failed to see that a great opportunity lay before him. The question was how to use it for the good of the Church. In circumstances not apparently so favourable Henry of Richmond had invaded England, defeated the King, married the rightful heiress, and established his dynasty upon the throne. If Pole had been a man of that type, he would have procured letters of censure upon Henry from the Pope, together with all the money he could raise, and would have embarked for England at once. But Pole's was no ignoble personal ambition, and, although he was not yet ordained, all his hopes and interests were bound up in the Church of Rome. Though he abstained from taking the vows of celibacy for many years, and was thus free to wed Mary if necessary, he never seems to have looked upon the hypothetical marriage as anything but a disagreeable duty which he might be called upon to perform for the good of the Church. As far as he himself was concerned he desired no part in the government of England.

Pole was no adventurer, but he was also no crusader. His heart did not leap up at the call to arms. He did not say to himself, "My countrymen are prepared to fight and die for the True Faith. I must be by their side." His idea of his own mission was that of a highly honoured ecclesiastic, returning, fully accredited, amidst the most respectful enthusiasm, to his native land to reconcile to a gracious Pope a deeply penitent monarch and a humbly joyful nation. His dream at last came true, but the Lincolnshire rising gave no immediate prospect of its fulfilment. In deciding whether or no to join the rebels, Pole was really forced to choose between his opinions and his prejudices. He had himself stated in his book that he believed subjects were sometimes justified in rebelling against their sovereign, and that Englishmen would in fact be justified in rebelling against Henry. But that was a strange and terrible opinion, which he had expressed more to frighten Henry than for any other reason. The book was kept a dead secret, and only his most intimate friends knew its contents. It was all very well to write such things in a book, but if it came to putting his theories into practice, he would be obliged to steal back to England secretly, in constant fear of arrest, to go marching about in the mud with a mob of undisciplined commons, to hold councils with their boorish leaders in unknown provincial towns; and in doing all this he would be acting openly and avowedly against Henry, the theologian, the musician, his own cousin and early patron. The idea was revolting

D.

to Pole, who was an aristocrat to his finger-tips. Accordingly he simply remained in Rome, awaiting developments.

When Paul III first heard of the rebellion he was anxious to take advantage of it. On 7 November he wrote to exhort Francis I to unite with other Christian kings against Henry[1], and about the same time the suggestion was made that Pole should be created a cardinal. The news of this proposal reached England on 18 November, and was received by Henry with the utmost indignation. Starkey wrote to Pole in the King's name and in the most positive terms forbade him to accept such promotion[2]. But Pole seems to have refused before the prohibition could have reached him. Perhaps the above suggestions as to his feelings are not wholly just, and his real reason for declining to stir may have done his heart more credit. His mother and brothers were in Henry's power, and he knew that any movement on his part might endanger their lives. Accordingly he declined the honour which the Pope proposed to bestow upon him expressly on account of his family[3]. Pole did not realise that he had already endangered their lives to such an extent that only the most vigorous action could save them. Henry would never forgive "De Unitate Ecclesiastica" and Pole's journey to Rome. Henceforward the King would bide his time, but in the end he would strike. The unfortunate Poles did not perceive this. They still thought that they had not gone too far for pardon, and thus, fearing to injure them, Reginald Pole lost the last chance of saving the lives of his nearest relatives.

On 21 November it was reported in Rome that the insurrection in England was nearly pacified, and that Henry had marched against the rebels in person[4]. This referred, however, only to the Lincoln-shire rising. Chapuys knew as early as 14 November that the Pope was thinking of sending Reginald Pole to England, and the ambassador encouraged the idea warmly[5].

On 24 November Cifuentes, the Imperial ambassador at Rome, told the Pope that according to despatches from England, part of the rebels had been crushed, and the rest were dispersing for want of a leader[6]. The Pope replied that he had had a letter from France, dated 3 November[7], from which it appeared that the rebels were holding their own, and that they had a leader whose name ended in

[1] L. and P. xi, 1012.   [2] Ibid. 1100, 1101.
[3] Haile, op. cit. chap. x.   [4] L. and P. xi, 1131.
[5] L. and P. xi, 1143; Cal. S. P. Spanish, v (2), 114, 116.
[6] L. and P. xi, 1159; Cal. S. P. Spanish, v (2), 120, 122.
[7] L. and P. xi, 976; cf. Cal. S. P. Venetian, v, 125.

" folc " (Norfolk). The Pope also said that he had sent the rebels money by means of a secret go-between in Picardy. There is no further record of this money. Perhaps the secret Picard stole it. At this time there was a rumour that the bull of privation against Henry VIII had been printed. It was not published in Rome, but it was suspected that the Pope intended to send it secretly to England[1].

On 26 November Faenza wrote that the insurrection in England was appeased, and that Pole could not go there now without manifest danger, but he ought to be in readiness, for it would be well to send him as soon as fresh disturbances arose, the people held him in so much esteem. Faenza proposed that Pole's writings should be disseminated in England to encourage people in the true faith[2]. The letter was sent from Paris, and cannot have reached Rome until at least a week after the date of writing. In the meanwhile, on 29 November a letter arrived at Rome from England which was dated 10 November. It does not appear who wrote it, but it contained the news that there were seventy or eighty thousand of the rebels, that the King's troops were disaffected, and that the leaders on both sides had determined to treat. Three honoured persons were sent from the rebels to the King, hostages being given for them, and they laid before him their demands:

(1) that the Pope should be acknowledged supreme head of the Church ;

(2) that Queen Katharine's marriage should be declared valid and Mary proclaimed the legitimate heir to the throne ;

(3) that the abbeys should not be suppressed ;

(4) that recent statutes should be repealed ;

(5) that Parliaments should be held as of old, without pensioners or placemen.

It was believed that the King would be compelled to grant these demands, although he was very reluctant to do so[3]. Naturally this news caused the greatest rejoicing in Rome. Next day arrived letters dated 12 November from the Regent of the Netherlands, in which it was reported that Henry had quelled the first rebellion by sending the Duke of Norfolk to the rebels with a promise of a general pardon, but that when the insurgents had dispersed, the King seized and executed fifty of the ringleaders. This caused a much greater insurrection all over the island, and the Duke of Norfolk, indignant at the King's breach of faith, had joined the rebels, who had seized several towns and forced the King to fly to

---

[1] Cal. S. P. Venetian, v, 125 ; L. and P. xi, 1160 ; see above, chap. i.

[2] L. and P. xi, 1173.   [3] Ibid. 1204 ; Cal. S. P. Spanish, v (2), 124.

London[1]. It is interesting to see how distorted the facts at the base of this spirited narrative have become as they passed from mouth to mouth.

A more sober version of events came from France in a letter announcing the betrothal of James V and Madeleine de Valois. In this it was said that the rebels in England were negotiating with Henry, and that the rising was practically at an end[2]. There was a story afloat on 16 December that the King of England had consented to James' marriage while the rebels were in arms, but that as soon as they dispersed he had written to forbid it, though his letter did not arrive until after the betrothal had taken place[3]. As a matter of fact Henry's consent had never been asked, and the rebels had not interested themselves in the subject. The satisfactory tidings from England and France encouraged the Pope to make an effort himself. Pole's hesitation was overcome, and on 22 December, 1536, he was made a cardinal[4].

It is clear from these despatches that foreign courts were bewildered between the English ambassadors' assurances that the rebellion was of no importance, on the one hand, and, on the other, the exaggerated successes attributed to the Pilgrims in the letters which from time to time eluded Henry's vigilance.

It is plain that neither Francis nor Charles had any real intention of moving in the matter, Francis because he was still half-tempted by the marriage between Mary and Orleans, and because in any case he would only act through Scotland, Charles because he was afraid of precipitating Mary's French marriage, and because he was exhausted by his disastrous Italian campaign.

The Pope was half inclined to take action, and any encouragement from him might really have had a good effect on the rebels, but there was no one to advise him as to the measures which he ought to take. Pole, having twice defied Henry, did no more, and the precious time was allowed to slip away. If Pole had accepted the Pope's first offer of the cardinalate he might have been in England by the time the news of the offer reached the King on 18 November, for it was easy then to travel as fast as a letter. Pole might have filled the pulpit at Pontefract in which Archbishop Lee proved so ignominious a failure. His presence could not, of course, have prevented the Reformation, but might have altered its whole progress in England, whether for better or for worse. But these are mere fancies. He did not come.

---

[1] Cal. S. P. Venetian, v, 126.   [2] Ibid. 127.
    Ibid. 129.   [4] Haile, op. cit. chap. x; L. and P. xi, 1353.

CHAPTER XIV

THE COUNCIL AT PONTEFRACT

At the great council which was now approaching, the Pilgrims were confronted by the very serious business of stating and justifying their position. Obedience to the government in the sixteenth century was not merely a theory or a convenience, as at the present day; it was a fundamental duty. There were none of the methods of peaceful opposition which are so common now. To resist the government meant civil war and social anarchy—cattle driven, houses burnt, women ravished, men slaughtered. The duty of non-resistance was the first principle of self-preservation, and the Pilgrims were not fulfilling that duty. They had risen in arms, and they were seriously anxious to show that they had sufficient grounds for this desperate step. Their justification was that the Church was in danger. The Church had always upheld the duty of obedience to the secular government, with but one important reservation, that the Pope had the power to release subjects from their allegiance if the King's conduct was such that to obey him was mortal sin. In the opinion of Pope Paul III, the crisis in England entitled him to use this extreme power. He had prepared a bull of deposition against Henry, but he lacked courage to publish it. Though the people of England had heard rumours of this bull, they knew nothing with certainty. The Pilgrimage of Grace had lasted for two months without the smallest sign of approval arriving from Rome.

It was of the utmost importance to the success of the movement that both gentlemen and commons should be convinced of the justice of their cause, for it was their unity in faith alone which held them together. As the Pope made no sign, the leaders resolved to obtain the sanction of the Church, if possible, from her chief representatives among themselves.

Even before the council at York, it had been proposed that the clergy of the northern parts should be asked to define clearly the ancient faith for which the Pilgrims had risen. After the truce at Doncaster, Aske requested Archbishop Lee to make a "book of the spiritual promotions," but Lee did not reply[1]. At York it was resolved that the spiritual men of the north should be bidden to prepare themselves for an assembly at Pontefract, where they were requested to declare their opinion touching the faith[2]. William Babthorpe took this order to the Archbishop, who was very reluctant to obey such a summons. He tried to persuade Sir Robert Constable to give him leave to remain at home, but Sir Robert would only agree to this if he would send his opinion to the council in writing. Shortly before the assembly at Pontefract Sir Ralph Ellerker, Robert Bowes and William Babthorpe waited on the Archbishop and told him that he was expected to draw up articles for the conference with Norfolk; Lee was very much alarmed, though they explained that they meant articles concerning the faith. He replied that he must first know on what points the Pilgrims wished to consult the clergy, and Babthorpe wrote to Aske for a statement of them, giving his own advice in the letter.

Aske with unsuspecting candour sent the Archbishop an outline of the articles which he thought should be considered[3]. This list of questions proposed to the clergy may be the one contained in an existing document, without heading or signature[4]. Most of the subjects mentioned in it were afterwards discussed at Pontefract, but there was one point of great importance which was not raised there. "If one oath be made and after one other oath to the contrary, and by the latter oath the party is sworn to repute and take the first oath void, whether it may be so by [spiritual] law or not[5]?"

This was a pressing question to most of the Pilgrims; nearly all, even the commons, had taken an oath of allegiance to the King, and although their new oath had been framed so that it should not directly contradict the former one, they could not hide from themselves that its meaning was very different. But this problem did not confront only the laymen. The English bishops had all taken an oath of canonical obedience to the Pope on their first installation, before the breach with Rome. The clergy had sworn to obey the

---

[1] L. and P. xii (1), 1022.   [2] See above, chap. xiii.
[3] L. and P. xii (1), 1022; 698 (3); 901 (107), printed in full, Eng. Hist. Rev. v, 570.
[4] L. and P. xi, 1182 (2); see note A at end of chapter.
[5] L. and P. xi, 1182 (2).

bishops in all lawful and canonical mandates, and to oppose all heresies condemned by the Church. But in February 1535 the bishops had made a solemn renunciation of any sort of obedience to the Pope, and in June of the same year the oath of the clergy had been altered to include a similar renunciation. In these cases also some attempt had been made to avoid a direct contradiction of their first oaths. The form laid before the bishops was not an oath, but a renunciation. The clergy had not sworn to obey the Pope, but only to obey their diocesans, who in turn obeyed the Pope[1]. The parallel of the Pilgrims' case with that of the clergy was obvious, and might be so inconvenient that it is no wonder they did not choose to argue the point.

When he sent his list of questions, Aske referred them wholly to the Archbishop as metropolitan[2], and begged that the clergy should determine the points "whereupon we may danger battle." Lee assured Cromwell that as soon as he read this he resolved to go to Pontefract, in order that he might explain to the misguided people that they had nothing to fight for, as the King had taken pains to have the faith clearly set forth in the Ten Articles, with the consent of the bishops and clergy[3]. It is impossible to avoid the suspicion that he really went because he found the Pilgrims were resolved to have either his written or his spoken word, and it was easier to explain away the latter than the former.

A letter was sent to all the northern clergy "that they should go a procession every day and send their minds, out of Holy Scripture and the four doctors of the Church, touching the commons' petition." Lee did not admit that he had anything to do with this letter, though it was issued in his name[4].

The leading north-country divines were summoned in person; the less important clergy were requested to send their opinions in writing[5]. Grice brought one of these written opinions to Pontefract, probably from a priest who lived near Wakefield[6]. Hallam brought two others from Watton. The alleged letter from the Archbishop was brought to Watton by William Horskey, and the curate of Watton forwarded it to a bachelor of divinity named Wade, who lived near by. When he received it Wade said that there was not time before the meeting to deal with such a difficult subject. The

---

[1] Dixon, op. cit. i, chap. iv.
[2] L. and P. xii (1), 901 (107); printed in full, Eng. Hist. Rev. v, 571.
[3] L. and P. xii (1), 1022.   [4] Ibid. 201 (3), (2).
[5] Ibid. 853, 1011.   [6] L. and P. xi, 1182 (1).

other theologians of the neighbourhood were not so diffident. Thomas Asheton, a young monk of Watton Priory, wrote a paper on the supremacy "comparing Peter and his apostles." Dr Swinburne, who lived thereabouts, also wrote out his opinion on the same subject[1].

As early as Tuesday 28 November the Pilgrims had begun to assemble at Pontefract, and Shrewsbury was alarmed by the report of their numbers. Sir Anthony Browne was sent by Norfolk to guard the bridges at Doncaster and Rotherham[2]. On 30 November Darcy wrote from Templehurst to Shrewsbury and Hastings to assure them that the meeting at Pontefract had no other object than to draw up articles to lay before Norfolk, that the truce should be observed, and that no treachery was intended at Doncaster, but all earnestly hoped for peace[3].

The leaders rode into Pontefract on Saturday, 2 December. Lord Darcy took up his abode at the Castle; Aske went to the Priory, and Lord Lumley to "Mr Henryson's, the late mayor," where he displayed the banner of the Five Wounds[4]. From all the districts concerned in the Pilgrimage the "worshipful men" had been summoned, as well as a certain number of yeomen and "well-horsed commoners."[5] These, with the gentlemen's servants, formed a picked force, which Norfolk had some reason to regard with misgiving, especially as more came than were summoned, a proof that the Pilgrims' zeal had not cooled. The towns were also represented. For York the lord mayor and his council had elected Sir George Lawson, the sheriff of the city, and six burgesses, with servants. They were given money for new coats, presumably of the city livery, ranging in price from 6s. 6d. for Lawson's to 2s. 4d. for the servants'. Their expenses were paid by the city which also provided them with a tent and all other necessaries[6]. With them came Richard Bowyer, who was a burgess but not one of the chosen delegates[7]. The companies marched into Pontefract well harnessed and bringing with them the latest achievement of military engineering, a bridge "to shoot over any arm of the sea in this realm." It was a device which had been constructed by "one Diamond of Wakefield, a poor man,"[8] and must have been designed to make the Pilgrims independent of the guarded bridges of the Don.

[1] L. and P. xii (1), 201, p. 99. [2] L. and P. xi, 1187.
[3] L. and P. xi, 1209, 1210. [4] Ibid. 1253.
[5] Ibid. 1155 (1) and (2).
[6] York City Records. House Book Vol. xiii, 23 Nov. 1536.
[7] L. and P. xii (1), 306.
[8] L. and P. xii (1), 946 (119).

Early on this morning the leaders at Pontefract wrote to Norfolk and Shrewsbury saying that as yet there were not above a hundred assembled there, that they intended no treachery, and were awaiting the safeconduct to treat with Norfolk. They expected the safeconduct to arrive on Sunday, 3 December[1].

The Pilgrims' council at Pontefract seems to have sat only from Saturday, 2 December to Monday, 4 December, 1536. Aske frequently remarked that the time was very short for all the work that had to be done.

Among those present were:

Lords. Scrope, Latimer, Conyers, Lumley, Darcy and Neville.

Knights. Robert Constable, James Strangways, Christopher Danby, Thomas Hilton, William Constable, John Constable, Peter Vavasour, Ralph Ellerker, Christopher Hilliard, Robert Neville, Oswald Wolsthrope, Edward Gower, George Darcy, William Fairfax, Nicholas Fairfax, William Mallory, Ralph Bulmer, William Bulmer, Stephen Hamerton, John Dawnye, Richard Tempest, Thomas Johnson, Henry Gascoigne.

Gentlemen. Robert Bowes, Robert Chaloner, William Babthorpe[2], John Norton, Richard Norton, Roger Lassells, Mr Place, Mr Fulthorpe, Richard Bowes, Delariver, Barton of Whenby, Richard Lassells, Mr Redman, Hamerton, Mr Ralph Bulmer, Rither, Metham, Saltmarsh, Palmes, Aclom, Rudston, Plumpton, Middleton, Mallory of Wothersome, Allerton[3], Marmaduke Neville[4].

Commons. Robert Pullen, Nicholas Musgrave and six others from Penrith[5], William Collins and Brown from the borough of Kendal, Mr Duckett, Edward Manser, Mr Strickland, Anthony Langthorn, John Ayrey and Harry Bateman from the barony of Kendal[6].

The only important captains who did not attend were Sir Thomas Percy, who was busy in Northumberland, and Sir Thomas Tempest, who had caught a chill "through being plunged in water in coming from York"; Tempest sent an apology for his absence, and as the best proof of his good faith he communicated his opinion on the various points to be considered to Robert Bowes in writing[7]; this was a length to which few of the gentlemen would go, as it was making permanent evidence against themselves.

[1] L. and P. xi, 1223.

[2] L. and P. xii (1), 901 (25); printed in full, Eng. Hist. Rev. v, 560.

[3] L. and P. xii (1), 6; printed in full, Eng. Hist. Rev. v, 340.

[4] L. and P. xii (1), 29.

[5] Ibid. 687 (2); printed in full, Wilson, op. cit. no. xxii.

[6] Ibid. 914.   [7] L. and P. xi, 1211.

It is not certain whereabouts in Pontefract the council was held, but probably it was at the Priory.

The first business was to choose a certain number of gentlemen, who should go to the Duke of Norfolk to lay before him the articles and to bring back the safeconduct for the three hundred who were to treat with the Duke[1]. The procedure was as follows: the Herald was sent to the Duke with the names of the first party, and brought back safeconducts for them on Sunday, 3 December[2]. The chosen gentlemen were Sir Thomas Hilton, Sir William Constable, Sir Ralph Ellerker, Sir Ralph Bulmer, Roger Lassells, Robert Bowes, Nicholas Rudston, John Norton, William Babthorpe and Robert Chaloner, each with two servants[3]. On Monday, 4 December, they were to take the articles to Doncaster and bring back the second safe-conduct. On Tuesday, 5 December, the great meeting was to take place, at which it was hoped the leaders on both sides would be able to make a satisfactory treaty.

After the gentlemen had been chosen, and the Herald despatched with their names, it was necessary to agree upon the articles. These had already been prepared by Aske in consultation with Darcy and the other leaders from lists of grievances brought in by the delegates, and from opinions in writing contributed by Sir Thomas Tempest, Babthorpe, Chaloner and others. Aske copied out the articles upon which they were all agreed, and returned the writings to their owners[4]. The list thus compiled was laid before the full assembly. Each article was read aloud, and when it was accepted the word "fiat" was written against it[5].

The articles may be divided into four groups, containing respectively: I. Religious, II. Constitutional, III. Legal, IV. Economic Grievances.

I. Religious Grievances.

Article (1) "To have the heresies of Luther, Wyclif, Husse, Melangton, Elicampadus, Burcerus, Confessa Germanie, Apologia Melanctonis, the works of Tyndall, of Barnys, of Marshall, Raskell, Seynt Germayne and other such heresy of Anabaptist destroyed."

The impressive list of heretics was probably drawn up from books which Richard Bowyer laid before the council as being heretical[6].

[1] L. and P. xi, 1246; printed in full, Speed, op. cit. bk ix, ch. 21.

[2] L. and P. xii (1), 901 (p. 409); printed in full, Eng. Hist. Rev. v, 566; cf. L. and P. xi, 1223.

[3] Ibid. 1243 (2).

[4] L. and P. xii (1), 901 (25); printed in full, Eng. Hist. Rev. v, 560.

[5] L. and P. xii (1), 6; 29.

[6] Ibid. 901 (30); printed in full, Eng. Hist. Rev. v, 560.

This was merely a general article to which the King would certainly
have agreed, and therefore it does not require further discussion.

(2) "The supremacy of the Church touching '*cura animarum*' to be
reserved to the See of Rome as before. The consecration of the bishops to be
from him, without any first fruits or pensions to be paid to him, or else a
reasonable pension for the outward defence for the Faith."

This was an article of the greatest importance. It was on this
point that the papers brought in by Grice and Hallam had been
written. Two other papers on the same subject were put into
Aske's hand, as poor men's petitions. One, written in Latin, he
gave to Archbishop Lee, but he did not receive the other, which
was in English, until the conference was over[1]. Sir Francis Bigod
wrote down his views in a paper which was a source of much future
trouble[2]. There also remain some fragments of a list of Articles
drawn up in the form of a petition to the King, which was doubtless
brought by some of the representatives to Pontefract, although it
cannot be ascertained from which district it came[3].

The number of papers on the question of the Supremacy shows
what deep feeling it aroused. Aske stated that every man grudged
against the Statute of Supremacy because it would cause England to
be divided from the universal Church[4]. The council of the Pilgrims
was ready to petition that the Act might be annulled altogether, but
Aske advised them to insert the clause "touching *cura animarum*."[5]
Even on this point there were differences of opinion among the
Pilgrims. It will be remembered that the commons of Caistor in
Lincolnshire had said that they were ready to take the King for
supreme head of the Church[6]. Darcy did not consider that excluding
the Pope from England was against the Faith[7], and Aske made it
appear that both Darcy and Constable agreed to include this among
the articles at his own request[8]. The papal scandals of the last
century and the growing spirit of nationality made Henry's proclamation of independence not altogether distasteful, and there was
a feeling that the authority of the Pope in England might be limited
in some way, if the King could come to an agreement with him to
preserve the unity of Christendom. The nameless petition accepted
the King's title of "supreme head of the Church in that it may

---

[1] L. and P. xii (1), 901 (23); printed in full, Eng. Hist. Rev. v, 565.
[2] See below, chap. xvi.   [3] L. and P. xi, 1182 (3).
[4] L. and P. xii (1), 901 (19); printed in full, Eng. Hist. Rev. v, 559.
[5] L. and P. xii (1), 901 (17); printed in full, Eng. Hist. Rev. v, 559.
[6] L. and P. xi, 853; see above, chap. v.   [7] L. and P. xi, 1086.
[8] L. and P. xii (1), 901 (44); printed in full, Eng. Hist. Rev. v, 570.

stand with the law of Christ," but complained that "heretics, bishops
...naughtily understanding that term...enforce your Grace through
flattery and blind fables to grant them commissions and authorities
to exercise all manner of jurisdiction as well against the laws of God
as the authority of those [*the Pope's*] councils, and so to make acts in
your parliaments and convocations to annul all laws and the sequel
that by the laws of God, of the Church, and of these councils should
be good throughout all the world approved and admitted for laws."[1]
In the list of questions which may be Aske's, it is suggested that
"where his Highness is recognised to be the supreme head of the
Church of England," yet as he is a temporal man and the cure of
souls and administration of sacraments are spiritual, "whereof necessity must be one head," and as the Bishop of Rome is the most
ancient bishop and has been admitted in all realms to have such
cure, it may please "our said sovereign lord" to admit him head
of spiritual matters, giving spiritual authority to the archbishops of
Canterbury and York, "so that the said bishop of Rome have no
further meddling[2]."

In after days a compromise on these lines was long a cherished
dream of the high church party in England, and if Henry would have
allowed the discussion of his title, such an arrangement might have
been effected.

(4)[3] "The suppressed abbeys to be restored to their houses, lands and
goods."

Here lay the chief cause of the rebellion. Aske constantly maintained that the suppression of the abbeys and the divisions among
the preachers were alone sufficient to have made the commons rise,
apart from any other real or imaginary grievances. The case for the
monasteries was set forth by Aske in the answer to an interrogatory
which he wrote in the Tower. The draft is hastily written, in some
parts corrected, in others scarcely grammatical, but the skilful use of
words, and the swing and balance of the sentences show that Henry
had reason to fear Aske's "filed tongue":

"[As] to the statute of suppression, he did grudge against the same and so
did all the whole country, because the abbeys in the north parts gave great alms
to poor men and laudably served God; in which parts of late days they had but
small comfort by ghostly teaching. And by occasion of the said suppression
the divine service of almighty God is much minished, great number of masses
unsaid, and the blessed consecration of the sacrament now not used and showed

---

[1] L. and P. xi, 1182 (3).   [2] Ibid. (2).
[3] See note B at end of chapter.

in those places, to the distress of the faith and spiritual comfort to man's soul; the temple of God russed[1] and pulled down, the ornaments and relics of the church of God unreverent used, the towns [*tombs*] and sepulchres of honourable and noble men pulled down and sold, none hospitality now in those places kept, but the farmers for the most part lets and taverns[2] out the farms of the same houses to other farmers, for lucre and advantage to themselves. And the profits of these abbeys yearly goeth out of the country to the King's highness, so that in short space little money, by occasion of the said yearly rents, tenths and first fruits, should be left in the said country, in consideration of the absence of the King's highness in those parts, want of his laws and the frequentation of merchandise. Also divers and many of the said abbeys were in the mountains and desert places, where the people be rude of conditions and not well taught the law of God, and when the said abbeys stood, the said people not only had worldly refreshing in their bodies but also spiritual refuge both by ghostly living of them and also by spiritual information, and preaching; and many their tenants were their fee'd servants to them, and servingmen, well succoured by abbeys; and now not only these tenants and servants want refreshing there, both of meat, cloth and wages and knoweth not now where to have any living, but also strangers and baggers of corn as betwixt Yorkshire, Lancashire, Kendal, Westmorland, and the Bishopric, [for there] was neither carriage of corn and merchandise [but was] greatly succoured both horse and man by the said abbeys, for none was in these parts denied, neither horsemeat nor mansmeat, so that the people were greatly refreshed by the said abbeys, where now they have no such succour; and wherefore the said statute of suppression was greatly to the decay of the commonwealth of that country, and all those parts of all degrees greatly grudged against the same, and yet doth, their duty of allegiance always saved.

"Also the abbeys were one of the beauties of this realm to all men and strangers passing through the same; also all gentlemen [were] much succoured in their needs with money, their young sons there succoured, and in nunneries their daughters brought up in virtue; and also their evidences and money left to the uses of infants in abbeys' hands, always sure there; and such abbeys as were near the danger of sea banks, [were] great maintainers of sea walls and dykes, maintainers and builders of bridges and highways, [and] such other things for the commonwealth."[3]

Even more enthusiastic evidence as to the virtues of the monasteries was given by a Yorkshireman who lived near Roche Abbey in the reign of Edward VI. He too praised the monks for repairing the highways, for lending money to the needy, and for their hospitality and charity. In addition he said that they were good landlords, who never enclosed the common lands, and when corn was scarce, would sell it "under the market" to bring down the price[4]. The Pilgrims' marching song sets forth their praises with the greatest simplicity:

---

[1] *injured.*   [2] *leases.*
[3] L. and P. xii (1), 901 (23); printed in full, Eng. Hist. Rev. v, 561-2.
[4] Cunningham, op. cit. i, bk. v, section 5.

```
" Alack, alack!                    For there they had
  For the church's sake            Both ale and bread
  Poor commons wake                At time of need
      And no marvel!                   And succour great
  For clear it is                  In all distress
  The decay of this                And heaviness
  How the poor shall miss              And well entreat.
      No tongue can tell.
```

```
              In trouble and care
              When that we were
              In manner all bare
                  Of our substance.
              We found good bate
              At churchmen's gate
              Without checkmate
                  Or variance."1
```

The anonymous petition is to the same effect, " Our petition is, the same [*the statute of suppression*] to be annulled and a new qualified order commodious to your Grace to be taken, so that the said monasteries may stand and your commonalty and poor subjects therein to be relieved, and the prayer for the founders and service of God maintained."2

It will be observed that the monks are praised for their public virtues. They might have done all this, except the education of children, even if their private lives were stained with as many vices as are mentioned in the Comperta. The people judged the monks by their deeds, and that their deeds were on the whole good is shown by the very fact that the King attacked them for their private lives, concerning which it was impossible that there should be very reliable evidence.

Allowance must be made for the fact that these eulogies were written by partisans of the monks. Even in Yorkshire all the monasteries did not attain this high standard, as for instance in the case of Whitby, where the Abbot lived on his cliff like a robber baron, in league with the pirates of the coast, and his fee'd men fought with the townspeople, and carried on feuds with the servants of the neighbouring gentlemen3. Nevertheless from the whole evidence it appears that in the north the abbeys still performed useful social duties, and that their destruction was therefore a severe blow. In the south, which was more civilised, their functions had been to a great extent superseded and consequently their loss was less felt.

---

1 Eng. Hist. Rev. v, 345.　　　　　　2 L. and P. xi, 1182 (3).
3 See above, chap. iii.

The wholesale suppression of all the monasteries, without more than nominal discrimination between the useful and the useless, was rightly felt by the Pilgrims to be a great injustice to the north.

In addition to the general objections to the suppression, Aske, being a lawyer, noticed a flaw in the printed version of the statute. He pointed out to Darcy and Constable that the Act granted to the King all monasteries under the value of £200, without any definition as to where the monasteries were situated, whether in England or abroad. In consequence of this Aske considered the statute in that form to be void, although he supposed that there might be "another statute" [i.e. the original] which was fully and legally drawn up[1].

(5) "To have the tenths and first fruits clearly discharged of the same [monasteries] unless the clergy will grant a rent-charge in generality to the augmentation of the Crown."

The arguments against the Act of Annates[2], which granted the first fruits to the King, were:

(a) that no King of England had ever received them before;

(b) that it had not been accepted by the Convocation of York;

(c) that in the case of monasteries it impoverished the monks unduly, as they had nothing to live on during the first year of a new abbot;

(d) that the money was sent out of the north, where there was too little coin already;

(e) that ecclesiastical benefices might by death, deprivation, or resignation become vacant several times in one year, and as the King demanded first fruits on each new appointment, the value of the benefice was for the time reduced to nothing, and in the case of monasteries the brethren were completely ruined[3].

This last complaint expresses the origin of the whole trouble. The King's argument was that tenths and first fruits had always been paid to the Pope, and that the clergy were just as well able to pay them to him. Also it was better that the money should be kept in the kingdom and spent on the needs of the government than that it should be sent abroad and nothing received in return. But the payments to Rome had only fallen due at reasonably long intervals; even then they had been a grievance, but now that they were collected by the King at close quarters, and made to yield as

---

[1] L. and P. xii (1), 901 (44); printed in full, Eng. Hist. Rev. v, 569.
[2] See above, chap. i.
[3] L. and P. xii (1), 901 (23); printed in full, Eng. Hist. Rev. v, 562–3.

much as could possibly be squeezed out of the Church, the grievance
became intolerable.

The clergy themselves naturally wished that all the payments
should be abolished[1], but the laymen were of the opinion that though
the Statute of Firstfruits was "a decay to all religion," the tenths
"might be borne well enough."[2] They were themselves petitioning
against the heavy taxes, and they did not intend that the clergy
should escape their share of the burden, although the laity were
willing to defend the clergy from extortion. The Pilgrims thought
that the case might be met by a fixed rent charge paid by the
Church to the Crown. The same idea is expressed in two of
the articles attributed to Aske. One complains of the "first fruits,
augmentations and other extortions that the lord Chancellor, lord
Cromwell and their servants yearly collect from all parts of the
realm." The other, which is mutilated at the beginning, proposes
that a charge should be reserved, probably upon the monastic lands,
"which is thought to be sufficient for defence of the said realm and
maintenance of lawful war, if it be kept for the same use."[3]

(6) "To have the Friars Observants restored to their houses."

As this order had been suppressed earlier than the others, by
different means and for different reasons[4], the repeal of the Act
of Suppression would not be sufficient to restore it, and it was
therefore mentioned separately.

(7) "To have the heretics, bishops and temporal, and their sect, to have
condign punishment by fire or such other, or else to try the quarrel with us and
our partakers in battle."

Aske said that this was taken from the Lincolnshire articles[5],
although it differed from them in naming none of the heretics. The
article was probably drawn up in this general form because the question
as to who were heretics was being very carefully discussed. The ten
articles of religion were accepted as being a satisfactory exposition of
the Faith. Archbishop Lee considered that they were all that could
be desired. Reginald Pole found no fault with their contents, which
he held to be in accordance with the Roman standard, although he
was shocked that they should be issued by the King's authority[6].
The Pilgrims evaded this last difficulty by laying stress on the part

---

[1] L. and P. xi, 1245.
[2] L. and P. xii (1), 901 (19); printed in full, Eng. Hist. Rev. v, 559.
[3] L. and P. xi, 1182 (2).   [4] See above, chap. iv.
[5] L. and P. xii (1), 901 (30); printed in full, Eng. Hist. Rev. v, 560.
[6] L. and P. xi, 376.

which Convocation had taken in drawing up the articles. In the propositions attributed to Aske, it is desired "that the book of articles lately commanded, by the advice of the Catholic bishops and doctors, be taught," and that those who offended against it should be punished. Among the supposed offenders are named the Archbishop of Canterbury, the Bishops of Rochester and Dublin, the Lord Chancellor, the Lord Privy Seal, and probably others whose names are lost[1].

In order that heresy should be clearly defined, Robert Chaloner laid before Aske, Constable, and the other leaders who drew up the Pilgrims' articles, a memorial on the subject. "In that book first were, as it had been interrogatories to the spirituality, touching our faith, to prove whose works and books were heresy by their opinion, and who of the bishops and others preached and maintained these books, being heresy, and by that means to have proved who, by their opinion, had been heretics, as then it was said friar Barnes was for his opinions put in the Tower."[2] Richard Bowyer laid before Aske certain books which he "articled to be heresy."[3] In the course of the discussion, Darcy declared that "he would be none heretic in consenting to the opinions" expressed in "the new preaching of certain new bishops."[4]

The books and the interrogatories were laid before the council of divines in order that they might pronounce on their doctrines, and meanwhile the laity expressed their opinion in this general resolution.

Although no names were entered in the petition, the commons "noted the bishops of Canterbury [*Cranmer*], Worcester [*Latimer*], Rochester [*Hilsey*] and St David's [*Barlow*] to be heretics."[5] It was objected against all of them that they had been named in the Lincolnshire petition, that they favoured the new learning and the opinions of Luther and Tyndale, that they preached against the religious orders and supported the Act of Suppression, disregarded the customs and ceremonies of the Church, preached against the Pope, and supported the royal supremacy. In particular it was alleged against the Bishop of Worcester that "he was before abjured, or else should have borne a faggot for his preaching,"

---

[1] L. and P. xi, 1182 (2).
[2] L. and P. xii (1), 901 (107); printed in full, Eng. Hist. Rev. v, 570.
[3] L. and P. xii (1), 901 (30); printed in full, Eng. Hist. Rev. v, 560.
[4] L. and P. xii (1), 945 (48); printed in full, Eng. Hist. Rev. v, 572.
[5] L. and P. xii (1), 901 (31); printed in full, Eng. Hist. Rev. v, 560-1.

and against the Archbishop of Canterbury that he had not received his pall from Rome, and that he had pronounced the divorce between the King and Queen Katharine[1]. It was also said, with a manifest allusion to the execution of More and Fisher, that the King should mingle mercy with justice, for though he had the power of life and death, he could not bring to life a man who had been executed, and therefore no one should be condemned without the counsel of the most virtuous bishops, not of those who were mere time-servers[2].

It is easier to unite in hate than in love; all the Pilgrims may not have been sound on the question of the papal supremacy, but none of them had a good word to say for the heretic bishops. Still the Pilgrims endeavoured to act fairly even by these men, for though it cannot be denied that they would dearly have liked to burn them, they referred their case for further consideration to the spirituality.

(11)[3] "That Dr Legh and Dr Layton have condign punishment for their extortions from religious houses and other abominable acts."

After the council at York, Aske sent orders into Cumberland and Westmorland that evidence should be collected as to the behaviour of the monastic commissioners[4]. The clergy in those parts were out of sympathy with the Pilgrims and would determine nothing[5], but similar orders were probably sent into other districts where the witnesses were more willing. Only one fragment of their evidence is preserved, and that not of a very serious character; it was said that the servants of the commissioners used the vestments from the suppressed abbeys for saddle-cloths[6]. It is not certain what further accusations were brought against Legh and Layton on this occasion, but in 1539 one of Bishop Tunstall's servants told a similar story. The commissioners stripped the gold and silver from the relics of the saints and threw the bones contemptuously away. On one occasion they gave some ornamented relics to a bystander and "bade him pluck off the silver and garnish his dagger withal," but he, horror-stricken, preserved what they gave him intact, and afterwards gathered up the bones they had dishonoured[7]. Such outrages against popular feeling aroused the greatest indignation and "in all parts of the realm men's hearts much grudge...against the visitors, especially against Doctors Legh and Layton."[8]

---

[1] L. and P. xii (1), 901 (32); printed in full, Eng. Hist. Rev. v, 567.

[2] L. and P. xi, 1244.　　　　[3] See note C at end of chapter.

[4] See above, chap. xiii.

[5] L. and P. xii (1), 687 (2); printed in full, Wilson, op. cit. no. xxii.

[6] L. and P. xii. (1), 786 (ii).　　　　[7] L. and P. xiv (2), 750.

[8] L. and P. xii (1), 6; printed in full, Eng. Hist. Rev. v, 342.

(18) "The privileges and rights of the Church to be confirmed by Act of Parliament. Priests not to suffer by the sword unless degraded. A man to be saved by his book. Sanctuary to save a man for all causes in extreme need, and the Church for forty days, and further according to the laws as they were used in the beginning of the King's days."

The first clause of this article is one of several which show the Pilgrims' respect for constitutional procedure. It was not enough that the King should promise to grant their petition, the articles must be ratified by the act of the whole nation.

The later clauses are frankly reactionary, but it may be urged in their favour that the laws at that time were very severe, and were enforced with great inequality. Any custom which tended to mitigate their severity had a certain use, and might serve to give the poor man a little protection against the rich. The abolition of privileges, even of those which were open to so much abuse as the right of sanctuary, made the weak more helpless.

In the case of the punishment of priests without degradation, it might fairly be maintained that a serious subject had been treated too hastily, as the clause which put an end to this privilege had been tacked on to the end of a re-enactment of some earlier statutes dealing with sanctuary and benefit of clergy[1].

(19) "The liberties of the Church to have their old customs, as the county palatine of Durham, Beverley, Ripon, St Peter of York, and such other, by Act of Parliament."

The policy of the Tudors was centralisation, but while the central government was still so ineffective, the advantages of centralisation were not as obvious as they are at present. Local feeling was very strong, and all of the "liberties of the Church" keenly resented any interference with their privileges, although with the passing of the feudal system the reasons for their exemption had disappeared. While the King was anxious to abolish privileges he was slow to grant the equivalent rights; for instance, most of the privileges of the county palatine of Durham were abolished, but the shire of Durham was not allowed to send representatives to the House of Commons. This article was included in deference to the feelings of the men of Durham, Beverley and elsewhere, but the point was not of much importance in itself.

II. Constitutional Grievances.

(3) "That the Lady Mary may be made legitimate, and the former statute therein annulled for the danger of the title that might incur to the crown of Scotland: that to be by parliament."

---

[1] See above, chap. i.

All Henry's efforts to obtain a legitimate male heir had ended in plunging the question of the succession into hopeless confusion. The acknowledgment of Mary was the solution which would be most acceptable to the nation at large. She was beloved for her own sake and for her mother's, she was undoubtedly Henry's daughter, she represented the old faith, and she stood between the crown and the detested Scots claim. The arguments in her favour were set forth as follows:

(*a*) Mary was legitimate "if any laws in Christendom may have place." The process by which her mother's marriage was declared void had been hurried through by the King while the cause was still before the Court of Rome, the authority which both the parties had acknowledged. "This cannot stand, a man to be both judge in his own case and party."[1] Although the Archbishop of Canterbury had pronounced the marriage null, yet he had no power to do so while the cause was being tried before his superior, the Pope, and the Archbishop's own consecration was doubtful, as he had not received the pall from Rome[2].

(*b*) The statute which pronounced Mary to be illegitimate was passed before the Pope's decision on her mother's appeal was known in England[3], and it was unjust to condemn her to the penalty before the judgment had been delivered[4].

(*c*) If the Pope's decision was in her favour, she would still be illegitimate by statute, from which it would appear that the statute had been made "more for some displeasure towards her and her friends, than for any just cause."[5] The wording of this objection shows that the decision of the papal Consistory Court was not generally known in England, although judgment had been given in favour of Katharine more than two years before, on 23 March 1534[6].

(*d*) She and her friends did not deserve displeasure; they ought rather to receive the highest consideration, as through her mother she was related to the greatest European monarch, whose family had long been allied with England[7].

(*e*) "The said Lady Mary ought to be favoured for her great

---

[1] L. and P. xi, 1182 (3).

[2] L. and P. xii (1), 901 (32); printed in full, Eng. Hist. Rev. v, 562.

[3] Froude, op. cit. i, chap. vii.

[4] L. and P. xii (1), 901 (23); printed in full, Eng. Hist. Rev. v, 562.

[5] Ibid.

[6] Pollard, op. cit. chap. xii.

[7] L. and P. xii (1), 901 (23); printed in full, Eng. Hist. Rev. v, 562.

virtues then and yet esteemed to be in her...for the said Lady Mary is marvellously beloved for her virtue in the hearts of the people."[1]

(*f*) She ought to be restored to the succession because her cousin, Charles V, might take up her cause, and prohibit the valuable trade with Flanders[2].

(8) " Lord Cromwell, the Lord Chancellor [Audley] and Sir Richard Riche to have condign punishment, as subvertors of the good laws of the realm and maintainers and inventers of heretics."

Aske said little against Cromwell and his underlings except in the matter of heresy[3]. The expressions of less moderate men may be learnt from the only one of the " books of advice " laid before the council of Pilgrims which has been preserved. Aske mentioned three such papers, Chaloner's, Babthorpe's and Sir Thomas Tempest's[4]. Chaloner's related principally to religion, and Babthorpe's "touched but few matters in the petitions; "[5] it therefore seems probable that the extant paper is the one which Sir Thomas Tempest sent to Pontefract because he was too ill to come himself. In form it is to some extent a reply to the King's letter to the gentlemen. The exordium is that " the King should [condescend to] our petition against the lollard and traitor Thomas Cromwell, his disciples and adherents, or at least exile him and them forth of the realm." The writer begins by discussing the question whether subjects have a right to appoint the King's Council, which Henry angrily denied. The Pilgrims, however, pointed out that it was essential for the welfare of the kingdom that the Council should be composed of patriots. If the King appointed men merely because they were personally pleasing to him, his subjects for his own sake must take some precaution, as in the case of "the council of Paris in France," for if the King preferred his favourites to the nobles, baronage and commonwealth of the realm, he would come to a miserable end like Rehoboam, Edward II, and Richard II. After touching on some other points, the writer enumerated Cromwell's offences. He was a traitor to the King, for he encouraged him to break his coronation oath, and caused him to lose the love of his subjects by pillaging them, and to lose the respect of foreign princes by his perjury. Cromwell had boasted that he would make the King the richest prince in Christendom, but instead of that he had made him the poorest, for

---

[1] L. and P. xii (1), 901 (23) ; printed in full, Eng. Hist. Rev. v, 562.   [2] Ibid.

[3] L. and P. xii (1), 901 (54); printed in full, Eng. Hist. Rev. v, 571.

[4] L. and P. xii (1), 901 (25) ; printed in full, Eng. Hist. Rev. v, 560.

[5] L. and P. xii (1), 901 (27 misprinted 107) ; printed in full, Eng. Hist. Rev. v, 570.

the riches of his kingdom were spent, his subjects were in rebellion, and his allies abroad had grown hostile. The writer concluded by a solemn warning that there could be no safety for any of the Pilgrims until Cromwell was dead. They saw what was the fate of the Lincolnshire rebels. Cromwell must be executed, and the treasure which he and his disciples had accumulated might be used for the good of the realm. If Cromwell were not put out of the way, it would be better to fight while the rebels' situation was so promising. The Duke of Norfolk and the other southern noblemen ought to help on the destruction of the arch-traitor, "for their part is not unlike to be in after this."[1]

This invective shows clearly how successful Henry had been in throwing the whole responsibility for his measures upon Cromwell's shoulders. The Pilgrims believed that they were saving both the King and the country from the power of a wicked man. They did not realise that Cromwell was the tool, not the principal.

Audley and Riche were not so much considered. They came in for a share of the hatred excited by Cromwell, because they were looked upon as his dependents. They had succeeded to the offices formerly held by the good Sir Thomas More, Audley as Chancellor and Riche as Speaker of the House of Commons[2].

(12) "Reformation for the election of knights of the shire and burgesses, and for the use among the lords in the parliament house after their ancient custom."

Henry asserted that Parliament had sanctioned everything which he had done. The Pilgrims retorted that "these parliaments were of none authority nor virtue, for if they should be truly named, they should be called councils of the King's appointment, and not parliaments."[3] Sir Thomas Tempest, if it was he, declared that members were no longer elected, but were appointed by the King. As an instance he mentioned Sir Francis Brian, who knew nothing about the affairs of the borough[4] which he nominally represented in the last parliament. His seat was given to him in order that he might speak against religion and make the grants which the King demanded. Moreover it was no longer permitted that the King's affairs should be discussed in parliament, although the whole realm suffered for the King's sin, as Israel did for David's[5].

[1] L. and P. xi, 1244.
[2] Dict. Nat. Biog. arts. Audley and Riche.
[3] L. and P. xi, 1244.   [4] Its name is illegible.
[5] L. and P. xi, 1244.

The propositions attributed to Aske mention the same points.

"Such persons as were elected to the said parliament were named in the King's letters....

Every burgess of parliament ought to be [an] inhabitant within the borough he represents; yet many were to the contrary, yea, that of the worst sort.

The old custom was that none of the King's servants should be of the Commons' House; yet most of that house were the King's servants.

If a knight or a burgess died during parliament his room should continue void to the end of the same[1]; and it is not unknown that—"

Here the manuscript is mutilated, but at the end the writer seems to be arguing that the acts of this packed House of Commons were all void[2].

Another parliamentary grievance was the insufficient representation of the north. This was not due to any malice on the part of the King, but rather to the poverty and indifference of the Yorkshire boroughs. Members were returned by fifteen boroughs, besides those for the shire and city of York, in the reigns of Edward I and Edward III[3], but of these all but two had become virtually disfranchised long before the reign of Henry VIII. In the case of Pontefract, it was recorded that in the time of Henry VI a return had been made for this place, but the inhabitants could not afford to send a member[4]. The other boroughs must have fallen off in the same way during the Scots wars and the Wars of the Roses. In 1529 Yorkshire sent to Westminster two knights of the shire, two members each from the city of York and the borough of Hull, which were separate counties, and two from the borough of Scarborough[5]. The returns for the parliament of 1536 are lost, but according to Aske's statement Scarborough was the only Yorkshire borough represented in it, apart from York and Hull[6]. It is interesting to see that reawakened interest in political affairs made the Yorkshire gentlemen regret the loss of their members, which was due to the indifference of their ancestors.

It was suggested at Doncaster that burgesses should be returned by Beverley, Ripon, Richmond, Pontefract, Wakefield, Skipton and Kendal[7], but it is not certain whether this point was discussed at Pontefract[8].

---

[1] See note D at end of chapter.
[2] L. and P. xi, 1182 (2). [3] See note E at end of chapter.
[4] Park, Parliamentary Representation of Yorkshire, Pontefract.
[5] Ibid. York, Hull, Scarborough.
[6] L. and P. xii (1), 6 (ii); printed in full, Eng. Hist. Rev. v, 343.
[7] Ibid.
[8] L. and P. xii (1), 901 (37); printed in full, Eng. Hist. Rev. v, 567.

As for the ancient customs of the House of Lords, Darcy described to Aske recent innovations. In the first place, matters touching the spiritual authority had formerly been determined in Convocation and not by the Lords.

Secondly, it had been usual for the Lords to begin their proceedings after mass, by reading the first chapter of Magna Carta, "touching the rights and liberties of the Church," but this custom had been discontinued. It seems to be alluded to in the list of propositions attributed to Aske, "that the Church of England may enjoy the liberties granted them by Magna Carta, and used until six or seven years past."[1] The Pilgrims anticipated the "discovery" of Magna Carta (so far as it affected the Church) by the parliamentary opponents of the Stewarts[2].

Thirdly, when any bill touching the prerogative of the crown was introduced into the House of Commons, it had been customary for the Lords to request to have a copy of it, that they might take counsel's opinion as to whether the bill was constitutional; but of late they had had great difficulty in obtaining copies of the bills, partly through "default in those of the Chancery in the use of their office amongst the lords," and partly because the bills were rushed through both houses without proper warning[3].

Thus the twelfth article in the Pilgrims' petition comprised the following points:

(*a*) that the King should not interfere in elections;

(*b*) that complete freedom of speech should be enjoyed in the House of Commons;

(*c*) that additional representation should be given to Yorkshire;

(*d*) that spiritual matters should be dealt with by Convocation;

(*e*) that the House of Lords should be supplied with copies of the bills laid before the House of Commons.

(15) "To have a parliament at Nottingham or York, and that shortly."

This was the necessary corollary of the last article. The reformed parliament must meet at once to undo the work of its corrupt predecessors, and it must be held at some place where it would not be so completely in the power of the King as it was at Westminster. The Pilgrims did not believe that there would be freedom of debate so near the Tower, but at York a brave man might venture to utter an opinion which it would be mere suicide to whisper in London.

---

[1] L. and P. xi, 1182 (2).   [2] Pollard, op. cit. chap. ii.

[3] L. and P. xii (1), 901 (39) and (40); printed in full, Eng. Hist. Rev. v, 568.

This article and the preceding one bear upon the vexed question of whether there was or was not freedom of speech in Henry VIII's parliaments. Without plunging into that controversy, we must simply note that the Pilgrims believed there ought to be freedom of speech, but did not believe that it existed. One scrap of evidence comes from Lord Montague, who used to talk over the business just transacted in Parliament with the Earl of Huntingdon. They both "did always grudge and murmur against things determined there," and "would say they were but knaves and heretics that gave over, and that such as did agree to things there did the same for fear."[1] This may have been merely the peevishness of a defeated opposition[2], but the Pilgrims had some grounds for their belief, as Darcy, after opposing a royal measure, had not been allowed to resume his seat in the House of Lords. In any case this demand of the Pilgrims is worth noting. Their expedient for securing free speech appears rather primitive, but it is necessary to bear in mind what a great difference there was at that period between the home counties and the more remote parts of England. Henry himself could not seize a man until he came within his reach, and the King's arm was not long. This makes it the more extraordinary that he was able to lure so many of his victims into his grasp.

(17) "Pardon by Act of Parliament for all recognizances, statutes and penalties new forfeited during the time of this commotion."

The general act of indemnity was the first work which the new parliament would be called upon to do.

(16) "The statute of the declaration of the crown by will to be repealed."

This statute aroused great indignation. Among the commons it was believed to have been framed in order that Cromwell himself might be brought into the succession[3]. Aske and his more enlightened colleagues were not deceived by this wild fancy, but they had substantial reasons to urge against the statute:

(a) First and most important from an Englishman's point of view, there had never been such a law before[4].

(b) Private men did not enjoy the right of bequeathing their lands as they pleased, although such a right would be very beneficial to them for the payment of their debts and provision for their younger children. It was unreasonable to give this power to the

---

[1] L. and P. xiii (2), 804 (6).   [2] Pollard, op. cit. chap. x.
[3] See above, chap. xiii.
[4] L. and P. xii (1), 901 (23); printed in full, Eng. Hist. Rev. v, 563–4.

King, who required it less than a private man, and thereby to make a distinction between inheritance of the crown of England and inheritance of private property in England[1]. This is an allusion to the unpopular Statute of Uses.

(c) Henry IV had made an entail of the crown, but Edward IV had repealed it, by the advice of his wise men. Henry VII had also wished to make an entail, but had been prevented, "and King Henry VII was bruited and called the wisest prince and king of the world."[2]

This point was characteristic of all the Lancastrian kings. As their title to the crown by descent was defective, they sought to have it confirmed by parliament[3]. It is curious that Aske should have thought that Henry VII did not make such a settlement, for the first statute of his first parliament confirmed the crown of England to himself and his heirs, as had been done in the case of Henry IV[4]. There is however a great difference between these acts and that of Henry VIII. In the earlier measures the crown was expressly entailed on the King's heirs according to the law of the land, whereas Henry was empowered to name his own heir.

(d) If the King willed the crown away from the rightful heir apparent, i.e. his next of kin, the result would be a war of succession, as it would be impossible to try the case, because there were no precedents[5]. One of the questions to be put to the clergy, in the list which is possibly Aske's, bears on this point,—"If the King by his last will will his realm after his death, especially out of the right line of inheritance, whether his subjects are bound by God's laws to obey the will?"[6]

In this objection Aske goes right to the heart of the position taken up by the defenders of the act. They are unanimous in saying that the nation delegated such power to the King in order to avoid civil war on his death. But it appeared to the Pilgrims that the act, far from averting a war of succession, made such a catastrophe almost inevitable. If the King merely named his natural heir as his successor, the act was pointless, for that person would have succeeded in any case. The late King's will might strengthen his or her position, but could have no material importance. The

---

[1] L. and P. xii (1), 901 (23, 2, 5); printed in full, Eng. Hist. Rev. v, 564.
[2] Ibid.
[3] Stubbs, Constit. Hist. of Eng. iii, chap. xviii, sect. 310, 313, 358.
[4] Pollard, The Reign of Henry VII from Contemporary Sources, ii, no. 8.
[5] L. and P. xii (1), 901 (23); printed in full, Eng. Hist. Rev. v, 564.
[6] L. and P. xi, 1182 (2).

only object of the statute, they thought, must be to enable the King to alter the succession " out of the right line of inheritance," and there could be no possible guarantee that the disinherited heir by birth would acknowledge the statute to be binding. The Pilgrims concluded from these arguments that the statute should either be annulled altogether, leaving the crown to descend according to the law of the land, or else that the King's heir should be named at once by act of parliament[1].

(*e*) The next objection brought against the statute shows the direction which the gentlemen's fears were taking. " If the crown were given by the King's highness to an alien, as we doubt not his grace will not do so, how should this alien by reason have it, for he in his person was not made able to take it, no more than if I would give lands to an alien, it is a void gift to the alien, because he is not born under the allegiance of this crown."[2]

The gentlemen did not believe that Henry could or would make Cromwell his heir, but they feared that he might bring into the succession the King of Scotland, or still more probably James V's half-sister, Lady Margaret Douglas. The idea of a Scots monarch sitting on the throne of England was detested in the north, and if Henry VIII had allowed his bitterness against his daughter Mary to carry him so far as to alter the succession in favour of her cousins, there can be no doubt that war would have followed.

(*f*) Finally it would appear very strange and ridiculous to other nations that in England there should be one law for the King and another for the people, and, what was still more inconvenient, that it should not be known who was the heir to the crown until after the King's death[3].

For all these reasons and many more " not necessary to be opened, unless it were in parliament," the Pilgrims determined that the statute ought to be repealed.

III. Legal Grievances.

(10) "The statute of handguns and crossbows to be repealed, except in the King's parks or forests."

This statute was a re-enactment of two earlier statutes, which prohibited the use of handguns and crossbows to persons whose income was less than £100 a year. Exceptions from its operation were made in favour of towns and fortresses on or within seven

---

[1] L. and P. xii (1), 901 (23, 2, 5); printed in full, Eng. Hist. Rev. v, 564.
[2] Ibid.   [3] Ibid.

miles of the coast, or the Scots marches, and also in favour of the inhabitants of Northumberland, Durham, Westmorland and Cumberland[1]. Its object was to keep up the practice of shooting with the long bow, which was falling into disuse, but all such attempts at coercion are inevitably unpopular, and this statute must have been particularly resented in Yorkshire, by reason of the contrast with the neighbouring counties which were exempted from its provisions.

Apart from any such local feeling there was a deeper motive in the opposition to this statute. The men of England dimly perceived that in their weapons lay their last hope of freedom. Legislation even about the nature of their weapons roused their suspicions. They felt that it would make a distinction between themselves and the regular soldiers whom the King might employ. The long bow, still the principal instrument of war in England, was becoming obsolete and the English bowmen respected if they did not fear the arquebus men used in the continental wars. The success of the Pilgrimage up to this point was in fact due to the absence of any trained soldiers in England. The revolt in Germany was crushed by the veterans who returned home from Italy after the battle of Pavia[2]. The Norfolk rebellion in 1549 was suppressed by means of German and Italian mercenaries[3]. Henry's foreign wars had been too brief to produce bodies of seasoned troopers, and it must be put to his credit that he had not yet employed mercenaries. But he might do so whenever he saw fit, and to equalise matters as far as possible the commons wished to be free to use whatever weapons they found most effective.

(20) "To have the statute that no man shall not will his lands repealed."

This was the Statute of Uses, which has already been discussed so fully[4] that it is not necessary to do more than recapitulate Aske's arguments against it. He seems to have considered that the law with respect to the inheritance of land held in chief of the King had been unsatisfactory before the statute was passed, and he said that this article would not have been included if it had not occurred in the Lincolnshire petition. When he went to court he declared his opinion of the old law fully to the King[5]. In the propositions

[1] 25 Hen. VIII, cap. 17.
[2] Bax, op. cit. 50, 322–4.
[3] Russell, op. cit. 91, 121, 141.
[4] See above, chap. i.
[5] L. and P. xii (1), 901 (23); printed in full, Eng. Hist. Rev. v, 563.

attributed to Aske there are two mutilated articles which appear to suggest that the King should cause inquisition to be made, and the Exchequer rolls to be searched, in order that it might be clearly ascertained which were the lands held in chief of the King, as at present much trouble and expense was caused by uncertainty on this point[1].

But Aske did not consider that the Statute of Uses was rightly framed to reform the old state of things. In the first place it gave a man in some ways more opportunity of defeating the royal claims on his lands; secondly, it altered the old forms of pleading at law and introduced great confusion; thirdly, it prevented men from raising money on their lands by making it possible for their sons to repudiate their debts[2].

The first objection roused the interest of his examiners, and they wanted to know how the King's rights might now be defeated[3]. Aske replied that it was difficult for him to set forth the matter, as he had been separated from his books for so long, but the judges and others deeply learned in the law could explain it, and there was one case which he himself could give from his own knowledge[4]. "If a man held land of the King as of his duchy or of the crown, and have licence to alien and do alien to an estranger to the use of the stranger, upon condition that he shall execute an estatute to him for term of his life, the remainder thereof to his son or heir apparent, and to the heirs of his body legitime, the remainder in fee simple to a younger of his sons or daughters or to an estranger, in this case his son cannot be in ward, nor the lands, for he comes in after his father as a purchaser; and collusion it cannot be, because the remainder of the fee simple is in a stranger."[5]

Aske was expressing the lawyer's point of view in this. Most of the gentlemen assembled at Pontefract would object to the Statute of Uses, not because it could be evaded, but because they did not for the moment see how to evade it. In the end Aske's view proved to be correct, and the effects of the statute were the very opposite to those which the King expected[6].

(21) "The statutes of treasons for words and such-like made since 21 Henry VIII to be repealed."

The chief reason that the people grudged against the treason

---

[1] L. and P. xi, 1182 (2).
[2] L. and P. xii (1), 901 (23); printed in full, Eng. Hist. Rev. v, 563.
[3] L. and P. xii (1), 945 (4); printed in full, Eng. Hist. Rev. v, 566.
[4] L. and P. xii (1), 901 (23).   [5] Ibid.   [6] Pollock, op. cit. 98.

laws was that they were prohibited from discussing the King's title of supreme head of the Church. They "thought it very strait that a man might not declare his conscience in such a great case," for it was a matter that touched the health of their souls[1]. There seem to be one or two allusions to the treason laws in the paper attributed to Sir Thomas Tempest. One has been noted above[2]. Another may be implied when the writer refers to the good days of Henry VII, who allowed men condemned to death to buy their pardons, and "if the faulter had amend[ed] his condition and grown to be a good man again, when he had amended the King would have withdrawn his wrath and by one mean or other have looked so of him that he should have had such a thing as should help him as much as his fine hindered him."[3] In the propositions attributed to Aske it is requested that "acts of parliament...contrary to the law of God may be avoided [made void] and the acts concerning high treason reformed."[4]

On the whole there was little discussion of these terrible laws, because no one ventured to criticise them. Aske's reply to a question on the subject breaks off suddenly, as if even his examiners in the Tower did not dare to hear all that an outspoken man could say on the subject[5].

(22) "That the common laws may have place as was used in the beginning of the reign, and that no injunctions be granted unless the matter has been determined in Chancery."

This and the following article are included in one among the propositions attributed to Aske: "that the laws may be used as at the beginning of the King's reign, and that injunctions, subpoenas, and privy seals be not granted so commonly and into countries distant from London as of late time they have been."[6] In another place Aske accused Audley the Lord Chancellor of "playing of ambedexter in granting and dissolving of injunctions."[7]

The theory which underlay the Chancellor's power to grant injunctions is well known. The Common Law courts administered justice according to law and precedent, but this, although sufficient in the average case, might bear hardly on individuals in special cases. When this happened, the individual had the power to appeal

---

[1] L. and P. xii (1), 901 (44); printed in full, Eng. Hist. Rev. v, 570.

[2] See article 7.   [3] L. and P. xi, 1244.

[4] Ibid. 1182 (2).

[5] L. and P. xii (1), 901 (23); printed in full, Eng. Hist. Rev. v, 565.

[6] L. and P. xi, 1182 (2).

[7] L. and P. xii (1), 6; printed in full, Eng. Hist. Rev. v, 343.

to the Chancellor who, as keeper of the King's conscience, was able to grant "grace," "conscience," or "equity," in the form of an injunction which bound the other party in the suit either to refrain from prosecuting in a particular court, or to cease from the conduct which was causing complaint[1]. There was no objection to this power in general, except the universal one that the remedy was in practice open only to the rich, but in the hands of such a man as Audley the granting of injunctions was liable to abuse. The Pilgrims' article " means that the chancery may interfere with an action at common law, only if that action is opening a question already decided in the chancery."[2]

At this particular period, however, the Chancellor's power had another and more dangerous aspect. There is some reason to believe that England was on the verge of a " Reception" of the Civil Code of Justinian similar to that which took place in Germany. Although Reginald Pole was an admirer of the Civil Law[3], yet its chief advocates were found among Henry's chosen servants, Gardiner, Bonner, Layton, Legh[4] and others, and " partly by injunctions, as well before verdicts, judgments and executions as after, and partly by writs of Sub Poena issuing out of the King's court of chancery" the " Common Laws of this realm...hath not been only stayed of their direct course, but also many times altered and violated by reason of Decrees made in the said court of chancery, most grounded upon law civil and upon matter depending in the conscience and discretion of the hearers thereof, who being civilians and not learned in the Common Laws, setting aside the said Common Laws, determine the weighty causes of this realm according either to the said Law Civil or to their own conscience ; which Law Civil is to the subjects of this realm unknown, and they not bound nor inheritable to the same law, and which judgments and decrees grounded upon conscience are not grounded nor made upon any rule certain or law written."[5]

The great bulwark of English Common Law against the Civil Law was the body of lawyers of the inns of court[6], and these champions were numerously represented among the Pilgrims, in whose ranks they carried on the struggle with weapons in their hands. Maitland says, "It will be seen that in 1536 the cause of 'the common laws'

---

[1] Baildon, Select Cases in the Court of Chancery (Selden Soc.), preface.
[2] Maitland, English Law and the Renaissance, note 51.
[3] Maitland, op. cit. ibid. note 11.   [4] Ibid. note 33.
[5] Acts of the Privy Council, 1547–50, pp. 48–50.   [6] Maitland, op. cit.

found itself in very queer company; illiterate, monkish and papistical company, which apparently has made a man of 'Anibaptist.'"[1] If the great jurist had gone more deeply into the Pilgrimage of Grace, he would have been surprised to find how familiar that company was to him.

(23) "That men north of Trent summoned on subpoena appear at York, or by attorney, unless it be directed on pain of allegiance, or for like matters concerning the King."

This article is closely connected with the preceding one. It is another illustration of the wide separation that there was between London and the North, when the journey was long, costly and dangerous, and the countryman in London found himself in a strange land.

(24) "A remedy against escheators for finding false offices and extorting fees."

This was one of the grievances connected with the Statute of Uses, and it is mentioned in the propositions attributed to Aske under that heading. As the lands held *in capite* are not certainly known "certain of the Exchequer for money finds untrue offices against the King and in like case oftentimes bribes and extortions the King's —." Here the manuscript is mutilated[2].

Complaints against escheators are older than the Statute of Uses, and occur among the grievances of the rebels in almost all revolts, both before and after the Pilgrimage. The escheators were the King's servants, who used their authority to bully and plunder the provincials. Another of the propositions attributed to Aske refers to the same injuries; it is against those who obtain "rooms" and "offices" "for maintenance of their authority and their children's blood," and who have "bribed and extortioned the King's subjects." It is requested that they may be punished and honourable men put in their places[3].

The Pilgrims associated all such abuses with Cromwell. The writer supposed to be Sir Thomas Tempest complained that Cromwell's servants and his servants' servants "thinks to have the law in every place here ordered at their commandment, and will take upon them to command sheriff, justices of peace, coram and of session in their master's name at their pleasure, witness Brabson and Dakyns."[4]

---

[1] Maitland, op. cit. note 51; see above, art. 1. [2] L. and P. xi, 1182 (2).
[3] Ibid. [4] Ibid. 1244.

IV. Economic Grievances.

(9) "That the lands in Westmorland, Cumberland, Kendal, Dent, Sedbergh, Furness, and the abbey lands in Mashamshire, Kirkbyshire, Netherdale, may be by tenant right, and the lord to have, at every change, two years' rent for gressom, according to the grant now made by the lords to the commons there. This to be done by Act of Parliament."

The "gressom," "ingressum" or "gyrsuma" was the fine paid by a tenant on entering upon his lands. In order to understand the peasants' grievances with respect to this fine, it is necessary to sketch the position of the tenant with regard to his landlord in these districts.

The commons of the districts named in the article held their lands by tenant right. "In this mode of tenure, the lord could not impose his will on the tenant—they were joint owners. The rights of lord and tenant were determined by the custom of the manor. When a tenant died, his estate escheated to the lord till the heir was declared as in tenure in capite. The lord was obliged to admit the heir, and the fine on admission was not arbitrary, like some other phases of tenure, but according to the custom of the manor." In the thirteenth century a fine of one year's rent seems to have been usual[1]. After the Black Death, when it was very difficult to find tenants, the lords of manors were often content with merely nominal fines; in 1358 at Pittington in Durham a tenant came in on payment of "one urchinne," i.e. a hedgehog[2]. But with the increase of enclosure and sheep-farming, the position of the lord altered completely. The tenant was no longer necessary to him, and the lord therefore began to disregard the custom of the manor and to demand much higher fines. If the tenant could pay, it was so much ready money into the lord's pocket. If he could not, he was evicted and the farm was thrown open as part of the lord's sheep pastures. This was going on all over the country. In a case which was brought before the Court of Star Chamber in 1527, the fine of land at Thingdon in Northamptonshire was raised from 6s. 3½d. to 30s.[3] The commons of Kendal complained that where the ingressum had been 4 marks it was now £40[4]. When they took

---

[1] Information supplied by the Rev. J. Wilson; cf. Leadam, Select Cases in the Court of Star Chamber, II, pp. lxiii–lxv; Cunningham, op. cit. I, bk. v, chap. 5, section 152, and references there; Tawney, The Agrarian Problem in the Sixteenth Century, 47, 50, 146–50, 297, 301.

[2] Booth, Halmota Prior. Dun. (Surtees Soc.), p. 21.

[3] Leadam, op. cit. pp. lxii–iii.

[4] L. and P. XII (1), 914; cf. Ibid. 478 and 687.

up arms the first thing they did was to force their landlord to promise that he would observe their ancient customs with regard to the ingressum. From the wording of the article it appears that such promises had been obtained in other districts also.

The commons of Westmorland demanded that "consernynge ye gyrsumes for power mens to bee layd aparte bot only penny farm penny gyrsum."[1] The fixing of the fine at two years' rent, as requested in the article, finally became law in 1781[2].

The rising in Cumberland and Westmorland bears a much closer resemblance to the various peasant revolts in Germany than do the movements in the other counties[3]. Thus in the proclamation drawn up at Penrith by Robert Thompson, the rebels were commanded to say daily five aves, five paters and a creed, which recalls the Bruchsal insurgents of 1502, who bound themselves to say five aves and five paternosters daily[4]. There is a striking correspondence between the petition of the commons of Westmorland dated 15 November 1536[5], and the Twelve Articles of the Swabian Peasants in 1525[6], despite the fact that the former were rising, nominally at least, on behalf of the Church, and the latter against it.

The first of the Twelve Articles required "that ministers should be chosen by the whole congregation,—If they misconducted themselves their parishioners should be empowered to remove them." The commons of Westmorland wished to turn out non-resident incumbents "ytt we may putt in yair rowmes to serve God oder yt wald be glad to keep hospytallyte for sum of yam ar no preestes yt hath ye benefyce in hand and oder of yam is my lord Cr[om]well chapplaynes."

The second of the Twelve Articles required that "only the great tithes [of wheat and other grain]...should be in future exacted, and not the small tithes [of the produce of animals and the minor crops]." The commons of Westmorland wished "all ye tythes to remayn to every man hys owne doynge yerfor accordynge to yair dewtye," which must mean that the tithes should be replaced by a voluntary subscription.

In the sixth article the peasants demanded that "no feudal services were to be exacted beyond those which could be proved to be of immemorial antiquity." This is paralleled by the demand of the Westmorland commons "to haffe nowte Gyelt and sargeant

[1] L. and P. xi, 1080.
[2] Leadam, op. cit. p. xc.
[3] See above, chap. ix.
[4] Eng. Hist. Rev. v, 73.
[5] L. and P. xi, 1080.
[6] Eng. Hist. Rev. v, 72.

corne layd downe qwyche we thynke war a Great welthe for all ye power men to bee layd downe." It is not necessary for the present purpose to go into the vexed question of the original significance which belonged to the payment of "nowt geld," i.e. neat [cattle] geld or cornage[1]. In Henry VIII's reign the feudal origin of the payments was forgotten, and the levying of cornage and serjeant corn, otherwise called bailiff oats, probably did not differ materially from what it was a hundred years later, when in 1634 the tenants made another effort to free themselves. The neat geld was a fixed annual payment made by the townships in the barony of Westmorland and varying from £5. 5s. 8d. paid by Milburn to 1s. paid by Croftormount. The serjeant corn was still paid in kind, the oats being collected by the bailiff between St Andrew's Day [30 November] and Candlemas [2 February]; the amount due from each township was measured in two ancient pecks, one containing 8 and the other 10 quarts. A perpetual quarrel raged between the bailiff and the tenants as to whether the measures ought to be "striked," i.e. filled level with the brim, or upheaped[2].

A comparison of the two articles shows how much further the English had advanced on the road to freedom than the Swabian peasants. In Germany the actual services were still demanded, and new ones might be exacted. In England the commons were trying to free themselves from the mere relics of the ancient services.

In the eighth article the Swabians required that "rents, which were in the majority of cases excessive, should be reduced to reasonable amounts." This may be compared with the complaint against the ingressum.

The tenth article required that "common land on which the lords had encroached should be restored to the community." This grievance was equally felt by the insurgents of both nations. In the Westmorland petition it is requested that "all the intakes yt [are] noysom for power men [ought] to be layd downe." On this point more will be said below.

One clause in the Westmorland petition has no parallel in the Twelve Articles, namely that "taxes [be] casten emongst ye benefest men as well yam in abbett within us as yai yt is nott incumbent." The clergy voted their grants of money to the King in convocation,

---

[1] See V. C. H. Dur. i, 272, art. Boldon Book, by T. G. Lapsley, and references there; V. C. H. Cumberland, i, 313, art. Domesday Book, by J. Wilson, and references there.

[2] Nicolson and Burn, op. cit. i, 292–4.

apart from the money bills in the House of Commons, and paid separately from the laity[1]. When the taxes were fixed sums raised by each district, as in the case of the tenth and fifteenth, it would be a relief to the small farmer if the clergy of the district shared in the lay taxes, instead of being assessed separately. The commons probably did not reflect that if clergy and laity paid together the King would demand a larger total than if the laity paid alone. As the subsidy was not levied in Cumberland and Westmorland all the taxes were paid in the old manner; none were assessed directly. In Germany the question of taxation cannot have arisen, as government taxes scarcely existed.

It is to be noticed that only two of the articles in the Westmorland petition, those relating to fines and to enclosures, were included in the list of articles drawn up at Pontefract. An assembly in which the knightly and clerical elements were so strong had little sympathy with demands drawn up entirely from the commons' point of view. The clergy could not be expected to acknowledge that parishioners might dispossess the incumbent, for although those particular incumbents were very unsatisfactory characters, still the principle, if once admitted, might easily be carried a great deal too far. The same argument applies to the question of tithes and taxation. The gentlemen, indeed, having accepted the great point of the fines, might have consented to waive the half-obsolete feudal dues, but the point may not have appeared of sufficient importance to be included in the Pilgrims' petition, as it applied only to one district, and might be settled privately between landlord and tenant.

(13) "The statute for enclosures and intacks to be put in execution and intacks since 4 Henry VII to be pulled down, except mountains, forests and parks."

This was a point on which the government was at one with the labourers, but both were powerless. Acts of parliament had been passed with a view to remedying the evil, but the King could not enforce them in the face of the passive resistance of the country gentlemen. During the rebellion the labourers sometimes took matters into their own hands, and pulled down the enclosures[2]. It is to be observed that the enclosure movement in the north was not quite the same as that in the south; "it was not the characteristic enclosure of the period, that of the open fields, which

---

[1] Dowell, op. cit. I, book III, chap. 1, part 2, section 1.
[2] L. and P. XI, 960, 1155 (2) (ii).

is most prominent [during the Pilgrimage of Grace], but the much older and long-continued enclosure of the commons."[1]

The gentlemen and their tenants at Pontefract must have united to insert this article in their petition, but it is perhaps not unjust to imagine that each of the gentlemen thought the reform ought to begin on somebody else's lands.

(14) "To be discharged of the quinzine and taxes now granted by Act of Parliament."

Something has already been said about the attitude of all classes towards taxation[2]. Briefly, they did not see why they should be taxed at all. Instead of looking upon the taxes as a necessary incident of government, they regarded them as something extraordinary, which were required only on account of the King's wilful extravagance. Therefore in every rising it was usual to demand that the taxes should be remitted[3]. Although the fifteenth is mentioned by name, the subsidy appears to have been the most keenly resented, because it was being assessed directly.

The leaders of the Pilgrimage might have been expected to know that it was absolutely necessary for the government to have money, and the article may have been included to please the rank and file. Some of the gentlemen, however, cherished the belief that the King could obtain what he needed without troubling them. The writer supposed to be Sir Thomas Tempest, dwells upon the means by which Henry VII increased his wealth; first, by selling pardons; secondly, by some rather obscure dealings in bishoprics, described as follows: "when a bishopric fell he would promote his chaplain, and thereby by such exchange he would have the profit of the temporalities of all the sees in the realm and content all his prelates by the same, for he amended all their lineage thereby, and hurt none, and yet increased his own riches marvellously"; thirdly, by encouraging foreign trade[4]. It is amusing to see how the gentlemen now turned fond eyes back to the reign of Henry VII, who while he lived was so bitterly hated for his extortion.

Such were the articles to be treated upon by the leaders of the Pilgrimage and the King's representatives. In reviewing them, it is evident that they were not the clamour of peasants driven mad

---

[1] Royal Hist. Soc. Trans. xviii, 196; cf. Tawney, op. cit. 88, 239–43, 322–7, 334–5, 360–1.

[2] See above, chap. i.   [3] Royal Hist. Soc. Trans. xviii, 199.

[4] L. and P. xi, 1244.

by suffering, but ignorant of the remedy for their wrongs; nor were they the work of blind fanatics who insisted on a complete reaction. The articles show willingness to accept a reasonable compromise on every important point.

The Pilgrims were ready to acknowledge the Ten Articles of Religion, as issued by the King. They were prepared to agree to his possession of all the substantial power attached to his title of Supreme Head of the Church, if he would lay down the unlimited pretensions which were implied in it. This was precisely what was done by his daughter Elizabeth. The Pilgrims suggested that the King should receive an annual rent charge from the monasteries, a permanent source of income which the wholesale suppression destroyed for ever. They asked the King to burn heretics, but he had never shown himself reluctant to perform that duty. They asked him to punish Cromwell, but Henry had no sentimental scruples about destroying a minister who had ceased to be useful. They desired the repeal of a number of statutes, but they were willing to refer that to a free parliament, and Henry always declared that he was glad to summon a free parliament at any time. The question of the succession was a thorny one, but it was to be solved next year by the birth of Prince Edward; consequently, if it had been referred to parliament it would not have proved a permanent obstacle.

It may be questioned whether it would not have been a wiser as well as a more honourable course if Henry had entered into serious negotiations with the Pilgrims, considered their demands, and established the Church of England on the basis of an agreement between the opposition and himself. That Church, when at last it was established, was the result of a compromise, and there seems to be no vital reason why some compromise should not have been made at once. No doubt the settlement would have been on more conservative lines than were adopted later, and therefore it would have had perhaps less chance of permanence, but it would have been a rallying-point for the moderate men of all parties in the troubled reigns which followed, and might have prevented much violent change and consequent suffering.

The King himself seems to have been swayed for a little while by this prospect. Stephen Gardiner, in a sermon preached at Paul's Cross on 2 December, 1554, said, "When the tumult was in the north, in the time of King Henry VIII, I am sure the King was determined to have given over the supremacy again to the Pope; but the hour was not then come, and therefore it went not forward, lest some would have said that he did it for fear."[1] Gardiner was on an embassy in France during the rebellion, and therefore cannot have been speaking from first-hand knowledge, but his opinion carries a certain weight.

A still more interesting witness to the King's hesitation is the draft for an act of parliament, which, it has been conjectured, was to be submitted to the free parliament which the Pilgrims demanded. It represents Henry's idea of a compromise on the subject of the monasteries. In the first place all the monasteries which had been suppressed were to remain so; the King would give up nothing which had come into his hands, but it was to be enacted that the grantees must reside upon the lands and maintain hospitality as the monks had done. In the second place, all houses north of Trent which had not yet been suppressed were to be expressly preserved by the act. The monks in these houses must observe the new rules for their conduct which had been drawn up in 1535, and a governor appointed by the King was to administer the revenues of every house. No monastery was to be permitted to have an income of more than 1000 marks a year. In the third place, the surplus revenue of the monasteries was to be made over to a court, to be called the Curia Centenariorum, presided over by the lord admiral. The funds belonging to this court were to be devoted to maintaining a standing army both in peace and war in the towns, castles and fortresses of the realm[2]. This scheme is stamped with Henry's own peculiar form of humour. In effect he said to the north:—"You insist on keeping the monasteries? Very well. But you shall keep a standing army too." It was easy to see that the greater part of this army would be garrisoned in the north. The project is a very striking one, but of no practical importance, as it was never carried out.

Against these symptoms of yielding, slight as they were, Henry's own argument may be used, that it would have been foolish to take serious notice of demands put forward by the ignorant and backward north. The policy of the government ought to be controlled by the more enlightened south. But it is clear that sympathy was felt for the northern movement all over the country. This was not a mere fancy of the Pilgrims. Apart from the abortive risings in other counties[3], there is abundant evidence that many, perhaps most,

---

[1] Foxe, Book of Martyrs (ed. Milner), p. 597.
[2] Cotton MSS. Cleopatra E 4, fol. 215. B.M.; quoted by Froude, op. cit. II, chap. XIII.   [3] See chap. XIX.

of the "southern men" would have rejoiced at a compromise of the kind suggested above[1].

In their negotiations with the King, the Pilgrims were handicapped by having among their leaders no nobleman above the rank of a baron. It was here that the Earl of Derby's loss was severely felt. He would at any rate have made a respectable figure-head for negotiations. The only ecclesiastical dignitary of importance with them was the Archbishop of York, whose timid, unstable character made him worse than useless.

Nevertheless, in spite of these drawbacks, the fact remains that the King was forced to enter into negotiations with the Pilgrims, even though they were northern men and lacked representatives in the peerage. Henry saved his honour, in his own opinion, by the mental reservation that he would not observe the terms any longer than he was compelled to do so by force. He was obliged to treat, but at least he need not do it sincerely. It was bad enough to be reduced to such an extremity, but he had not fallen so low as to make a serious treaty and to keep his promises. In this spirit, therefore, he rejected the opportunity of establishing the Church of England upon the consent of the people. For the remaining nine years of his reign his will was absolute in ecclesiastical matters. The doctrines of the catholic faith were to be accepted by his subjects not on the authority of "the Holy Church throughout all the world" but on that of the reigning king. There was therefore no security for the conservatives that the King would not alter these doctrines at his pleasure, and in fact there is reason to believe that Henry contemplated further changes of a more sweeping character in the doctrine and practice of the Church at the time of his death. The most probable explanation of his attitude in ecclesiastical matters seems to be that he overrated his own power. He believed that he could establish a church upon his own absolute will, and that yet, after his own death, the church would stand. The event showed his mistake. On his death religion in England fell into chaos.

The council at Pontefract had already done a good day's work, but it was not yet ended. In addition to agreeing upon the articles, a list of instructions was drawn up for Sir Thomas Hilton and his companions[2]. One of these alone requires comment here: "That

---

[1] See chaps. III and XIII.

[2] L. and P. XI, 1244; printed in full, Speed, Hist. of Great Britain, bk. IX, chap. 21.

Richard Cromwell nor none of his kind nor sort be at our meeting at Doncaster." This was resolved upon because—

(*a*) Norfolk had stated that he was coming to Doncaster unaccompanied save by Sir Anthony Browne's band, and the Pilgrims were annoyed to hear that Richard Cromwell was also with him.

(*b*) There was great danger that if the commons knew that Cromwell's men were there they would insist upon attacking them.

(*c*) One of Robert Bowes' servants, while in London, had quarrelled with one of the Lord Privy Seal's servants, and would pursue the feud if he had the chance.

(*d*) Richard Cromwell had "spoken extreme words against the commons of Lincolnshire."[1]

Before the council broke up, Lord Latimer suggested that the Archbishop and the divines now assembled should be requested to "show their learning whether subjects might lawfully move war in any case against their prince."[2] There was no debate on the question, but Aske undertook to lay it before the clergy, and it was hoped that the Archbishop would deal with the problem in the sermon which he was to preach next day[3].

Lee had already arrived at Pontefract. The first thing that he did was to attempt to play the same trick on Darcy which had succeeded so well with Aske. His chaplain, Dr Brandsby, carried a verbal message to Darcy that the Archbishop wished to have his written opinion as to how the divines there assembled should show their learning. But Darcy was not to be caught. He answered Dr Brandsby not in writing but by word of mouth, and "like a knight, and neither as an orator nor lawyer nor dissembler."[4] From this it may be inferred that his language was forcible, not to say profane. At any rate he upset Lee's plan for collecting the treasonable opinions of the Pilgrims without stating his own.

Meanwhile the other priests were assembling at Pontefract. Richmond was represented by John Dakyn and the rector of Wycliffe, who was probably Dr Rokeby[5]. The rector of Wycliffe was not popular with his parishioners, as one of his uncles was a surveyor of the abbeys. On the outbreak of the rebellion the commons had threatened Rokeby, calling him a lollard and a puller down of abbeys[6]. It was Sir William Tristram, the warlike chantry priest

---

[1] L. and P. xii (1), 1175.

[2] Ibid. 945 (100–1); printed in full, Eng. Hist. Rev. v, 573.

[3] L. and P. xii (1) 901 (102); printed in full, Eng. Hist. Rev. v, 572.

[4] L. and P. xi, 1336.   [5] See note F at end of chapter.

[6] L. and P. xii (1), 1011; see above, chap. ix.

of Lartington, who told him that he must go to Pontefract with Dakyn. On this news Rokeby went to consult Dakyn, and they both appealed to Robert Bowes for advice. He assured them that the Archbishop wanted their counsel, and they therefore both went to Pontefract. They arrived in the afternoon on Saturday 2 December, and waited on the Archbishop in his chamber[1]. He seems to have been at the Priory, as he refused to go to the Castle[2]. On seeing Dakyn and Rokeby he expressed some surprise. They told him that they understood from Bowes that he sent for them. He denied that he had summoned anyone to a conference, although the letters had been sent out in his name. He admitted, however, that he had received a list of articles from the rebels, and had been requested to pronounce on their truth. Although he would not acknowledge that he possessed the articles, he sent Rokeby and Dakyn to Dr Brandsby for a copy. These seem to have been the articles that Aske had sent to him[3].

After this, the laymen's conference having broken up, Lord Latimer came to the Archbishop and asked him to declare next day in his sermon whether it was lawful for subjects to wage war against their sovereign, and to do it briefly, as there was to be a council at the Castle at nine o'clock. Lee felt himself driven into a corner. With the resolution of despair he promised to obey and asked Latimer to attend the sermon instead of the council[4]. Richard Bowyer, who seems to have acted as clerk to the council, came to the Archbishop the same night with the articles which had been passed by the Pilgrims that day. To him Lee assumed the pose of a martyr: " Ye do see I cannot better it. How I am entreated ye know."[5]

It has been said before, and may here be repeated, that it is incredible that Archbishop Lee should have been allowed to preach at this critical point if he really uttered all the loyal sentiments and made all the protests which he afterwards attributed to himself. There were many prominent divines at Pontefract who were heart and soul with the Pilgrims. One of these, Friar John Pickering for example, would have been asked to preach if it had been known that the Archbishop was such a convinced supporter of passive obedience. In spite of his subsequent protests, Lee was regarded on all hands as the ecclesiastical leader of the opposition to Cromwell's innovations.

---

[1] L. and P. xii (1), 1011.   [2] Ibid. 1022.
[3] Ibid. 1011.   [4] Ibid. 1022.
[5] Ibid. 306.

So long as conservatism was safe, he had been a bigoted conservative[1]. He had vigorously attacked the very moderate reforming tendencies of Erasmus[2]. He is supposed to have burnt a man and a woman at York for heresy, although the evidence in this case is defective[3]. It was at this very time reported in the host on the authority of Sir Robert Oughtred that Lee had said " that there was no way for the commons but battle."[4] His determination to preach was opposed by three of his chaplains and his suffragan, but it does not appear whether they knew what he was going to say, or merely did not wish him to preach at all[5].

Service was held in the parish church of Pontefract on the morning of Sunday 3 December before nine o'clock. Lord Darcy was not present[6], but everyone else thronged to hear the Archbishop's sermon. It seems that the gentlemen and divines filled the body of the church, and that most of the commons were in a gallery, "up a height in the church."[7]

Lee afterwards represented himself as coming to the pulpit "indifferent to live or die," resolved only to save the bodies and souls of his flock by telling them at any cost that they did evil in resisting the King[8]. But this was not what his audience anticipated, and it was some time before the drift of his sermon appeared. His text unfortunately has not been preserved, but he began his discourse by speaking of the sacraments of baptism, penance and communion, and of the creed, which had been set forth in the Ten Articles of Religion[9]. This was non-controversial matter, as the Ten Articles were accepted by both parties. He next ventured on the rather bolder assertion that lands which were given to the Church might not be put to profane uses. This was what the congregation expected, and they waited eagerly for what followed. The Archbishop continued that priests ought not to fight in any circumstances[10]; as for making a " peregrynage "—and on this word he paused[11]. There was a little stir and bustle round the door, and Lancaster Herald came into the church. He had arrived with the safeconduct, and very properly attended divine service on Sunday morning at the first opportunity[12].

---

[1] Dic. Nat. Biog. art. Edward Lee.
[2] Seebohm, The Oxford Reformers, chap. xvi, sections iv, ix.
[3] Duff, op. cit. p. 45.   [4] L. and P. xii (1), 532, 533.
[5] Ibid. 1022.   [6] L. and P. xi, 1336.
[7] L. and P. xii (1), 1021; see note G at end of chapter.
[8] L. and P. xi, 1300.   [9] L. and P. xii (1), 1021.
[10] Ibid. 786 (ii, 2).   [11] Ibid. 1021.
[12] Ibid. 901 (102); printed in full, Eng. Hist. Rev. v, 572.

The appearance of the Herald had a decisive influence on the Archbishop's sermon. It either gave him courage to carry out his purpose of condemning the Pilgrimage[1], as he said, or drove away the little courage that he had and prevented him from blessing it, as his audience believed[2]. After this little pause he took up his discourse again and declared that in the King's Book of Articles the Faith was sufficiently determined, that the sword was given to none but a prince, and that no man might draw it but by his prince's orders.

At this the fury of the commons broke loose. They cried out that the Archbishop was a false dissembler[3], and in the midst of the uproar Aske and the other gentlemen hurried Lee away[4]. He afterwards dwelt pathetically on the danger that he had incurred[5], but it cannot have been very great, as it appears that the commons were some distance from him in the gallery, and that he was surrounded by the gentlemen, who, however angry they might be, would do him no bodily harm. Darcy did not think much of his peril. He told the Archbishop that he reckoned that the King and his honourable councillors would accept him after the true meaning of that and all his sermons, without his seeking the King's favour by desiring, in letters, to die for his faith. "Whosoever desires such high perfection may, with the King's licence, be sped in Africa or Turkey."[6] Darcy obtained "such high perfection" much nearer home, but it was denied to Archbishop Lee.

It was natural that the gentlemen should resent Lee's sermon. When a man is risking his lands and life for a cause, it is very annoying to be told by the representative of that cause that he is acting wickedly, and that the cause has no need of him. Lee dined with Darcy that Sunday, and begged him to use his influence for peace[7], but it may be imagined that he was not very warmly received. He heard many unfavourable opinions of his sermon in the next few days. Sir Robert Constable used "cruel words far unfitting to be uttered by his mouth against me that have the cure of his soul," complained the aggrieved Archbishop[8]. To appease the commons and perhaps to give vent to his own feelings, Constable had said that the Archbishop would make amends hereafter. As soon as he was safely home at Cawood, Lee wrote to remonstrate with Sir Robert for using

---

[1] L. and P. xii (1), 1022.
[2] Ibid. 901 (102); printed in full, Eng. Hist. Rev. v, 572.
[3] L. and P. xii (1), 1011, 1021.   [4] L. and P. xi, 1300; xii (1), 1021.
[5] L. and P. xi, 1300; xii (1), 1022.   [6] L. and P. xi, 1336.
[7] L. and P. xii (1), 1022.   [8] L. and P. xi, 1300.

such words, and declared that he had nothing to make amends for[1]. Robert Aske was reported to have said that if he had known what the sermon would be he would have pulled Lee out of the pulpit[2], but what he really said was that if he had known " my lord of York would preach as he did, he should not have preached."[3] Lee was told that when Darcy heard that he had said no one might lawfully resist the King, he exclaimed " By God's mother that is not true."[4] Lee wrote to complain of this to Darcy, who denied the words ; but the bitterly contemptuous tone of his letter shows what he thought of the Archbishop[5].

All this chorus of condemnation arouses a certain amount of sympathy for the Archbishop in the modern mind. The doctrine of non-resistance at its highest is perhaps the noblest conceivable. Lee was upholding non-resistance, and there is an odd resemblance between his position and that of the Tolstoian hero in Zangwill's *War God*. But the likeness breaks down when tested. In order to win acceptance the professor of non-resistance must be unflinchingly brave and absolutely consistent. Lee did not fulfil either of these conditions. He had not dared to proclaim his doctrine, or he would not have been allowed to preach that day, and he did not protest against all war. On the contrary, he praised those who fought for the King and condemned only rebellion. Finally even non-resisters agree that a body of men may unite to indicate peacefully but firmly that they disapprove of the government's action. At this crisis of the Pilgrimage there was a reasonable hope that the Pilgrims would obtain all they desired by peaceful means if they stood firmly together. Lee's sermon did a great deal to destroy that hope. This was far from being his intention. Whatever may be thought of his conduct, it is quite certain that he sincerely desired peace. Yet he had adopted a very unfortunate method of bringing it about. His sermon not only exasperated the commons, but increased their constant suspicion of the gentlemen. After the fiasco in Lincolnshire they naturally feared that the gentlemen would make their own peace with the King and abandon the commons to Cromwell's vengeance. Lee's condemnation of the Pilgrimage increased this distrust. It seemed only too probable that he had been inspired by the leaders, who might already have secretly come to terms with Norfolk. If this were so, they were now anxious to dismiss the commons to their homes in order that,

---

[1] L. and P. xii (1), 33.
[3] Ibid. 786 (ii, 2).
[5] Ibid. 1336.
[2] Ibid. 1022.
[4] L. and P. xi, 1300.

disunited and helpless, they might fall into the hands of the royal troops. On account of these inevitable suspicions Aske deeply regretted that he had allowed the Archbishop to preach. The sermon had the air of an official statement, and though Lee might have made himself safe with the King, he had embarrassed the position of the leaders. Quarrelling broke out among the commons, and tumults arose. Aske's servants cut the red crosses off the coat of Richard Bowyer, who was in the coat at the time. It does not appear what he had done to annoy them, but he seems to have been a meddlesome fellow. Sir George Lawson expressed a wish to know what the assembly of divines resolved upon, and Bowyer tried to be present at their meeting. He succeeded in entering the room while they were at dinner, but when they came back, they declined his offer to act as secretary and turned him out[1].

The convocation of divines met in the Priory on Monday 4 December[2]. They were summoned to the Priory church by Dr William Cliff, chancellor to the Archbishop of York, chaunter of York and rector of Waverton in Cheshire[3], who was acting for his master, and were led by the Prior of Pontefract into a private chamber. The persons present were John Ripley[4], Abbot of Kirkstall; his chaplain; Dr Sherwood, chancellor of Beverley minster[5]; Dr Cliff; Dr Langrege, Archdeacon of Cleveland[6]; Dr Geoffrey Downes, Chancellor of York; Dr John Brandsby, the Archbishop's chaplain and master of the collegiate church of Sutton[7]; Dr Cuthbert Marshall, Archdeacon of Nottingham; James Thwaites, Prior of Pontefract; Dr Waldby, rector of Kirk Deighton and prebendary of Carlisle; Dr Pickering the Friar Preacher; Dr Rokeby; a friar; Dr George Palmes, rector of Sutton-upon-Derwent[8]; and Dr Dakyn, rector of Kirkby Ravensworth and vicar-general of York, who was requested to sit in the midst and take the minutes. The Prior of Pontefract and the friar seem to have been the only persons present who were not doctors either of law or of divinity[9].

The divines had before them the questions and propositions which Aske had originally sent to Lee, but Aske said that they made no direct reply to his list, and that he could not remember who drew up

[1] L. and P. xii (1), 306.   [2] Ibid. 786 (ii, 1).
[3] Valor Eccles. v, 207.
[4] Baildon, Monastic Notes (Yorks. Arch. Soc. Rec. Ser.), i, 107.
[5] Valor Eccles. v, 132.   [6] Ibid. 95.
[7] Ibid. 110.   [8] Ibid. 140.
[9] L. and P. xii (1), 786 (ii, 1) ; 1021.

the questions which they answered[1]. These questions may perhaps have been Chaloner's interrogatories concerning heresy[2].

The divines' first resolution was :—

"We thynke yt preachynge agaynste purgatory, worshuppynge of Sayntes, pylgrymage, Images and all bookes set forth agenst ye same or sacramentes or sacramentallis of ye Churche be worthy to be reproved and condempned by Convocacion, and ye payne to be executed yt is devysed for ye doars to ye contrary, and proces to be made herafter in heresye as was in ye dayes of kynge henry ye 1111 th and ye new statutes wherby heresyes now lately have ben greatly norysshed to be annolled and abrogated, and yt ye holydaes may be observed accordyng to ye lawes and lawdable Custumes, and yt ye byddynge of beadys and preachinge may be observed as hath ben used by olde Custume."[3]

Over this there was little debate, for even Archbishop Lee objected to the abolition of holydays[4], but the second resolution was that

"ye kynges highnes ne any temporall man may not be supreme hedd of ye churche by ye lawes of god to have or exercise any jurysdiccons or poer spirituall in ye same, and all actes of parliamente made to ye contrary to be revoked."

There was a long discussion over this. Marshall, Pickering, Brandsby and Waldby maintained the papal cause, urging the primacy of St Peter. The three last-named had been present in Convocation when the momentous resolution in the King's favour was passed. They took out of their purses protests which had been made then[5], and complained that the saving clause "in quantum per legem Christi licet[6]" was omitted. Dakyn, Cliff and Rokeby thought that the question ought to be referred to a General Council. Dakyn was not opposed to some limitation of the Pope's authority, for he had been in the Court of Arches and had learnt there how much trouble and delay were caused by appeals to Rome. Dr Sherwood was more inclined to the royal supremacy than the rest. Finally they agreed that the King might retain the title of " Caput Ecclesiæ," but that he might exercise no jurisdiction such as visitation[7].

The third question seems to have referred to Mary's legitimacy, upon which they resolved

" we be not suffycyently instructed in ye facte ne in ye proces therin made but we refarre it to ye determynation of ye Churche to whom it was appealed."

[1] L. and P. XII (1), 945 (97); printed in full, Eng. Hist. Rev. v, 573.
[2] L. and P. XII (1), 901 (107) ; printed in full, Eng. Hist. Rev. v, 570.
[3] See note H at end of chapter.   [4] L. and P. XII (1), 786 (6).
[5] Ibid. 786 (ii, 2), 1021.   [6] See above, chap. I.
[7] L. and P. XII (1), 786 (ii, 2).

The other resolutions were

"yt no clerke oughte to be put to death withoute degradacyon by ye lawes of ye Churche.

yt no man ought to be drawen owte of sentuary but in certayne causes expressed in ye lawes of ye Churche.

To ye vi[th] we saye yt ye clargye of ye northe parties hath not graunted nor consentyd to ye pamente of ye tenthes or ffyrste frutes of benefices in ye Convocan and also we may make no suche personall graunte by ye lawes of ye Churche and we thynke yt no temporall man hathe auctoryte by ye lawes of god to claym any suche tenthes or ffyrst frutes of any benyfyce or spirituall promocyon.

To ye vii[th] we thinke yt landis gyven to god, ye churche or relygyouse men ma not betaken away and put to prophane uses by ye lawes of god.

To ye viii[th] we thynke yt dispensacons upon Iuste causes lawfully graunted by ye pope of Rome to be good and to be accepted, and pardons have ben allowed by generall Counsels of lateran and Vyenna and by lawes of ye churche.

To ye ix[th] we thynke yt by ye lawes of ye Churche, Generall counselles, interpreta [*torn*] ys of approved doctors and consente of Crysten people ye poope of Rome hath ben taken for ye hedd of ye Churche and Vycare of Cryste and so oughte to be taken.

To ye x[th] we thinke yt ye examynacon and Correxion of dedly synne belongith to ye mynisters of ye Churche by ye lawes of ye same, wch be consonante to goddes lawes."

This was the conclusion of the interrogatories, which were ten in number. In the debate Cliff and Palmes were most eager for the repeal of the various statutes, and Dakyn for the restoration of the monasteries, as he had been very much shocked by the profanation of sacred things[1].

In the afternoon Aske himself brought the laymen's articles to the divines. He found them sitting with their books before them, and with their articles almost ready[2]. They read over the laymen's petition to the King, but they did not consider the temporal articles within their province. Aske offered to lend them a book written by the Bishop of Rochester [Fisher], which would assist them if they were in any difficulty[3], and besought them to speak their minds on all points openly and without fear[4]. He himself was ready to fight and die for the old faith and the papal supremacy[5].

On Tuesday 5 December the divines debated on the first eight articles of the petition, namely (1) the suppression of heresies, (2) the supremacy of the Pope, (3) the legitimacy of Mary, (4) the restoration of the abbeys, (5) the abolition of tenths and first fruits, (6) the

---

[1] L. and P. xii (1), 786 (ii, 2).
[2] Ibid.; and 698 (3).
[3] Ibid. 1021.
[4] Ibid. 698 (3).
[5] Ibid. 786 (ii, 2), 1021.

restoration of the Friars Observants, (7) the punishment of heretics, (8) the punishment of Cromwell, Audley and Rich.

In this they were going over the same ground as on the day before, and they had only to confirm the lay articles. In addition to their answers to the questions which they had received, the divines passed some resolutions of their own :—

"ffarther we thynke it convenyente yt ye lawes of ye churche may be openly redde in Unyversyties as hath ben used here to ffore, and yt suche clarkys as be in pryson or ffledde owte of ye realme for withstandyng ye kynges supporyorite in ye Church may be set at lybertye and restored withoute danger and yt suche bookys and workes as do entreate of ye primacye of ye Churche of Rome may be ffrely kepte and redde notwithstandyng any prohybyssion to ye contrary and yt ye artycles of praemynire may be declared by actes of parlamente to the entente no man be in daunger therof withoute a prohibicyon fyrste awarded and yt suche apostataes as be goon from relygion withoute suffycyente and lawfull dyspensacyon of ye See of Rome may be compelled to returne to theyre howses, and yt all Sommes of mony as tenthes fyrste frutes and other Arreragis [*torn*] graunted unto ye kynges highnes by parlyamente or convocacyon and dew to be payed before ye fyrst day of ye nexte parliament may be remytted and forgyven for ye causes and reasones above expressed.

And we ye saide clargie saye yt for lacke of tyme and instruccyon in thies artycles and wante of bookys we declare this our opynyon for this tyme refarrynge our determynacon in ye premysses to ye nexte Convocacyon.

Also we desyre yt ye statute Cammanndynge ye clergye to exhibyte ye dyspensacons graunted by ye pope byfore ye ffeaste of michelmas nexte commynge may be revoked at ye nexte parliamente."

On Tuesday evening the articles were ready, and the assembled divines carried them to the Archbishop[1]. Aske was present[2], as Lee had been urging him to come to terms with Norfolk, to disclose everything, and to inquire whether Lee should proceed with the collection of the tenth[3]. The Archbishop read over the articles, but when he came to the declaration of the papal supremacy, he objected that it was unnecessary. There was a long debate over this. Marshall and Pickering defended the article[4]. Aske questioned the Archbishop as to what he really believed on this point. Lee replied that the supremacy touching the cure of souls did not belong to the King, but the punishment of sin rested with him as the head of his people, and therein he was supreme head. Aske was surprised at the distinction, as he had never before heard anyone make it[5]. In the end Lee permitted the clause to stand, as it expressed the consent of Christian people[6]. The articles were then delivered to Aske[7].

[1] L. and P. xii (1), 786 (ii, 3).   [2] Ibid. 698 (3).   [3] Ibid. 1022.
[4] Ibid. 786 (ii, 3).   [5] Ibid. 698 (3).
[6] Ibid. 786 (ii, 3).   [7] Ibid. 698 (3).

That night, probably after they had left Lee's presence, Aske laid before the divines the problem which the Archbishop had solved in so unexpected a fashion. Was it ever lawful for subjects to resist their sovereign? To this they returned no answer[1], but on the whole their attitude was much more satisfactory, from Aske's point of view, than Lee's had been. Their resolutions were certainly bold enough; probably the timid spirits were encouraged and hurried on by the ardour of Pickering and the more enthusiastic priests. It is true that afterwards they all represented themselves as having been in terror of the commons, but the statement of Dakyn, who was a very simple-minded man, throws some light on that point. He explained that when he, Marshall and Cliff were summoned to court to account for their conduct, they agreed together that they would say they had done everything from fear; and Dakyn innocently goes on to repeat exactly the words they had agreed upon, that every man came through fear, and was weary of his part, and doubtful what to do[2]. If this were true, the reason of the Pilgrims' failure is not far to seek. No one could drag to victory such very flabby and reluctant upholders of the Church. But a statement made with such an obvious motive does not command much belief. No doubt the priests were anxious and afraid. An assembly of elderly clergymen are very uncomfortably situated in the midst of a rebel army, and very dangerously employed in drawing up a manifesto hostile to the government. But it was the King, not the commons, whom they chiefly feared.

On this point Aske was closely interrogated. After some questions as to the matters laid before the clergy, he was asked, " Was it not a double iniquity to fall into rebellion and also after to procure matter to be set forth to justify that rebellion? "[3] To which he replied with that touch of humour which is sometimes perceptible in his answers, " If the clergy did declare their minds contrary to the laws of God, it was a double iniquity," and again, " as he thinks, the spiritual men were willing enough of themselves to declare their minds as they did in those points that they answered unto, but in that point, whether subjects might fight against their prince, he thinks they were not willing, because they made no determination at all touching the same."[4]

. In short, it is an injustice to the learned men to say that they did

[1] L. and P. xii (1), 945 (100–5); printed in full, Eng. Hist. Rev. v, 573.
[2] L. and P. xii (1), 789 (ii).
[3] Ibid. 900 (93); printed in full, Eng. Hist. Rev. v, 555.
[4] L. and P. xii (1), 945 (93, 104, 105); printed in full, Eng. Hist. Rev. v, 573.

not mean what they resolved. Aske expressed the confidence of all the Pilgrims when he said, " They thought none other like but that the said clergy would have showed their minds according to their learning and conscience, and [they] had no violence offered them in the world to do the contrary."[1]

NOTES TO CHAPTER XIV

Note A. The points which indicate that this paper was drawn up by Aske are :

(1) The questions are not the same as those which were laid before the clergy at Pontefract, and Aske said afterwards that his questions were not used there[2].

(2) Several of the questions are on points on which Aske was examined, e.g. the contradictory oaths, the rights of the Church according to Magna Carta, and the Statute of Uses. The opinions expressed in the questions agree with those in Aske's replies.

(3) The questions were found together with a paper in Latin on the clause in the Creed "Credo in Sanctam Ecclesiam Catholicam."[3] This paper would probably be given to Archbishop Lee, who also had Aske's questions in his possession[4]. He may have sent both to the King together.

Note B. The Articles of Pontefract are printed in the Letters and Papers, xi, 1246, in Speed's History of Great Britain, Book ix, chap. 21, and in Froude's History of England, ii, chap. xiii, in a foot-note. In the present work the articles have been grouped in a new order, but the numbering of the original order has been retained for convenience of reference.

Note C. Against this article is written "ney," but it is uncertain when or by whom the note was made. It is difficult to believe that there was a division of opinion among the Pilgrims as to the conduct of the notorious commissioners, and there seems to be no reason to suppose that this article was opposed or rejected after it was laid before the general council, for Aske stated that "they all agreed to the Articles and none to the contrary of them."[5] Possibly the word may have been written when Aske was being examined to indicate that he had not yet been interrogated on this article, as his reply to it occurs in his last examination[6].

"Non" is written in the margin against article 9, probably for a similar reason.

Note D. Bye-elections were not accepted as a constitutional practice even as late as the seventeenth century[7].

---

[1] L. and P. xii (1), 945 (94, 95) ; printed in full, Eng. Hist. Rev. v, 573.
[2] L. and P. xii (1), 945 (97); printed in full, Eng. Hist. Rev. v, 573.
[3] L. and P. xi, 1182 (1). [4] L. and P. xii (1), 1022.
[5] Ibid. 901 (23); printed in full, Eng. Hist. Rev. v, 566–7.
[6] L. and P. xii (1), 1175 (ii). [7] Pollard, op. cit. chap. xii.

Note E.　The boroughs were Ripon, Doncaster, Tickhill, Ravenspur, Yarm, Pickering, Hedon, Beverley, Thirsk, Northallerton, Malton, Knaresborough, Pontefract, Hull and Scarborough[1].

The other northern counties had electoral grievances as well as Yorkshire, for instance, Durham was not represented at all.　The members for Cumberland in 1523 were nominated by the King but this was because no one would volunteer to stand[2].

Note F.　The name is illegible in his confession[3], and as he had received his benefice in August 1536 it cannot be discovered from the Valor Ecclesiasticus. Dakyn, however, mentions that Dr Rokeby was at Pontefract[4], and the unknown writer names his uncle William Rokeby.　Friar Pickering adds to the list of divines, Mr Bachelor of Meux and a secular man.　He also says that the friar was an Observant[5].

Note G.　There are galleries in All Hallows, the parish Church of Pontefract, at the present day[6], but as the church was almost completely destroyed during the Civil War it is impossible to say whether there were galleries in the original building[7].

Note H.　These articles are printed by Strype, Memorials, I (ii), 266, and by Wilkins, Concilia, III, 812, but as neither of these copies is very accurate a fresh one has been made from the original in the British Museum, Cotton MS. Cleop. E. v, 381 (old numbering), 413 (modern numbering).　A very much condensed summary is printed in the Letters and Papers, XI, 1245.　The Articles are also printed in "The Acts of the Northern Convocation" (Surtees Soc.), but they are erroneously represented as being the reply of the Northern Convocation to the King's Ten Articles.

---

[1] Park, op. cit. under the respective boroughs.
[2] L. and P. III, 2931.
[3] L. and P. XII (1), 1011.
[4] Ibid. 786 (ii, 1).
[5] Ibid. 1011; 1021.
[6] Yorks. Arch. Journ. XIII, 390.
[7] Boothroyd, Pontefract, 346.

END OF VOLUME ONE.

For EU product safety concerns, contact us at Calle de José Abascal, 56–1°,
28003 Madrid, Spain or eugpsr@cambridge.org.

www.ingramcontent.com/pod-product-compliance
Ingram Content Group UK Ltd.
Pitfield, Milton Keynes, MK11 3LW, UK
UKHW050226270426
470322UK00031B/557